"This edited book uniquely combines all aspects of Chinese students' experiences, ranging from developing cultural identities to being educated by Chinese parents to learning academic subjects and thus helps readers see the interplay of various aspects and gain a better understanding of the complexity of academic and non-academic experiences of Chinese students."

*Hong Xu, Professor of Teacher Education,
California State University, Long Beach, USA*

"As I read through this important new collection of studies … what struck me was the incredible diversity of communities and contexts, families and young people brought together under the umbrella of 'Chinese-heritage' students. It depicts the actual diversity in Chinese socioeconomic and migration background, first and second language and dialect resources, spatial/geographic dis/placement, and, indeed, everyday educational experience. This is a question of cultural homogeneity and heterogeneity, of difference within difference—of how we can talk about 'Chinese-heritage' or 'Chinese' or, for that matter, 'Chinese-American' communities in ways that capture the complex lived dynamics of common cultural experiences, practices, and schemata—and, indeed, the differences between and within these communities."

*Allan Luke, Emeritus Professor, Queensland University of Technology, Australia;
Adjunct Professor, University of Calgary, Canada;
Honorary Professor, Beijing Normal University, PRC, from the Foreword*

"The 'Chinese' have carried the stereotypical status of being excellent in test taking globally for a long time. This rich collection of studies reveals the diversity and complexity of Chinese students in North America. It clearly shows that Chinese students are much more than test scores…. However, the value of this volume goes way beyond demystifying Chinese students…. I am hopeful it will serve to inspire similar efforts in the entire field of education and one day we can move beyond test scores as the only outcome measure in education."

Yong Zhao, Presidential Chair and Director of the Institute for Global and Online Education, and Professor in the Department of Educational Measurement, Policy, and Leadership, College of Education, University of Oregon, USA, from the Afterword

CHINESE-HERITAGE STUDENTS IN NORTH AMERICAN SCHOOLS

This comprehensive look at Chinese-heritage students' academic, sociocultural, and emotional development in public schools examines pertinent educational theories; complex (even inconvenient) realities; learning practices in and outside of schools; and social, cultural, and linguistic complications in their academic lives across diverse settings, homes, and communities.

Chinese-heritage students are by far the largest ethnic group among Asian American and Asian Canadian communities, but it is difficult to sort out their academic performance because NAEP and most state/province databases lump all Asian students' results together. To better understand why Chinese-heritage learners range from academic role models to problematic students in need of help, it is important to understand their hearts and minds beyond test scores. This book is distinctive in building this understanding by addressing the range of issues related to Chinese-heritage K–12 students' languages, cultures, identities, academic achievements, and challenges across North American schools.

Wen Ma is an Associate Professor of Education at Le Moyne College, USA.

Guofang Li is a Professor and Canada Research Chair (Tier 1) in Transnational/ Global Perspectives of Language and Literacy Education of Children and Youth at the University of British Columbia, Canada.

CHINESE-HERITAGE STUDENTS IN NORTH AMERICAN SCHOOLS

Understanding Hearts and Minds Beyond Test Scores

Edited by Wen Ma and Guofang Li

NEW YORK AND LONDON

First published 2016
by Routledge
711 Third Avenue, New York, NY 10017

and by Routledge
2 Park Square, Milton Park, Abingdon, Oxon, OX14 4RN

Routledge is an imprint of the Taylor & Francis Group, an informa business

© 2016 Taylor & Francis

The right of the editors to be identified as the authors of the editorial material, and of the authors for their individual chapters, has been asserted in accordance with sections 77 and 78 of the Copyright, Designs and Patents Act 1988.

All rights reserved. No part of this book may be reprinted or reproduced or utilized in any form or by any electronic, mechanical, or other means, now known or hereafter invented, including photocopying and recording, or in any information storage or retrieval system, without permission in writing from the publishers.

Trademark notice: Product or corporate names may be trademarks or registered trademarks, and are used only for identification and explanation without intent to infringe.

Library of Congress Cataloging in Publication Data
Ma, Wen, editor. | Li, Guofang, 1972- editor.
Title: Chinese-heritage students in North American schools : understanding hearts and minds beyond test scores / edited by Wen Ma and Guofang Li.
Description: New York, NY : Routledge, 2016. | Includes bibliographical references and index.
Identifiers: LCCN 2015034423 | ISBN 9781138999268 (hardback) | ISBN 9781138999275 (pbk.) | ISBN 9781315658438 (ebook)
Subjects: LCSH: Chinese American students. | Chinese Americans--Education--Social aspects. | Chinese--Education--Social aspects--Canada. | Children of immigrants--Education--Social aspects--United States. | Children of immigrants--Education--Social aspects--Canada.
Classification: LCC LC3071 .C58 2016 | DDC 371.829/951--dc23
LC record available at http://lccn.loc.gov/2015034423

ISBN: 978-1-138-99926-8 (hbk)
ISBN: 978-1-138-99927-5 (pbk)
ISBN: 978-1-315-65843-8 (ebk)

Typeset in Bembo
by Saxon Graphics Ltd, Derby

Printed and bound in the United States of America by Publishers Graphics, LLC on sustainably sourced paper.

This book is dedicated to our children, Xiaoya, Francis, Patrick,
and Amanda, and millions of Chinese-heritage learners like them.
We hope they will grow up to achieve their full potential,
and become happy, well-rounded, global citizens, free of bias
and stereotypes.

CONTENTS

Foreword: Who and What Are "Chinese" Students? *Allan Luke*	*xiii*
Acknowledgments *Wen Ma and Guofang Li*	*xix*

Introduction: Understanding "Difference within
Differences" in Chinese-Heritage Students' Educational
Experiences across School, Home, and Community
Contexts   1
Guofang Li and Wen Ma

PART I
Chinese-Heritage Students' Language and Literacy Learning   9

1   Chinese Students' Heritage-Language Learning in the
United States: Issues and Challenges   11
Keying Wen and Guofang Li

2   A Chinese Student's Early Education in U.S. K–12 Schools:
A Multilevel Perspective   25
Yalun Zhou, Rebecca L. Oxford, and Michael Wei

x Contents

3 Ordinary Moments Tell Extraordinary Stories: Children's
Multimodal Literacy Explorations   41
Xiaoxiao Du, Rosamund Stooke, and Rachel M. Heydon

4 Looking through the Lens of Chinese ELLs on Academic
Writing in Secondary School   55
Ravy S. Lao, May Y. Lee, and Araceli Arzate

PART II
Chinese-Heritage Students' Learning across the Curriculum   71

5 Culture and Everyday Life Experiences of Chinese Immigrant
Students Learning Science from Classroom Discourse   73
Shu-Wen Lan and Luciana C. de Oliveira

6 Disaggregating Secondary-Level Chinese Immigrants'
Academic, English, and School Success   88
Lee Gunderson and Reginald Arthur D'Silva

7 Between Classes and Schools: Time, Space, and Languages   103
Yamin Qian

8 Opportunities to Learn at Home and Chinese-American
High School Students' Mathematics Achievement   120
Keqiao Liu and Xiufeng Liu

PART III
Chinese-Heritage Students' Cultures and Identities   135

9 (Re)Positioning the "Chinatown" Default: Constructing
Hybrid Identities in Elementary Classrooms   137
Joseph C. Rumenapp

10 Heterogeneity and Differentiation behind Model Minority
Discourse: Struggles of Chinese Students in Canadian
Schools   153
Dan Cui

Contents **xi**

11 "I Feel Proud to Be an Immigrant": How a Youth Program
Supports *Ibasho* Creation for Chinese Immigrant Students in
the U.S.   164
Tomoko Tokunaga and Chu Huang

12 Of Cowboys and Communists: A Phenomenological
Narrative Case Study of a Biracial Chinese-White Adolescent   180
Mary B. McVee and Zachary C. M. Zhang

PART IV
Other Sociocultural Variables Confronting
Chinese-Heritage Learners   **195**

13 A Bioecological Model of Chinese American Children's
Socio-Emotional and Behavioral Adjustment   197
Stephen H. Chen, Jennifer Ly, and Qing Zhou

14 Cultivating Creativity among Chinese-Heritage Students in
North America   211
Cecilia S. Cheung

15 Who Are Their Parents? A Case Study of the Second-
Generation Chinese American Students' Middle-Class Parents
and Their Parenting Styles   224
Xuan Jiang and Gwyn W. Senokossoff

16 Cantonese Emergent Bilinguals in the "Latino/Mandarin"
U.S. Education Landscape: A Critical Case Study in Chicago   239
Jason Goulah

Conclusion: Looking beyond the Stereotypes and
Moving Forward: Cultivating the Hearts and Minds of
Chinese-Heritage Learners   254
Wen Ma and Guofang Li

Afterword: Redefining Education Outcomes   262
Yong Zhao

Contributors   *266*
Index   *271*

FOREWORD

Who and What Are "Chinese" Students?

Who and what are "Chinese" or "Chinese-heritage" students in North American schools? Are they first or second English language speakers? From recent waves of wealthy professional business and academic migrants or, perhaps, longstanding urban working-class families? Do they speak Putonghua, Cantonese, or perhaps Hokkein, or English, or even Malay or Spanish as first languages? Are they religious? Christian, Buddhist, or Muslim? Do they live and go to school as "majorities" in the many longstanding urban and *nouveau* suburban Chinatowns or as "minorities" in White, Hispanic, or African-American communities? Are we to assume, following a "default" model of Chinese ethnicity, that they are of Han Chinese origin or, perhaps, are they from one of China's many *Minzu* (minority) groups, or Taiwan's Indigenous minorities, or, for that matter, from the substantive population of racially blended new American and Canadian families?

There are, of course, many published historical, sociological, and cultural analyses of the Chinese-American and Chinese-Canadian communities (e.g., Wu & Chen, 2010). This corpus of work was founded by the postwar generation of Chinese immigrants, often working with Japanese, Koreans, Filipinos, Indians, and others in a shared struggle for civil rights, educational and economic access, and political and social enfranchisement. Despite the model minority discourses and stereotypes, and now complicated by the ideological and economic effects of the geopolitical rise of China—these North American struggles for political and economic justice for Asian-Americans and Asian-Canadians continue (Lee, 2008).

As I read through this important new collection of studies of "Chinese-heritage" students and youth engaging with schooling, language, and literacy issues, what struck me was the incredible diversity of communities and contexts,

xiv Allan Luke

families, and young people brought together under the umbrella of "Chinese-heritage" students. Some are, like myself, kin of the longstanding Chinese migrant communities established over a century of successive waves of immigration. Others arrived as part of the large-scale South East–Asian immigration in the aftermath of the Vietnam War. Yet others trace their origins back to pre-"handover" Hong Kong or from Kuomintang-era Taiwan. Finally, there are more recent migrants, part of the ongoing and expanding transnational flows of academics, professionals, and workers from the Chinese mainland to Canada and the United States. Yet others are newcomers from the Chinese diaspora of Malaysia, Indonesia, and Singapore.

Many of us have worked to make the case that the "between-two-worlds" binary models of first-wave multiculturalism have their historical and interpretive limits (Luke, 2009a). These models tacitly set the grounds for deficit explanations, disguising the complex "difference within difference" and heterogeneity of Chinese communities and lived experience.

The studies here describe "Chinese-heritage" students from a diverse range of social class, ethnolinguistic, and, indeed, cultural backgrounds dealing with language, literacy, and cultural transitions to mainstream American and Canadian schooling. Yet there is a subtle, unresolved tension across this volume. For some chapters refer to the students as "Chinese-heritage" while yet others refer to "Chinese," "Chinese-Canadian," "Chinese-American," and so forth. Like the 1990s Hong Kong-based descriptions of "Chinese learning styles" (Watkins & Biggs, 1996), the risk here is that the attempt to describe a distinctive institutional or cultural experience unintentionally sets the grounds for another set of culturally debilitating and empirically misleading stereotypes. The products of history and society, Roland Barthes (1972) insisted, should never be construed as given by nature.

In these brief comments, I want to raise key definitional and epistemological questions—questions that ultimately are political and cultural—about what might count as "Chineseness." My case is that we cannot take the category "Chinese heritage" as an unproblematic, empirically descriptive category.

Because of the historical baggage of empire, nation, and language, one of the residual traditions in everyday cultural life is the assumption that there are homogeneous races and singular cultures: explained by reference to genetic phenotypes and physical appearance, skin color, inter-generationally shared cultural practices, common languages, and so forth. The legacy of European empire, Stuart Hall (1993) often reminded us, was premised on a simple equation: 1 nation = 1 culture = 1 nation. Hence, the slogans and rationales of right-wing, xenophobic political parties in Europe and North America today.

It is also worth noting that the modern term *identity* is in fact derived from seventeenth-century European mathematics, describing equivalence between sets of numbers. The search for national, cultural, ethnic, and, indeed "individual" identity is thus premised on concepts of singularity/multiplicity and in/equality.

Nor is this a wholly Anglo-European move. As Kam Louie's (2002) remarkable study of the history of Chinese masculinity pointed out, there are powerful traditions in Chinese literature and history of attempts to define and assert a singular Han Chinese lineage, masculine identity, and, relatedly, political, and national unity. While the Qin Dynasty nominally marks the formal unification of China, since 1949 political rule has continued to be dominated by the perceived imperative to hold together an ethnically diverse and potentially unruly China. Current state policy is focused on the status, recognition, and, from the government's point of view, necessary integration and assimilation of *Minzu*: the Indigenous and non-Indigenous ethnic minorities who compose slightly less than a decile of the mainland population. In China, Han Chinese culture and bodily *habitus*[1] remain the unmarked, hegemonic norm. Within China and Chinese history, then, there are ongoing issues around cultural, linguistic, and, indeed, religious diversity and heterogeneity.

Nor within Chinese-American or Chinese-Canadian communities is there singular identity, common language, or history. I grew up around Los Angeles Chinatown in the 1950s. My grandparents had been part of the massive Guangzhou migration of the turn of the twentieth century—driven by the push/ pull effects of large-scale famine in Southeastern China,[2] and the demand for migrant labor to build the railroads and work the farms and mines. We were part of a Cantonese-speaking minority, our parents without citizenship rights until the 1940s, and without full employment and access rights until the Civil Rights legislation of the 1960s.

Yet even the nomenclature "Chinese-American" and "Chinese-Canadian," like that of other hyphenated migrant minorities in North America, is at best a congregation or amalgamation of diversity and difference. Many of my childhood friends were from the waves of migration that followed 1949—they spoke a different dialect of Chinese than my parents, some had parents who had attended the best American and Chinese universities, and their cultural practices and, indeed, dispositions were visibly and audibly different than ours. We didn't need social science to tell us about differences that we could see and hear, taste, smell, and experience every day. As we grew up, we witnessed some pretty heated political disagreements within the Chinese-American community, with fractures amongst us about Taiwan/China allegiances, about solidarity with the Black-led Civil Rights Movement, and other issues. And yet, we assumed, what we shared was that we were all "Chinese."

The "model minority" stereotype has reared its head yet again in the U.S. media hype around "Tiger Mothers." And it is complicated by the advent of an acute case of Western educational "Asia-envy" as PISA, TIMMS, and other international comparative measures underline the ostensive educational success of Singapore, Korea, Japan, and Shanghai. These new stereotypes and generalizations risk writing over the complexity of Chinese communities inside and outside of Chinatown—where many Chinese-Americans struggle alongside and with

Latinos, African-Americans, and other "minoritized" Asian communities, fighting for basic economic and social justice and, indeed, educational access (Chang & Lee, 2012).

To return to my opening point: What counts as *Chineseness*? And how is this made to "count"? The sociological contribution to the critique of race by Omi and Winant (2015) was to shift focus from "race" as an essential unifying characteristic of a given community or group, to an understanding that racism occurred through racializing practices (cf. Luke, 2009b). Likewise, dominant societies and culture never consist of minorities but rather minoritize particular communities as outside an unmarked, dominant ethnic/cultural/linguistic norm.

We are indeed all human beings, and much of our common sense about "race" was a destructive artifact of colonialism and imperialism, genocide and racism—North and South, East and West. But if there are no essential, singular, and generalizable racial characteristics, then perhaps how and when we are identified and positioned, how and when we identify and position ourselves as "Chinese" matters even more (Ang, 2001). This is a continuing case for what Gayatri Spivak (1999) terms *strategic essentialism*: the assertion of cultural and racial identity and solidarity as deliberate political, cultural, and social action in an ongoing struggle for equity and social justice.

Taken together, the studies in *Chinese-Heritage Students in North American Schools* depict the actual diversity in Chinese socioeconomic and migration background, first and second language and dialect resources, spatial/geographic dis/placement, and, indeed, everyday educational experience. This is a question of cultural homogeneity and heterogeneity, of difference within difference—of how we can talk about "Chinese-heritage" or "Chinese" or, for that matter, "Chinese-American" communities in ways that capture the complex lived dynamics of common cultural experiences, practices, and schemata—and, indeed, the differences between and within these communities.

To conclude, an illustrative story: While I was working and teaching in Singapore, an idealistic White Australian colleague asked me for advice on how to understand local culture and context. I explained to him something of my background: that I was less than successful in weekend Cantonese school and did not speak Chinese, not that my parents' Cantonese would have counted in the context of Singapore's aspirations towards an English/Putonghua bilingual elite. I further explained that when I worked and lived in China, Hong Kong, and Singapore, there is much that I could see, hear, understand, and, indeed, feel on the basis of my own embodied history. But, I explained, there were core elements of vernacular, local Chinese cultures that remained inaccessible and unknowable, despite my Han Chinese appearance.

I offered him a useful question he (and other outsiders) could ask himself: "How many different kinds of Chinese do I see and hear around me each day?"

His response was, "I don't understand the question?"

I paused: "You've answered it."

What we are able to see and hear, sense and feel—what we take as history and what we take as nature—depends on our cultural, linguistic, and epistemic standpoints and histories. Wen Ma and Guofang Li have brought together these meticulous case studies of young people and children engaging with schooling and education, language and literacy in what remain White-dominated societies. Whether you as a reader are of "Chinese heritage" or not—it is my hope that you recognize and engage with the diversity of Chinese experience here, with an eye for which cultural and community differences make substantive educational differences, where and when, and for whom.

Allan Luke
Brisbane, Australia
August 12, 2015

Notes

1 See Mu (2015) and Cui (2015) on Chinese "*habitus*," drawing on the sociology of Pierre Bourdieu.
2 See Davis (2001) for a fascinating new account of the role of climate change, imperialism, and political economy in late-nineteenth-century Chinese and Indian famines.

References

Ang, I. (2001). *On not speaking Chinese: Living between Asia and the west*. London, UK: Routledge.
Barthes, R. (1972). *Mythologies* (Trans. A. Lavers). London, UK: Paladin.
Chang, B., & Lee, J. (2012). Community-based? Asian American students, parents, and teachers in the shifting Chinatowns of New York and Los Angeles. *AAPI Nexus: Policy, Practice and Community, 10*(2), 99–117.
Cui, D. (2015). Capital, distinction and racialized habitus: Immigrant youth in the educational field. *Journal of Youth Studies, 18.* doi:10.1080/13676261.2015.1020932. Retrieved from www.tandfonline.com/doi/full/10.1080/13676261.2015.1020932# abstract
Davis, M. (2001). *Late Victorian holocausts: El nino and the making of the third world*. London, UK: Verso.
Hall, S. (1993). Culture, nation, community. *Cultural Studies, 7*(3), 349–363.
Louie, K. (2002). *Theorizing Chinese masculinity: Society and gender in China*. Cambridge, UK: Cambridge University Press.
Luke, A. (2009a). Race and language as capital in school: A sociological template for language education reform. In R. Kubota & A. Lin (Eds.), *Race, culture and identities in second language education* (pp. 286–308). New York, NY: Routledge.
Luke, A. (2009b). Another ethnic autobiography? Childhood and the cultural economy of looking. In R. Hammer & D. Kellner (Eds.), *Media/Cultural studies: Critical approaches* (pp. 482–500). New York, NY: Peter Lang.
Mu, G. M. (2015). *Learning Chinese as a heritage language: An Australian perspective*. Clevedon, UK: Multilingual Matters.

xviii Foreword

Omi, M., & Winant, H. (2015). *Racial formation in the United States* (3rd ed.). New York, NY: Routledge.

Spivak, G. (1999). *Critique of postcolonial Reason*. Boston, MA: Harvard: Harvard University Press.

Watkins, D., & Biggs, J. (Eds.). (1996). *The Chinese learner: Cultural, psychological and contextual influences*. Hong Kong, China & Melbourne, AUS: Hong Kong University Press & the Australian Council for Educational Research.

Wu, J., & Chen, T. (Eds.). (2010). *Asian American studies now: A critical reader*. New Brunswick, NJ: Rutgers University Press.

ACKNOWLEDGMENTS

There are so many individuals that we would like to thank for helping bring this book into fruition. First of all, we are grateful to all the chapter authors who share their research on the educational experiences and lives of all kinds of Chinese-heritage students. It is their scholarly insights that fill the pages of this edited volume and, we believe, will contribute to the well-being of Chinese and other minority learners in North American schools. We also appreciate their willingness and time to review each other's work. We are most thankful to the invaluable contribution of Allan, who gave us the honor to have his "last Foreword," and Yong for his not last but important Afterword. As editors, we feel a genuine pleasure working with Naomi, Brianna, and other Routledge staff. We really cannot ask for a better editor than Naomi, who has guided us through the lengthy review and publication process. Finally, we could not have done it without our families' love and support—a big *thank-you* to our spouses and children, who had been our biggest support while we worked on the book through late nights and weekends. You have made our work all the more worthwhile!

INTRODUCTION

Understanding "Difference within Differences" in Chinese-Heritage Students' Educational Experiences across School, Home, and Community Contexts

Guofang Li and Wen Ma

Chinese-heritage students (we use this term to refer to students of Chinese descent, including earlier migrant Chinese, diasporic Chinese, and current Chinese moving and living across borders) are by far the largest ethnic groups among Asian-American and Canadian communities. They are often viewed as high achievers, lumped under the single category of "Asian students" in most federal and state databases, such as the National Assessment of Educational Progress data in the United States, and in most federal and provincial databases in Canada, despite disseminated reports about cultural difficulties, academic pressures, and socialization problems confronting individual learners from Chinese backgrounds (see Lee, 2009; Li & Wang, 2008). Popular media have also depicted Chinese-heritage students (along with other Asian students) as academically single-minded and socially inept hard-workers, spurred by their tradition and culture. The new Chinese-heritage students, as the highly controversial "Too Asian" article (Findlay & Köhler, 2010) in *Maclean's* magazine and the "Too Smart" article (Chen, 2012) in *The New York Times* indicate, have also been seen as a threat to the White mainstream students and society in both Canada and the United States. As well, the new Chinese-heritage students are seen as "rich" and a threat to native-born Asian Americans and Canadians (Kuo, 2014). While a lot of these new and old myths surrounding Chinese-heritage students have been focused on students at the college level, much less attention has been given to Chinese-heritage students in the K–12 schools. Obviously, to unpack these myths about K–12 Chinese-heritage learners in these complex social realties in both the United States and Canada, it is important to understand their hearts and minds beyond test scores.

2 Guofang Li and Wen Ma

Objectives of the Book

We see an urgent need for a close examination of the educational experiences of this under-researched population. First of all, the growing number of Chinese-heritage students in the United States and Canada has generated broad interests and necessities for the educational community to learn more about the successes and struggles to dispel the myths surrounding their academic performance. Second, contrary to the popular perception that they are a homogenous group, Chinese-heritage learners come from very diverse origins, and the diversity of this population and its impact on Chinese-heritage language learners' educational experiences has not been adequately addressed in the research literature. Therefore, there is a need to look comprehensively at their different academic, sociocultural, and socio-emotional development in the public schools.

With this intention, this book addresses the different issues related to Chinese-heritage K–12 students' languages, cultures, identities, and challenges beyond academic achievements across North American schools. Our goal is to "capture difference within differences" (Luke & Luke, 1999, p. 240) among Chinese-heritage K–12 students, while acknowledging the historical, generational, cultural, social, geographical, and demographic complexities. Specifically, this book examines Chinese-heritage learners' pertinent educational experiences, complex (even inconvenient) realities, and language and literacy practices in and outside of schools, as well as the multi-dimensional sociocultural and socio-emotional complications in Chinese-heritage students' lives across divergent K–12 settings, homes, and communities. It aims to address the following overarching questions:

1   What are Chinese-heritage students' experiences in learning language and literacy and across content areas?
2   What unique educational challenges and difficulties do they encounter as they navigate the complex relationships of race, class, and culture in North American schools?
3   How do they make sense of their ethnic and cultural identities in and out of school?
4   What variables are at work that make the Chinese-heritage students range from academic role models to problematic students in need of help, and anything in between?
5   What implications can be drawn to inform their teachers, fellow students, parents, and educational communities?

Focusing on these central questions, individual chapters in the book wrestle with language and literacy challenges; learning across the curriculum; social, cultural, and personal identities; prices for academic pursuits; acculturation and socialization; socio-emotional and psychological development; and other critical topics confronting Chinese-heritage students.

"Difference within Differences" **3**

As the chapters will demonstrate, we address several strands of differences among K–12 Chinese-heritage learners, including differences in language use and choices (between English and Chinese, between early arrivals and late arrivals, among Cantonese, Chinese, and other dialects, and between ELLs [English language learners] and non-ELLs); in identities (between the Chinese and the White mainstream, between the rich and the poor, between the high achievers and the under-achievers, and between individuals who are ethnic Chinese and those from hybrid backgrounds); in achievements (between those who fit the model minority stereotypes and those who do not); and in the learning context (between the early 1990s and the early 2000s and later, between affluent schools and inner city schools, between Chinatown and mainstream suburbs, among the home, community and schools, and among ESL [English as a second language] classes, content classrooms, and youth programs). By addressing the nuanced sociocultural, socio-linguistic, and socio-emotional differences confront these learners as they navigate complex race, culture, and class landscapes in North American schools and communities, we strategically construct the book as one that moves beyond the indiscriminate model minority stereotypes that render them faceless, emotionless, and self-sufficient. As such, this book will offer valuable insights about the lives and educational experiences of a significant cohort of students in and out of school in North America. This will in turn provide useful insights for their teachers to better teach them (and hopefully other peer groups, too).

Organization of the Book

In addition to the Foreword, Afterword, Conclusion, and this Introduction, there are sixteen chapters, divided into four sections. Specifically, Part I addresses Chinese-heritage students' language and literacy learning across K–12 grades. Chapter 1 opens the section with an expansive review of research on learning Chinese as a heritage language (HL) in the United States across three contexts: home, community-based Chinese schools, and K–12 schools. It is found that there are huge variations in parental practices at home to support HL development and multiple challenges confronting Chinese Weekend Schools, and there is inadequate Chinese-language instruction at K–12 schools to meet learners' needs. The chapter concludes with suggestions for parents, Chinese schools, and K–12 schools to overcome students' HL loss. Chapter 2 offers a longitudinal case study of how one Chinese-American immigrant family (Zeta and her parents) helped her transition from a beginning ESL student to a high-achieving student in the mainstream classroom. Such efforts provide valuable insights in the importance of parental involvement in a language minority child's second language (L2) learning as well as the powerful impact of home literacy context on L2 development. Chapter 3 shifts to a Canadian context to look at first-grade Chinese-heritage children's spontaneous literacy practices. Drawing on Holland's notion of "identities in practice," the chapter critically analyzes two narrative ensembles depicting child-initiated, multimodal literacy events. The results call into question the current obsessional practices with standardized achievement tests, which often constrain educators' efforts to listen to and learn from children. Chapter 4 sets the stage back in the United States on secondary students' writing experiences. Based on 150 writing assessments and questionnaires, the chapter shows that recent Chinese immigrant students can benefit from direct instruction in argumentative writing. The findings shed light on what secondary educators can learn about these students' experience in English writing prior to immigration in order to support their learning of academic writing genres in American schools. The chapters in this section not only offer us conceptual lenses to tackle the sociocultural, pedagogical, ideological, and logistical issues related to learning Chinese as a heritage language, but also provide authentic portraits of Chinese-heritage students' situated experiences and challenges in learning English reading and writing. These insights, in turn, will help us better facilitate diverse learners' development in multiple languages and literacies beyond test scores.

Part II delves into Chinese-heritage students' learning across different content areas. Chapter 5 describes cultural and linguistic challenges and adjustment difficulties confronting recently arrived Chinese immigrant students in their participation in mainstream science classroom discourse. The chapter reveals why and how a Chinese immigrant student, Yuna, encountered challenges of content learning when the teacher drew on everyday knowledge associated with mainstream American household and community life to teach targeted science concepts. Understanding cultural differences between learners' and mainstream American everyday experiences helps teachers to be more aware of how to scaffold Chinese immigrant students' content learning in the mainstream English-speaking classroom. Chapter 6 centers on disparities in achievements among a large cohort of Chinese-heritage students in a Canadian context. The chapter documented differential achievement patterns among Chinese learners by analyzing such variables as first language, country of origin, age, age on arrival, length of residence, initial English-language skill levels, and long-term records of academic achievement. The chapter also compared achievement patterns among Mandarin and Cantonese speakers from China, Hong Kong, and Taiwan, and with learners from other Asian immigrant groups. Drawing on data from multiple sources including interviews and achievement data from large databases, the authors find that many of them struggle academically. The chapter's findings suggest that lumping diverse Chinese-heritage students all as high achievers masks the disparity among them. Chapter 7 further discusses 10 Chinese-heritage adolescents' participation in and perspectives of their positions in ESL, language arts, and content area classes such as mathematics and science in Canadian schools in relation to their language and cultural barriers. The adolescents perceived the school as a distant space constituted of "their" (i.e., English, literature, and social studies that often require more English proficiency and group interactions) and

"Difference within Differences" **5**

"our" (e.g., math and science) classes, and they remained silent in "their" classes and were more active in participation in "our" classes. These findings require teachers to carefully consider social interaction and classroom-participation structure concerning new immigrant students in instruction. Chapter 8 uses two national data sets to analyze how home variables are related to twelfth-grade math performance among Chinese-heritage high school students in the United States. For students in the early 1990s, better prior math performance, higher socioeconomic status (SES), more siblings, never being in a math remedial class, and having married parents were associated with better twelfth-grade math performance, but for students in the early 2000s, better prior math performance and being first-generation students were associated with better twelfth-grade math performance. This study reveals the different variables that affect Chinese-heritage students' mathematical achievements in different historical times. All in all, the chapters in this section further testify that aggregated test scores reinforce the myth that Chinese-heritage students are all "naturally strong" in math, science, and other STEM areas, and that results from more nuanced analyses such as those in this section help to portray tremendous complexity and diversity in Chinese-heritage learners' learning struggles across the curriculum.

Part III wrestles with issues related to Chinese-heritage students' cultures and identities. Chapter 9 features Chinese and non-Chinese-heritage elementary students and their teachers from an American "Chinatown" school who contest several stereotypes including assumed homogeneity that all students are Chinese, thus complicating the notion of *Chinese* in this particular sociocultural context. Through examples of students' resistance to racial stereotypes about people in Chinatown (i.e., seen as "foreigners" against "the United States people") and the "antiquated" Chinatown itself, the study further complicates the assumed hegemonic and homogeneous views of Chinese-heritage learners in Chinatowns. Chapter 10 expounds on a variety of struggles experienced by Chinese-heritage students in Canadian schools. The chapter challenges the model minority discourse that represents Chinese-heritage students as a homogenous group of high-academic achievers privileged with strong parental support yet socially deficient by identifying issues of differential treatment and discrimination in their social interaction with teachers and peers at school. The findings caution us to guard against reproducing racism confronting Chinese-heritage learners. Chapter 11 presents ways in which "CYLP," a Chinese immigrant youth program run by a community-based organization, supports the creation of *Ibasho*, or a place to feel safe, secure, and accepted, for 18 first-generation Chinese-heritage high school students from China. While the students often felt a sense of confinement and isolation at home, school, and in their neighborhood, CYLP assisted them to expand their Ibasho through acknowledging the students as cultural brokers and training them as potential leaders. These efforts facilitated their linguistic, cultural, and social-emotional adjustment to life in the United States. Chapter 12 is a phenomenological narrative case study of a Chinese-White youth's bicultural identity development across preschool, early grades, middle school, and high school. The chapter explores biracial identity as a constructed, fluid, and often in-between space, and concludes with a discussion of how phenomenological narrative inquiry can assist educators and researchers to probe identity issues pertaining to multiracial youth with Chinese heritage. In sum, these chapters highlight issues and complications compounded by non-academic-related sociocultural, linguistic, and racial variables that affect Chinese-heritage students' lives in and out of school as they navigate across multidimensional borderlines. The chapters in this section further inform of Chinese-heritage learners' difficult cross-cultural journey and their equally arduous sense-making of their evolving identities and personhood.

Finally, Part IV grapples with other sociocultural variables that affect Chinese-heritage students' cognitive, emotional, and psychological development. Chapter 13 reports findings from the University of California-Berkeley's Kids and Family Project, a longitudinal investigation of psychological and academic development in Chinese-heritage families in the United States. Using Bronfenbrenner's bio-ecological model as a conceptual framework, the chapter presents findings on the socio-emotional and behavioral processes that influence Chinese-heritage children's performance in the classroom. Specifically, the authors report the children's socio-emotional and behavioral development patterns from four aspects: individual-environmental processes (children's relationships with parents and teachers), person characteristics (children's self-regulatory processes), contexts (neighborhoods and cultural orientations) and time (periods of development and acculturation). Chapter 14 reviews the literature on Chinese-heritage students' development in creativity, drawing on recent research on the characteristics of Chinese-heritage students, at the personal, familial, and societal levels that distinguish these students' learning experiences from their European American counterparts. The chapter further explains the unique challenges and distinct pathways of creativity development among Chinese-heritage students. Chapter 15 deals with how parenting styles affect second-generation Chinese-heritage students' academic performance. Based on an analysis of the parenting styles of five families whose children were in gifted programs in the United States, the chapter finds that the parents attributed their dedication, high expectations, and hard work to their children's academic success. In addition to paying attention to their children's academic achievements, the parents were also highly attentive to the maintenance of Chinese culture and language, and held high importance of the children's emotional and psychological well-being. Finally, Chapter 16 examines one "low-performing" public high school's efforts to meet the socio-linguistic and academic needs of the growing population of Cantonese-speaking Chinese-heritage students in a Spanish-speaking Latino community in Chicago. The chapter suggests that despite substantial school efforts, the Cantonese-speaking students were no longer just "up against Whiteness," they were also competing for resources with Latinos and Mandarin-speaking Chinese-heritage students. In conclusion, all these chapters broaden the contexts from mainstream public schools to other settings, such as Chinatown and Latino community, and extend our attention from academic achievements to other critical areas, such as creativity and socio-emotional and psychological development. The section helps us recognize the breadth, depth, and diversity of the challenges and potential opportunities for Chinese-heritage students' holistic development and growth beyond the academic realm.

As we can see, Chinese-heritage students in North American K–12 schools are a very diverse cohort of learners. Some of them have outstanding test scores, some of them struggle academically, and many more are in the middle. Just like their academic performance, their non-academic-related conditions, such as emotional and psychological health, creativity, peer relations, cultural affiliations, and social identities, also range widely. The implications of these findings will be further discussed in the Conclusion. We are confident that all the studies and the insights that emerge from them will help us better understand the hearts and minds of these students beyond test scores.

References

Chen, C. (2012, Dec. 20). Asians: Too smart for their own good? *The New York Times*, p. A43.

Findlay, S., & Köhler, N. (2010, Nov. 10). The enrollment controversy: Worries that efforts in the U.S. to limit enrollment of Asian students in top universities may migrate to Canada. *Maclean's*. Retrieved from www.macleans.ca/news/canada/too-asian/

Kuo, L. (2014). *Are US universities choosing rich Chinese students over Asian Americans?* Retrieved from http://qz.com/203273/are-us-universities-are-choosing-rich-chinese-students-over-asian-americans/

Lee, S. J. (2009). *Unraveling the "model minority" stereotype: Listening to Asian American youth* (2nd ed.). New York, NY: Teachers College Press.

Li, G., & Wang, L. (Eds.). (2008). *Model minority myth revisited: An interdisciplinary approach to demystifying Asian American educational experiences.* Charlotte, NC: Information Age.

Luke, C., & Luke, A. (1999). Theorizing interracial families and hybrid identity: An Australian perspective. *Educational Theory, 49*(2), 223–249.

PART I

Chinese-Heritage Students' Language and Literacy Learning

1

CHINESE STUDENTS' HERITAGE-LANGUAGE LEARNING IN THE UNITED STATES

Issues and Challenges

Keying Wen and Guofang Li

The increasing language diversity in the United States over the past few decades suggests the continuing and growing role of non-English languages, such as Chinese, "as part of the national fabric" (Ryan, 2013, p. 15). According to a U.S. Census Bureau report of language use in the United States, in 2011, almost 3 million people aged five or older spoke Chinese at home, an increase of 354.3% from 1980 to 2010 (Ryan, 2013). With the emergence of China's international power and the potential of business cooperation, more and more American schools offer instruction of Chinese as a foreign language (Zhang & Slaughter-Defoe, 2009). As one of the less commonly taught languages, Chinese is believed to be indispensable for national defense, international business, and local government services in the United States (Marcos, 1999).

Different from Chinese as a foreign-language learner, Chinese as a heritage-language[1] learner (HLL) is a person who has proficiency in Chinese or a Chinese cultural connection studying Chinese (Kelleher, 2010a). Chinese HLLs vary widely in their Chinese proficiency. Most Chinese HLLs who are born in the United States or immigrate at young ages develop Chinese proficiency below native level; and some Chinese HLLs who immigrate to the U.S. at older ages "maintain native level or close to native level Chinese" (Jia, 2008, p. 190).

As the second most commonly spoken heritage language (HL) in the United States (U.S. Census Bureau, 2011), Chinese has many sub-varieties. It is an umbrella term that "subsumes numerous dialects which are grouped under Wu, Xiang, Gan, Min, Cantonese, Hakka, and Mandarin" (He, 2008, p. 3). Among these varieties, Cantonese was mostly spoken by the early Chinese immigrants from Hong Kong and Guangdong Province while Mandarin is mostly spoken by recent Chinese immigrants from mainland China and Taiwan (Wiley et al., 2008).

Chinese HL learning takes place within the family, community-based heritage-language schools (CHLSs), and mainstream schools in the United States. Informal, everyday learning of Chinese at home is "indispensable" for Chinese HL learning (He, 2008, p. 2), while CHLSs are the major efforts for Chinese HL instruction and development. Influenced by several waves of Chinese immigrant influxes, CHLSs were documented to be growing in the past century (Chang, 2003; Chao, 1997; Lai, 2004; McGinnis, 2005; Pan, 1997). According to the two main organizations of Chinese CHLSs in the United States, the National Council of Associations of Chinese Language Schools (NCACLS) (formed by Taiwan and Hong Kong CHLSs for traditional Chinese characters instruction), and the Chinese School Association in the United States (CSAUS) (formed by PRC Chinese CHLSs for teaching Mandarin and simplified Chinese characters), NCACLS's member schools served about 100,000 students (NCACLS, 2010), and the CSAUS had more than 500 member schools in the U.S. with more than 8,000 teachers and 100,000 students (CSAUS, 2014). This means, in total, there were approximately 200,000 students enrolled in Chinese CHLSs in recent years. In addition, more and more students of Chinese descent are taking Chinese within the U.S. educational system from kindergarten to college (He, 2008). According to Dillion (2010), there were approximately 1,600 U.S. mainstream schools (including public schools and private schools) that taught Chinese as a foreign language in 2010 and the number has been increasing. There are also a growing number of Chinese immersion programs in the mainstream schools.

Chinese language maintenance is seen as "the most important element" in the process of HL and culture transmission from one generation to the next (Wang & Green, 2003, p. 171). As well, Chinese as a HL is both the emotional connection between Chinese students and their families and a critical factor that helps Chinese students establish positive ethnic identity and brings them practical advantage in the job market in the future (Lao, 2004). Despite the fact that developing Chinese as a HL benefits both HL individuals and the nation as a whole, Chinese maintenance cannot be easily achieved. It is commonplace that Chinese learners' fluency in their HL declines as English improves—by the end of the high school years, children are at best semi-speakers of their HL (Hinton, 2001; Liu, 2008). In addition to HL attrition, research (e.g., Zhang, 2008) has also showed most school-aged Chinese children developed unbalanced bilingualism and biliteracy with their English proficiency much higher than their HL proficiency. The majority of these children understood Chinese when spoken to and some could speak Chinese fluently, but most of them had "a low level of Chinese literacy" (Zhang, 2008, p. 93) because they did not have adequate reading or writing skills in Chinese.

Many Chinese HLLs are reported to be less motivated on maintaining a HL in an English-dominant society. Their interest on learning Chinese has been found to descend with age, and they increasingly perceived learning Chinese "as a tedious and unprofitable task" (Zhang & Slaughter-Defoe, 2009, p. 89). Indeed, at young ages, many HLLs find the learning activities in CHLSs "interesting and entertaining" (Zhang & Slaughter-Defoe, 2009, p. 89) and with less academic pressure from public school they are able to attend CHLS. However, as the difficulties of learning Chinese increase, especially the difficulty of learning the complex Chinese written system (Liu, 2008; Zhang & Slaughter-Defoe, 2009), HLLs are reluctant to learn Chinese after a few years of attending CHLS. Many young HLLs cannot foresee the potential of usefulness of Chinese in the academic arena and job market, nor do they feel connected with Chinese language and culture as their parents do (Zhang & Slaughter-Defoe, 2009). The "pressures for linguistic and cultural conformity in the school environment" increase as the academic tasks in public school become challenging (Zhang & Slaughter-Defoe, 2009, p. 90). As a consequence, many young Chinese students gradually shift their language preference from Chinese to English. Yet, older HLLs who have motivation to learn Chinese perceive being able to interact with their ethnic peers in Chinese and understanding heritage culture as an important ability (Lei, 2012; Lu & Li, 2008). Many second- or 1.5-generation Chinese immigrants express the regret of not having a high level of proficiency in Chinese after they go to college, and want their children to learn Chinese (Hinton, 2001; Huang, 2012). HLLs' experience of HL attrition and the challenges that they face to maintain Chinese HL suggest that we need to better learn the practices and processes in Chinese maintenance in the United States and the impeding factors of HL maintenance. In the following sections, we will discuss Chinese students' HL learning in the family, CHLS, and mainstream school contexts. We hope to frame an agenda that can guide education and research in supporting school-aged Chinese students' HL learning in the future.

In order to include a broad range of research in this review, literature search strategies were adopted. Relevant research from 1990 to 2015 concerning Chinese HL education in home, CHLS, and K–12 school contexts was identified by searching databases like ProQuest for primary research materials. As well, key journal articles were obtained from *Heritage Language Journal*, and foreign language education or bilingual education journals. Reports published by Center for Applied Linguistics, the National Foreign Language Center, Asian Society, and other organizations were also included. Besides, books about Chinese HL education were also included. Finally, we conducted a comprehensive Internet search and included various kinds of resources. Resources were eligible for this review if: (a) the focus of the study, review article, or report was Chinese HL education in the U.S.; and (b) at least one of the three contexts (i.e., family, Chinese language school, and K–12 school) was discussed. Among them, empirical studies on Chinese HLLs' learning were the major resources. Focusing on sociocultural and practical aspects of HL learning, studies only focused on linguistic aspects of HL learning were excluded. Since the focus age group of this book is K–12 students, studies on Chinese HL learning at post-secondary level were also excluded.

Heritage Language Learning at Home

Family and parents play an important role in supporting individual HLLs' HL maintenance. This is especially true in Chinese immigrant families. Interestingly, Asian parents, including Chinese parents, are found to not expect mainstream schools to be responsible for bilingual education; rather, they think "family should play the most important role" (Liu, 2008, p. 41). This section discusses research on parents' attitudes towards Chinese children's HL maintenance and their practice of Chinese literacy at home.

Research has revealed that most Chinese parents have positive attitudes toward HL maintenance and their positive attitudes were positively correlated with children's HL development (Lao, 2004; Liu, 2008; Luo & Wiseman, 2000; Lü & Koda, 2011; Zhang & Slaughter-Defoe, 2009). The studies found that parents who held positive attitudes toward HL maintenance believed: (a) in HL's practical value, such as its value on academic advancement and better career in the future; (b) HL was important for developing positive ethnic identity; and (c) HL increased HLLs' cohesion with their family and ethnic group. These positive attitudes were "instilled in children via daily contact" and served to enhance HL maintenance (Liu, 2008, p. 42).

In families where parents hold a positive perspective toward Chinese, parents believe that speaking Chinese at home consistently, especially after children attend mainstream school, is an effective way of instilling the HL in these children (Zhang & Slaughter-Defoe, 2009). Some parents enforce a Chinese-only policy and require their children to only speak Chinese at home. They convey the message that Chinese is "the only language in the family" (Zhang & Slaughter-Defoe, 2009, p. 87). Many parents, especially the well-educated ones, are reported to teach their children Chinese by themselves and assign Chinese homework to their children. They rely on Chinese communities and libraries to access Chinese teaching materials or purchase textbooks from China, and they also support their children's Chinese development by organizing family gatherings, providing daily TV exposure in Chinese, and reading with children in Chinese (Lü & Koda, 2011).

Studies have also found that in general, Chinese parents value CHLSs' critical role in preserving and developing HL proficiency and cultural knowledge of ethnic communities (Liu, Musica, Koscak, Vinogradova, & Lopez, 2011, p. 1). Many parents view CHLSs as a resource to learn Chinese systematically. For example, Zhang and Slaughter-Defoe's (2009) study of Chinese parents' and children's attitude toward CHLSs showed that many Chinese parents favored CHLS and anticipated their children to learn HL systematically, formally, and consistently in CHLS, even though some of the older Chinese children did not necessarily share these views.

Research has also found that Chinese parents with positive attitudes toward HL maintenance also strongly support Chinese education in the mainstream schools (Lao, 2004; Liu, 2008). Some even demand Chinese instruction be included in

Heritage-Language Learning in the U.S. **15**

mainstream schools. For example, Wang (2009) documented how 12 Chinese parents in a Midwestern small university town requested adding Chinese as a foreign language in the high school their children attended. The Chinese parents in the study viewed the opportunity for their children to speak or learn to speak their HL in school as the right to pursue educational equality and social justice as well as maintain their Chinese culture and identity. The Chinese parents also viewed the Chinese language as an important communication tool their children should have so they could be competitive in the future international job market.

Although most Chinese parents' attitude toward HL maintenance has been positive, research has reported discrepancy between parents' attitudes towards HL maintenance and actions they actually take in supporting HL development at home, resulting in "a gap between a general desire for Chinese to be spoken and actual practice" (Lao, 2004, p. 114). These discrepancies can be best explained in the two Chinese immigrant families documented in Li's (2006) study. Although the parents wanted their children to learn Chinese, they perceived Chinese as an interference of children's English acquisition and emphasized the importance of English development over HL maintenance at home; nor did they make full use of community resources to facilitate their children's HL maintenance. The parents' attitude toward HL agreed with the "English only" message the children received in school. As a result, both of the focal students were succeeding in English, but they "quickly lost their HL with only one year of public school experiences" (Li, 2006, p. 27).

Therefore, both parental attitudes and actions and mainstream school language policies and ideologies are critical factors that influence children's HL development (Li, 2006). In order to promote HL development, efforts must be devoted to foster positive attitudes among both parents and mainstream teachers and educators who "need to work collaboratively in helping learners become bilingual and biliterate" (Li, 2006, p. 30).

Heritage-Language Learning in Heritage-Language Schools

It has been historically recognized that "the strongest efforts for the teaching of heritage languages have occurred outside of mainstream schooling" (Kelleher, 2010b, p.1), notably through CHLSs. CHLSs are often established by ethnic communities to "pass on their language and culture from one generation to the next" and "to maintain connection within families and communities" (Kelleher, 2010b, p. 1). At the macro level, CHLSs support "multilingualism and linguistic diversity" (Compton, 2001, p. 162). It has been "the major provider for Chinese language instruction in the U.S. over the past several decades" (Liu, 2010, p. 1). At the micro level, CHLSs play an important role in preserving HLs and promoting ethnic identity of HLLs (Huang, 2012).

CHLSs' positive influence on Chinese children's ethnic identity construction has been well documented. First, the opportunity of interacting with a number of fellow ethnic friends weekly becomes an important way of identity construction for the children and youth (Du, 2007). Many students found it was "fun" to gather with other Chinese people by attending the school (Du, 2007, p. 157). Although some students were critical of the outcome of attending CHLS and did not see the connection between what they learned in CHLS and their daily life in the U.S., attending the school itself "reaffirmed their ethnic identity to the youth" (Du, 2007, p. 157). In addition to the opportunity for Chinese children to socialize with their ethnic peers, the curriculum content can also help foster positive ethnic identities. In another multiple-case study by Wu (2011), Chinese CHLS teachers implemented culturally relevant pedagogy to connect the instruction with students' prior knowledge and daily experience in order to develop students' cultural understanding. As a result, the CHLS was considered by the students as an important context to "speak their heritage languages and experience Chinese culture" (Wu, 2011, p. 950). Further, CHLS has been reported to help students reconcile with both their Chinese and Western identities. For example, Huang (2012) documented a successful example of CHLS in constructing Chinese children's positive ethnic identities and Western identities. The teachers and administrators perceived students would "have identities with both American traits and Chinese traits" (Huang, 2012, p. 150). Holding this perception, teachers guided students to switch positions of being Chinese or being American according to the context. To establish positive ethnic identity and "nurture a sense of belonging to Chinese culture" (Huang, 2012, p. 127), the teachers used Chinese moral tales to promote Chinese role models, asked students to do projects that helped them explore Chinese culture and strengthen their Chinese identity, and required students to bow to teachers in order to practice respect in traditional ways. Huang reported that the teachers did not want to over-emphasize the Chinese side of their identity and helped students make a connection with their daily life in the U.S. and China and Chinese culture so that students could "learn the essence of both Chinese and Western cultures" (Huang, 2012, p. 113).

Although Chinese CHLSs' contribution to students' positive ethnic identity construction has been clear from research, reports on their effectiveness on Chinese HL maintenance have been mixed. While there are some successful examples, many Chinese CHLSs did not fulfill parents' expectations of children's HL-learning outcomes. For example, in P. S. Wang's (1996) survey study of Chinese parents' expectations of their children's Chinese proficiency at a Chinese CHLS in Delaware, the parents reported that they were merely requiring the children to know "basic Chinese," which meant that "their children could speak Chinese with any native speaker, understand Chinese movies or TV news, and read Chinese newspapers or magazines" (p. 64). These expectations can be too high for CHLS to achieve because this range of activity is considered advanced or native-like proficiency rather than rudimentary Chinese, as claimed by the parents (P. S. Wang, 1996). Reports on students' perceptions are also mixed. For example, Du's (2007) study revealed that although the Chinese youth had fun in CHLS, they believed they learned "nothing" in terms of Chinese proficiency (Du, 2007, p. 156). And parents chose to "tolerate" the way their children made use of the CHLS as long as their children could socialize with other Chinese people (Du, 2007).

These issues mirrored a variety of difficulties CHLSs face in promoting HL education that include a lack of both physical and human resources. According to Liu et al. (2011), CHLSs' challenges included (a) seeking program funding; (b) finding enough meeting space; (c) addressing students' diversity on language skills and backgrounds; (d) recruiting and retaining students; (e) getting parents' cooperation on developing students' HL proficiency; (f) recruiting and training qualified teachers; and (g) finding teaching materials that are appropriate for Chinese HLLs in the United States. Specifically, shortage of funding has been identified as one of the major difficulties that most CHLSs face (Gallagher, 1996; Liu et al., 2011). Although CHLSs receive funding through tuition and donations, the funds are not enough to fully cover the expense of developing teaching materials, providing professional development for teachers, updating teaching technologies, or the rent of meeting space (Liu et al., 2011).

Student retention is also a challenge for Chinese CHLSs (Du, 2007; X. Wang, 1996; Zhang & Slaughter-Defoe, 2009). The dropout rate increases with a student's age. A large number of students are found to withdraw from their Chinese CHLS around the middle-school years (X. Wang, 1996). Du (2007) also reported that many students complained and neglected the homework of CHLS and eventually withdrew from the Chinese CHLS. Like many Chinese parents, the parents in Du's study complied with their children's dropout.

Lack of appropriate teaching materials is another problem that many Chinese CHLSs need to tackle (Du, 2007; P. S. Wang, 1996). The Chinese CHLS principal in Du's (2007) study perceived that the lack of appropriate teaching materials hindered teachers' contribution to Chinese teaching; since the compensation that the school can offer was limited, teachers do not have sufficient time to prepare for the classes or make up the shortcomings of the textbooks. The textbooks that some CHLSs use are not cultural-related materials and do not address Chinese HLLs' different backgrounds or learning needs (P. Wang, 1996).

Among the challenges that Chinese CHLSs face, lacking qualified teachers might be the most imperative one for the schools. As Liu et al. (2011) stated, "recruitment and training of teachers is a challenge that most heritage language programs face" (p. 10). Most CHLS teachers do not receive formal preparation as mainstream teachers do. In fact, several studies (Chao, 1997; Li, 2005; X. Wang, 1996) have found that most of the teachers were parents or university/college volunteers who did not receive any professional training on teaching Chinese as a HL. Since CHLSs excessively depend on parents and volunteers for staffing the classes, it is difficult to recruit high quality teaching and adequately prepared teachers (Li, 2005).

Teachers' volunteering status affects their motivation for teaching and innovating in the CHLS as it is seen as a volunteer-oriented position, "rather than a strong committed profession" (Li, 2005, p. 203). Many of the teachers had full-time jobs and used their teaching as a means to stay close to the Chinese community, or "do it just for recreation and socializing" (Li, 2005, p. 203). Regarding teacher recruitment, no "widely agreed teacher recruitment criteria" (Li, 2005, p. 203) is available for the Chinese CHLSs. Although some teachers had teaching experiences in China, most of them had no teaching certificate in China or in the United States.

Classroom instruction was problematic too. Li (2005) found classroom instruction in Chinese CHLSs has been "dominated by repetitive drills and exercise coupled with memorization of texts" (Li, 2005, p. 203). Although the CHLSs' teachers might have a high level of proficiency in the Chinese language, few of them "have the knowledge of the structure of the language or teaching methodology and assessment" (Liu et al., 2011, p. 10). Essentially, Li argues that the teaching approaches for HLLs are not appropriately differentiated from those for native Chinese speakers or traditional foreign language learners.

Another challenge for the CHLS is to address the diversity of its students in terms of their age, family background, and level of their Chinese proficiency (Chao, 1996). While CHLSs typically group together "students of similar age with compatible levels of Chinese" (Chao, 1996, p. 10) there are different Chinese dialect speakers (such as Cantonese, Hakka, and others) as well as Chinese as a second language learners (e.g., adopted Chinese children in non-Chinese households). As well, there are simplified Chinese users typically from mainland China and traditional Chinese users typically from Taiwan and Hong Kong. Also, there are learners who study in the CHLS systems and aim for Chinese-language high school foreign-language or Advanced Placement (AP)-credit classes. These different learners often require different strategies and materials, which CHLSs often struggle to provide due to problems listed above, especially the lack of resources, qualified teachers, and professional development.

In summary, CHLSs as an organization critical to Chinese children's HL and positive identity development face a myriad of challenges in further achieving their full potential. It is clear that CHLSs cannot solve these difficulties alone. Further efforts must be made to seek policy support for funding, close collaboration between CHLSs and the formal education system (such as mainstream schools), and teacher education institutions for teacher development and curriculum development. As well, CHLSs must raise public recognition on CHLS and HL education that can generate broader impact on HL maintenance.

Heritage Language Learning in K–12 Schools

Chinese instruction in mainstream schools provides another possibility of learning Chinese language, developing Chinese literacy, and constructing Chinese ethnic identity for Chinese-descent students. The number of Chinese programs in U.S. schools has increased dramatically in recent years while other foreign language programs fade (Asian Society, 2012; Dillion, 2010; Weise, 2013). Other than offering Chinese as a foreign language in school, many schools provide Chinese immersion programs. Chinese immersion programs aim to produce results in "high levels of proficiency at relatively low cost" (Asian Society, 2012, p. 5). Most Chinese immersion programs start in kindergarten or first grade and aim to develop both "oral and written proficiency in Chinese" (Asian Society, 2012, p. 5). The number of Chinese immersion programs grew dramatically in the last few years. According to Weise (2013), as of November 2013 there were 147 U.S. schools that offered Mandarin immersion programs to K–12 students, and about 22,050 students enrolled in these programs. Over half of the programs were established after 2009.

There are two types of Chinese immersion programs in American schools: one-way immersion and two-way immersion. One-way immersion is for English speakers and Mandarin would be the only instructional language, while two-way immersion is taught in both English and Mandarin. Weise (2013) identified 83% of Mandarin immersion programs were one-way immersion (123) and 16% of them were two-way immersion programs (24).

Several factors have contributed to the increase. One was that being fluent in Chinese brought more opportunities in the future (Dillion, 2010). The other was that the Chinese government has been very supportive on improving Chinese education all over the world. Through Hanban, a language council affiliated with the Chinese Education Ministry, American schools were able to get qualified teachers who were partially paid by the Chinese government. A third reason was that since 2007, Chinese language and culture has been included as a subject in AP tests, and has become the third most-tested AP language after Spanish and French (Dillion, 2010).

Despite the rapid growth, current Chinese programs have been found to not sufficiently fulfill Chinese students' HL development. First, American schools in general do not provide a supportive environment for HL maintenance due to their educational policies. In the English-dominant society, many Chinese bilingual children are found to change their language preference in the first days of their school because of "the pressures for language assimilation and the negative social attitudes toward the children's heritage language" (Zhang, 2008, p. 7). Even children in bilingual programs do not practice bilingual speaking. Some children feel unable to use Chinese as skillfully as English because they lag behind on Chinese vocabulary. Others find Chinese too hard to learn. Zhang (2008) argued the main cause of Chinese HL loss is the "language hegemony favoring English over other minority languages in the larger society" (p. 92).

In addition to the lack of policy support for HL, Chinese programs in K–12 are not specifically designed for Chinese HLLs to develop their HL and positive ethnic identity (He, 2008). To date, although there is no official data on the number of students of Chinese descent enrolled in Chinese programs, in many Chinese programs, there are only a small number of Chinese students. In the Chinese immersion program in a Midwestern elementary school, for example, there are only 14 Chinese students through Pre-K to Grade 6 out of the total number of 278 students in the program. These Chinese students usually do not receive differentiated instruction based on their family connection with Chinese and their prior knowledge of Chinese. However, there are many differences between HLLs and traditional foreign language learners. For example, HLLs have different learning needs than the foreign language learners; therefore, language programs should apply strategies of "screening such students and placing proficient HL learners in a separate track" (Kondo-Brown, 2005, p. 576). Right now, however, Chinese HL learners are placed within the same classes as non-Chinese speaking foreign language learners who have little prior knowledge of the target language.

Another reason that the Chinese programs do not fully support maintaining Chinese students' HL is because they lack continuous instruction on students' Chinese development. Many Chinese programs end in fifth or sixth grade. After finishing the program, students will study in regular classrooms that do not provide any Chinese instruction. After the Chinese instruction is withdrawn, these students' Chinese proficiency might stay at their current level or gradually attrite.

Implications

Although multilingualism is desirable in the U.S. and mainstream monolingual children are encouraged to learn languages other than English, ironically, immigrant children have been urged to become monolingual English speakers "even at the expense of their HL maintenance or development" (Kondo-Brown, 2006, p. 6). This is also true for Chinese HLLs who struggle to learn and maintain their HL.

The different issues and challenges presented in the home, CHLSs, and Chinese programs in K–12 school contexts have important implications for research and practice. For Chinese families, efforts must be made to develop a positive attitude towards HL and create a literacy-rich environment that not only provides English books but also age-appropriate Chinese books. Besides, insisting on using Chinese language at home is an important message that parents should send to their children. Parents also need to be aware of the discrepancy between their belief on HL and their actual practice at home. For families that can get access to Chinese CHLSs, parents may encourage their children to attend a Chinese language school. Importantly, parents need to facilitate their children's Chinese-literacy practice at home. In this way, children will get consistent support on Chinese development. In terms of the cooperation with public school, parents can consider sending children to schools that have Chinese programs.

For CHLSs, they need to seek the articulation with local schools, Chinese families, and universities (McGinnis, 2005). Finding qualified teachers is one of the most important factors that CHLSs should take into account. Also, professional training of new teachers can be very helpful. Teachers should be encouraged to join organizations such as the Chinese Language Teachers Association (CLTA) to get access to more teaching resources and updates of development on Chinese teaching. Besides, Chinese CHLSs also need to improve the public recognition of HL education and CHLSs. By doing so, they find solutions to many challenges they face such as lacking meeting space and enrolling and retaining students. We suggest CHLSs should gather more demographic data of Chinese communities and Chinese CHLSs and publicize Chinese CHLSs in academic fields to promote more studies on HL education. In addition, CHLSs can utilize organizations and programs that support foreign language teaching and learning in the U.S., such as STARTALK, one of the programs that aims to facilitate the development of less commonly taught languages. Many Chinese CHLSs benefit from the STARTALK program in the form of financial support, summer camps, and teacher professional development. They can also benefit from the practical guidance about curriculum developing and lesson planning on the STARTALK website (https://startalk. umd.edu/resources/).

For K–12 schools, whether there is a Chinese program or not, teachers and school administrators should work together to foster bilingual children's positive attitude toward HL by creating a home-language-welcome environment in school. Teachers' positive attitudes toward language diversity and expertise working with language diverse learners are desirable. Schools with a Chinese program must consider identifying HLLs and their needs and designing an appropriate track for them to address their language learning needs and develop positive identity.

Note

1   Oftentimes, terms such as *"heritage language," "home language," "ethnic language," "mother tongue,"* and *"first language"* are used interchangeably.

References

Asian Society. (2012). *Chinese language learning in the early grades: A handbook of resources and best practices for Mandarin immersion.* Retrieved from http://asiasociety.org/files/chinese-earlylanguage.pdf

Chang, I. (2003). *The Chinese in America.* New York, NY: The Penguin Group.

Chao, T. H. (1996). Overview. In X. Wang (Ed.), *A view from within: A case study of Chinese heritage community language schools in the United States* (pp. 7–14). Washington, DC: National Foreign Language Center.

Chao, T. H. (1997). Chinese heritage community language schools in the United States. *ERIC Digest.* Retrieved from http://files.eric.ed.gov/fulltext/ED409744.pdf

Compton, C. J. (2001). Heritage language communities and schools: Challenges and recommendations. In J. K. Peyton, D. A. Ranard, & S. McGinnis (Eds.), *Heritage languages in America: Preserving a national resource* (pp. 145–166). McHenry, IL: Center for Applied Linguistics and Delta Systems.

CSAUS. (2014). *Introduction of the Chinese School Association in the United States*. Retrieved from www.csaus.net/about12.asp

Dillion, S. (2010, January 20). Foreign language fade in class except Chinese. *The New York Times*. Retrieved from www.nytimes.com/2010/01/21/education/21chinese. html?_r=1&

Du, L. (2007). *Community-based education and the formation of ethnic identity: Case study in a Chinese American community* (pp. 97–160). (Doctoral dissertation). Retrieved from ProQuest dissertation and theses database. (UMI No. 3291583)

Gallagher, M. W. (1996). Optimizing unique opportunities for learning. In X. Wang (Ed.), *A view from within: A case study of Chinese Heritage community language schools in the United States* (pp. 69–76). Washington, DC: National Foreign Language Center.

He, A. W. (2008) Chinese as a heritage language: An introduction. In He, A. W. & Xiao, Y. (Eds.), *Chinese as a heritage language: Fostering rooted world citizenry* (Vol. 2, pp. 1–12). Honolulu, HA: University of Hawaii Press.

Hinton, L. (2001). Involuntary language loss among immigrants: Asian–American linguistic autobiographies. *Georgetown University Round Table on Languages and Linguistics 1999*, 203–252.

Huang, Z. D. (2012). *Chinese heritage school's role in Chinese language maintenance and identity formation in the U.S.* (Doctoral dissertation). Retrieved from ProQuest. (UMI Number: 3545635)

Jia, G. (2008). Heritage language development, maintenance, and attrition among recent Chinese immigrants in New York City. In A. W. He & Y. Xiao (Eds.), *Chinese as a heritage language: Fostering rooted world citizenry* (Vol. 2, pp. 189–203). Honolulu, HA: University of Hawaii Press.

Kelleher, A. (2010a). *Who is a heritage language learner?* Center for Applied Linguistics. Retrieved from www.cal.org/heritage/pdfs/briefs/Who-is-a-HeritageLanguage-Learner.pdf

Kelleher, A. (2010b). *What is a heritage language program?* Center for Applied Linguistics. Retrieved from www.cal.org/heritage/pdfs/briefs/what-is-a-heritage-language-program.pdf

Kondo-Brown, K. (2005). Differences in language skills: Heritage language learner subgroups and foreign language learners. *The Modern Language Journal, 89*(4), 563–581.

Kondo-Brown, K. (2006). Introduction. In K. Kondo-Brown (Ed.), *Heritage language development: Focus on East Asian immigrants* (pp. 1–12). Amsterdam, NLD: John Benjamins.

Lai, H. M. (2004). *Becoming Chinese American*. Lanham, MD: AltaMira Press.

Lao, C. (2004). Parents' Attitudes toward Chinese–English Bilingual Education and Chinese-Language Use. *Bilingual Research Journal: The Journal of the National Association for Bilingual Education, 28*(1), 99–121. doi: 10.1080/15235882.2004.10162614

Lei, J. (2012). Socio-psychological factors affecting heritage language education: Case studies of Chinese American adolescents. *New Waves—Educational Research & Development, 15*(1), 62–88.

Li, G. (2006). The role of parents in heritage language maintenance and development: Case study of Chinese immigrant children's home practices. In K. Kondo-Brown (Ed.), *Heritage language development: Focus on East Asian immigrants* (pp. 15–31). Amsterdam, NLD: John Benjamins.

Li, M. (2005). The role of parents in Chinese heritage-language schools. *Bilingual Research Journal, 29*(1), 197–207. doi:10.1080/15235882.2005.10162831

Liu, N. (2010). The role of heritage language schools in building a multilingual society. *Heritage Briefs*. Retrieved from www.cal.org/heritage/pdfs/briefs/the-role-of-heritage-language-schools.pdf

Liu, N., Musica, A., Koscak, S., Vinogradova, P., & Lopez, J. (2011). Challenges and needs of community based heritage language programs and how they are addressed. *Heritage Briefs*. Retrieved from www.cal.org/heritage/pdfs/briefs/challenges-and%20needs-of-community-based-heritage-language-programs.pdf

Liu, R. (2008). Maintaining Chinese as a heritage language in the United States: What really matters? *Arizona Working Papers in SLA & Teaching, 15*, 37–64

Lu, X., & Li, G. (2008). Motivation and achievement in Chinese language learning: A comparative analysis. In A. W. He & Y. Xiao (Eds.), *Chinese as a heritage language: Fostering rooted world citizenry* (Vol. 2, pp. 89–108). Honolulu, HA: University of Hawaii Press.

Luo, S. H., & Wiseman, R. L. (2000). Ethnic language maintenance among Chinese immigrant children in the United States. *International Journal of Intercultural Relations, 24*(3), 307–324.

Lü, C., & Koda, K. (2011). The impact of home language and literacy support on English biliteracy acquisition among Chinese heritage language learners. *Heritage Language Journal, 8*(2), 44–80.

McGinnis, S. (2005). From mirror to compass: The Chinese heritage language education sector in the United States. In D. M. Brinton, O. Kagan, & S. Bauckus (Eds.), *Heritage language education: A new field emerging* (pp. 229–242). London, UK: Routledge Taylor & Francis Group.

Marcos, K. (1999). *Are we wasting our nation's language resources? Heritage languages in America.* ERIC/CLL Language Link, October 1999.

NCACLS. (2010). *NCACLS introduction.* Retrieved from www.ncacls.org/ncacls_introduction.htm#history

Pan, S. (1997). Chinese in New York. In O. Garcia & J. Fishman (Eds.), *The multilingual apple: Languages in New York City* (pp. 231–255). New York, NY: Mouton de Gruyter.

Ryan, C. (2013). Language use in the United States: 2011 [PDF file]. *U.S. Census Bureau.* Retrieved from www.census.gov/prod/2013pubs/acs-22.pdf

U.S. Census Bureau. (2011). Statistical abstract of the United States: 2011. Retrieved from www.census.gov/compendia/statab/2011/tables/11s0053.pdf

Wang, P. S. (1996). Academic curriculum. In X. Wang (Ed.), *A view from within: A case study of Chinese heritage community language schools in the United States* (pp. 21–26). Washington, DC: National Foreign Language Center.

Wang, S. C. (1996). Improving Chinese language schools: Issues and recommendations. In X. Wang (Ed.), *A view from within: A case study of Chinese heritage community language schools in the United States* (pp. 62–67). Washington, DC: National Foreign Language Center.

Wang, S. C., & Green, N. (2003). Heritage language students in the K–12 education system. In M. Hayford-O'Leary (Ed.), *Heritage languages in America: Preserving a national resource* (pp. 167–196). *The Modern Language Journal, 87*(4), 631–632.

Wang, X. (1996). Forging a link: Chinese heritage community language schools and the formal education system: A case study. In X. Wang (Ed.), *A view from within: A case study of Chinese heritage community language schools in the United States* (pp. 77–89). Washington, DC: National Foreign Language Center.

Wang, Y. (2009). Language, parents' involvement, and social justice: The fight for maintaining minority home language: A Chinese-language case study. *Multicultural Education, 16*(4), 13–18.

Weise, E. (2013, November 20). *Mandarin immersion schools in the United States in 2014.* Retrieved from http://miparentscouncil.org/2013/11/20/mandarin-immersion-schools-in-the-united-states-in-2014/

Wiley, T. G., De Klerk, G., Li, M., Liu, N., Teng, Y., & Yang, P. (2008). Language attitude towards Chinese "dialects" among Chinese immigrants and international students. In A. W. He & Y. Xiao (Eds.), *Chinese as a heritage language: Fostering rooted world citizenry* (Vol. 2, pp. 67–87). National Foreign Language Resource Center, University of Hawaii at Manoa, Honolulu, HA: University of Hawaii Press.

Wu, H. P. (2011). Constructing culturally relevant pedagogy in Chinese heritage language classrooms: A multiple-case study. *Online Submission.* Retrieved from http://eric.ed.gov/?id=ED529916

Zhang, D. (2008). *Between two generations: Language maintenance and acculturation among Chinese immigrant families.* El Paso, TX: LFB Scholarly..

Zhang, D., & Slaughter-Defoe, D. T. (2009). Language attitudes and heritage language maintenance among Chinese immigrant families in the USA. *Language, Culture and Curriculum, 22*(2), 77–93.

2

A CHINESE STUDENT'S EARLY EDUCATION IN U.S. K–12 SCHOOLS

A Multilevel Perspective

Yalun Zhou, Rebecca L. Oxford, and Michael Wei

Understanding the involvement of Chinese American families in their children's education is becoming increasingly important, as this ethnic group is the largest among the fast growing Asian American population in the United States (U.S. Census Bureau, 2012). In the last 2 decades, there exists prolific research literature that either depicts the stereotypes of Asian American (including Chinese) students as "model minority" students or demystifies the myth of model minority students (Wu, 2014). Some other researchers investigated the experiences of Chinese American students (Ma & Wang, 2014) or their parents (Park, Endo, & Rong, 2009). However, there is scant research on the hearts and minds of Chinese American students and their parents regarding their children's early ESL (English as a second language) education in K–12 schools.

This chapter intends to fill this gap by triangulating personal accounts of Zeta (pseudonym; a 1.5-generation Chinese American student) and her parents about Zeta's early second language (L2) literacy development immediately after their arrival in the United States. The accounts guide readers to take a closer look at the efforts and pursuits of Zeta and her parents over 4 years when she went from an ESL student to an achieving student in the mainstream classroom. Instead of depicting the stereotype of or demystifying the myth of model minority of Asian American students, the purpose of this chapter is to present rich data of a Chinese immigrant family's early L2 home literacy experiences—a case study of what Luke and Luke (1998) described as accounting "difference within difference" or "how families identify themselves" (p. 728). This case study intends to interpret the emergent cohesive literacy activities of this uniquely different family via the small culture approach (Holliday, 1999). Zeta's objective evaluations of parental involvement and ESL learning strategies are particularly useful for newly arrived Chinese immigrant parents or those who have lived in the U.S. but speak Chinese at home. Considering the parents' academic background and that 47% of Chinese immigrants (ages 25 and above) had a bachelor's degree or higher (Hooper & Batalova, 2015), this unique family's efforts and strategies in early L2 literacy are informative for K–12 ESL teachers in respect to beginning ESL students' language skills interventions and suggestive for educated Chinese immigrant parents. At the end of the chapter, the authors discuss intervention strategies for Chinese immigrant parents wishing to help with their children's adjustment from ESL to mainstream education. They also draw implications and recommendations for L2 literacy professionals that might speed up the acquisition of ESL proficiency for immigrant children.

Theoretical Framework

Two interrelated theoretical frameworks guide the study. The Family as Educator model (Snow, Barnes, Chandler, Goodman, & Hemphill, 1991) states that families can be the most effective literacy educators. Children have higher achievement in reading, writing, and language performance when their families establish a positive home literacy environment, directly teach relevant skills, create literacy opportunities, and communicate high expectations. Moreover, cultural traditions and culturally specific ways of learning can be integrated into the family's literacy efforts (Li, 2005). This model assists us to analyze the family's specific daily-routine literacy activities such as storybook reading and parents' explicit letter-sound teaching of new vocabulary.

The Home Literacy model (Sénéchal, 2006; Sénéchal & LeFervre, 2001, 2002) indicates the importance of parental home literacy involvement. This model recommends that parents provide two types of home literacy experiences: informal, meaning-based storybook reading and formal, explicit letter-sound instruction, both of which aid receptive language, emergent literacy, and phonological awareness. It guides us to examine the role of parental involvement through the eyes of Zeta and her parents and to interpret details of Zeta's linguistic and educational development that go beyond test scores. This model also functions as the base to draw implications and propose recommendations for involving Chinese immigrant parents into their children's literacy development.

Under these two frameworks, we explore the multilevel parental involvement and its effect during Zeta's early L2 literacy acquisition and perspectives of this family about their endeavors beyond test scores. The rationale is that "the next stage of parental involvement research should ... focus on questions that address the dynamics of parental involvement and its effect on education outcomes. Among them are questions about the conditions and personal attributes that prompt parental involvement" (Seigner, 2006, p. 39). Ultimately, the research questions guided by the theoretical framework are: (a) What are the strategies and perspectives of Zeta's parents regarding their involvement in Zeta's education?

and (b) Beyond test scores, what are Zeta's evaluations regarding her parents' and her own efforts for her achievements?

Review of the Research

We focus our review of literature on: (a) parental involvement in children's education, and (b) parental involvement in L2 home literacy. These key areas provide the research-based background for the study.

Parental Involvement in Children's Education

Parental involvement is a critical factor in a child's academic success and literacy development (Darling, 2008; Sénéchal & LeFevre, 2002). Research shows that, regardless of socioeconomic status (SES) and language background, many language–minority parents had strong educational interests and high expectations for their children (Drummond & Stipeck, 2004). In addition, the educational background and Confucian esteem for education of Asian American parents affects the ways these parents deal with their children's education (Li & Wang, 2013). They are highly supportive of their children's education (especially for literacy skills and mathematics learning) outside of school (Li & Wang, 2013), instilling in their children beliefs about individual achievement, hard work, and discipline from a young age (Roessingh, 2006).

Parental Involvement in L2 Home Literacy

Parental literacy practices are often more important than socioeconomic class or ethnicity in predicting academic and literacy outcomes (August & Shanahan, 2008; Snow et al., 1991). Over the past 20 years, individuals living in the United States with Limited English Proficiency (LEP) have grown by 81% since 1990, reaching 25.3 million in 2011. Among the LEP population, 9% was ages 5 to 15 (Whatley & Batalova, 2013). Immigrant children's successful literacy learning, therefore, depends on parents' knowledge of their children's literacy instruction in school (Risko & Walker-Dalhouse, 2009) or is influenced by their parents' educational background (Li & Wang, 2013). In addition, parents' literacy interactions with children at home are closely related to children's literacy acquisition and language performance at school (Dudley-Marling, 2009). Chen and Harris (2009) suggested that language–minority parents should be taught effective literacy strategies to use at home with their children in order to support school literacy instruction.

However, although there is considerable evidence that parents are positively disposed to helping their children, August and Shanahan (2008) insightfully pointed out that the impact of social dimensions (e.g., parental involvement) on L2 literacy acquisition is not well studied; not much is known about the likely effects on language-minority children's literacy development (Goldenberg, Rueda, & August, 2008). The hearts and minds of Zeta and her parents revealed in this chapter provide important research data in this regard and contribute to the understanding of social dimensional impact on L2 literacy acquisition and the effect of L2 home literacy in an ESL child's educational development.

The Study

Background

This study explores perspectives of Zeta and her parents regarding their family's longitudinal effort in Zeta's L2 literacy acquisition and educational development. Zeta was born in China and moved to the United States at the age of 7 and a half. The study considers her progress over 4 years (2001–2005), from that time until she was more than 11 years old. In January 2002, Zeta entered an East Coast public elementary school in a school district that is among the largest and most diverse in the nation. At first, Zeta received the school's standard 2-hour pullout ESL instruction daily. After one semester, due to a school boundary change, Zeta was assigned to another elementary school that had more ESL students than her previous one. In this school, Zeta's ESL teachers believed her English was too advanced to receive pullout ESL instruction and quickly arranged for her transfer to a mainstream classroom after 2 months of independent ESL study. In this second elementary school, the teachers and the PTA collaborated to promote school-wide reading activities in school and at home. Students were encouraged to keep weekly reading logs to earn the "Husky Reader" title, a magnet to take home, and coupons for free pizza from the local Pizza Hut.

Zeta's parents, Brian and Heather (the English nicknames of the third and first authors), were actively engaged in every aspect of her schooling. Like many other Chinese American parents embracing the Confucian heritage, they viewed literacy development as highly important and involved themselves extensively in Zeta's education and linguistic development. One factor made their home literacy involvement special, enriching the study: Brian and Heather had both been English teachers before coming to the United States and were seeking U.S. graduate education in English teaching at the time of the study. They devoted as much time as possible to Zeta's education, supporting her English learning at home, capitalizing on every opportunity to enrich her early learning of English, and gathering longitudinal data.

Data Collection

Data collection spans 2001 to 2005. The data included (a) in-depth, longitudinal field notes of parent–child interactions and parent records of Zeta's work and books read; (b) completed homework papers, in-class assignments, journal entries, and other school-mandated written work; (c) standardized test scores; (d) completed exercises that were parent-created; and (e) phone interviews conducted by the second author from each family member. These interviews included two with Brian, three with Heather, and two with Zeta, 1 hour long each. The interviews (in a friendly, chat-style format) with Zeta provided a worry-free arena for the child to express her perspectives about parental literacy involvement. The interviews with the parents were about their past and present experiences, cultural beliefs, and personal attitudes regarding parental involvement in literacy development at home. To perform a member check, each family member reviewed the interview transcripts and validated them as meaningful and correct.

In the longitudinal data collection process, we followed Adler and Adler's theorization of "parent-as-researcher participant observation" (1996) and their reminder to parent-researchers that "protection, safety, and affection take precedence" (1987, p. 58). Such an ongoing ethical consideration helps keep the priority between researcher and parent balanced on the side of the parent. Most of the data, such as homework, notes about reading to and reading with Zeta, and journal writing, came from the normal family routine. There was no authoritative force from the parents.

Data Analysis

We analyzed the data into the following categories: parental beliefs in education, Zeta's language experiences and evaluation, literacy activities at home, ESL and literacy activities at school, and teacher–parent communication. The overarching themes emerged from data coding are multilevel perspectives of Zeta and her parents, Zeta's English skills development, and strategies of home literacy activities.

Results and Discussion

Zeta started her U.S. schooling with "no English," as diagnosed by the county ESL Office. With Zeta's strong motivation and active L2 home literacy intervention, Zeta exhibited remarkable progress in ESL class and moved on to mainstream learning within a short time. Table 2.1 shows Zeta's status of ESL learning within the first two semesters of her schooling.

Within 11 months, Zeta had reached the fourth level in oral proficiency (out of six possible levels) on the IDEA Oral Proficiency Test. This was remarkable oral progress in less than a year. In addition, it is clear from the IDEA results that Zeta's progress was also very significant in writing and reading. Based on the test scores, in November 2002, her ESL teacher had placed Zeta out of the ESL program. Zeta became an independent ESL student seeing the teacher twice a month. Being independent means longer hours of study in mainstream classrooms and higher expectations from teachers, which demands more family support. The

30 Yalun Zhou, Rebecca L. Oxford, and Michael Wei

effect of continued home literacy involvement, after Zeta exited the ESL program and attended mainstream classes, was witnessed by test results demonstrated in Table 2.2.

The rapid progress of Zeta in both ESL and mainstream classroom learning is, of course, inseparable from school education and family effort in her L2 literacy

TABLE 2.1 IDEA Language Proficiency Test (IPT) Scores in ESOL Placements

Time of Testing	Reading	Writing	Recommendation for ESOL Placement
Jan., 2002 (1st diagnosis)	NA	NA	ESL level 1; "She speaks no English"
May, 2002 (2nd grade)	25/51	5/12	Attending the 1 month summer school for ESL students
Nov., 2002 (3rd grade)	41/51	11/12	Out of ESL program; becoming an independent student

Note: The *IDEA Language Proficiency Test* is an examination Zeta's school district used for initial enrollment and annual assessment for students with limited English proficiency. It is also the exit assessment for ESL students who are to transfer to the mainstream classroom at Zeta's school district. There are six possible Oral proficiency levels on the *IDEA Language Proficiency Test*. The maximum Reading score is 51 and the maximum Writing score is 12.

TABLE 2.2 Grades in ESL and General Education

Year	Subject	Quarters and Grade			
		1	2	3	4
2nd semester, 2nd grade Jan.–June '02	Reading	—	ESOL	Progress★	Progress★
	Oral & Written	—	ESOL	Needs time	Progress
	Mathematics	—	Progress	Progress	Progress
	Science	—	NA	Progress	Progress
	Social Studies		Progress	Progress	Progress
3rd grade Aug. '02–June '03	Reading	A	A	A	A
	Oral & Written	A	A	A	A
	Mathematics	A	A	A	A
	Science	A	A	A	A
	Social Studies	A	A	A	A
1st semester, 4th grade Aug.–Dec. '03	Reading	A			
	Oral & Written	A			
	Mathematics	A			
	Science	A			
	Social Studies	A			

acquisition. To get insiders' views of the L2 home literacy that goes beyond the test scores, we discuss the factors in the order of research questions:

Research Question 1: What are the strategies and perspectives of Zeta's parents regarding their involvement in Zeta's education?

The home literacy environment Brian and Heather facilitated for Zeta stemmed from their cultural beliefs, which had a significant impact on their parenting. Like many Chinese American parents, they were heavily influenced by Confucian values and viewed Zeta's education the priority of the family. As Brian stated in an interview,

> Confucius' famous motto, "Everything else is inferior to education," is a lifelong guideline for us. My parents repeatedly reminded me, "A person who receives an education can always find a good life. Otherwise you have to work as a laborer."
>
> *(February 20, 2005)*

Heather expressed the same perception of education:

> My family values education as something that cannot be substituted by anything else. It is always the first priority. I was not asked to do any chores at home, because my parents felt I should spend my time studying.
>
> *(March 1, 2005)*

Propelled by these strong notions of education, Brain and Heather helped Zeta with homework daily and arranged family activities around Zeta's learning. An important factor they mentioned that affected Zeta's swift English acquisition was her teachers' guidance to the parents and their willingness to pay attention to that guidance. They credited their knowledge of after-school literacy resources to Zeta's teachers. They thought Zeta's classroom teachers and ESL teachers were experienced in helping new students and parents navigate the educational system. The teachers taught the parents how to follow the school's voicemail to track the daily homework, introduced them to free after-school ESL homework tutoring and to the community volunteer homework center (in case Heather was busy), and informed them of the services offered by the public libraries, including a reading program for immigrant youth.

Strategies for oral skills. Obviously, as former English teachers Brian and Heather could both speak English. Therefore, the school district's ESL office suggested that the parents speak English with Zeta at home for "quick" English acquisition. This time, however, Brian and Heather had a different approach from the schoolteacher's advice. Heather explained in an interview, "[If we spoke to her

32 Yalun Zhou, Rebecca L. Oxford, and Michael Wei

in English,] she would have a Chinese accent in English, more or less like we do" (April 1, 2005). Brian was even more emphatic:

> We refused to do it [speak English with Zeta at home]! She was just at the verge of being able to acquire native-like pronunciation of English, and we didn't want to harm that. We hoped she could catch the tail of acquiring native-like accent through authentic learning. Also, she would lose her native language if we stopped speaking Chinese with her.
>
> *(April 8, 2005)*

To compensate for not speaking English at home, they borrowed audiobooks and videotapes from public libraries for Zeta. In addition, they helped her by watching children's TV channels together, and encouraged her to talk with friends over the phone daily. Considering that Zeta had a minimal vocabulary, they tried to borrow books and videos that Zeta already knew in her native language. The series *Arthur* was the first that she found meaningful in English because she had already watched the Chinese version of this series. Since she knew the plots of the stories very well, she could guess the content in English when familiar episodes were played.

In Zeta's spare time, Brian and Heather encouraged her to make friends with peers, regardless of whether they were ESL students. Zeta enjoyed the time she spent daily talking with friends over the phone after finishing her homework. Her friendships drove her to use the limited English she learned for real life purposes, which indirectly motivated her to acquire English for free communication.

Facilitating reading. Brian and Heather did not put reading and writing as the top priority for Zeta's home education at the beginning. They thought they did not have to emphasize this as much because both of the elementary schools Zeta attended had a heavy emphasis on reading. Additionally, keeping a weekly reading log was mandatory for both schools' Language Arts classes. To help Zeta complete the weekly homework of reading logs, Brian and Heather consulted Zeta's language arts teacher, ESL teacher, and librarians as to what kind of books she should read. The teachers suggested borrowing picture storybooks for younger children as opposed to the more challenging material found in storybooks for second graders. The librarians in the public libraries suggested that they start from books with sight words. For this, Heather expressed her gratitude:

> We found the teachers' guidance in using library books to be very beneficial to our home literacy activities, and we followed this guidance. Hadn't the teachers told us how to start Zeta's English reading, we would never know the function of the American public library, nor the existence of audiobooks to help Zeta's listening and pronunciation. Being informed to make use of the public library is crucial for us new immigrant families.
>
> *(March 1, 2005)*

Strategies in early reading. At first, the pictures illustrated in the picture books and storybooks did not make any sense to Zeta; she barely knew any of the words in the books, and the pictures contained a remarkable amount of new cultural information that she had yet to encounter or experience in daily life. Zeta's English book "reading" in the beginning weeks actually consisted of listening to parents' translation of the books. The focus was the meaning and cultural ideas contained within the picture books.

After a month had passed, they felt Chinese should only serve as a transitional tool for Zeta to get a sense of reading English books. They needed to find a way to start her English reading. However, they encountered a dilemma here. Since they did not want to interfere with Zeta's English accent by speaking English with her, how, then, could they help Zeta read English books without her being influenced by their accents? They, again, went to the public library for help. One librarian suggested borrowing picture books with audiotapes. She thought that in this way, Zeta could develop the habit of reading while being exposed to authentic English pronunciation by native speakers at the same time. Brian and Heather were very excited to discover the existence of audiobooks, a mode of reading to which they had never been exposed. This form of reading, which persisted for several months, lasted until Zeta entered third grade in the second elementary school. This strategy appeared to improve her reading skills in English. Table 2.3 demonstrates the progression of Zeta's reading in the first semester of her ESL learning, the early stage of L2 literacy development:

TABLE 2.3 Summary of Reading Logs in the First Semester with ESL Program

Week	Titles of Books	Minutes Read
Jan. 14–20	My friends; Off to grandma's house; Chuck; Sleepy dog; Safety at home; Traffic safety	32
Jan. 21–27	Komobo; The cream and the cat; The name jar; Arthur writes a story; Tacky the penguin; Something wonderful; What will the weather be?	103
Feb. 4–10	The mystery …; Wally Walrus; The Wednesday …; Arthur's new …; The little red hen; The elves and …; Arthur goes to …	145
Mar.11–17	How to be a friend; Fire fighters; Garbage collectors; Arthur's birthday; Pig, pig grows up; Christmas surprise; Homework! Oh, homework	121
Apr. 15–21	Who lives here? My first Halloween; Arthur makes …; The magic school bus …; The magic school bus taking …; Franklin fibs; Franklin and Harriet	145
May 6–12	Anansi's narrow waist; Flash, crash, rumble and roll …; Each orange had 8 slices; Snow day; Sun up, sun down; We come the ice	123

After entering the third grade (The Husky Reader school), each student in Zeta's class was required to bring in a "chapter book," not a picture book, to read during the Drop Everything and Read (DEAR) time at the end of the school day. In addition, students were required to keep an annotated reading log about their reading at home, recording not only the time but also the author and a brief storyline of each book they read. To fulfill this daunting assignment for Zeta who had just exited from the ESL program, again, Brian and Heather started with the books with which Zeta was familiar, namely, the *Arthur* series and the *Magic School Bus* series. The reading log assignment and the DEAR program were excellent sources of motivation for Zeta to read more difficult books than those targeted toward younger children. The focus of reading at home in this period for Zeta and her parents was the print and comprehension of the print. They sometimes read together and other times read in turns. Heather was fond of playing a game called "Pop Corn" that Zeta taught her when reading in turns. In the game of reading, whenever the listener had questions, she had to say "Pop Corn," and the one who was reading had to stop for questions. Heather described questions asked when playing the "Pop Corn" reading game:

> The questions Zeta had for us were mainly regarding reading comprehension or cultural orientation. Our questions for Zeta were geared toward checking the meaning of certain words she had learned in school, requesting that she reread a word she may have mispronounced (e.g., evergreen as "everygreen"), or that she revisit any phonemes she had omitted (e.g., "-s," "-ed," or "-ing") in the sentence.
>
> *(March 2, 2005)*

With all this help, Zeta's reading comprehension rapidly improved. When taking the *IDEA Language Proficiency Test* 11 months after she started learning English, Zeta scored 41points out of 51, placing her into the "competent reader" category. The speedy transition from "learning to read" to "reading to learn" served as a catalyst for Zeta's overall academic achievement, making it a short route compared to the slow and tedious route of most ESL students.

Vocabulary and journal writing. When Zeta was able to communicate with teachers and friends in English and was able to follow the daily instruction, her parents focused on helping her improve her writing skills. They decided to start with spelling first, not only because spelling was part of her school grade, but also because they believed that spelling was foundational to writing development.

The following parent journal recorded the steps of weekly vocabulary learning for the family:

A Chinese Student's Early Education **35**

> *11/19 Tues.*
> Rearrange spelling list. This week's vowel is /ɔ:/, such as law, brought, already, daughter, chalk.
>
> *11/20 Wed.*
> Review spelling list; can remember all of the words. First time finish homework on her own. When reading [Zeta's] journal, found she could convey her meaning with complete sentence.
>
> *11/21 Thu.*
> Read *Magic School Bus* and *Arthur's April Fool's Day* together.
>
> *11/22 Fri.*
> Review all the words with /ɔ:/ again in the morning in preparation of this week's spelling test. She spelled the word wrong at first: caught cought. After reminding her to self-check, she realized the mistake. Prepare four bags of muffin for Salvation Army's food collection. She asked the reasons for donation. Explained the significance of charity to her.

This systematic method was very efficient and effective. Zeta's English vocabulary expanded quickly using this method. In turn, her excellent spelling scores inspired her to accept her parents' advice.

After Zeta had accumulated a certain amount of vocabulary, Zeta's parents noticed the teacher's morning warm-up exercise of journal writing. They decided to ask Zeta to write a journal entry at home after finishing daily homework. This was viewed as good practice in spelling, writing, and thinking. Their daily journal requirement was to write at least two sentences. At the beginning, Zeta needed her parents' help with spelling and felt reticent about writing. In time, Zeta started feeling satisfaction in writing, and they did not have to remind her or ask her to write; she did so voluntarily.

Research Question 2: Beyond test scores, what are Zeta's evaluations regarding her parents' and her own efforts for her achievements?

As a highly motivated child, Zeta is nevertheless the driving force for this family to achieve. Without her strong will and motivation, it would not have been possible for the school–parent collaboration to have had such positive effects on Zeta's L2 literacy development. Zeta explained the following in an interview:

> Do you know how much harder I had to try [than other kids]? Don't underestimate my efforts. I started learning English late. I compared myself

with the better kids, those born in America, not the ESL kids. Only hard work can help me catch up. I was disadvantaged. I must try harder and harder so that I can catch up and survive in American schools. It was a necessity, a must!

(May 24, 2005)

Her awareness of her own efforts and goals is indicative of her internal motivation. The sense she had of needing to "catch up" reveals how the proficiency of fluent English speakers provided an external impetus. Her high goals are evident in the fact that she compared herself not to ESL students but to native English speakers. One thing she constantly checked with her parents was: "Are you sure I can catch up?"

Zeta imbibed her parents' optimism, dedication, and esteem for education. As she stated,

I always felt confident with my math due to the extra practice of math worksheets my parents gave to me. After I exited the ESL program, they kept on monitoring my homework and grades so that I got A's in all subjects. For Language Arts, after years of hard work, I saw hope when I was in fifth grade. After sixth grade, I think I am above the native speakers.

(November 6, 2005)

In terms of parent expectations, it was natural for her to follow the parental requirement that after school she must finish her homework before watching TV or eating dinner. She told in an interview:

About school, I think they always expected me to complete my homework and stuff, but I would have done that anyway. I would not count that as strict. So I wouldn't say they were very strict.... . I was raised this way. I can only do like this. I don't know other ways to act with learning. I don't have a choice, because now it [learning] is automatic. I cannot stop doing it.

(July 5, 2005)

After Zeta was used to writing English journals at home, her parents had an extra task for her in addition to daily reading and spelling lists: reading her journal entries aloud, hoping that she would be aware of the errors she made earlier. Zeta expressed the benefits of journal writing and reading-aloud:

When I [was asked to] go back to read my journals, I noticed that I got a lot of misspelled words, but I went along and my parents told me that I made those mistakes. I then wrote them down on my notebook, and those corrections of my misspelled words were kept in my memory. The other strategy that I still use today is to spell the word out, like, b-e-c-a-u-s-e. This way, I can remember word spellings.

(July 5, 2005)

The family's long-term commitment to supporting their school's literacy instruction and general education led to Zeta's good academic standing. She was able to complete homework independently from year two and maintained all A's in her subjects. She reached the proficient level or higher in reading and mathematics in the yearly state mandatory assessment starting in 2004 (see Table 2.2). At the end of the 2004–2005 school year Zeta performed as a team captain, leading the team to win the county Science Bowl championship. When asked her perspective on the role of her parents' involvement in her ESL and general education, Zeta commented,

> They are very, very involved in my education. They may be more involved than other parents in other kids' education. One reason I think is maybe I came a little bit late. They wanted me to catch up fast. On a scale of 1 to 10, they are like 9, which is pretty good. They got involved, like when following my teacher's advice to find help in the library, sorting spelling words on a list for memorization, making sentences with spelling words, checking my homework, and having me write a journal, which I guess is a lot of help … and I like their communication with teachers … If I were to give suggestions to new ESL kids for learning English, I would tell them about activities I did that can involve parents, to give them a hint.
>
> *(July 5, 2005)*

Conclusion

English literacy is the key for immigrant children's academic success in the United States, and family is the educational unit wherein early literacy occurs (Leichter, 1984). This longitudinal study of Zeta's early L2 literacy development provides a rich case of how parental involvement might influence their children's L2 literacy acquisition. It expands existing research findings on the dynamics of social dimensions (e.g., parental involvement) on L2 literacy acquisition. The first-hand data of parent-as-researcher contributes to the understanding of hearts and minds of Zeta and her parents, beyond a group profile of Chinese immigrant families. This family's L2 literacy strategies and unique parental involvement are informative and suggestive to schoolteachers, literacy practitioners, university teachers, researchers, and policy makers. When working with educated, English-speaking immigrant parents, schoolteachers and practitioners could inform them of resources that they could utilize, just as Zeta's teachers did for her parents. Moreover, reminding parents to use their mother tongue to help with spelling lists and vocabulary will alleviate the overwhelming translation burden of ESL students and possibly accelerate the speed at which students are able to memorize new words. Zeta's home literacy activities remind schoolteachers and literacy practitioners of the vitality and validity of involving educated Chinese immigrant parents in their children's ESL acquisition and the dynamic extent of some immigrant parents' knowledge of school literacy education. Furthermore, more than 270,000 Chinese international students are receiving graduate and undergraduate education in America in 2013/14, with a 31% increase than the prior academic year (Institute of International Education, 2014), and more than 47% of current Chinese immigrants hold a bachelor's degree or higher (Hooper & Batalova, 2015). The rise of the Chinese immigrant population makes this realization particularly important because it is possible that K–12 teachers will be working with increased numbers of well-educated Chinese immigrant parents in the near future.

When working with Chinese immigrant parents who do not speak much English, teachers could advise parents on how to make use of multilingual books and videos that scaffold their children's learning. Some practices Brian and Heather used with Zeta, such as sitting beside her while doing her homework, periodically going to public libraries, checking out bilingual audiobooks, and asking for tell-back readings, are applicable for many immigrant parents, regardless of their English proficiency.

Based on the data and Zeta's achievements, we draw three implications to inform L2 literacy professionals and Chinese immigrant families. First, explicitly balanced teaching is essential for beginning ESL students. They need informal literacy exposure, such as reading together and multisensory avenues for learning to read, and they require formal instruction in vocabulary, narrative writing, and phonological awareness. An integrated skill-based ESL intervention may lead to positive ESL learning outcomes, especially when utilizing ESL parents' social capital.

Second, literacy instruction emphasizing vocabulary development in terms of word-level and sentence-level usage is helpful for early L2 literacy development. Language teachers benefit by finding out their students' language backgrounds, looking up information on students' linguistic systems, and discovering the immigrant parents' literacy levels and needs.

Third, guided home literacy activities are necessary for L2 reading and writing development. Zeta and her parents' activities such as the "Pop Corn" game, a review of a spelling list, or comments on journal writing are effective for educated parents when they read with their children or when they teach reading-writing-speaking connections to their children at home.

The value of this study lies in the fact that this study opens up windows for second language researchers and L2 literacy practitioners to see the impact of family involvement. It is important to appreciate immigrant families' value on education and to integrate that in their literacy instruction for "family must be a part of the solution in closing the achievement gap" (Darling, 2008, p. 245). Zeta's home literacy and educational attainment reveal that much literacy acquisition can happen outside of school and that immigrant parents can become agents of their child's education by providing a home literacy environment, opportunities for second language literacy learning, and direct teaching of literacy skills (August & Shanahan, 2008).

The results beyond test scores and first-person accounts of Zeta's L2 literacy development suggest the importance of involving immigrant parents in their children's English learning, as well as the necessity of teachers and family program practitioners to utilize immigrant parents' potential for providing home literacy activities. In addition, teachers could work to ensure that they understand each student's language background, parental language proficiency level, and linguistic needs. If stakeholders could find an effective way to educate immigrant parents and help them become involved in their children's education, ESL students and society as a whole will benefit. If parents are provided the necessary literacy strategies and/or resources that Zeta's teachers pointed to, they can be active agents for their children's education, catalyzing stronger academic performance and higher long-term achievement.

References

Adler, P., & Adler, P. (1987). *Membership roles in field research*. Thousand Oaks, CA: Sage.

Adler, P. A., & Adler, P. (1996). Parent-as-researcher: The politics of researching in the personal life. *Qualitative Sociology, 19*(1), 35–58.

August, D., & Shanahan, T. (2008). Introduction and methodology. In D. August & T. Shanahan (Eds.), *Developing reading and writing in second-language learners: Lessons from the report of the National Literacy Panel on language-minority children and youth* (pp. 1–18). New York, NY: Routledge, the Center for Applied Linguistics, and the International Reading Association.

Chen, H., & Harris, P. (2009). Becoming school literature parents: An ESL perspective. *Australian Journal of Language and Literacy, 32*(2), 118–135.

Darling, S. (2008). Family must be a part of the solution in closing the achievement gap. *Clearing House, 81*(6), 245–246.

Drummond, K. V., & Stipeck, D. (2004). Low-income parents' beliefs about their role in children's academic learning. *The Elementary School Journal, 104*(3), 197–213.

Dudley-Marling, C. (2009). Home-school literacy connections: The perceptions of African American and immigrant ESL parents in two urban communities. *Teachers College Record, 111*(7), 1713–1752.

Goldenberg, C., Rueda, R. S., & August, D. (2008). Sociocultural contexts and literacy development. In D. August & T. Shanahan (Eds.), *Developing reading and writing in second-language learners: Lessons from the report of the National Literacy Panel on language-minority children and youth* (pp. 95–129). New York, NY: Routledge, the Center for Applied Linguistics, and the International Reading Association.

Holliday, A. (1999). Small cultures. *Applied Linguistics, 20*(2), 237–264.

Hooper, K., & Batalova, J. (2015). *Chinese immigrants in the United States*. Retrieved from www.migrationpolicy.org/article/chinese-immigrants-united-states/

Institute of International Education. (2014). *Top 25 places of origin of international students, 2012/13–2013/14*. Retrieved from www.iie.org/opendoors

Leichter, H. J. (1984). Families as environments for literacy. In H. Goelman, A. A. Oberg, & F. Smith (Eds.), *Awakening to literacy* (pp. 38–50). Portsmouth, NH: Heinemann Educational Books.

Li, G. (2005). Family as educator: A Chinese-Canadian experience of acquiring second language literacy. *Canadian Children, 30*(2), 9–16.

Li, G., & Wang, J. (2013). Chinese immigrant parents' perspectives on literacy learning, homework, and school-home communication. In E. Grigorenko (Ed.), *Handbook of US immigration and education* (pp. 337–354). New York, NY: Springer.

Luke, C., & Luke, A. (1998). Interracial families: Difference within difference. *Ethnic & Racial Studies, 21*(4), 728–754.

Ma, W., & Wang, C. (Eds.). (2014). *Learner's privilege and responsibility: A critical examination of the experiences and perspectives of learners from Chinese backgrounds in the United States.* Charlotte, NC: Information Age.

Park, C., Endo, R., & Rong, X. L. (Eds.). (2009). *New perspectives on Asian American parents, students, and teacher recruitment.* Greenwich, CT: Information Age.

Risko, V. J., & Walkder-Dalhouse, R. (2009). Parents and teachers: Talking with or past one another—or not talking at all? *The Reading Teacher, 62*(5), 442–444. doi: 10.1598/TR.62.5.7

Roessingh, H. (2006). The teacher is the key: Building trust in ESL high school programs. *Canadian Modern Language Review, 62*(4), 563–590.

Seigner, R. (2006). Parents' educational involvement: A developmental ecology perspective. *Parenting: Science and Practice, 6*(1), 1–48.

Sénéchal, M. (2006). Testing the home literacy model: Parent involvement in kindergarten is differentially related to grade 4 reading comprehension, fluency, spelling, and reading for pleasure. *Scientific Studies of Reading, 10*(1), 59–87.

Sénéchal, M., & LeFevre, J.-A. (2001). Storybook reading and parent teaching: Links to language and literacy development. In P. R. Britto & J. Brooks-Gunn (Eds.), *The role of family literacy environments in promoting young children's emerging literacy skills* (pp. 39–52). San Francisco, CA: Jossey-Bass.

Sénéchal, M., & LeFevre, J.-A. (2002). Parental involvement in the development of children's reading skill: A five-year longitudinal study. *Child Development, 73*(2), 445–460.

Snow, C., Barnes, W. S., Chandler, J., Goodman, I., & Hemphill, L. (1991). *Unfulfilled expectations: Home and school influences on literacy.* Cambridge: MA: Harvard University Press.

U.S. Census Bureau. (2012). The Asian population: 2010. Retrieved from www.census.gov/prod/cen2010/briefs/c2010br-11.pdf

Whatley, M., & Batalova, J. (2013). Limited English proficient population of the United States. Retrieved from www.migrationpolicy.org/article/limited-english-proficient-population-united-states

Wu, E. D. (2014). *The color of success: Asian Americans and the origins of the model minority.* Princeton, NJ: Princeton University Press.

3

ORDINARY MOMENTS TELL EXTRAORDINARY STORIES

Children's Multimodal Literacy Explorations

Xiaoxiao Du, Rosamund Stooke, and Rachel M. Heydon

Today's children are growing up in "a globally interlinked economy" (Suárez-Orozco & Suárez–Orozco, 2009, p. 62) in which education grows ever more important and competition among school systems grows ever more intense. Indeed, corporations make decisions about where to locate their operations based on the "level and type of skill associated with a national population" (DeVault, 2008, p. 12). No wonder politicians pay such close attention to test scores. We argue, however, that a preoccupation with test scores threatens the ability of teachers and parents to respond to children in thoughtful and caring ways and we further argue that international league tables and other highly visible comparisons of academic achievement can be particularly harmful to children. For example, when test scores are used to compare populations, they tend to reinforce stereotypes. Many scholars have pointed to the harm done by stereotypes that represent minoritized groups as deficient, but we are increasingly aware that positive stereotypes can be harmful too (e.g., Li & Wang, 2008). As a group, students from Asian backgrounds tend to score highly on tests, but within this diverse population are many students who do not do well at school and many who face economic, social, or emotional challenges. In fact, all stereotypes tend to mask the diversity within a group.

Our chapter seeks to honor the diversity that existed among a group of first-grade students from Chinese backgrounds studying in Ontario, Canada. In the chapter we present and discuss data excerpts collected during a year-long Canadian case study of first-grade Chinese[1] children's literacy practices at school, at home, and in their neighborhoods (Du, 2014). Through a close examination of some seemingly ordinary moments in the lives of three children, we demonstrate that looking closely at their everyday interactions with people and things creates opportunities for educators and parents to promote children's well-being.

Theoretical Framework

Murphy (2015) reminds us that "assessments are bound up in values, which in turn are bound up in shared systems of knowing" (p. 26). As former teachers we acknowledge a role for standardized tests in educational policy making, but we believe that standardized tests, like all forms of assessment, tell incomplete stories. In preparing the chapter we asked ourselves: What kinds of looking and listening might help us learn about the interests and concerns of children? What theories might help us make sense of what we observe? Reflecting on the first question we concluded that educators benefit from looking and listening closely as an ethnographer looks (e.g., Dyson & Genishi, 2005) and from looking *with* children at events of significance to them (e.g., Wien, 2013). For example, Du took a keen interest in child-initiated, informal interactions and she was able to glimpse the "messy wonder that regularly occurs during child-directed play and exploration" (Wohlwend, 2008, p. 127). Du also spent time in the children's homes and she noticed that although all parents were positively disposed toward schooling, each parent's attitude toward schooling seemed to be shaped by their access to economic resources and their intentions to stay in Canada or return to China. To address the second question we drew on concepts from New Literacy Studies (NLS) (see e.g., Barton & Hamilton, 2000; Kress, 2003; Street, 1984). Important among NLS concepts are *literacy practices*, *literacy events*, and *domains*. According to Barton and Hamilton (2000), literacy events are "observable episodes which arise from [literacy] practices and are shaped by them" (p. 8) while domains are the "structured, patterned contexts" (p. 11), in which literacy events are situated. A teacher's question to the class about where to print the date on a journal entry can be described as an event arising from the literacy practice called *journal writing* that takes place in the primary classroom domain. Barton and Hamilton noted too that an event occurring in one domain can be re-contextualized in another—as when a child creates a dramatic retelling of a school literacy lesson during a game of "school" that takes place at home. Multiliteracies theory builds on NLS theory. We are indebted to the multiliteracies theorist Gunther Kress (2003) for his observation that all forms of expression are multimodal. Although one mode is often foregrounded in a literacy event (e.g., the visual mode in a drawing), people always draw on a "range of social semiotic resources ... including image, sound, number, the manipulation and choreography of physical materials, and body movement" (Hamilton, Heydon, Hibbert, & Stooke, 2015, p. 2). As multimodality gains acceptance in literacy education, the definition of a literacy event expands to include any occasion in which a person mobilizes any combination of social semiotic resources and the definition of a text is expanded to include a drawing, a song or dance, and so on.

Important to our discussion is the idea that looking closely at multimodal literacy events can reveal clues about children's identities. Rowsell and Pahl (2007) skillfully brought together concepts from multimodal literacy theory,

Bourdieu's (1977, 1990) notion of *habitus*, and the idea that identities are formed within culturally shaped activities (Holland, Lachicotte, Skinner, & Cain, 1998) to argue that children's identities are laid down or "sedimented" (p. 388) in the texts they create. Following Holland et al. (1998), Rowsell and Pahl noted that people navigate "tensions between past histories that have settled in them and the present discourses and images that attract them or somehow impinge upon them" (2007, p. 4). They invoked the idea of habitus because it helps us to see how identities can be passed from one generation to the next. They then proposed that literacy events and the texts children produce contain traces of the text maker's habitus. Hence, looking closely at literacy events in which children participate can provide insights into their *identities in practice* (Holland et al., 1998, p. 270).

Literature Review

A large body of research in English has examined culturally and linguistically diverse children's literacy practices in English-speaking countries (e.g., David et al., 2000; Gregory, 1996, 1997, 2008). Many of the studies pertaining to children from Asian backgrounds focus on American contexts (e.g., Li, 2009; Park, Endo, & Rong, 2009), but there are several notable Canadian exceptions. Chen and her colleagues investigated Chinese children's reading and writing development in Ontario schools (Anderson & Chen, 2013; Chen & Lin, 2008; Hao, Chen, Dronjic, Shu, & Anderson, 2013; Luo, Chen, Deacon, Zhang, & Yin, 2013; Luo, Chen, & Geva, 2014).

Studies that addressed issues of identity often employed a sociocultural perspective. Li (2001, 2003, 2006a, 2006b, 2007, 2009) identified home factors in children's biliteracy learning. Toohey (2000) examined ways in which primary-grade children negotiated relationships with people and texts at school. Moore (2010) examined the multilingual literacy practices of 14 young Chinese children enrolled in French immersion programs. Dagenais, Day, and Toohey (2006) showed how a child's identity construction in classroom literacy activities was tied to teacher expectations. Of particular note is the work of Cummins (e.g., Cummins et al., 2005; Cummins, 2006; Cummins & Early, 2011) who has demonstrated ways in which children's out-of-school literacies can be pedagogical resources. Our chapter aims to contribute to this literature through a close examination of formal and informal literacy events.

Methodology

As noted earlier, the chapter draws on a larger case study (Yin, 2003) conducted by Du (2014) in a mid-sized, southwestern Ontario city (population of approximately 350,000 people) that was home to many people of Chinese heritage, including Canadian citizens, immigrants, international students, visiting scholars, and post-doctoral fellows (Citizenship and Immigration Canada, 2014).

44 Xiaoxiao Du, Rosamund Stooke, and Rachel M. Heydon

We revisit portions of the data set to respond to the question: What can educators and parents learn about children's *identities in practice* (Holland et al., 1998) by looking at what children actually say and do?

Study participants were recruited using purposive sampling. With assistance from the teachers in two Grade 1 classrooms, Du distributed Letters of Information and Consent forms to all parents of Chinese children in the two classes. All the invited families lived in a neighborhood that included single family homes, apartment buildings, and university-owned student housing, and the children attended a public school where 21 teachers and three assistants taught 270 children between the ages of 4 and 12 years. While seven families agreed to participate in the original study, for the purposes of the chapter, we constructed narrative vignettes featuring three children: Brian, Jiajia, and Shasha[2] (see Table 3.1).

The study addressed trustworthiness (Lincoln & Guba, 1985) in several ways: prolonged and varied field experience, triangulation of data sources, member checking, peer examination, interview techniques, dense descriptions, and low inference descriptors. Du also collected a range of artifacts (e.g., literacy-related work samples) and photographs of artifacts made by the children outside of school. Her Chinese cultural and linguistic background helped her to establish rapport with the children and their parents. She encouraged children to share ideas in self-chosen ways and at their own pace, and asked open-ended questions. She kept a reflective journal, invited comments, and enlisted colleagues as critical friends. She then conducted an interpretational analysis using the constant comparison approach (Bogdan & Biklen, 2006).

In the next section we introduce the three children and present two narrative ensembles that respond to the themes of this book. The narratives are composed from data collected in semi-structured interviews with parents and participant observation with the children at the public school and the Chinese community school, in the children's homes, and at a community playground.

TABLE 3.1 The Participants

Pseudonym	Family Information
Brian	Brian was an only child born in Canada. His father was a doctoral fellow in science at the local university and his mother worked part time in a private school residence.
Shasha	Shasha was an only child whose family was new to Canada. Her father was a master's student in computer science and her mother was a homemaker.
Jiajia	Jiajia was an only child. Born in China, she had lived in another Canadian city prior to this one. Her mother was a postdoctoral fellow in science and her father worked in China.

Ordinary Moments, Extraordinary Stories **45**

The Narratives

Brian

Brian was born in Canada. He had received English language support during junior and senior kindergarten, after which he was ineligible. The public school teachers described him as a student who exhibited mild behavior problems and needed more time to complete his work. He was sometimes inappropriately loud and his efforts to gain acceptance into games on the playground were often rejected. At the Chinese community school he experienced more success. The family had recently returned from a 2-month stay in Beijing and Brian had been able to communicate well with his extended family. The trip was not without difficulties though. Brian's cousins were involved in many extra-curricular activities and they were not often available to play with him. The trip had led Brian's mother to reflect on differences between the Canadian and Chinese school systems. In Canada there was less homework, less pressure, and less competition. She liked the relatively relaxed pace, but she had no money for extra-curricular activities and she felt unable to help Brian with his schoolwork. Her assessment of Brian as a learner did not match the assessment of the public school teachers. She felt he was doing well and commented that he was interested in math, joking that he was probably interested in money because the family did not have a lot of it. All the same, Brian did not bring home the leveled books assigned by his teacher. Instead the family visited the public library where Brian enjoyed illustrated books on science topics. He would pore over the illustrations and match single words with the corresponding images. By contrast, at school there was a lot of test-preparation work and the children were grouped for literacy lessons according to their assigned reading levels. Brian's reading was assessed at the kindergarten level, which meant that he was grouped with kindergarteners rather than with his age peers. He was aware that he was not doing as well as the other Chinese children in his class and this made him self-conscious and reluctant to accept help from classroom volunteers.

At school it seemed as if Brian was always short of time. On the morning when his teacher gathered the children on the carpet to watch a 1-minute YouTube video about water filters, he arrived without his planner. Now he was seated in the back row. The video was an advertisement for a water filter system. When it was over, the teacher, Ms. K, asked the children to "talk with your elbow partners about what you see and what you think they are trying to sell." Brian talked with the boy next to him in an animated way using gestures to mimic the people in the video. He was having fun! Yet when the teacher asked the children to comment on what the video was communicating, he was silent and just looked up at the ceiling.

Brian's teacher closed the discussion by saying, "They are trying to get us to stop using water bottles." She told the children to return to their desks and write "a couple of 'I think' sentences in your Quick-Write books." Brian scrunched up his face as he dawdled back to his desk. He looked over to the chalkboard, opened his book, and slowly copied the date. While he was writing, Ms. K spoke to the group: "Start out with 'I think' or 'I wonder.'" Brian looked to the ceiling before writing "I think." Then he stopped, looked around the room and noticed me sitting nearby. Du, who was a participant observer in the class, was unsure if she should try to help. In the past when she had offered to help, Brian's facial expression told her this made him uncomfortable. She decided to give him some space.

One afternoon, Du observed Brian at work during the Literacy Centers period. The children were expected to work independently or with a partner at a designated center. After 10–15 minutes, the teacher would ring a bell to signal that it was time to move to a new center. When the bell rang, Brian was writing a response to the picture book, *Rosie's Walk* (Hutchins, 1971) (see Figure 3.1). Brian did not stop writing even when a classmate leaned over and said, "Time to

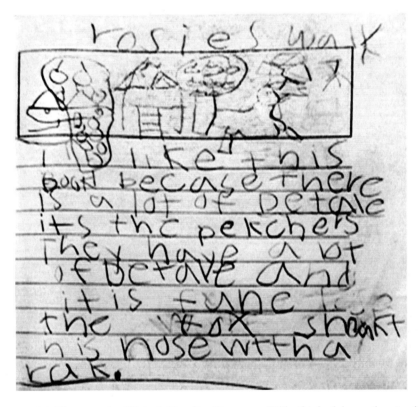

FIGURE 3.1 Photograph of Brian's Reading Response (*I like this book becase there is a lot of detale its the pekchers. They have a lot of detale and it is fune the fox shoakt his nose with a rak*).

Ordinary Moments, Extraordinary Stories **47**

stop." Only when he had completed his sentence did Brian get up from his chair and place his notebook into the assignment basket.

Brian's next center was Read with Someone. He walked to where the folders were kept, but seeing many children ahead of him, he hung back, wandering around the room until his reading partner, Emily, called him to the carpet. Emily had already picked up the folder and had the book open to where the two of them were to start reading. She told him she would read two pages and then it would be his turn. Brian snuggled up against Emily. He looked at the book and appeared to be engrossed in the story as Emily read with confidence, but when his turn came, he hesitated frequently and looked to Emily for help. The bell rang during his turn and again, he seemed reluctant to move on.

A glimpse into his home life can help us to think about Brian's identities in practice. During Du's fourth visit to the home, Brian's mother initiated a game of school to encourage him to share his experiences at school and his feelings about them. "We are at school," she said in a forceful voice. She sat down at the table across from him and asked, "B, 你今天在学校学什么了?" ("B, what did you learn at school today?") Brian commanded, "Mum, I am the teacher." She replied, "哦，对。Teacher, 我们今天学什么?" ("Oh, yes. What are we going to learn today, teacher?") Brian smiled, cleared his throat, and pronounced, "Look up here and tell me how to spell the word interesting." Brian's mother looked to be thinking about it and answered slowly, "I-n-t-e-r-s-t-i-n-g." Brian wrote down the letters on a white board that was fixed to the living room wall. When he finished, he looked at the word, looked back at his mother and reviewed the word again. Miming frustration he said, "No, that's not the word interesting. Think about it and try again." Looking sad, Brian's mother paused and said, "Okay. I-n-t-e-r-e-s-t-i-n-g 这回对么? Is it right this time?" Brian looked closely at the word he had written down and turned to his student, "对了。Correct." Brian's mother smiled at him, but he did not congratulate her. Instead, he directed his student to write a story using the word *interesting* to which she asked, "我的本子在哪?" ("Where is my notebook?") Brian pointed, "在那。" ("Over there.") Brian's mother asked, "我写什么呀?怎么开头呀?" ("What should I write about? How should I start?") Brian answered in an authoritative voice. "Just write! You can write anything you want. Remember: you need to use the word I-N-T-E-R-E-S-T-I-N-G. And you can start with I." Nodding, Brian's mother pretended to write. Brian walked around the table and checked her work to see if she was "doing okay." He returned to his side of the table and announced, "It's time for recess. Tidy up and go outside." Then he said, "You did not finish the writing. I need to call your parents."

The final narrative in this ensemble describes a literacy event at the Chinese community school. The children were seated in a circle led by their teacher, Ms. Q. Ms. Q talked about her weekend then asked the children about theirs. After several children had taken a turn, she looked at Brian who was sitting beside her and asked, "你能给大家讲一讲你的周末么?" ("Could you please tell us about

48 Xiaoxiao Du, Rosamund Stooke, and Rachel M. Heydon

your weekend?") Brian did not answer immediately. He looked up at Ms. Q then looked down again. His head rested in his hands. Ms. Q continued, "你待在家里么?" ("Did you stay at home?") Brian answered, "没有，我去Nick家。" ("No, I went to Nick's place.") In response to Ms. Q's questions, "谁是Nick?" ("Who is Nick?") and "你们一起玩么?" ("Did you play games together?") Brian replied, "Nick 是我的neighbour." ("Nick is my neighbor.") "He invited me to his birthday party." Brian paused, sat up, and code switched, "他请我去他的 birthday party. 我们吃蛋糕，一起玩。他妈妈关灯，Batman 来了，我们都笑了，我们一起玩。" ("We had cakes and played games. His mother turned off the light, Batman showed up. We all laughed and played.") Ms. Q recapped Brian's story, "你周末参加了一个生日聚会，很开心。" ("On the weekend, you went to a birthday party and had a good time.") Looking happy, Brian said, "Yes, it's fun," then added, "很好玩!" ("It's really fun!") Ms. Q congratulated Brian, "不错。你讲得很好。谢谢你。" ("Good for you. Well done! Thanks for sharing.") Brian smiled.

Jiajia and Shasha

Having recently arrived in Canada, Shasha was shy and cried easily. She looked to the outgoing and confident Jiajia for guidance. Jiajia participated actively at school, asked questions, and improvised strategies for dealing with her emergent English vocabulary. She was succeeding academically and socially and she was seen as a leader by her peers. The story begins at the community playground where 10 or so children of varying ages were playing near the slide.

Jiajia and Shasha arrived at the playground. The girls parked their bikes and ran directly over to the group. Jiajia asked a tall girl, "What are you playing?" The tall girl appeared older than the others. She explained that they were trying to stay together on the slide to form a train. They were taking turns being the "bottom" person whose job was to hold the train back. They wanted to see who could hold the train back for the longest time. Jiajia asked if she and Shasha could play and the girls agreed. The tall girl seemed to be the leader and she told the others they should begin a new round with Jiajia and Shasha. The girls came down from the slides and stood in a circle. They put their hands behind their backs and played rock-paper-scissors to decide who would go to the bottom first.

A similar game called 石头-剪刀-布 is played in China. Recalling the Chinese version, Jiajia asked, "How about a bradawl? A bradawl is a sewing tool like scissors. It can beat paper, but it cuts cloth. Rock can beat scissors. Scissors can beat paper and the paper can cover up the rock." But the tall girl said, "No." There could just be scissors, rock, and paper. Jiajia turned to Shasha and said, "这个和中国的不一样。 不是我们的那个剪刀，石头，布。我们就听她的吧，我们现在不是在加拿大么。" ("This is different from the one we had in China. Let's just listen to her since we are in Canada.") Shasha agreed. "是，有点不一样，我们的多好呀。" ("Yes, it's different, but ours is better.") The tall

Ordinary Moments, Extraordinary Stories   49

girl asked Jiajia what Shasha was saying. "We were talking about the differences between your game and ours in China. And we will do your way. It's Canada." After playing rock-paper-scissors, one girl became the bottom person and the others ran up to the platform at the top of the slide. The bottom girl slid first, stopping about half way down. The other girls slid down, one after the other. Jiajia was in the middle. Shasha was not sure about this "squeezing together" game, but Jiajia called to Shasha, "没事的，玩么。" ("It's okay. It's just for fun.") The other girls called Shasha too and finally she joined in, sliding down gingerly. Eventually the girl at the bottom could not hold the others any longer and they tumbled into a heap on the gravel surface of the playground, laughing and screaming. When it was Jiajia's turn, she told the girls that they needed to slide more slowly. First she slid down, carefully controlling her speed to stop just above the bump at the halfway mark. Then she called the next girl, saying, "It's your turn now. Remember to slow down." The second person tried to be slow. Jiajia moved a little bit further down. She smiled and said, "Told you! Slow will work." After a few turns, Shasha looked more comfortable. When it was her turn she waved to Jiajia and said, "Here I come." Jiajia turned to Shasha and said, "You need to slow down." Shasha said, "Sorry, I forgot. Next time." Then Jiajia asked the others, "Who's next?" The remaining girls up on the slide asked Jiajia if they could go together, but Jiajia said, "No. One by one. Nice and slow!"

The story continues at school. The children were on their way outside for recess. Shasha found Jiajia in the school hallway rummaging through her backpack. She asked her, "What are you doing?" Jiajia smiled mischievously, raised her arms and shouted, "Surprise!" Then with her hands behind her back, she asked, "想知道我手里有什么?" ("Do you want to know what's in my hand?") Shasha nodded. Jiajia slowly uncurled her fingers to reveal a large red button about the size of a quarter, a smaller blue button about the size of a dime, and a tiny yellow one plus two stones striped in shades of red and dark brown. "Wow!" Shasha exclaimed. Noticing that Du was watching, Jiajia turned to her and said, "美吧！" ("Beautiful, right?") Du nodded and enthused, "是的。" ("Yes, they are.") Shasha looked at Jiajia, "你从哪找的?" ("Where did you get them?") to which Jiajia answered, "纽扣是从家里拿的，石头是从小区里的捡的。" ("I got the buttons from home and picked up those stones from the playground.") Shasha checked if she heard right, "家里?" ("Home?") Jiajia explained. "昨天我妈妈在缝睡衣的时候，我发现的。" ("Yesterday, I found them when my mum was fixing her pajamas.")

After a discussion in Chinese about the contents of the buttons, Shasha asked, "你是在学校的playground 发现这些石头的?" ("Did you find the stones on the school playground?") Jiajia corrected, "不是，是小区的那个。我们常去的那个。" ("No, the community one. The one we always go to.") Shasha lamented, "我知道呀，我怎么没有发现像你那样的石头呢。" ("I know that one, but I never find any stone like yours.") Jiajia consoled Shasha, "咱俩一起玩吧。" ("We can play with these buttons and stones together.")

Later, on the playground, Jiajia and Shasha held the buttons, moving them to catch the light. Jiajia could not wait to show Du the game, "看，很亮，美吧!" ("See, it is shiny. Beautiful. Right?") Du smiled at her, "是呀，确实很美。" ("Yes, indeed.") Shasha looked proud and happy, "他们很特别。" ("They are really special.") Jiajia pointed to the blue button and offered, "这个不亮，不过它的中间有两个洞，你看看?" ("This one is not shiny but there are two holes in the middle, and you can see through them. Want to try?") Du held the button up to her eyes and peered through the holes at Shasha's nose. Guessing that she had set this up, Du joined in the joke. Du asked, "那些石头哪去了?你放哪了?" ("Where are the stones? What did you do with the stones?") Returning to class, the children explained that they were trying to build a house by using the "regular grey stones from the school playground." Shasha described it: "我们做了个圆形房子。" ("We made a house and the shape was a circle.") Jiajia added, "我们用那些特别的石头做窗户和门。" ("We used my special stones for the windows and the door.") Du queried further, "很好呀。房子用来做什么?" ("That is a good idea. What is the house for?") Shasha said, "给小动物。" ("Small animals.") Jiajia added, "昆虫。" ("Insects.") "你是说虫子，像蚂蚁和瓢虫。" ("You mean bugs like ants or lady bugs.") Shasha affirmed, "是的" ("Yes"), but Jiajia wasn't sure, saying "什么小动物都可以呀，大家一起快乐地住在一起。" ("It could be anything. You know bugs live happily together.") After agreeing to continue the game after lunch, Jiajia carefully sealed her treasures into a bag and stored them safely in her backpack.

The last narrative also takes place at school. Jiajia put her backpack on the hook, opened her bag, and took out a small parcel. She hid the parcel behind her back and went to find Shasha who was looking for her planner. Jiajia tapped Shasha who smiled and asked, "干什么?" ("What's up?") Jiajia presented the parcel to surprise Shasha who asked, "这是什么?" ("What is it?") Jiajia said, "我给你做的卡。" ("It's a card. I made it for you."). The girls hugged for at least 10 seconds after which Shasha said, "谢谢!" ("Thanks!") Jiajia announced, "我们是好朋友么。" ("We are good friends.")

Shasha's eyes were on the parcel. She could see her name and a drawing of a heart. She looked at Jiajia and told her, "你是我最好的朋友!" ("You are my best friend!") "我可以打开么?" ("Can I open it right now?") Jiajia smiled, "当然可以呀。" ("Of course.") Shasha gently removed the red wrapping paper to find a card that said, "朋友" ("Friends"). It featured drawings of hearts and girls playing. Shasha was about to say something, but the teachers reminded the children that they needed to hurry up and not forget their planners. Jiajia whispered to Shasha that it was a secret friendship card. They gathered their things and went back to the classroom. Later that afternoon, Shasha used class time to color rainbows. She showed her coloring to Jiajia and asked Jiajia to keep it. Jiajia had not told Shasha she was returning to China to visit her father and she did not know whether she would come back to Canada.

Discussion

Children's daily lives are lived through/in myriad stories, some of them imagined, like Shasha and Jiajia's stories, in secret worlds and most taking place beyond the awareness of parents and teachers. We would like to highlight four themes in the above stories. First, the stories illuminate ways in which the children navigated between cultural and linguistic worlds. Jiajia's skillful use of pragmatic cues to gain acceptance into the "train game" stands out among these negotiations. Her decision to accept the Canadian version of rock-paper-scissors and her inaccurate translation of Shasha's negative comments about the Canadian version of the game showed diplomacy. Second, the stories show children drawing on a range of multimodal resources to tell stories about themselves and their worlds, and to reposition themselves in those worlds. For example, Brian's actual world of school was peppered with abrupt transitions over which he had little control. In the dramatic retelling for his mother, he took the teacher's part, but his final words—I need to call your parents—suggest that being "too slow" was very much on his mind. Third, the stories accentuated ways in which the children negotiated identities across domains. At home Brian took control of the school game. At school he frequently needed direction, but resisted being directed. At Chinese school, he seemed like another child again. He responded to Ms. Q's prompts and told a story that identified him as a boy who relished jokes and spectacles.

Finally, and most importantly, the stories show how the children's identities were connected to their interests and concerns. In Shasha and Jiajia's case the stories reveal a friendship that was all consuming. They collected and created many artifacts together to symbolize friendship and placed a high value on friendship. As Jiajia explained when Du asked her who would live in the bug house, "Bugs live happily together." Brian's written response to *Rosie's Walk* (Hutchins, 1971) (see Figure 3.1) and his book choices at the library revealed an interest in visual details. His library book choices may have also been motivated by a desire to present himself as knowledgeable in spite of his reading difficulties. Unlike the kindergarten-level books he was supposed to take home from school (but didn't), his library books contained age-appropriate content as well as stunning visuals.

What might educators learn from these stories? First and foremost, we hope they show how important it is to recognize who children are, who they can/could be, and what they can/could do. The need to do well on tests impinges on children and educators as never before and stands to deny children their full personhood. By assembling these stories and reflecting on what the stories suggested to us about each child as an individual, we offer an alternative way to look at and learn from children. We concede that we were selective in choosing stories for our chapter, but in offering them, we hope to contribute to an ongoing conversation aimed at honoring children's identities in practice (Holland et al., 1998).

Notes

1 The signifiers "Chinese" and "children" do not go together unproblematically. In Du's study, all the participating children's parents had been born and raised in mainland China and had chosen to visit, study, or live in Canada. All the children could understand, read, and speak Mandarin Chinese, as well as write simplified Chinese characters. The children were navigating both the English and Chinese languages and cultures to make meaning.
2 All names have been changed.

References

Anderson, R. C., & Chen, X. (2013). Chinese reading development in monolingual and bilingual learners: Introduction to the special issue. *Scientific Studies of Reading, 17,* 1–4.

Barton, D., & Hamilton, M. (2000). Literacy practices. In D. Barton, M. Hamilton, & R. Ivanič (Eds.), *Situated literacies: Reading and writing in context* (pp. 7–15). New York, NY: Routledge.

Bogdan, R. C., & Biklen, S. K. (2006). *Qualitative research for education: An introduction to theory and methods* (5th ed.). Needham Heights, MA: Allyn and Bacon.

Bourdieu, P. (1977). *Outline of a theory of practice* (R. Nice, Trans.). Cambridge, England: Cambridge University Press.

Bourdieu, P. (1990). *The logic of practice.* Stanford, CA: Stanford University Press.

Chen, X., & Lin, P. Y. (2008). Literacy interventions for Chinese children. *Encyclopedia of language and literacy development.* London, Canada: Canadian Language and Literacy Research Network.

Citizenship and Immigration Canada. (2014). *Facts and figures 2013 — Immigration overview: Permanent and temporary residents.* Retrieved from www.cic.gc.ca/english/resources/statistics/menu-fact.asp

Cummins, J. (2006). Identity texts: The imaginative construction of self through multiliteracies pedagogy. In O. Garcia, T. Skutnabb-Kangas, & M. E. Torres-Guzman (Eds.), *Imagining multilingual schools: Language in education and globalization* (pp. 51–68). Toronto, Canada: Multilingual Matters.

Cummins, J., Bismilla, V., Chow, P., Cohen, S., Giampapa, F., Leoni, L., … Sastri, P. (2005). Affirming identity in multilingual classrooms: By welcoming a student's home language into the classroom, schools actively engage English language learners in literacy. *Educational Leadership, 63*(1), 38–43.

Cummins, J., & Early, M. (Eds.). (2011). *Identity texts: The collaborative creation of power in multilingual schools.* Stoke on Trent, England: Trentham Books.

Dagenais, D., Day, E., & Toohey, K. (2006). A Multilingual child's literacy practices and contrasting identities in the figured worlds of French immersion classrooms. *International Journal of Bilingual Education and Bilingualism, 9*(2), 205–218.

David, T., Raban, B., Ure, C., Goouch, K., Jago, M., Barriere, I., & Lambirth, A. (Eds.). (2000). *Making sense of early literacy: A practitioner's perspective.* Stoke on Trent, England: Trentham Books.

DeVault, M. (2008). *People at work: Life, power, and social inclusion in the new economy.* New York, NY: New York University Press.

Du, X. (2014). Navigating Chinese and English multiliteracies across domains in Canada. (Doctoral dissertation). Retrieved from *Western Postdoctoral and Graduate Studies Electronic Thesis and Dissertation Repository.* Paper 2347. http://ir.lib.uwo.ca/etd/2347

Dyson, A. H., & Genishi, C. (2005). *On the case.* New York, NY: Teachers College Press.

Gregory, E. (1996). *Making sense of a new world: Learning to read in a second language.* London, England: Paul Chapman.

Gregory, E. (Ed.). (1997). *One child, many worlds: Early learning in multicultural communities.* London, England: David Fulton.

Gregory, E. (2008). *Learning to read a new language: Making sense of words and worlds* (2nd ed.). Los Angeles, CA: Sage.

Hamilton, M., Heydon, R. Hibbert, K., & Stooke, R. (Eds.). (2015). *Negotiating spaces for literacy learning: Multimodality and governmentality.* London, England: Bloomsbury.

Hao, M., Chen, X., Dronjic, V., Shu, H., & Anderson, R. C. (2013). Chinese children's development of morphological awareness. *Applied Psycholinguistics, 34,* 45–67.

Holland, D., Lachicotte, W., Skinner, D., & Cain, C. (1998). *Identity and agency in cultural worlds.* Cambridge, MT: Harvard University Press.

Hutchins, P. (1971). *Rosie's walk.* New York, NY: Aladdin.

Kress, G. (2003). *Literacy in the new media age.* London, England: Routledge.

Li, G. (2001). Literacy as situated practice. *Canadian Journal of Education, 26*(1), 57–75.

Li, G. (2003). Literacy, culture and politics of schooling: Counter-narratives of a Chinese Canadian family. *Anthropology and Education Quarterly, 34*(2), 182–204.

Li, G. (2006a). *Culturally contested pedagogy: Battles of literacy and schooling between mainstream teachers and Asian immigrant parents.* Albany, NY: State University of New York Press.

Li, G. (2006b). Biliteracy and trilingual practices in the home context: Case studies of Chinese Canadian children. *Journal of Early Childhood Literacy, 6*(3), 355–381.

Li, G. (2007). Parenting practices and schooling: The way class works for new immigrant groups. In L. Weis (Ed.), *The way class works: Readings of school, family and the economy* (pp. 149–166). New York, NY: Routledge.

Li, G. (2009). *Multicultural families, home literacies and mainstream schooling.* Charlotte, NC: Information Age.

Li, G., & Wang, L. (2008). *Model minority myth revisited: An interdisciplinary approach to demystifying Asian American educational experiences.* Charlotte, NC: Information.

Lincoln, Y. S., & Guba, E. A. (1985). *Naturalistic inquiry.* Beverly Hills, CA: Sage.

Luo, Y., Chen, X., Deacon, H., Zhang, J., & Yin, L. (2013). The role of visual processing in learning to read Chinese characters. *Scientific Studies of Reading, 17,* 22–40.

Luo, Y. C., Chen, X., & Geva, E. (2014). Concurrent and longitudinal cross-linguistic transfer of phonological awareness and morphological awareness in Chinese-English Bilingual Children. *Written Language & Literacy, 17,* 89–115.

Moore, D. (2010). Multilingual literacies and third script acquisition: Young Chinese children in French immersion in Vancouver, Canada. *International Journal of Multilingualism, 7*(4), 322–342.

Murphy, S. (2015). Beyond governmentality: The responsible exercise of freedom in pursuit of literacy assessment. In M. Hamilton, R. Heydon, K. Hibbert, & R. Stooke (Eds.), *Negotiating spaces for literacy learning: Multimodality and governmentality* (pp. 25–42). London, England: Bloomsbury.

Park, C., Endo, R., & Rong, X. L. (Eds.). (2009). *New perspectives on Asian American parents, students, and teacher recruitment.* Charlotte, NC: Information Age.

Rowsell, J., & Pahl, K. (2007). Sedimented identities in texts: Instance of practice. *Reading Research Quarterly, 42*(3), 388–404.

Street, B. V. (1984). *Literacy in theory and practice.* Cambridge, England: Cambridge University Press.

Suárez-Orozco, M. M., & Suárez-Orozco, C. (2009). Globalization, immigration, and schooling. In J. A. Banks (Ed.), *The Routledge international companion to multicultural education* (pp. 62–76), New York, NY: Routledge.

Toohey, K. (2000). *Learning English in school: Identity, social relations and classroom practice.* Clevedon, England: Multilingual Matters.

Wien, C. (2013). *Making learning visible through pedagogical documentation.* Toronto, Canada: Queens Printer for Ontario. Retrieved from www.edu.gov.on.ca/childcare/Wien.pdf

Wohlwend, K. E. (2008). Play as a literacy of possibilities: Expanding meanings in practices, materials, and spaces. *Language Arts, 88*(2), 127–136.

Yin, R. K. (2003). *Case study research: Design and methods* (3rd ed.). Thousand Oaks, CA: Sage.

4

LOOKING THROUGH THE LENS OF CHINESE ELLS ON ACADEMIC WRITING IN SECONDARY SCHOOL

Ravy S. Lao, May Y. Lee, and Araceli Arzate

Children from immigrant families are the fastest growing demographic in the United States, and research suggests that one in five children in America today is the child of immigrant parents (Rumbaut & Portes, 2001; Fuligni, 2004). In the case of Asians (and Chinese in particular) their sustained migration to the United States resulted in the sharp demographic growth of Asian children in public schools. While many children of Asian immigrants (including Chinese) have been very successful in their schooling as represented through their high test scores, an area of difficulty confronting them is composing academic essays.

Education in the United States is often viewed as a means of achieving social mobility for immigrant families as it allows for the acquisition of academic credentials needed to further economic prospects in an increasingly complex economy (Fuligni, 2004; Suárez-Orozco & Suárez-Orozco, 2001). Thus, immigrant children can potentially gain a great deal from school success, and some research has found that many first- and second-generation immigrant children are doing quite well, on the whole, achieving higher than their peers from American-born families (Fuligni, 2004).

Asian students (regardless of length of residency in the U.S.) are often viewed within an Asian American collective that assumes all Asian-descent students are academically successful, as propagated by the model minority stereotype of Asian American students (Lee, 1996). As a result, recent Asian immigrant students are not well attended to in the research literature (Ngo, 2006). To address this oversight, this exploratory study will shine light on recent secondary Chinese immigrant students and their writing issues and needs. This discussion will be viewed in light of the Common Core State Standards (CCSS), which stress students to use and produce complex academic literacy and the California High

School Exit Examination (CAHSEE), which these students must pass in order to obtain their high school diploma.

In order to get to know the hearts and minds of this group of Chinese English Language Learners (ELLs) through the lens of writing, we ask the question: What can secondary educators learn about these students' experiences with English language writing prior to immigration by looking beyond immediate test scores in order to support their learning of American English academic writing genres?

Situating English Language Learners in High School Settings

In their book titled *A Synthesis of Research on Second Language Writing in English*, Leki, Cumming, and Silva (2008) reviewed published literature on secondary level second language (L2) writing over the past 35 years going back to the 1980s and concluded that "this adolescent population has generally suffered from a lack of attention to its writing needs in L2 ..." (p. 17). Sharing similar concerns, Harklau (2006) noted that in the context of U.S. K–12 education, English Language Learner students at the secondary level are an under-researched population, whereas the processes of English language learning are best documented in the elementary grade levels. While there are emerging research on this population (Faltis & Wolfe, 1999; Fu, 1995), not much is known about how these secondary English Language Learners navigate high school content-area academics, learn a new language, and come of age in U.S. society (Harklau, 2006, p. 103). This chapter contributes to this field of study by focusing on recent Chinese immigrant high school students and their writing issues and needs.

Contextualizing English Writing Instruction in China

In order to contextualize these Chinese English Language Learners' experiences with English language writing prior to immigration, it is important to understand English language writing instruction in the home country in comparison to the practices of American classrooms. In recent years, there have been studies that examined (K–12 level) English writing instruction in China. Whether focusing on the writing instruction on students (Wang, 2011) or by teachers (Fu & Matoush, 2012; Spalding, Wang, Lin, & Hu, 2009), these studies came to similar conclusions. Spalding et al. (2009) echoed many of their research peers' findings by stating "writing in English, when taught at all, has primarily been seen as a matter of filling in blanks, following pattern drills, and producing error-free text of the type associated with linguistically controlled writing and that the present teaching force in China is ill-prepared to teach English writing" (p. 25). Wanting to understand how English writing is taught at the K–12 level across China, Fu and Matoush's (2012) survey study included 123 teachers representing 30 schools in 13 cities and districts. Based on their findings, they concluded that, "It appears that teaching English writing in China is a brand new field in which few teachers have either much knowledge or experience" (p. 32). Similarly, several studies carried out by Hu (2005) found that a linguistically controlled approach to L2 English language and writing instruction appears to dominate in China.

Exploring how first language (L1) writing instruction may impact composition produced in English as a foreign language (EFL) classrooms in China, Wang's (2011) qualitative study investigated 50 Chinese students to learn how they were taught to write in their L1 (Chinese). This study shows that Chinese high school students lack training in the process of writing. Without an outline and even the thesis statement, students may start the composition from unrelated information, diverge from the topic, or be indirect. When they go to college, students tend to transfer their L1 writing practice to EFL writing. Thus, helping students develop the writing process is necessary. Specifically, due to the difference in rhetorical features of the two languages, teachers should introduce the English rhetorical features in class.

Chinese "Parachute Kids" in Californian Secondary Schools

A large percentage of the ELLs focused on in this chapter are of Chinese heritage and some belong to a particular group scholars have termed *parachute kids* (Chang & Shyong, 2015; Lee & Zhou, 2004). The term *parachute kids* refers to children sent to a new country to live alone or with a caregiver while their parents remain in their home country (Chang, 2004; Lee & Zhou, 2004). In the case of the Chinese parachute-kid phenomenon, Chang and Shyong (2015) traced it back to the 1980s and 1990s when wealthy Chinese families in Taiwan and Hong Kong sent their children to live in upscale Chinese enclaves in Southern California while the parents remained in their country. In terms of living arrangement, these youngsters either lived with relatives or alone in the home purchased by their parents.

Today, however, there is a surge of Chinese parachute youngsters coming from mainland China (Chang & Shyong, 2015). In contrast to the past, these recent parachute kids may come from either modest or wealthy families. They stay in private homes, paying for room, board, transportation, and guardians who act as their parents while their own parents remain in China (Chang & Shyong, 2015). Although not every student participant in our study is Chinese and a parachute kid, many are, and they came from mainland China as our survey found (see Table 4.1).

Theoretical Perspectives: The Situated Nature of Literacy Learning and Teaching

Good writers would say that writing is like any craft; it requires practice, effort, and time in order for a person to become good at it. Thus, effective writing ability is not something that one is born with but a skill that is learned. To support the success of English Language Learners (ELLs) in the process of acquiring the English language and at the same time be expected to compose lengthy academic writing, educators need to know that these students are capable learners who will acquire the necessary skills when they are instructed with effective writing strategies.

To construct a theoretical framework that supports the aforementioned assumptions, we adopted what Lea and Street (2006) called the "study skills approach" to writing. This model conceptualizes "writing and literacy as primarily an individual and cognitive skill" and focuses on "the surface features of language form and presumes that students can transfer their knowledge of writing and literacy unproblematically from one context to another" (pp. 368–369). Furthermore, "the study skills model is concerned with the use of written language at the surface level, and concentrates upon teaching students formal features of language; for example, sentence structure, grammar, and punctuation" (p. 369).

In addition, we also drew on various scholars who view literacy as social and cultural practices that vary with context (Barton & Hamilton, 1998; Street, 1984, 1995). In this chapter, for example, we viewed these Chinese ELL students' already developed Chinese literacy to be their "funds of knowledge" which U.S. literacy educators can draw on to support these students' learning of American English academic writing genres.

Understanding literacy instructors and their teaching practices, we drew on Smagorinsky (2006) who proposed that writing educators are working with an expanded understanding of literacy that includes "new questions about the situated nature of teaching and learning as they are enacted amid competing political agendas, constructed subjectivities, social goals and structures, discourses, and value systems" (p. 12). Thus, writing instructors' preference for one writing strategy over the other is based on their students' needs and their instructional goals.

Situating the Study

The study for this chapter was part of a California Writing Project site, located on a California State University campus, that provided professional development training in writing to a school district situated in a large Chinese enclave in Southern California where there is a large number of Chinese-speaking students. In order to get to know the hearts and minds of a group of secondary Chinese English Language Learners through the lens of writing, we ask the question: What can secondary educators learn about these students' experiences with English language writing prior to immigration by looking beyond immediate test scores in order to support their learning of American English academic writing genres?

The professional training occurred in the 2013–2014 academic school year. Three high schools in this school district participated in the professional development. However, the data included in the study for this chapter came

Looking through the Lens of Chinese ELLs **59**

from one of the schools, which will be named Valley High School (VHS) hereafter. All three of the authors are connected to the aforementioned high school and university. While Author B and Author C are both teachers in the English Language Development (ELD) department at VHS, Author A is a lecturer at Hillview University (a pseudonym). Although the professional development training has ended between the Writing Project and VHS, Hillview University continues its university–community school partnership by holding a writing center at VHS since January 2015. Thus, the relationship between the people and the schools continues.

According to the 2010 U.S. Census data, the community where VHS is located has a population of 60,937 with a median household income of $48,000. The primary ethnicity of the city is Asian, comprising 64.9% of the population; Hispanics make up 27.7% of the residents; White/Caucasian 4.9%; and other races less than 3% combined. Because of the high concentration of Chinese residents, Li (2009) has referred to this area as an *ethnoburb*, a suburban residential and business area with a notable cluster of a particular ethnic minority population. Also according to the 2010 Census data, this Chinese ethnoburb where VHS is situated has a foreign-born population significantly above the state average: 54% of the residents are foreign born; 43.6% Asian, 7.3% Latin American, with the total for California as a whole being 26.9% foreign born.

Student enrollment at VHS reflects the community's population make-up. According to the school's 2013–2014 report for the Western Association of Schools and Colleges and the California Department of Education, the majority of the 2,356 students enrolled are Asian (71.7%), while 23.3% are Hispanic, 1.4% Caucasian, and 3.6% other. Over one-third of the students are Limited English Proficient. As for primary languages, the largest groups in order of numbers of students are Cantonese, Mandarin, and Spanish. VHS receives Title I funding and approximately 62.6% of its students are part of the Free/Reduced Lunch program.

Who are the ELLs at Valley High School? They consist of two groups: Long-term English Learners (LTELs) and recent immigrants. The LTELs are identified early in the year by all their teachers and given assistance or tutoring as needed in the specific area of concern, even in their English classes. The recent immigrant students are placed in Structured English Immersion (SEI), depending on individual students' level of proficiency according to the scores on the California English Language Development Test (CELDT) and given Specially Designed Academic Instruction in English (SDAIE) classes to help with the transition to Academic English in all their courses. SDAIE is a method for teaching both the English language and academic content to English Language Learners.

Over 90% of the SEI students come from China with Mandarin (Putonghua), followed by Cantonese, as their native language. Students may also come from Taiwan (who also speak Mandarin), Vietnam, Philippines, Korea, Mexico, and other South American countries, but only in small numbers. With the majority of the students sharing the same home language, students typically do not communicate with one another in English; therefore, language acquisition may be delayed in addition to various academic issues.

Many of the students appear to have unaddressed learning differences or disabilities but addressing these issues can be extraordinarily challenging. Because of cultural beliefs and the stigma attached to learning disabilities or psychological conditions, parents typically deny services and do not pursue further testing to determine the students' needs. At the same time, testing for learning disabilities in students' native language can be difficult because of funding and lack of resources.

As mentioned earlier in the chapter, some of our students are parachute kids (Chang, 2004; Chang & Shyong, 2015; Lee & Zhou, 2004). They may reside with guardians who typically receive a monthly stipend in exchange for legal custody of the student. The purpose is to set up residency for the student in order to register in school with limited or no parental support. Once the guardian enrolls a student, academic responsibilities rest solely in the hands of the student. Most of these paid guardians rarely attend conferences and do not monitor the student's academic progress. The students become, essentially, neglected minors in a foreign country with limited language abilities. The struggles to acquire a new language and to assimilate are further compounded by lack of parental involvement or guidance. They become vulnerable to drugs, gangs, and chronic absenteeism.

Assessments and Placement of ELL Students at Valley High School

Valley High School teachers and staff use a variety of assessments to monitor student academic progress and achievement. The *California English Language Development Test* (CELDT) is administered each year to formally assess and identify ELLs' proficiency level in English. Students take CELDT in late July and the results are shared with teachers, parents, and students to determine proper placement within the Structured English Immersion (SEI) department or mainstream English instruction. Based on these results, ELL students are categorized into four levels of classes: SEI 1–2 (beginning), 3–4 (intermediate), 5–6 (intermediate advanced), and 7–8 (advanced). Students progress from SEI 1–2 to SEI 3–4, and so on, but are allowed to skip levels in subsequent years if their test scores indicate it. If students test as fluent or higher on the CELDT, they become eligible for the Initial Fluent English Proficient (IFEP) label, and they are moved into a mainstreamed class. Their progress is monitored for an additional year. Within the classroom, teachers identify their ELL students and take note of their strengths and weaknesses to place them in instructional settings to address those needs, including flexible groupings of diverse target language fluency and placement of EL students near fluent English speaking students to encourage better fluency. The goal is to move students up at least one level each year, and eventually graduate them from the SEI program altogether.

Methods

The data in this chapter come from an ongoing study that focused on enhancing ELLs' strategic reading and text-based analytical essay writing. In fall 2013, a California Writing Project site was invited to work with the Norrington School District (a pseudonym) to provide a series of professional development to the English departments of their three high schools. The focus of the professional development was for the writing project staff to work with the high school teachers in developing whole holistic writing rubric, writing assessment of their students, and writing strategies to enhance the teaching of analytical student writing.

Although the professional development training was carried out among the three high schools in the district, the focus of this chapter is on Valley High School, where 70% of the student body are Asians, particularly Chinese who live in the Chinese ethnoburb.

Two types of data were gathered and informed this chapter. The first are 146 exploratory surveys completed by ELL students in winter 2015, and the second consists of 152 ELL student writing assessments in the fall of the 2013–2014 academic year. Except for the seniors who graduated, the same cohort of ELL students completed the surveys and wrote the writing assessment which became the data set used for this chapter. In the following sections, we provide details about the surveys administered and discuss information on the 152 student papers.

Student Surveys

To ascertain the demographics of ELL students enrolled in the VHS English Language Development (ELD) program, a survey was administered in the classes taught by three teachers including Author B and Author C. Two of the instructors administered the paper-based surveys in class while the third posted the survey on the class's website through Google Forms, and the students completed the questionnaire at their leisure at home. After a week period, a total of 146 students of whom 88 (60%) were males and 58 (40%) were females completed the survey (see Table 4.1). In this high school student sample, based on grade level distribution, 34% ($N = 51$) of them were tenth-graders, followed by an even number 25% ($N = 37$) for both the eleventh- and twelfth-graders, and finished up with 14% ($N = 21$) of the ninth-graders.

Of the total 146 students surveyed, interestingly, 89% ($N = 130$) of the students reported China as their country of birth with five of the 130 explicitly writing *Hong Kong* next to the word *China*. By noting this clarification, it appears that these students wished to distinguish themselves from mainland China. By this huge percentage, clearly the majority of students enrolled at Valley High School are Chinese students coming from mainland China. Another interesting discovery is that of the 146 respondents, seven (5%) reported the United States as

TABLE 4.1 Student Demographics

Gender		Grade Level		Country of Birth	
M	88 (60%)	9th	21 (14%)	China (including 5 from Hong Kong)	130 (89%)
F	58 (40%)	10th	51 (35%)	Taiwan	3 (2%)
		11th	37 (25%)	South Korea	1 (.7%)
		12th	37 (25%)	Southeast Asia	4 (2.7%)
				Mexico	1 (.7%)
				USA	7 (5%)
Total	146 (100%)		146 (100%)		146 (100%)

their country of birth. This indicates that although these seven students are U.S. born, in terms of English ability, they are placed in the ELD program because English is not their native language and these students have received instruction, primarily, outside of the United States. Thus, it is most likely that these students, having been raised and growing up in a Chinese enclave, will have retained their home language.

In terms of racial identity, the majority of students (99%) are Chinese and were born in mainland China. However, there are a few from countries such as Burma/Myanmar, Cambodia, the Philippines, and Vietnam, as well as Mexico.

The exploratory questionnaire, consisting of 14 items, was grouped into three main sections: demographic questions, background of English language study, and student perception of English literacy. The questionnaire was provided in English only, because the assumption based on the selection criteria was that the informants were English proficient. The demographic questions ask for students' gender, place of birth, and length of U.S. residency.

The section on English language study background asks if students have studied English in their home country and if they were taught to write English essays by their English teachers. The construction of these questions was informed by the literature on English instruction in K–12 level in China, particularly by studies conducted by Fu and Matoush (2012) and Hu (2005). The final section on student perception of English literacy elicits their self-assessment of their English literacy (e.g., "Do you like to write essays in English? Why or why not?" and "What part of writing essays in English do you find the most difficult and why?") (see Table 4.2). Since the survey was constructed as an exploratory means to capture the full range of answers and to understand who are the English Language Learners at Valley High School, the questions were open-ended in nature, especially as to not limit their answers. Thus, not all the questions on the survey had predetermined options or choices on a Likert scale.

Looking through the Lens of Chinese ELLs 63

TABLE 4.2 Student Linguistic Profile

	Yes	No	Total		Yes	No	Total
Learned English in home country?	129 (88%)	17 (12%)	146 (100%)	Were taught to write English essays when learning English in own country?	41 (32%)	88 (68%)	129 (100%)
Total			**146**	*Total*			**129**

	Yes	No	Total
Do you like to write essays in English?	54 (37%)	92 (63%)	146 (100%)
Total			**146**

	English Section	Math Section	Not taken		Reading	Writing	Both
What part of the CAHSEE do you find the most difficult?	128 (88%)	2 (1%)	16 (11%)	What part of the English section do you find most difficult?	55 (40%)	46 (34%)	35 (26%)
Total			**146**	*Total*			**136**

Means and frequencies of the ELL students' answers were calculated to assess student demographics and English-language study patterns. Student responses to the open-ended questions about their perception of English language literacy were coded for themes that relate to student assessment writing and literature findings. Furthermore, the responses of the students are presented to provide a deeper understanding of their perceptions and needs to inform the instruction on writing to meet the Common Core State Standards and in preparing them for the CAHSEE exam.

Having discussed data from our student surveys in detail, we now turn to the student writing assessments, which was the impetus for this study. Explanation of its genesis and what was learned are presented below.

Student Writing Assessments

The other portion of the data set came from student writing assessments. As part of a multi-year collaboration, the California Writing Project site at Hillview

University supports Norrington School District teachers in developing and using a text-based, district-wide assessment of argumentative writing. The first-year partnership took place during the 2013–2014 academic school calendar. In the fall semester, as part of a district-wide argumentative writing assessment, students were to respond in the form of an argumentative essay to Jeffrey Rosen's essay "The Importance of Societal Forgetting." Although all students at VHS participated in the assessment writing, only papers written by ELL students in the English Language Development department were included in this chapter. A total of 152 student papers were gathered for closed linguistic analysis. The papers were analyzed using an analytic rubric based on holistic scoring on a scale from 1 to 6, where 6 indicates commands of attention and 1 shows severely limited English reading and writing. The essays received a score of 1 to 6 on how well the student addressed these six categories: (a) understanding the task; (b) understanding the text; (c) content; (d) coherence; (e) stylistics; and (f) mechanics, usage, grammar, and syntax. This analytic rubric was collaboratively developed by the teachers at Norrington School District.

Results and Discussion

Student Surveys: English Language Study and Perception of English Literacy

In order to examine how the students perceived their English language skills and their study of English back in their home countries, they were asked to not only answer with a yes or no but also to provide explanations for their answers.

As shown in Table 4.2, a summary of the students' answers is provided. When asked if they learned English in their home countries, the majority of the students, 88% (N = 129), stated that they did. Of the 129 students who responded in the affirmative when asked a followed-up question if they were taught to write English essays when they learned English in their home country, 68% (N = 88) of them said no. One female twelfth-grader summed up what students in China learned when they studied English: "Teachers teach to write sentences and paragraphs, not essays." Their response to not being taught to write essays while they learned English in China corroborates Fu and Matoush's (2012) study of teachers' perceptions of English language writing instruction in China. They found that the majority of pre-service teachers in the K–12 level in China were not taught how to teach writing. Thus, when they have their own classroom, these teachers did not teach the writing skills to their students. Having not been taught how to compose essays in their prior schooling coupled with their limited English, it is not surprising that the majority, 63% (N = 92), of the ELL students at VHS stated that they did not like to write essays in English. However, as high school students, they are not only expected to be able to compose academic essays but to do so in different rhetorical modes, such as argumentative, narrative, compare and contrast, and to utilize complex academic language to convey their ideas in their writings. Only learning to write sentences and paragraphs in English does not fulfill the rigorous expectations of the new Common Core State Standards and high-stakes tests such as the California High School Exit Examination (CAHSEE), which students need to pass in order to graduate from high school. Thus, it is not surprising that when asked what part of the CAHSEE they found the most difficult, an overwhelming majority—88% (N = 128) of these ELL students—answered the English (language arts) section of the CAHSEE was the most difficult for them.

Writing Issues as Revealed through Student Writing Assessment

Of the 152 student papers analyzed and scored, 31 (20%) received a score of 4 rating, which was satisfactory, and the rest received a score of 3 (unsatisfactory) or lower. Considering the majority of the ELL students have been living and attending U.S. schools on an average of 2.6 years as indicated by the surveys, the results of this timed student writing assessment were not surprising. It is important to note, however, the median scores of the SEI students are comparatively similar to their mainstream counterparts in ninth- and tenth-grade English classes. Furthermore, since their English writing instruction in China was devoted to filling in blanks, following pattern drills, and producing error-free text of the type associated with linguistically controlled writing (Spalding et al., 2009) or were not taught the English rhetorical features such as argumentative essay writing in this case, it was not surprising that not too many papers received higher scores.

Closely examining these ELL student assessment papers revealed several areas of weakness. In terms of understanding the task for writing this argumentative essay, these ELL students failed to address adequately the task, purpose, and/or audience. In terms of content, they expressed unclear ideas, little or inappropriate information, and/or poorly chosen examples and/or evidence. There was poor logic, lack of appropriate organization, and incoherence when it came to expressing themselves in their papers. As for stylistics, frequently there were imprecise word choices, little sentence variety, and little or detrimental use of rhetorical devices or appeals. In terms of mechanics, usage, grammar, and syntax, these papers contained a few major errors or many minor errors in Standard English conventions.

After dissecting and locating areas of trouble found in these Chinese ELL students' writing, we now turn to instructional strategies that foster ELL writing. These instructional strategies are grounded in Carol Booth Olson's research on the reading–writing connection (Olson, 2011) and in hers and her colleague's professional development trainings with secondary English teachers (Olson & Land, 2007). Their work foregrounds the need in "making visible for … students the thinking [and writing] tools experienced readers and writers access in the process of meaning construction" (Olson & Land, 2007, p. 269). These tools

Ravy S. Lao, May Y. Lee, and Araceli Arzate

include "explicitly teaching, modeling and providing guided practice in a variety of strategies to help students read and write challenging texts" (p. 269). The following section explicates the aforementioned instructional writing strategies.

Implementing Research-Based Instructional Strategies to Support ELLs in Writing

For English Language Learners, especially those that come from countries where writing follows a different rhetorical style or structure (cyclic and the thesis is mentioned last) compared to the linear one stressed in Western writing, explicit and direct instruction is needed (Olson, 2011; Olson & Land, 2007). This is of the utmost importance as the Common Core State Standards now stress text-based analytical writing where students read from complex texts (usually nonfiction) and compose academic writing corroborated with textual evidence to bolster their argument. Since the majority of the ELLs in this study indicated that they were not taught to write English essays in their survey responses, and also evident in their receiving a low score on their writing assessment papers, explicit and direct writing instruction and strategies are needed. In our professional development training, we coached English teachers to make visible to students, especially ELLs, the particular structure in English academic writing and its various parts as explained below. Furthermore, within these different parts, *specific* information and language are used to convey the paper's argument and idea. In addition, the 2014–2015 academic school year was the first school-wide attempt at VHS to implement the Jane Schaffer writing instruction curriculum where SEI teachers adopted the basic premise of this curriculum to provide explicit instruction with models. The Jane Schaffer writing instruction strategy and the literacy strategies proposed by Carol Booth Olson and colleagues work in tandem to support ELLs' writing. As mentioned earlier, as part of their writing assessment, students at VHS had to read the article "The Importance of Societal Forgetting" by Jeffrey Rosen and then compose an argumentative essay where they argued for or against the use of the Internet and social media. Working with the same writing prompt and article, we explicate step by step below how instructors of writing can make visible to their ELL students the specific information and language needed to compose an academic essay.

In the introduction of an essay we would explicitly tell the ELL students that it consists of three features and they are a hook, a TAG (title, author, genre), and a thesis statement. We would point out that the first sentence of an introductory paragraph requires a hook or an attention-grabber to capture the reader's interest. A hook can be a quote, a description, a question, or a statement to make people think. Then follow the hook with a TAG (title, author, genre). To make visible to students what this may look like, we provided various examples as models so they could see what a sentence containing a TAG looks like. Thus, the three TAG sentences could be: (1) In the article "The Importance of Societal

Forgetting," Jeffrey Rosen describes a serious problem of using the Internet that …; (2) Jeffrey Rosen's article "The Importance of Societal Forgetting" deals with …; or (3) Reminding the reader of one of the perils brought on by the technological advances that exist today, Jeffrey Rosen, a law professor, focuses on … in his article "The Importance of Societal Forgetting." Students also need to summarize the author's claim in the article. Lastly, the introduction, usually the last sentence of that section, contains a thesis statement. Explain to the students that the thesis statement in an essay is the claim the writer makes in response to the prompt. We explicitly divide the THESIS into two parts: the subject of the student's essay and the student's opinion of this subject to anchor the rest of the body paragraphs. Some teachers further guide students to form compound opinions whereby each opinion is the premise of each body paragraph that follows in the paper. We also drive home the message that the thesis statement is the "key" that will "drive" our essay because it tells the reader where you as a writer will take them.

Once again, being explicit and direct as in the instruction of the introduction, we continued with the main body paragraphs of the essay. We would instruct the ELL students that after the introduction comes the main body of the essay, and it can consist of multiple paragraphs. These multiple paragraphs focus on different things. We also used universal language so that from SEI to mainstream English classes, instruction of essay writing used the same terminology of concrete details and commentary to support the thesis in the introductory paragraph. In addition, universal color-coding was adopted to help students visually process the various components of a paragraph to effectively support the thesis with text-based evidence as well as student analysis. Again, referring back to Rosen's essay, we instructed them to ask themselves: What is the author claiming? In order for the student to express an opinion, he or she needs to understand what Rosen's position is on social media and the Internet. Thus, the student needs to analyze the author's use of language, point out specific types of language he uses, and discuss why he makes these comparisons. Teachers emphasize to students to write in formal, academic tone, include quotes from the text or cite examples from personal life or outside research, and follow with commentary sentences to explain the significance of cited evidence. A common practice in SEI classes is to provide sentence frames where teachers provide a list of phrases to introduce quotes and examples. For instance, words to introduce quotes can be something like *Rosen states, points out, comments, remarks*, and so forth. As these are high school students, we would go further by introducing academic vocabulary when discussing language use. Thus, teachers remind students of the academic language deemed appropriate for the audience of the essay. For example, to discuss what the author does, students can use words such as *depict, portrays, illustrate*, or *suggest*. Similarly, to provide examples, students should use phrases such as *for example, for instance*, or *furthermore* in their paper. On the timed portion of the writing assessment, students are allowed to use a bilingual glossary—CAHSEE glossary—that includes commonly used academic vocabulary.

After showing ELL students ways and words to introduce quotes, we would explicitly demonstrate words to use after a quotation, along with sentence starters, such as (a) "This suggests that …," (b) "This is significant because …," (c) "Rosen's point is that …," or (d) "These words communicate that …"

The last paragraph of an essay is the conclusion. In their writing assessment, Valley High School students were asked to revisit and restate the author's theme and to express why it was important. For English Language Learners it is important to show and model to them what a conclusion sentence looks like. Here are a few sentence starters that were suggested to our students: (a) "To sum up, Rosen's message is …"; (b) "Rosen wants us to come away from his article believing that …"; (c) "In conclusion, Rosen's article teaches us that …"; or (d) "Ultimately, the central lesson we learn from Rosen is …" By providing students with sentence starters, teachers are not only helping with sample sentences but also reinforcing them with the academic language being used.

English Language Learners face layers of obstacles when asked to compose academic writing. Firstly, they are still learning the English language, which entails acquiring vocabulary, recognizing grammatical patterns in the target language, and piecing together the correct words and grammatical rules in order to produce the correct syntax. Secondly, if these ELL students came from a writing tradition where their L1 rhetorical feature is very different from the linear style of Western writing, they need to be aware of this difference. By explicitly making visible to students the various components that make up each part of an essay, writing instructors are arming them with a clear road map where ELL students can navigate the complex path of composing academic essays. Furthermore, although ELLs are developing their language in English, students are capable of dissecting challenging texts and comprehending complex writing demands. In hearing the complex and rich academic vocabulary teachers use in their instruction of writing, ELL students will not only be exposed to new words but will, hopefully, acquire them (Wong-Fillmore & Fillmore, 2012; Zwiers, O'Hara, & Pritchard, 2014). As young adult writers, their writing needs to sound academic. Thus, academic vocabulary should be taught in tandem with writing instruction.

Conclusion and Directions for Further Research

This study which focused on a group of English Language Learners in Southern California both corroborates and also extends our understanding of the writing issues, needs, and instructional process for English Learners at the high school level. Although this study focused on Chinese ELL students in particular, the writings issues, needs, and instructional strategies discussed and mentioned here can be applied to other ELLs of various language backgrounds, as well as language-minority students who may have grown up speaking a register different from the one taught in school (Wong-Fillmore & Fillmore, 2012). With the adaption of

Common Core State Standards by more and more states in K–12 levels and with the demand for high-level writing by colleges and universities in the Unites States and abroad, ELLs are expected to perform at a competent level if they want to obtain their high school diploma (in the case of California) or be a competitive candidate to enter a good university or get a good job. Thus, active measures need to be taken to pass on the writing skills to English Language Learners. Findings from this study suggest some measures that can be taken to support secondary ELLs in writing.

This research is an exploratory study that examined writing issues confronting recently arrived Chinese students on their timed writing assessment. In order to capture and understand how writing interventions, in the case of using direct and explicit instructional strategies, affect these students' writing performance, a pre- and post-test design should be implemented in order to measure any difference. This is a direction that we are looking forward to in our future study.

References

Barton, D., & Hamilton, M. (1998). *Local literacies*. London, UK: Routledge.

Chang, C., & Shyong, F. (2015, July 2). Teens' attack on Chinese girl draws comparison to "Lord of the Flies" from judge. *Los Angeles Times*. Retrieved from www.latimes.com

Chang, I. (2004). *The Chinese America: A narrative history*. New York, NY: Penguin Books.

Faltis, C., & Wolfe, P. (Eds.). (1999). *So much to say: Adolescents, bilingualism, and ESL in the secondary school*. New York, NY: Teacher College Press.

Fuligni, A. J. (2004). The adaptation and acculturation of children from immigrant families. In U. P. Gielen & J. Roopnarine (Eds.), *Childhood and adolescence: Cross-cultural perspectives and applications* (pp. 297–318). Westport, CT: Greenwood.

Fu, D. (1995). *My trouble is my English*. Portsmouth, NH: Boynton/Cook.

Fu, D., & Matoush, M. M. (2012). Teacher's perceptions of English language writing instruction in China. In C. Bazerman, C. Dean, J. Early, K. Lunsford, S. Lull, P. Rogers, & M. Sandsell (Eds.), *New directions in international advances in writing research: Culture, places and measures* (pp. 23–39). West Lafayette, IN: Parlor.

Harklau, L. (2006). From the "good kids" to the "worst": Representations of English language learners across educational settings. In P. K. Matsuda, M. Cox, J. Jordan, & C. Ortmeier-Hooper (Eds.), *Second-language writing in the composition classroom: A critical sourcebook* (pp. 103–130). Boston, MA: Bedford/St. Martin's.

Hu, G. (2005). Professional development of secondary EFL teachers: Lessons from China. *Teachers College Record, 107*, 654–705.

Lea, M. R., & Street, B. V. (2006). The "Academic Literacies" model: Theory and applications. *Theory into Practice, 45*(4), 368–377.

Lee, J., & Zhou, M. (Eds.). (2004). *Asian American youth: Culture, identity, and ethnicity*. New York, NY: Routledge.

Lee, S. J. (1996). *Unraveling the "model minority" stereotype: Listening to Asian American youth*. New York, NY: Teachers College Press.

Leki, I., Cumming, A., & Silva, T. (2008). *A synthesis of research on second language writing in English*. New York, NY: Routledge.

Li, W. (2009). *Ethnoburb: The new ethnic community in urban America.* Honolulu, HA: University of Hawaii Press.

Ngo, B. (2006). Learning from the margins: The education of Southeast and South Asian Americans in context. *Race, Ethnicity and Education, 9*(1), 51–65.

Olson, C. B. (2011). *The reading/writing connection: Strategies for teaching and learning in the secondary classroom* (3rd ed.). Boston, MA: Pearson.

Olson, C. B., & Land, R. (2007). A cognitive strategies approach to reading and writing instruction for English language learners in secondary school. *Research in the Teaching of English, 41*(3), 269–303.

Rumbaut, R. G., & Portes, A. (2001). *Ethnicities: Children of immigrants in America.* Berkeley, CA: University of California Press.

Smagorinsky, P. (2006). Overview. In P. Smagorinsky (Ed.), *Research on composition: Multiple perspectives on two decades of change* (pp. 1–14). New York, NY: Teachers College Press.

Spalding, E., Wang, J., Lin, E., & Hu, G. (2009). Analyzing voice in the writing of Chinese teachers. *Research in the Teaching of English, 44*(1), 23–50.

Street, B. V. (1984). *Literacy in theory and practice.* Cambridge, UK: Cambridge University Press.

Street, B. V. (1995). *Social literacies: Critical approaches to literacy development, ethnography and education.* London, UK: Longman.

Suárez-Orozco, C., & Suárez-Orozco, M. M. (2001). *Children of immigration.* Cambridge, MA: Harvard University Press.

Wang, Z. (2011). *Chinese high school students' L2 writing instruction: Implications for EFL writing in college: A qualitative study.* Chinese English Language Education Association. Retrieved from www.celea.org.cn/pastversion/lw/pdf/wangzhaohui.pdf

Wong-Fillmore, L., & Fillmore, C. J. (2012). *What does text complexity mean for English learners and language minority students?* Stanford, CA: Stanford University School of Education.

Zwiers, J., O'Hara, S., & Pritchard, R. (2014). *Common Core Standards in diverse classrooms: Essential practices for developing academic language and disciplinary literacy.* Portland, ME: Stenhouse.

PART II

Chinese-Heritage Students' Learning across the Curriculum

5

CULTURE AND EVERYDAY LIFE EXPERIENCES OF CHINESE IMMIGRANT STUDENTS LEARNING SCIENCE FROM CLASSROOM DISCOURSE

Shu-Wen Lan and Luciana C. de Oliveira

Schools throughout the United States have recently witnessed a growing population of English language learners (ELLs). In fact, ELLs continue to outpace the non–ELL population in K–12-school enrollment (de Jong, 2013). ELLs at varying English proficiency levels are placed in mainstream English-medium classrooms with their native English-speaking peers—the current mainstream classroom context (Li, 2013). These K–12 classes are generally taught by monolingual English speakers with limited experience of working with culturally and linguistically diverse immigrant students (Zeichner, 2009). Indeed, many mainstream content-area teachers have not had university coursework on the integration of language and content instruction; nevertheless, they face students who are not only learning English as a new language but also studying subjects through English at the same time (de Oliveira & Pereira, 2008). Without appropriate subject-specific instructional support, most ELLs placed in mainstream content-area classrooms struggle with the challenging content-area literacy tasks of learning English, learning different subjects through English, and adjusting to White mainstream culture. Although Chinese and other Asian immigrant students face the challenges that all ELLs from diverse backgrounds encounter, this specific group of students is stereotyped as high achievers (e.g., Ma, 2009; Ma & Wang, 2014) who smoothly integrate into American life and English-speaking classroom discourse (e.g., Chen & Stevenson, 1995; Ma, 2009). However, not all Chinese immigrant students adjust easily to the White mainstream English-speaking culture or become high achievers within a short period of time. Nevertheless, these students have been consistently overlooked in research on challenges encountered by ELLs in their transitional adjustment and educational experiences, specifically the content-area literacy challenges faced by being ELLs in mainstream English-speaking content-area classrooms.

Recognizing the needs of Chinese immigrant students in today's K–12 schools, a growing number of researchers have investigated educational and socialization issues confronting Chinese immigrant students in U.S. K–12 mainstream content-area classrooms (e.g., Han & Hsu, 2004; Ma, 2010; Ma & Wang, 2014). Specifically, Chen et al. (2014) found that acculturation of immigrant children during their early school years was important for their adaptation and assimilation into mainstream classes. Furthermore, the more acculturated students behaved better and interacted better socially. However, studies have recognized that because their prior everyday experiences in China are so different from those in the United States, Chinese immigrant students, and particularly those newly arrived Chinese students, often struggle with their mainstream classroom interactions, participation, and socialization. Therefore, this chapter focuses on cultural and linguistic challenges and adjustments confronting recently arrived Chinese immigrant students in their participation in mainstream science classroom discourse. Specifically, we provide a detailed account of Chinese immigrant student Yuna (pseudonym) and examples from the fourth-grade science classroom discourse data to reveal the learning challenges Yuna encountered in the mainstream English-speaking classroom instruction and interactions. Mrs. Dalloway's (the teacher) instruction was shaped by a textbook approach to science and drew on everyday knowledge to teach the science textbook content. The teacher attempted to support her students learning science by connecting what students most likely would have habitually experienced in everyday life to what they were learning in science. However, everyday life experience is not uniform for all students, especially for ELLs with diverse language and cultural backgrounds. In particular, Yuna's life experience from a developing country was different from that of her native English-speaking peers from a developed country. Consequently, due to the differences in their everyday lives, there was a disparity between Yuna's everyday knowledge and that of her native English-speaking teacher and peers. Such incongruence became critical as Yuna was expected to participate in the science classroom discourse. Given that the teacher tended to draw on everyday knowledge associated with household and community activities to teach the targeted science concepts, such a pedagogical strategy posed unexpected challenges to Yuna's learning. Exploring the challenges Yuna encountered in the mainstream English-speaking content-area classroom will help us consider how to enhance teachers' knowledge for scaffolding Chinese immigrant students learning science from mainstream English-speaking classroom discourse.

Literature Review

Challenges for ELLs in U.S. K–12 Content-Area Classrooms

In U.S. K–12 mainstream content-area classrooms, all students encounter the challenging literacy task of developing their curriculum knowledge and academic language simultaneously (Irujo, 2007). This task becomes even more challenging and complex for ELLs. Compared to their English-speaking peers, most ELLs in primary grades, unaware of how sounds associate with written symbols, face challenges in decoding written texts (Cummins, 2000). Furthermore, upper elementary ELLs have a more challenging task of learning *academic English* to read increasingly complex content-area texts. Recently, there has been great interest in ELLs' learning in mainstream content-area classrooms (e.g., Carrasquillo, Kucer, & Abrams, 2004; de Oliveira, Lan, & Dodds, 2013). Some researchers have identified challenges faced by many ELLs and their struggles with developing disciplinary knowledge and discipline-specific language (Fang & Schleppegrell, 2008). ELLs who achieve a certain level of English proficiency attend mainstream English-medium classes alongside native speakers of English and no longer receive language services and instructional language support. However, they might struggle with participating in mainstream content-area classroom instruction and interactions (Gibbons, 2003; Schleppegrell, 2004). Furthermore, although ELLs rapidly acquire *everyday English* and appropriately use it in their daily communication, they still need extended time and continuing instructional support to develop academic English for school subject learning (Cummins, 2000).

Given the increasing number of ELLs in mainstream classrooms, it is crucial that educators, researchers, and policy makers continue examining how current educational policies result in academic language and literacy challenges and affect educational opportunities for ELLs (Williams, 2001). To date, many mainstream content-area classrooms do not represent a promising atmosphere for either language development or content learning for culturally and linguistically diverse students (e.g., Bunch, 2006). Teaching ELLs and native speakers of English together in mainstream classrooms demands that teachers have a high level of skills and knowledge about language (Heritage, Silva, & Pierce, 2007). However, as noted above, most mainstream content-area teachers rarely have professional training in teaching ELLs and are not prepared to teach a diverse population (Menken & Antunez, 2001). Furthermore, the current curriculum in mainstream content-area classrooms is primarily designed for native speakers of English, and there are rarely instructional strategies to meet the needs of ELLs. Noticing many ELLs' limited participation and interactions during mainstream classroom discussions, some researchers have detailed the linguistic, social, and cultural challenges ELLs encounter as participants in these classrooms (de Jong & Harper, 2005; Gibbons, 2003). ELLs' limited classroom participation and low-quality interactions, perhaps resulting from the differences between their everyday life experiences and those of their native English-speaking teachers and peers, may become critical in the pedagogical process in school (e.g., Colombo, 2005; Duff, 2001; Hasan, 1996; Macken-Horarik, 1996). Everyday life experience is defined by Macken-Horarik (1996) as "the world of the home and the community into which children are born and which provides them with their primary formation ... [and it] is not uniform" (pp. 235–236). In

76 Shu-Wen Lan and Luciana C. de Oliveira

fact, the disparity of everyday life experience between teachers and their students has resulted not only in uncomfortable classroom experiences for some students and teachers but also in poor performance by students in school contexts because of the incongruence between what was expected at school and what they brought from home (Hasan, 1996).

Bunch (2006) highlighted the importance of everyday uses of English for ELLs in mainstream content-area classrooms to engage in academic tasks. ELLs in middle school social studies classrooms were expected to use both academic and everyday English, thereby smoothly participating in group discussions and presenting to the whole class. The students used two ways to achieve the academic tasks of answering group discussion questions: the language of ideas (conversational and everyday use of English in discussions among group members) vs. the language of display (more academic-like English to present their answers to the entire class). In addition to the need to improve their academic English, Bunch highlighted the need for ELLs, with limited access to conversational English in interactive settings, to develop their everyday English and eventually to successfully negotiate content-area coursework.

The reviewed studies on ELLs' challenges in mainstream content-area classrooms and the issues related to the dissimilarity between everyday life experience of ELLs and those of their native English-speaking teachers and peers provide useful lenses for understanding the issues explored in this research. Pertinent to this study, there is now a growing body of literature on the educational and socialization issues confronting ELLs in U.S. K–12 schools. However, more research in this area is needed. Researchers and teachers still have a very limited understanding of ELLs, especially Chinese immigrant students, who have moved from bilingual or English as second language (ESL) instructional contexts to monolingual English mainstream content-area classrooms (Carrasquillo et al., 2004).

Challenges for Chinese Immigrant Students in U.S. K–12 Schools

Among ELLs in different racial and ethnic groups, Chinese immigrant students from China, Taiwan, Hong Kong, and other regions of East and Southeast Asia are the fastest growing ethnic group (Yamamoto & Li, 2012). In 2012–2013, 55,000 more international students enrolled in U.S. higher education institutions compared to 2011–2012, with most of the growth from China (Institute of International Education, 2013). Many of these Chinese graduate students bring their children and enroll them in schools near their universities. After getting their diplomas, most Chinese remain in the United States, and their children become Chinese immigrant students in U.S. K–12 schools. Although these students face the challenges all immigrant students with diverse language and cultural backgrounds encounter in mainstream content-area classrooms, including learning English, learning content-area knowledge through English, and adjusting to the White mainstream culture, many Chinese immigrant students attain higher levels of academic achievement such as higher grades and test scores in a relatively short period of time compared to other immigrant students (Han & Hsu, 2004; Ma, 2009).

On the one hand, due to their higher academic achievement and the perceived "smooth adjustment" into English-speaking classroom discourse, Chinese immigrant students are often stereotyped as high academic achievers (Kim, 2014). On the other hand, however, most teachers in K–12 mainstream classrooms tend to view them as quiet or passive learners and poor communicators (Yamamoto & Li, 2012). As a result, concerned about perceptions of these students ranging from academic role models to problematic students in need of help, researchers have examined the educational experiences of Chinese-background learners in the U.S. (e.g., Ma, 2009; Ma & Wang, 2014; Wang, 2009). Ma's (2009) longitudinal case study examined the educational journey of Yutong, a Chinese immigrant student, over a 12-year period and traced her process from a newly arrived student not knowing any English to a so-called academic achiever in U.S. schools and in a mainstream content-area classroom context. Nevertheless, in spite of Yutong's successful academic performance, Ma (2009) revealed that Yutong did not express her feelings or needs as much as her native English-speaking peers. Because asserting one's needs and desires is expected and valued in Western societies, native English-speaking teachers and peers tend to view quiet students as passive and inhibited communicators (Yamamoto & Li, 2012). These perceptions might lead to reduced attention from and interactions with native English-speaking teachers and peers; therefore, Chinese immigrant students might feel they are not accepted as belonging in the mainstream classroom context.

As the reviewed studies suggest, Chinese immigrant students, along with their excellent academic performance, do not appear to suffer from adjustment problems in White mainstream English-speaking classroom learning. Nevertheless, helping to frame the current research, these studies provide insights into Chinese immigrant students' cultural and linguistic challenges and adjustments, which range from limited participation in mainstream classroom discourse to not being accepted as belonging in the classroom.

This current study focuses on Yuna, a Chinese immigrant student, and her struggles to participate in science classroom discourse. Specifically, we examined how Yuna was challenged to participate due to an incongruence between her everyday knowledge (acquired through her life experience) and language and that of her native English-speaking teacher and peers. Exploring Yuna's challenges in the mainstream English-speaking content-area classroom may help us enhance teachers' knowledge for scaffolding Chinese immigrant students' participation and engagement in mainstream classroom instruction and interactions.

The Study

Setting and Participants

This study was conducted in Mrs. Dalloway's fourth-grade mainstream classroom situated in Lakeview Elementary School (a pseudonym), an Indiana public school which, according to the school's website, had approximately 40% culturally and linguistically diverse students and 60% White students. Lakeview is located near Midwestern University, where the international student population is ranked the second largest among U.S. public universities. A great number of these international graduates bring their children and enroll them in the schools around the university. Thus, many of the ELLs at Lakeview come from families whose parents are associated with Midwestern University. Furthermore, the population of culturally and linguistically diverse students at Lakeview, especially those from Asia, has steadily grown. As shown in the Lakeview student ethnicity statistics, 23% were from Asia (statewide 2%), 5% multiracial (statewide 4%), 4% Black (statewide 12%), 4% Hispanic (statewide 8%), and 64% White (statewide 73%) (Indiana Department of Education, 2011).

Despite the extra academic support given by parents of Asian immigrant and Asian American students (Carrasquillo & Rodriguez, 1995), these students often appear to be less verbal and expressive at social occasions, including teacher–student interactions, and they are often left out of the mainstream classroom talk (Duff, 2001). Furthermore, Asian immigrant students are said to be more accustomed to structured and passive learning conditions than to active classroom participation and discussion characteristic of U.S. classrooms (Yao, 1985). Therefore, concerned about *silently struggling* immigrant Asian students mainstreamed in U.S. schools and ELLs from different ethnic backgrounds, as our research site, we selected Lakeview Elementary School, where ELLs, primarily Asian immigrant students, comprise about one fourth of the student population. The participants of this observed science classroom, including the teacher and students, will be further described in the following paragraphs.

Teacher. Mrs. Dalloway had been teaching fourth grade at Lakeview since 2002. She holds a bachelor's degree and a teaching license in elementary education and a master's degree with a focus on Literacy and Language Education. Mrs. Dalloway has consistently had ELLs in her classroom and always seeks more opportunities to improve her instruction of these students.

The Targeted ELLs. At the beginning of the study, we targeted the Asian-origin ELLs at their varying English proficiency levels. Out of a total of 25 students in the classroom, we originally selected five focal ELLs for more focused observation and artifact collection. Later, during the months of data collection, Mrs. Dalloway told us in both formal and informal interviews that she was particularly puzzled and concerned about the disruptive and distracting classroom behaviors of Yuna, one of the selected five focal ELLs. Yuna was said to constantly interrupt the flow of classroom discourse by persistently asking questions about the content just explained. We thus followed this focal ELL, observed her more closely, and gathered more data.

Focal ELL. At the time of the study, Yuna was 9 years old and in the fourth grade. She is a fair-skinned little girl who, until a few months previously, had been adapting to her new life in Texas. She grew up in China, moved to Texas with her parents, played with new friends, and attended a new school where she was enrolled in the second grade. Suddenly, after 2 years in her new environment, her life changed once again. Her parents moved from Texas to Indiana driving a U-Haul moving van. Figure 5.1 presents the focal ELL's autobiography. Even though Yuna did not elaborate on her difficulties and adjustments, during our classroom observations, she appeared withdrawn and had infrequent face-to-face interactions with her classmates.

Data Collection and Analysis

During 4 months we collected a variety of data including audio recordings and transcriptions of classroom observations, field notes, and interviews with Yuna's teacher. Initially, we informally conversed with the teacher on general issues such as her common teaching strategies. We also carried out formal, semi-structured, audiotaped interviews (Bernard, 2000). The teacher talked about her impressions of students' overall performance and especially Yuna's in participating in the observed science classroom discussions and classroom activities.

To code interview data, we followed Merriam's (1998) suggested procedures: we first reviewed all interview transcripts and field notes and then read through

---

Hello, I am Yuna. I'm now 9 years old and live in Indiana. I will tell you about ME!

I was born in 2002 1/25 in China. I doodle when I was older, like 4 or 5. The pictures look like this. Or ... I forgot. Then I moved to Texas *[according to Mrs. Dalloway, that would be three years before they moved to Indiana].* **The first day, I was on the plane. Maybe I should make this smaller** *[the drawing Yuna did on the 1st page of notebook].* **Ok! Now where was I. Oh yes the plane, it was my first flyt? At night, I couldn't sleep! So mnay times I NEED TO GO TO THE BATHROOM! After the second flyt, MY EARS IS NOT ... like something stuck to it! But it's better fast. That night, we ate dinner in a friend's house, and we went to our new home. Flip a page! The second day we went shoping. Days had gone, I ... lets see. I went to school, I had a art teacher, then. My parents move here** *[Indiana].* **By DRIVING! The wheels on the Bus go round and round. We passed a lot of states. I got many friends. Yayh I sent to Lakeview Elementary School! Mrs. Dalloway is my teacher. I had a lot of fun!**

FIGURE 5.1 Yuna's Autobiography (Yuna's Original Writing)

them carefully. Recurrent issues were identified, and emergent categories and themes were recorded. Next, the recurrent issues previously identified in interview data were cross-checked with classroom observation data. This enabled us to explore the teacher's impression of students' and especially the ELLs' participation vital for selecting extracts of classroom discourse containing instances of incongruence in Yuna's everyday life experiences.

Due to the interrelatedness of the interview and classroom observation data, we used the constant comparative analytic method, an inductive data coding process used to classify, compare, and analyze qualitative data (Glaser & Strauss, 1967). Broadly, an inductive method begins with particular instances and moves toward generalizations. With this method, we compared all the identified recurrent issues, themes, patterns, and categories. Constantly comparing the results enabled us to identify the convergent and divergent components—the elements for constructing our understandings and descriptions of Yuna's challenges in the science classroom as well as the support the teacher provided (or not) in response.

Results and Discussion

Our descriptions begin with the teacher's perspectives on Yuna's participation performance and then explore some examples. They show (a) how Yuna was judged by the teacher as disorganized and distracted with behavior problems; and (b) how Yuna encountered challenges in participating in the science classroom discourse due to a disparity between her everyday knowledge and language and that of her native English-speaking teacher and peers.

Constant Questions and Interruption: Being Judged Disorganized for Behavior Problems

According to Mrs. Dalloway, Yuna was a recently arrived Chinese immigrant student and newly integrated into mainstream classes. Yuna spoke Mandarin Chinese with her family, and due to her mother's limited English skills, her mother relied on Yuna to translate for the parent–teacher conferences. The teachers were puzzled by Yuna, who seemed to have high oral English proficiency but did poorly engaging in classroom instruction and discussion. Yuna was said to constantly interrupt the flow of classroom discourse by persistently asking questions about previously explained content. Mrs. Dalloway commented on the student's overall performance:

> One teacher said she had just gone over something. And she feels like Yuna always raises her hands. She feels like Yuna knows more than [she lets on]. We go over the information with her. But ... It's hard to tell [why Yuna persistently raises her hands and asks questions].

(Interview with teacher, 11/23/2011)

Puzzled by Yuna's constant questions and interruptions, Mrs. Dalloway judged Yuna disorganized and distracted for behavior problems. As Mrs. Dalloway put it in one interview:

> She interrupts constantly. It would be a topic we just discussed; we just went over the definitions thoroughly. And she would ask a question that we just went over exactly the same answer.... I don't know. It can be the behavior problems because the kids would just look at her and say, 'Yuna, we just went over this.' And she would have the smile.
>
> *(Interview with teacher, 11/23/2011)*

We present this teacher's puzzlement about Yuna's disruptive classroom behavior in the following analysis of the science classroom discourse. Close investigation of what Yuna said, did, and asked in the classroom interactions provides us with a better sense of the complexity beneath the teaching, learning, and classroom participation of Chinese immigrant students.

Disparity of Everyday Life Experiences for the Focused Chinese Immigrant Student

Disparity between Yuna's everyday knowledge and language and that of her native English-speaking teacher and peers led to Yuna's limited participation in the mainstream classroom discourse and low-quality interactions. Evidence of this incongruence comes from one oral and one written response. Below, in the first excerpt, Yuna raised an unexpected question about cereal in the middle of classroom discussion. The second excerpt illustrates an unexpected idea in her written response to an essay question about energy transformation in a clothes dryer.

Excerpt 1. In the introductory unit, the teacher introduced students to procedures of experimentation. She explained the importance of building specific steps to construct procedures through everyday knowledge, everyday language, and recounting events from everyday experiences. Initially, Mrs. Dalloway guided students to reflect on their familiar events (e.g., how to eat a banana) and to include specific steps for constructing their own procedures by drawing on those experiences. Mrs. Dalloway then asked a few students to read aloud their written procedures without revealing the procedure titles. Afterwards, their peers were told to guess the procedure titles. As shown in Excerpt 1, during the teacher–student exchanges of the guessing procedures related to "how to eat cereal," Yuna raised her hand and asked, "What's cereal?" Her native English-speaking peers were flabbergasted at Yuna's question.

82 Shu-Wen Lan and Luciana C. de Oliveira

Excerpt 1: One Example of Mismatch

Turn	Speaker	Topic on Procedures
1	Teacher	Diana, go ahead.
2	Diana	Okay! Step 1—first pick up your favorite kind of brand to eat. Next, lots of materials in your refrigerator if you have one. And pick up fat milk or skim milk not recommended for kids. Take the milk and open it. Then pick any bowl you want to pour the brand and then the milk. Finally, if you have a drawer where you keep the silverware …
3	Students	Ooh, that's easy.
4	Diana	Take out a spoon nothing else except a napkin in case you spill.
5	Paula	How to eat cereal!
6	Teacher	Did you have the step that says to mix the milk and then cereal together?
7	Diana	Yeah, I just said, just mixing it!
8	Yuna	**What is cereal?**
9	Students	**Huh?** [Students are incredulous that Yuna is asking about this.]
10	Teacher	Okay.
11	Students	**You don't know what's the cereal?** [Students sound skeptical.]
12	Teacher	No, I think … see! **This is the perfect example about why you have to be specific. Okay. Because maybe not everybody, just like what I say about banana. I saw you guys laugh … but some people might have not had banana before.** Diana … you want to explain "cereal"?
13	Diana	Okay. Cereal is a kind of thing that comes out with all different types. And you could eat. You could put it in chocolate milk, fat milk is good with Vitamin D, skim milk is not recommended for kids. It's like the thing. Well, you know, for breakfast. Like …
14	Teacher	It's usually breakfast. You mix it with milk. A lot of times it's made with corn … okay guys, Carol, are you the "Word Wizard"? [Students take turns to look up the vocabulary in the dictionary.]
15	Carol	A grass as wheat, edible grain, suitable for food, it's grain, the breakfast food esp. [Reading aloud from the dictionary]
16	Teacher	Especially the breakfast food?
17	Carol	Yeah! Especially the breakfast food. It's fare from original grains.
18	Students	**Cereal? She doesn't know cereal?** [Students continue to express skepticism about Yuna's lack of knowledge.]

A close look at the students' responses to Yuna's vocabulary question (as boldfaced in Excerpt 1) highlighted that Yuna's question seemed to interrupt the flow of classroom discourse. Although it would appear that an appropriate pedagogical strategy was followed—Yuna's teacher presented and explained the targeted science concept of *procedures*, and Yuna's peers constructed procedures through everyday knowledge, everyday language, and recounting events from everyday experience—this pedagogical approach may not be as effective as desired, especially in an

English-speaking mainstream classroom with ELLs. A disparity appears to have existed in the different life experiences of Yuna and her native English-speaking teacher and peers. While Westerners might be used to cold cereal with milk for breakfast, Asian immigrants, including Chinese immigrant families, might habitually eat congee (rice porridge) with some hot bean juice instead. Yuna might not have experienced cereal in her household, not to mention not knowing how to eat it. Another example of the disparity of everyday life experience between Yuna and her native English-speaking teacher and peers follows.

Excerpt 2. In the context of reflecting on Yuna's unexpected ideas shown in Figure 5.2, Mrs. Dalloway explained why she was so puzzled. She noted that Yuna had tried to answer a question about energy transformation in a clothes dryer.

Mrs. Dalloway was sure that Yuna understood that energy can be transformed in many types of machines. However, she was puzzled that "the sun" or "the clothes line" in Yuna's written response seemed to be unrelated to the essay question. The teacher ventured that Yuna probably did not understand what a clothes dryer is or how a clothes dryer can work, not to mention not knowing how a clothes dryer uses different types of energy to work. So the teacher had the following conversation with Yuna.

> Question: Describe how electrical energy is transformed in a clothes dryer.
> Yuna: **The sun gives out heat and that heat goes to the clothes line which dries the clothes.**

FIGURE 5.2 Yuna's Written Response to a Fourth-Grade Essay Question in Science

Excerpt 2: Another Example of Disparity

Turn	Speaker	Topic on Energy Transformation
1	Teacher	**Do you know clothes dryer?** [Pointing to the essay question]
2	Yuna	Mrs. Dalloway, **what's a clothes dryer?**
3	Teacher	**Do you have a machine at your home to wash them and then to dry the clothes?**
4	Yuna	**[Shaking head]**
5	Teacher	Um … Do you hang them to dry them?
6	Yuna	[Nodding head]
7	Teacher	Well, you know there is a machine used to dry [the washed clothes]. It's just like a washing machine! It looks like this! [Mrs. Dalloway draws a picture to explain.] There is a door and when you put clothes in it spins the clothes around and around over there! And there is heat …

Yuna had never had a clothes dryer in her household. Growing up in China, Yuna was taught to hang clothes on lines to dry. While Westerners might be used to using clothes dryers, many Chinese immigrant families might habitually use clotheslines instead. Thus, Yuna might have never seen a clothes dryer used, not to mention not knowing how it works.

As evidenced, the teacher perceived Yuna as a constant interrupter. Yuna constantly offered unexpected ideas and questions as she attempted to participate. The teacher attempted to support her students' learning by connecting what students could and should have habitually experienced in everyday life to what they were learning in science. However, everyday life experience is not uniform for all students and especially for Chinese immigrant students in that their prior educational and life experiences in China are so different from those in the U.S. Although it seems obvious that Mrs. Dalloway could explain the targeted science concepts using everyday knowledge, everyday language, and so-called everyday life experience, this issue is not completely straightforward, especially in mainstream content-area classrooms with Chinese immigrant students where an incongruence might exist between their everyday knowledge and language and that of their native English-speaking teachers and peers. Yuna had no experience with cereal or a clothes dryer. Such a dissimilarity of everyday knowledge and everyday language between Yuna, her English-speaking teacher, and peers led to Yuna's limited classroom participation, low-quality interaction, and uncomfortable classroom experiences. Unlike many native English-speaking students who arrive at elementary classrooms and find familiar environments and a teacher who speaks their language, many Chinese immigrant students might feel like they are moving "from one world to another" as they go from home and community to school (Colombo, 2005, p. 1). Their teachers often differ from their families in race, culture, language, and everyday life experiences. Classroom expectations and patterns of communication may also differ from those at home.

Conclusion and Implications

In this chapter, we described how Yuna was challenged to participate in and learn from the observed mainstream science classroom discourse. Close investigation of what she said, did, and asked and her native English-speaking teacher and peers' responses provides us with a better sense of the complexity beneath the teaching, learning, and classroom participation of Chinese immigrant students. Future research should consider also collecting data pertinent to students' previous educational and cultural experiences from the students' families. Additionally, so that students' individual voices might be better heard, future research might consider collecting direct reflections from students on their perspectives on their educational experiences.

This chapter's findings and analyses suggest the need for explicit attention to the cultural and linguistic challenges and transitional adjustments confronting

Learning Science from Classroom Discourse **85**

recently arrived Chinese immigrant students. It is important to note that not *all* Chinese immigrant students can smoothly adjust to the White mainstream English-speaking culture or become high achievers within a short period of time. Because their prior experiences in China are so different from those in the U.S., exploring their previous educational and life experiences and current learning needs can help educators better understand and teach all students to maximize their learning. At first glance, in the two excerpts of the disparity of everyday life experiences, puzzlement, and questions raised by Yuna, she seems to be confused or to be missing the point, and yet, as we further reflect, we perceive that we are constrained by our own assumptions. When we use what we assume are the best teaching practices such as connecting everyday life experience to teaching science and they do not work for some students, especially Chinese immigrant students, we generally blame these immigrant students' lower English proficiency, sometimes without even realizing it.

However, because of the distance between the life experiences of teachers and Chinese immigrant students, teachers are often unfamiliar with these students' out-of-school lives and the perspectives they bring to learning, the ways they use language to communicate what they know and don't know, and the ways they interact socially. To align this incongruence, we need to center on the educational experiences and perspectives of Chinese immigrant students (Ma & Wang, 2014). In addition, at a micro level, teachers can help ELLs learn the labels for certain everyday words already known by their native English-speaking peers (August, Carlo, Dressler, & Snow, 2005). Furthermore, teachers should attend professional development workshops promoting more meaningful interactions with immigrant families and promoting teachers' greater understanding and empathy for cultural diversity (Colombo, 2005). It is an educator's responsibility to assist students and especially ELLs in reconciling the disparity and focusing on their learning tasks in science classroom discourse.

References

August, D., Carlo, M., Dressler, C., & Snow, C. (2005). The critical role of vocabulary development for English language learners. *Learning Disabilities Research & Practice, 20*(1), 50–57.

Bernard, H. R. (2000). *Social research methods: Qualitative and quantitative approaches.* London, UK: Sage.

Bunch, G. C. (2006). "Academic English" in the 7th grade: Broadening the lens, expanding access. *Journal of English for Academic Purposes, 5*, 284–301.

Carrasquillo, A., Kucer, S. B., & Abrams, R. (2004). *Beyond the beginnings: Literacy interventions for upper elementary English language learners.* Clevedon, UK: Multilingual Matters.

Carrasquillo, A., & Rodriguez, V. (1995). *Language minority students in the mainstream classroom.* Clevedon, UK: Multilingual Matters.

Chen, C., & Stevenson, H. W. (1995). Motivation and mathematics achievement: A comparative study of Asian-American, Caucasian-American, and East Indian high school students. *Child Development, 66*(4), 1215–1234.

Chen, S. H., Hua, M., Zhou, Q., Tao, A., Lee, E. H., Ly, J., & Main, A. (2014). Parent–child cultural orientations and child adjustment in Chinese American immigrant families. *Developmental Psychology, 50*(1), 189.

Colombo, M. W. (2005). Empathy and cultural competence: Reflections from teachers of culturally diverse children. *Journal of the National Association for the Education of Young Children,* 1–8.

Cummins, J. (2000). *Language, power, and pedagogy: Bilingual children in the crossfire.* Clevedon, UK: Multilingual Matters.

de Jong, E. (2013). Preparing mainstream teachers for multilingual classrooms. *Association of Mexican American Educators Journal, 7*(2), 40–49.

de Jong, E., & Harper, C. (2005). Preparing mainstream teachers for English language learners: Is being a good teacher good enough? *Teacher Education Quarterly, 32*(2), 101–124.

de Oliveira, L. C., Lan, S.-W., & Dodds, K. (2013). Reading, writing, and talking science with English language learners. In J. Nagle (Ed.), *English learner instruction through collaboration and inquiry in teacher education* (pp. 3–23). Charlotte, NC: Information Age.

de Oliveira, L. C., & Pereira, N. (2008). "Sink or swim": The challenges and needs of teachers of English language learners. *INTESOL Journal, 5*(1), 77–86.

Duff, P. A. (2001). Language, literacy, content, and (Pop) culture: Challenges for ESL Students in Mainstream Courses. *The Canadian Modern Language Review, 58*(1), 103–132.

Fang, Z., & Schleppegrell, M. J. (2008). *Reading in secondary content areas: A language-based pedagogy.* Ann Arbor, MI: The University of Michigan Press.

Gibbons, P. (2003). Mediating language learning: Teacher interactions with ESL students in content-based classroom. *TESOL Quarterly, 37*(2), 247–273.

Glaser, B., & Strauss, A. (1967). *The discovery of grounded theory: Strangers for qualitative research.* Chicago, IL: Aldine.

Han, A., & Hsu, J. (Eds.). (2004). *Asian American X: An intersection of 21st century Asian American voices.* Ann Arbor, MI: University of Michigan Press.

Hasan, R. (1996). Literacy, everyday talk and society. In R. Hasan & G. Williams (Eds.), *Literacy in society* (pp. 377–424). London, UK: Longman.

Heritage, M., Silva, N., & Pierce, M. (2007). Academic language: A view from the classroom. In A. L. Bailey (Ed.), *Language demands of students learning English in school: Putting academic language to the test* (pp. 171–210). New Haven, CT: Yale University Press.

Indiana Department of Education. (2011). *DOE Compass.* Retrieved from http://compass. doe.in.gov/dashboard/statereports.aspx?type=school&id=8135

Institute of International Education. (2013). *Open doors 2013: International students in the United States and study abroad by American students are at all-time high.* Retrieved from www.iie.org/Who-We-Are/News-and-Events/Press-Center/Press-Releases/2013/2013-11-11-Open-Doors-Data

Irujo, S. (2007). What does research tell us about teaching reading to English Language Learners? Haverhill, MA: *The ELL Outlook.* Retrieved from www.usc.edu/dept/education/CMMR/543/543IrujoResearchReadingELLs.pdf

Kim, E. (2014). When social class meets ethnicity: College-going experiences of Chinese and Korean immigrant students. *The Review of Higher Education, 37*(3), 321–348.

Li, G. (2013). This issue. *Theory into Practice, 52*(2), 77–80.

Ma, W. (2009). Beyond learning literacy at school: One Chinese adolescent's educational journey. *American Secondary Education, 37*(3), 52–69.

Ma, W. (2010). Bumpy journeys: A young Chinese adolescent's transitional schooling across two sociocultural contexts. *Journal of Language, Identity, & Education, 9*(2), 107–123.

Ma, W., & Wang, C. (2014). *Learner's privilege and responsibility: A critical examination of the experiences and perspectives of learners from Chinese backgrounds in the United States.* Charlotte, NC: Information Age.

Macken-Horarik, M. (1996). Literacy and learning across the curriculum: Towards a model of register for secondary school teachers. In R. Hasan & G. Williams (Eds.), *Literacy in society* (pp. 232–278). New York, NY: Addison Wesley Longman.

Menken, K., & Antunez, B. (2001). *An overview of the preparation and certification of teachers working with limited English proficient students.* Washington, DC: National Clearinghouse of Bilingual Education. Retrieved from www.usc.edu/dept/education/CMMR/FullText/teacherprep.pdf

Merriam, S. B. (1998). *Qualitative research and case study applications in education* (Revised and expanded). San Francisco, CA: Jossey-Bass.

Schleppegrell, M. J. (2004). *The language of schooling: A functional linguistics perspective.* Mahwah, NJ: Erlbaum.

Wang, S. (2009). *Academic discourse socialization: A case study on Chinese graduate students' oral presentations* (Unpublished doctoral dissertation). University of Cincinnati.

Williams, J. A. (2001). Classroom conversations: Opportunities to learn for ESL students in mainstream classrooms. *The Reading Teacher, 54*, 750–757.

Yamamoto, Y., & Li, J. (2012). Quiet in the eye of the beholder: Teacher perceptions of Asian immigrant children. In C. Garcia Coll (Ed.), *The impact of immigration on children's development* (pp. 1–16). New York, NY: Karger.

Yao, E. L. (1985). Adjustment needs of Asian immigrant children. *Elementary School Guidance and Counseling, 19*(2), 222–227.

Zeichner, K. (2009). *Teacher education and the struggle for social justice.* New York, NY: Routledge.

6

DISAGGREGATING SECONDARY-LEVEL CHINESE IMMIGRANTS' ACADEMIC, ENGLISH, AND SCHOOL SUCCESS

Lee Gunderson and Reginald Arthur D'Silva

One of the overall purposes foundational to the discussions in this volume is to explore differences within categories such as "Chinese learners" that dispel notions of potentially damaging stereotypic homogeneity. Our purpose in this chapter is to explore differences related to the academic achievement of the two largest populations of Chinese immigrant students in our local school district: Cantonese and Mandarin speakers. We are convinced that the analyses that follow will dispel the notion that there is any veracity in the stereotypic view that all Chinese students are members of a "model minority."

Background

Chua (2011) generated a great deal of discussion and debate around "Chinese" students and their "tiger mothers" on the basis of the findings of a "study" of her two children. Chua's narrative self-study and its results exemplify the perils of generalizing findings to broad populations. We will not enter into the debate concerning Chua's generalizations since they are not relevant to the focus of this chapter. Chua's study included two individuals, both born in the United States, from an affluent family. Her generalizations add to the misconceptions related to the "myth of the model minority," and are neither necessarily valid nor reliable for Chinese immigrant students in general. There is evidence that the children of less affluent Chinese immigrant families are not as successful in school (e.g., Qin & Han, 2014). The difficulty is that category errors often lead to faulty or erroneous implications.

Individuals who speak a language at home that is not English have been categorized using the acronyms ESL, ESOL, EAL, or more recently, ELL. ESL (English as a second language) and ELL (English language learner) are misrepresentative categories because they include incredibly diverse populations, but are often used to refer to the individuals they include as though they are homogenous (Gunderson, D'Silva, & Murphy Odo, 2014). ESL students, for instance, have been accused of lowering achievement (Asimov, 1997; Frallic, 2014). Frallic notes, "What that means, simply, is that thousands of public school students arrive in classrooms these days unable to read, write, speak or comprehend English." Such statements ignore the fact that ESL, as a category, contains human beings who can read, write, and speak English, and some succeed well in school. Indeed, it also contains the motivated children of so-called tiger mothers.

Review of the Literature

There is a persistent mythology surrounding the notion that some groups of students apparently have little difficulty achieving at high rates. They are often called the "model minority" (Lee, 1996). The general notion is that such students do not struggle in school. Lee (1996) contends that difficulties in school are often overlooked because of the erroneous view of them as members of a model group. It has been noted, however, that the reality is that the discrepancies in families' access to educational resources within the Asian population makes any single characterization of the group inappropriate (Kao, 1995).

The belief that Asian students are all high achievers obscures the disparity among different first language and cultural groups included in the category (Ngo, 2006). Ngo found higher secondary school and college graduation rates for South and Northeast Asians than he did for Southeast Asians. He also notes that the 2000 U.S. Census data reveal that a larger proportion of Cambodian, Hmong, Lao, and Vietnamese Americans aged 25 and over do not graduate from high school compared to Indian, Japanese, and Chinese Americans. While 42.7% of all Asian Americans aged 25 and over hold a bachelor's degree or higher, less than 10% of Cambodian, Hmong, Lao, and Vietnamese Americans hold a bachelor's degree or higher (Ngo, 2006). This finding demonstrates the discrepancy in educational attainment among individuals in the group of immigrants typically aggregated together in a category labeled "Asian."

Lee (2006) argues that the Asian category is diverse and includes as many as 50 different ethnic groups and concludes that there is no single, homogeneous Asian American culture. The problem, in his view, is that the label "Asian American" implies that they share some kind of unified culture, which is not the case. Some Asian groups have higher academic achievement than others. Chinese students are viewed as high achievers (Abada & Tenkorang, 2009; Louie, 2001) along with Korean (CCL, 2008), and South Asian (e.g., Indian and Pakistani) (Pfeifer & Lee, 2004). The Canadian Council on Learning (CCL, 2008) found that Chinese and Korean students had significantly higher levels of achievement than other language groups in math and science at the high school level. Abada and Tenkorang (2009) also found that Chinese and South Asians appeared to demonstrate higher levels of integration and achievement than other Asian groups since they adapted more quickly and had higher long-term achievement as a result.

Pang, Kiang, and Pak (2003) found that school districts with high numbers of Southeast Asian students have a higher proportion of Asian students with failing scores than did districts with majorities of Chinese and South Asian students. Gunderson (2007) discovered that Vietnamese speakers did not achieve as highly as Mandarin and Cantonese speakers. They also disappeared from academic classes at a much higher rate. Similar results have been observed for Cambodian, Hmong (Pfeifer & Lee, 2004), and Filipino learners (CCL, 2008).

It has been suggested that the success of Chinese students is due, in part, to the support of their parents (e.g., Chao, 1995; Jose, Huntsinger, Huntsinger, & Liaw, 2000; Louie, 2001). Chinese parents influence their children's success in school by setting high expectations and communicating that education is valuable (e.g., Hao & Bonstead-Bruns, 1998; Peng & Wright, 1994; Schneider & Lee, 1990). There is evidence, however, that not all Chinese students are highly successful in school and there are differences related to first language (L1) backgrounds (Gunderson, 2007; Gunderson, D'Silva, & Murphy Odo, 2012; Murphy Odo, D'Silva, & Gunderson, 2012). Gunderson (2007), for instance, found that Mandarin speakers received statistically significant higher grades than Cantonese speakers in many secondary-school academic classes. Murphy Odo et al. (2012) concluded that "Cantonese males appear to be least likely to qualify" for post-secondary education among the groups categorized as Mandarin and Cantonese speakers (p. 263). They also found that in their sample Mandarin-speaking girls were four times more likely to be eligible for post-secondary admission than the other Chinese speakers. Another study of secondary-level academic achievement found that, "Chinese speakers retain a performance advantage over all other ethnolinguistic groups in English and math and overall scores" (Garnett, Adamuti-Trache, & Ungerleider, 2008, p. 320). The difficulty is that results are often based on studies of fairly broad categories of human beings. Our purpose in this chapter is to disaggregate findings related to the broad category labeled "Chinese" speakers and, in addition, to explore scores within the ethnolinguistic categories labeled "Mandarin" and "Cantonese." To achieve this objective we have revisited databases and conducted new analyses.

The Databases

The research was conducted in a school district in Western Canada that enrolls approximately 58,000 students in 18 secondary and 90 elementary schools and annexes (Gunderson, 2007). Data were collected following a protocol that included items concerning such issues as personal development, literacy learning background, first and second language interactions, school history, English study, and health history. Interviews were conducted in English or the immigrants' first languages. Students' English skills were assessed using various standardized and holistic instruments, beginning with an individual oral language assessment. Elementary students who had some English ability were administered the word recognition and comprehension sections of the *Woodcock Reading Mastery Test* (Woodcock, Various). Older students were administered the "*GAP*" (McLeod & McLeod, Australia: Heinemann, 1977) or the *Comprehensive English Language Test* (Harris & Palmer, New York: McGraw-Hill Book Company, 1986). All students were administered a math skills test developed by local curriculum consultants. They were also asked to write essays following different prompts in both first and second languages (L1 and L2) when they were able to do so (see Gunderson, 2007). The databases used in the present chapter include 24,890 school-aged students (Grades 4 to 12), 1,307 primary-level students (kindergarten to Grade 3), 5,000 randomly selected, secondary-level immigrant students, and 407 randomly selected secondary immigrant students. These will be referred to as the Immigrant Study Group (ISG), the Primary Group (PG), the Secondary Random Sample Group (SRSG), and the Secondary Interview Group (SIG).

The Immigrant Study Group (ISG)

There were students who spoke 158 different L1s in this database, including 9,106 Cantonese and 2,882 Mandarin speakers identified during family interviews (Gunderson, 2007). Other Chinese languages such as Foochow, Fukien, Hokkien, Taiwanese, Shanghaise, Yanping, Chiuchow, and Hockchew were identified but not included in the present analyses. It is important to note that the categories labeled "Mandarin" and "Cantonese" are extremely broad and include human beings who are quite diverse. Immigrants entering Canada were classified according to official documents as being "regular immigrants," "business or entrepreneurial immigrants," "refugees," "student visa" (their parents entered as students at a post-secondary institution), "diplomat," "visitor," and "Canadian." Overall, 74.20% entered as regular immigrants, 13.10% as entrepreneurs, 7.50% as refugees, and 3.20% Canadians. The definition of *refugee* is complex because it contains both socioeconomically advantaged and disadvantaged families.

Students on entry into the country were administered different English assessments depending on their age. For this chapter, we broke down their scores by Cantonese versus Mandarin speakers and tested for significance. Differences in means were tested by computing t tests. Such an approach is appropriate because the populations for the different measures are different.

The assessments were administered when students first entered Canada. There were statistically significant differences between Cantonese and Mandarin speakers' Woodcock word recognition and comprehension scores (see Table 6.1) favoring Cantonese speakers with an effect size of .67 and .52. The CELT and GAP scores were significantly higher for Cantonese than for Mandarin speakers. Effects sizes were small and moderate respectively.

92 Lee Gunderson and Reginald Arthur D'Silva

TABLE 6.1 Woodcock Recognition and Comprehension, CELT, and GAP Means by Cantonese- and Mandarin-Speaking Students

	Woodcock Recognition		Woodcock Comprehension		CELT		GAP	
		t-Test		*t-Test*		*t-Test*		*t-Test*
	N	*Results*	*N*	*Results*	*N*	*Results*	*N*	*Results*
Cantonese	550	*t* = 9.297	1,154	*t* = 9.783	2,754	*t* = 2.915	2,291	*t* = 12.94
		p = .000		*p* = .000		*p* = .004		*p* = .000
		df = 862		*df* = 1612		*df* = 3887		*df* = 3196
Mandarin	314	*d* = .67	460	*d* = .52	1135	*d* = .10	907	*d* = .49

Mean L1 (Cantonese and Mandarin) composition scores (rated on a scale of 1 to 5) were tested and Mandarin speakers' L1 scores were significantly higher than Cantonese speakers', while the opposite was true for scores on an English composition (effects sizes were both small). There was a significant difference favoring Cantonese speakers on an English preposition test (strong effect size), but no significant differences in math scores (see Table 6.2). Mandarin speakers from China had significantly lower scores than Mandarin speakers from Taiwan and those from rural schools had lower scores than those from urban schools. It was reported that students from Hong Kong began reading instruction at about 3 years of age (36.90 months), while in both China and Taiwan reading instructions started on average about a year later (49.84 and 45.25 months).

The Secondary Random Sample Group (SRSG)

A random sample of 5,000 immigrant students was selected from the ISG database. The sample was designed to include students who were within an age range that would normally assure that they had all been enrolled in Grades 8 to 12 (secondary level in the school district) (Gunderson, 2007). Grades were recorded for English, math, social studies, and science classes following a conversion protocol varying

TABLE 6.2 L1 Composition, L2 Composition, English Prepositions, and Math Scores by Cantonese- and Mandarin-Speaking Students

	L1 Composition		L2 Composition		Prepositions		Math	
		t-Test		*t-Test*		*t-Test*		*t-Test*
	N	*Results*	*N*	*Results*	*N*	*Results*	*N*	*Results*
Cantonese	1,324	*t* = -5.567	1,347	*t* = 7.118	849	*t* = 15.297	2,855	*t* = -.743
		p = .000		*p* = .000		*p* = .000		*p* = .457
		df = 2057		*df* = 2023		*df* = 1315		*df* = 4084
Mandarin	735	*d* = -.25	678	*d* = .34	468	*d* = .88	1,231	

Disaggregating Success **93**

from 0 (fail) to 4 (A). These scores were recorded for the two languages groups and are shown in Table 6.3. A score of 2.00 is equivalent to a grade of "C," which is the expected "average" grade. As shown in Table 6.3, Cantonese speakers' scores fall below a mean of 2.00 for Grade 12 English and Social Studies (see Figures 6.1 and 6.2). Mandarin speakers' grades were significantly higher than Cantonese speakers' grades in a number of cases, for example in English achievement in Grades 8 to 11 (see Table 6.4). One difficulty with these data is that the underlying numbers decrease significantly from Grades 8 to 12.

It was noted that the overall drop in the number of regular immigrant students who took English 12 was 32% of the number who took English 8. The pattern was the same for math (37%), and science (33%); however, 94% chose not to take social studies 12. This is an extraordinary drop in the number of students who took social studies in Grade 12. It seems apparent that Grade 12 social studies is not very appealing to immigrants (Gunderson, 2007, p. 167).

TABLE 6.3 Grade-Point Averages and Standard Deviations for Cantonese- and Mandarin-Speaking Students in Academic Classes from Grades 8 to 12

Language	Subject	Grade 8	Grade 9	Grade 10	Grade 11	Grade 12
Cantonese	English	2.30 – .99	2.3 – .96	2.2 – 1.00	2.0 – .98	1.7 – 1.10
Mandarin	English	2.80 – .77	2.7 – .73	2.5 – .80	2.4 – .75	2.1 – .78
Cantonese	Social Stds	2.40 – 1.00	2.60 – 1.00	2.40 – 1.10	2.00 – .99	1.70 – 1.70
Mandarin	Social Stds	3.00 – .80	2.80 – .78	2.80 – .97	2.40 – 1.00	2.33 – .41
Cantonese	Science	2.60 – 1.20	2.50 – 1.14	2.60 – 1.10	2.30 – 1.20	2.30 – 1.30
Mandarin	Science	2.90 – 1.10	2.80 – 1.00	2.70 – 1.00	2.60 – .96	2.70 – .70
Cantonese	Math	2.90 – 1.00	2.70 – 1.20	2.50 – 1.20	2.60 – 1.20	2.40 – 1.40
Mandarin	Math	3.30 – .99	2.90 – .90	3.00 – 1.00	3.19 – 1.20	3.00 – 1.20

TABLE 6.4 Tests of Significance for Comparisons of Cantonese- and Mandarin-Speaking Students' Scores for Academic Classes in Grades 8 to 12

	Grade 8	Grade 9	Grade 10	Grade 11	Grade 12
English	$F = 5.1\star$	$F = 5.20\star$	$F = 4.06\star$	$F = 5.90\star$	$F = 1.90$
	$p = .026$	$p = .024$	$p = .045$	$p = .017$	$p = .177$
Social Studies	$F = 6.10\star$	$F = 1.24$	$F = .371$	$F = 5.40\star$	$F = .77$
	$p = .016$	$p = .268$	$p = .543$	$p = .022$	$p = .400$
Science	$F = 1.03$	$F = 2.130$	$F = .660$	$F = 2.65$	$F = 2.41$
	$p = .313$	$p = .147$	$p = .420$	$p = .105$	$p = .125$
Math	$F = 4.10\star$	$F = 1.45$	$F = 9.40\star$	$F = 6.50\star$	$F = 4.60\star$
	$p = .045$	$p = .229$	$p = .002$	$p = .011$	$p = .034$

Note: *Significant at alpha .05

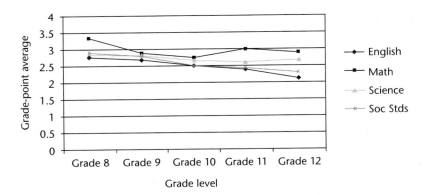

FIGURE 6.1 Grade-Point Averages for English, Social Studies, Math, and Science for Mandarin Speakers in Grades 8 to 12

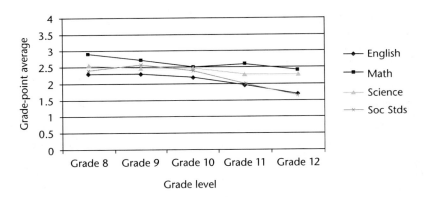

FIGURE 6.2 Grade-Point Averages for English, Social Studies, Math, and Science for Cantonese Speakers in Grades 8 to 12

The Primary Group (PG)

Primary students, kindergarten to Grade 3, were assessed, but not placed in ESL support classes on the principle that they were young and would acquire English quickly and easily. The 1,307 students entered Canada from 82 countries. Canada (12.90%), China (15.10%), Hong Kong (20.00%), the Philippines (7.11%), and Taiwan (11.80%) were the most common countries of origin. Immigrants born in Canada were individuals who were taken back to home countries until they were old enough to return and enter school. The boys numbered 665 and the girls 642. About 72% were immigrants, and 4% were refugees. These students should have graduated from secondary school in 2010 (Gunderson et al., 2012). For the present chapter we selected students from this group who remained in the school district and who had received a grade for English 12, which is an important course for determining eligibility for acceptance at a university or college. We found scores for English 12 for Mandarin ($n = 34$) and Cantonese ($n = 42$) speakers. A 75% (B+) grade in English 12 was used to determine a dichotomous variable that indicated whether the students would qualify for admission to post-secondary institutions in the province. We chose to limit our analysis to English 12, because students' performance in the language of instruction, English, "constitutes the most decisive evidence of the likelihood of doing well in post-secondary educational programs" (Looker & Thiessen, 2004, p. 13). Logistic regression was employed to explore variables that significantly predict students' eligibility for post-secondary studies. "Mandarin-speakers performed on average better than Cantonese speakers" and "Mandarin speakers were on average" eligible for university at a higher rate than Cantonese speakers. Cantonese-speaking boys were the least likely to be eligible for post-secondary admission. Cantonese girls were significantly more likely to be eligible than Cantonese-speaking boys, while Mandarin-speaking girls were overall the most likely to be eligible (Murphy Odo et al., 2012).

The Secondary Interview Group (SIG)

A random sample of 1,000 was selected for a study of secondary students. After receiving parental permission interviews were conducted by a research team including research assistants with 407 immigrant students over a period of 3 years (Gunderson, 2007). The five most frequent countries of origin were Hong Kong (39.30%), Taiwan (15.20%), Vietnam (11.20%), China (5.50%), and El Salvador (3.10%) (Gunderson, 2007). The school district in these studies operates 18 secondary schools located in a city of approximately 603,000 people in an urban area of approximately 1,200,000. Schools are located in different neighborhoods varying in mean incomes reported by Statistics Canada (www.statcan.ca/english/IPS/Data/13C0015.htm). There are eight low-, two mid-, and eight high-income neighborhood schools. Students' socioeconomic status was assessed according to immigration information supplied by their families when they entered Canada. Overall, 28% of the Cantonese speakers and 39% of the Mandarin speakers entered Canada with an entrepreneurial immigration status. About 95% of the students in the high socioeconomic or entrepreneurial category reported that they wished to continue on to college or university. Many specified their academic goals, for example to become a doctor, an engineer, or a lawyer. A large majority of "regular" immigrants in low-income schools responded that they wanted to get good jobs after graduating from high school. It was found that

> a majority of students from entrepreneurial families (75%) stated that they were not doing very well in school. However, rather than finding fault in

themselves as many of the other students in the study did, they faulted the teachers, the curriculum, and the differences in teaching and learning they found in Canada for their difficulties. An interesting finding was that every entrepreneurial student interviewed had at least one tutor, many had as many as three or four. Tutors were normally university students, most of whom were members of the student body of the author's university. English and Math tutors were the most widely hired. Teachers reported that they believed many of the tutors actually did students' homework for them, particularly their writing assignments.

(Gunderson, 2007, p. 191)

Students often succeeded in this group because of their culturally related view of the importance of education, because of the strong support they received from tutors, because of their parents' unrelenting drive to have them succeed in school, and because of their strong work ethic and their willingness to spend long hours working on school related tasks. They were not more intelligent than other immigrants, but their success was a result of drive, cultural values related to education, hard work, and the available financial support to enable them to have the resources to help them in their studies. All of these features "worked" for them. However, some entrepreneurs did not succeed as well, in spite of the economic advantages available to them. In Grade 12 English, for instance, 65.50% of the students received a grade of C or less. In Grade 8 English, the overall means were 1.50 for students from China, 2.50 for Hong Kong, and 2.80 for Taiwan.

Financially advantaged students had negative views concerning ESL courses. Generally, they viewed such courses as interfering with their preparation for university admission. For instance, some comments were that "ESL classes don't help you to learn to read" or "ESL classes take up too much time," and others noted that "ESL classes make students second-class."

High socioeconomic students, both Cantonese and Mandarin, had fairly negative views of schooling in Canada. For instance, one noted:

In Hong Kong all we do, memorize, memorize, memorize, day and night, 5 hours homework every day. In XXXXX all we do is think, think, think, nothing more. It's hard to think when the teacher doesn't tell you what to do (female, Cantonese, 18 years).

(Gunderson, 2000, p. 695)

It was noted that, "In China the teacher always gives you homework. School starts at 7 a.m. and you have to get up at 6:00 a.m. You have to memorize and be ready for the exams" (male, Mandarin, 15 years). It was also concluded that:

The schools in Canada have no rules. Student can just do what they want and this is not a good thing. The school is too loose. It seems like the students is not studying, they are playing in the classrooms and they do not respect the teachers and they can even swear.

(Female, Cantonese, 16 years)

It was noted that, "Schools in Canada are more free. I remember the school in China. We weren't allowed to move at all, just sit all day and listen" (male, Mandarin, 14 years). One student opined that:

You don't have any freedom in Taiwan. You can't have too long hair, no ear rings, you have to wear uniforms, the same shoes, socks, you have to do lots of homework and you have tests every day.

(Male, Mandarin, 16 years)

It was also argued that "the labs are better equipped in Canada, but the teachers don't show us what to do with them" (female, Cantonese, 16 years). One advantage student noted "there aren't enough parking spaces at school" (male, Mandarin, 18 years), while another argued that "Canada is really stupid because it builds big beautiful super highways but only let's you go 50 K an hour. That's a waste of money."

There were differences in views related to socioeconomic status. A student from the "regular immigrant category" noted, for instance, that "in Canada school is better than in China. In China it sometimes very dirty and always sick. Here better than in China" (female, Mandarin, 17 years). Comments about school and schooling suggested that there were significant differences in views of the teaching and learning occurring in Canada related to socioeconomic status. These views were similar in the Cantonese- and Mandarin-speaking entrepreneurial groups, while regular immigrant students viewed schools more positively. Entrepreneurs had university admission as a goal at a much higher rate than regular immigrant students who were more likely to express their goal as getting a good job after graduation. Students in lower socioeconomic areas suggested that ESL classes were helpful. They complimented the teachers as being concerned and interested in their students' welfare, while just halfway across the city students and parents complained bitterly that ESL classes were roadblocks to students' success and they interfered with the learning of academic courses that would gain them admission to university (Gunderson, 2007).

The foundational study was not designed to explore parental views. However, there was great interest in the results of the study, primarily from entrepreneurial families. These parents objected to their children being enrolled in ESL support classes for a number of reasons. Academic credit was not associated with ESL classes, so taking them did not contribute to students' graduation. Both students and parents argued that they should not be enrolled in such classes. Interestingly, when they left ESL classes, their grade-point averages declined. In many respects, these parents, mostly Mandarin speakers but including Cantonese speakers, resembled to a degree Chua's description of the "tiger mother."

Discussion, Conclusions, and Limitations

Our purpose in this chapter was to disaggregate findings related to the broad category labeled "Chinese" speakers and, in addition, to explore scores within the ethnolinguistic categories labeled "Mandarin" and "Cantonese." The first somewhat surprising finding was that there were statistically significant differences in English achievement between the groups when they entered Canada. Woodcock recognition and comprehension scores were both significantly higher for Cantonese speakers. The same was true for CELT and GAP scores (see Table 6.1). There was a strong effect size for the significant difference related to knowledge of English prepositions. These findings are not surprising, however, if they are contextualized. The majority of the Cantonese group entered Canada from Hong Kong where their schooling was in most cases English-based, while Mandarin speakers, primarily from Taiwan and China, were mostly from Mandarin-medium schools. The Cantonese speakers had been immersed in teaching and learning involving English. It is also not a surprise that they would show an advantage in knowing about English prepositions.

Students were asked to write compositions in English and their L1s when they were able to do so. The quality of English compositions was significantly higher for Cantonese speakers, while Mandarin speakers' L1 compositions were judged as significantly higher in quality. It appears this finding reflects the instruction they received; L2 instruction in the first case and L1 in the second. Scores on a math skills test, one not involving English word problems, revealed no significant differences between the two groups (see Table 6.2).

ISG students arrived in Canada as students in Grade 4 and higher. Their achievement in secondary school (Grades 8 to 12) was assessed using course-achievement data from a random sample of 5,000 from the ISG. Mandarin speakers received statistically significant higher grade-point averages in English courses in Grades 8, 9, 10, and 11. They also had higher averages in social studies in Grades 8 and 11 and in math in Grades 8, 10, 11, and 12. There were no differences in their science achievement scores in any of the grade levels (see Tables 6.3 and 6.4 and Figures 6.1 and 6.2). The surprise is that on entry into Canada Cantonese speakers scored significantly higher on English achievement measures than Mandarin speakers, while high school achievement scores revealed that Mandarin speakers had higher grades in a number of courses at a number of grade levels. On entry there were no significant differences between the groups on a math skills assessment, but in secondary school there were in all grades favoring Mandarin speakers except ninth grade. It is our speculation that early differences are a reflection of instructional practices, while long-term differences were likely due to the scaffolding their families could afford such as hiring tutors.

Disaggregating Success **99**

This inference is based on an analysis of the responses received during interviews with the 407 randomly selected SIG students.

PG students arrived in Canada when they were very young (6 to 9 years old) and did not receive ESL support. Their long-term achievement as measured by grades in high school and their eligibility for admission to post-secondary education differed in various ways. From Grades 8 to 12, Mandarin grades were higher than Cantonese grades (Murphy Odo et al., 2012). Logistic regression analysis revealed that L1, age on arrival, and gender were predictors of whether or not Asian immigrant students would be eligible for post-secondary education (p. 263). We concluded that, "It is clear that the Cantonese speakers are at a disadvantage in terms of qualifying for College" and "It also appears that while both Cantonese males and females were least likely to qualify for college, Cantonese males appear to be the least likely to be eligible for college when all subgroups related to L1 and students' gender are considered" (p. 263).

It has been suggested that immigrants who arrive at a younger age struggle more to develop their academic language than older-arriving students (Roessingh & Kover, 2004). These researchers found that older-arriving students were able to transfer language and literacy concepts that they had already developed in their first language. Comparing achievement for the two groups this finding does not appear to have occurred. However, significant differences were found between Cantonese and Mandarin speakers.

We had the goal in writing this chapter to explore scores within the ethnolinguistic categories labeled "Mandarin" and "Cantonese." It turns out that these are quite complex categories that have some features in common. The most striking difference is that in this school district the Mandarin-speaking immigrant sample had a higher percentage of entrepreneurs than the Cantonese-speaking group. A larger percentage of them attended schools in high economic neighborhoods and were more likely to have the goal of attending a university after graduation. However, differences between Cantonese and Mandarin entrepreneurial students were not so clear.

Findings of these studies are in many respects troubling. The most troubling finding is that immigrant students have a very high disappearance rate from academic courses in the secondary schools in the studies. Indeed, in Grade 12 about 60% were missing from the district (Gunderson, 2007). We explored this phenomenon with the assistance of the British Columbia Ministry of Education. We attempted to track the students in the PG until they graduated. We selected students who had been born in 1989 or 1990 (there were 401). Our rationale was that they would have graduated from secondary schools by the end of 2010. The Ministry maintains records of all students in BC, including those in private schools and those who are home-schooled, so individuals in this sample should have been in their database. A total of 269 (67.10%) graduated, while (32.90%) could not be located. The status of the missing students is not clear. It is not clear whether they returned with their families to their home countries, moved with their families to other provinces, moved to other countries such as the United States, or dropped out. A 60% decrease represents a significant threat related to study mortality, which means findings should be evaluated with caution. We have also been aware of multicultural classrooms that have population changes of 100% over an academic year. We have named the phenomenon "kinetic diversity" (D'Silva & Gunderson, 2014).

It is abundantly apparent from this research that in the school district we studied Cantonese-speaking boys were the least likely to be eligible for post-secondary education. · Cantonese-speaking male immigrants were in some educational jeopardy in the jurisdiction where our study took place.

There were significant differences among groups when immigrants entered the study school district. In measures of English Cantonese students were significantly higher than Mandarin speakers in English word recognition and comprehension, although effect sizes were low. Cantonese speakers' English composition scores were of significantly higher quality than Mandarin speakers' and the effect size was large. Mandarin speakers produced Chinese compositions of higher quality than Cantonese speakers, but the effect size was low. There were also significant differences in these measures across type of school and type of immigration status for both populations. Cantonese speakers scored higher in initial English measures because a majority of the individuals in this category were from Hong Kong where they received English instruction, while the Mandarin speakers from China and Taiwan did not. They, on the other hand, scored higher on the Chinese writing measure. In addition, the immigrants from Hong Kong started learning to read when they were about 3 years old. Long-term achievement was generally higher for Mandarin speakers because this category had a larger proportion of affluent families that could afford to scaffold their children's development. Findings are in accord with Qin and Han's (2014) study showing that Chinese students in lower socioeconomic groups do not succeed as well as those from families in higher levels.

One of the difficulties of long-term research, in addition to loss of numbers over time, is that immigration demographics also change. When initial data were collected, beginning in the mid-1990s, the two highest numbers of immigrants entered Canada from Hong Kong and Taiwan. However, over the last 10 years the number of immigrants from China has been greater than both Hong Kong and Taiwan combined (see www5.statcan.gc.ca/subject-sujet/result-resultat?pid=30000&id=-30000&lang=eng&type=DAILYART&pageNum=1& more=0). What this means for schools in 2015 and when students begin to graduate is unknown, although the present findings suggest they might not do as well in school as those in the present studies.

Another limitation of the studies is that the categories Cantonese and Mandarin are broad and include incredibly diverse populations that are clearly not homogenous. Students in these categories came from various countries other than Hong Kong, China, and Taiwan. Some immigrants were not included in either category because they spoke a different Chinese dialect. We hope these studies have shown how complex these categories are. It is clear to us that the results of these studies demonstrate that the use of terms such as "Asians" or "Chinese" is highly questionable since they obscure significant diversity features.

References

Abada, T., & Tenkorang, E. Y. (2009). Gender differences in educational attainment among the children of Canadian immigrants. *International sociology, 24*, 580–608.

Asimov, N. (1997, January). California schools rate D-minus in report: Exhaustive study blames Prop 13 for the damage. *The San Francisco Chronicle*, p. A2.

Canadian Council on Learning. (2008). *Lessons in learning: Understanding the academic trajectories of ESL students.* Toronto, CAN: Author.

Chao, R. K. (1995). Chinese and European-American cultural models of the self-reflected in mothers' child-rearing beliefs. *Ethos, 23*, 328–354.

Chua, A. (2011). *Battle hymn of the tiger mother.* New York, NY: Penguin Press.

D'Silva, R., & Gunderson, L. (2014). Teaching to kinetic diversity: Multicultural Canadian classrooms in the 21st century. *Education Canada, 54.* Retrieved from www. cea-ace.ca/education-canada/article/teaching-kinetic-diversity

Frallic, S. (2014). ESL, the trouble with our schools: Looking past altruism, and political correctness. *Vancouver Sun.* Retrieved from www.vancouversun.com/life/trouble+with+schools/10203596/story.html

Garnett, B., Adamuti-Trache, M., & Ungerleider, C. (2008). The academic mobility of students for whom English is not a first language: The roles of ethnicity, language, and class. *Alberta Journal of Educational Research, 54*, 309–326.

Gunderson, L. (2000). Voices of the teenage diasporas. *Journal of Adolescent and Adult Literacy, 43*, 692–706.

Gunderson, L. (2007). *English-only instruction and immigrant students in secondary school: A critical examination.* Mahwah, NJ: Lawrence Erlbaum.

Gunderson, L., D'Silva, R., & Murphy Odo, D. (2012). Immigrant students navigating Canadian schools: A longitudinal view. *TESL Canada Journal, 29*(6), 142–156.

Gunderson, L., D'Silva, R., & Murphy Odo, D. (2014). *ESL(ELL) literacy instruction: A guidebook to theory and practice* (3rd ed.). New York, NY: Routledge.

Hao, L., & Bonstead-Bruns, M. (1998). Parent-child differences in educational expectations and the academic achievement of immigrant and native students. *Sociology of Education, 71*, 171–198.

Jose, P., Huntsinger, C., Huntsinger, P., & Liaw, F. (2000). Parental values and practices relevant to young children's social development in Taiwan and the United States. *Journal of Cross-Cultural Psychology, 31*, 667–702.

Kao, G. (1995). Asian Americans as model minorities? A look at their academic performance. *American Journal of Education, 103*(2), 121–159.

Lee, S. J. (1996). *Unraveling the 'model minority' stereotype: Listening to Asian American youth.* New York, NY: Teachers College Press.

Lee, S. J. (2006). Additional complexities: Social class, ethnicity, generation, and gender in Asian American student experiences. *Race Ethnicity and Education, 9*(1), 17–28.

Looker, D., & Thiessen, V. (2004). *Aspirations of Canadian youth for higher education (Final Report SP-600-05-04E)*. Gatineau, QC: Human Resources and Skills Development, Canada.

Louie, V. S. (2001). Parents' aspirations and investment: The role of social class in the experience of 1.5 and second-generation Chinese Americans. *Harvard Educational Review, 71*, 438–474.

Murphy Odo, D., D'Silva, R., & Gunderson, L. (2012). High school may not be enough: An investigation of Asian Students' eligibility for post-secondary education. *Canadian Journal of Education, 35*(2), 249–267.

Ngo, B. (2006). Learning from the margins: The education of Southeast and South Asian Americans in context. *Race Ethnicity and Education, 9*, 51–65.

Pang, V. O., Kiang, P. N., & Pak, Y. (2003). Asian Pacific American students: Challenging a biased educational system. In J. Banks (Ed.), *Handbook of research on multicultural education* (2nd ed., pp. 542–563). San Francisco, CA: Jossey-Bass.

Peng, S., & Wright, D. (1994). Explanation of academic achievement of Asian American students. *Journal of Educational Research, 87*, 346–352.

Pfeifer, M., & Lee, S. (Eds.). (2004). *Hmong population, demographic, socioeconomic, and educational trends in the 2000 Census*. Washington, DC: Hmong National Development.

Qin, D. B., & Han, E.-J. (2014). Tiger parents or sheep parents?: Struggles of parental involvement in working-class Chinese immigrant families. *Teachers College Record, 116*(8). Retrieved from http://tcrecord.org ID Number 17501

Roessingh, H., & Kover, P. (2004). Variability of ESL learners' acquisition of cognitive academic language proficiency: What can we learn from achievement measures? *TESL Canada Journal, 21*, 1–21.

Schneider, B., & Lee, Y. (1990). A model for academic success: The school and home environment of East Asian students. *Anthropology & Education Quarterly, 21*, 358–377.

Woodcock, R. (Various). *The Woodcock Reading Mastery Test*. New York, NY: Pearson.

7

BETWEEN CLASSES AND SCHOOLS

Time, Space, and Languages

Yamin Qian

Usually, Chinese learners in North America are regarded as a "Model Minority," a group of hard-working, submissive, and quiet learners (Li & Wang, 2008). This self-sufficient image is further reinforced by the comparatively higher rate of high school graduation and university entrance. Studies have focused on this group's experiences between school and home (Qin, 2007; Li, 2006; Moje, Overby, Tysvaer, & Morris, 2008; Song, 2010), as well as between school and community (Leander, 2002; Moje et al., 2004). School, home, and community are recognized as spaces of discourses and practices distinctive from each other. In particular, home and community produce daily life knowledge and lived experiences contradicting school space of dominant middle-class English discourses and practices (Fine & Weis, 2003).

Critical spatial theory highlights the interface between social space and humans' daily lives, none of which should be regarded independently from each other. Social spaces are social products of, and a process of, social relations and activities (Bourdieu, 1989; Lefebvre, 1991). Space not only mediates, but also is defined by, people's daily life literacy and language practices. On the other hand, daily literacy and language practices reveal the spatial aspect of human life (e.g., school and community). This theory opens to new insights and interpretations for the studies of discourses and practices in educational spaces (Robertson, 2010), as well as in and out of educational spaces (Leander & Sheehy, 2004).

Taking a class as a social space, studies investigated Chinese learners' experiences at one specific class such as (a) ESL/EFL classes (Baynham & Simpson, 2010; Li & Giran, 2004; Liaw, 2007), (b) content-based classes (Moje, 2008; Wallace, 2004), and (c) English language arts classes (Benson, 2010; Gutiérrez, 2008; Lee, 2009). Those studies found a class has its particular set of social relations and practices, enabling and/or disenabling certain aspects of, if not all, Chinese learners' daily life knowledge and practices, through curriculum and pedagogy embedded in the courses.

Within the framework of critical spatial theory, this study attempts to uncover the complex nature of school as one collective yet disruptive space with multiple classes as sub-spaces. The author argues that classes, as one segment of school geographical space, are not necessarily complementary to the whole school space. Each class has its own social relations and social activities unique to its curriculum and pedagogy, while school space is a product of dominant discourses and practices of the society. Through the data, this study first wishes to address how a group of late-arriving Chinese learners spatialize their language practices in different classes in Canadian high schools. Second, this study explores the nature of school as one dominant educational space and classes as respective spaces, and investigates how the nature of those spaces impacts learning experiences. This study argues that late arrivals' language experiences and practices reveal the learners' negotiation with North American schools and classes at the present time, but also the juxtaposition of the past and the present with school education in general.

This chapter will first discuss school and classes as discrete social spaces, and then late-arriving Chinese learners' learning experiences at high schools. Then I will introduce the research method, followed by the findings categorized under two major themes: (a) school as one dominant "their" space, and (b) classes as disruptive sub-spaces. This chapter concludes with a theoretical discussion on the divergent nature of school and classes as discrete social spaces, and suggestions for teachers and educators.

Review of the Literature

Doing with Languages at School and Classes

Chinese immigrant adolescents' experiences at school, in and between various classes, are the products and process of both physical and social movements in and between separate social spaces, each of which contains varied social-temporal relations and symbolic systems.

One social space is a sociocultural setting (Hélot & de Mejía, 2008), and a social product (Lefebvre, 1991), evolved from people's perception of and experiences with a geographical place, within certain social relations during a period of time (Soja, 1996). A social space usually has one dominant discourse (Bourdieu, 1989; Lefebvre, 1991), and advantages certain daily life knowledge within a particular set of social-temporal relations, which further supports such relations and practices. Specifically, one social space recognizes certain language practices (Blommaert, Collins, & Slembrouck, 2005). Such dominance reveals the traces of inclusion/exclusion of social-temporal relations and practices.

Therefore, every space bears the traces of the time and place of its sociocultural relations and practices, and reveals its interaction with other times and places (Blackledge & Creese, 2010).

School and classes are different sociocultural settings, within which learners use languages as a mediation tool to negotiate. In this lens, school is one social space containing different social-temporal relations and practices, within which learners position themselves, and are positioned, differently in different languages (i.e., L1/L2). It is important to point out that the combination of sociocultural and critical spatial theory is necessary for the study of immigrant adolescents' experiences at school as well as in and between classes. This theoretical stand highlights the dynamics between learners and the space they lived in, manifested in a form of learners' sense of social-temporal relations and practices, in particular, their mediation with various space(s), and their definition of the spaces through language use.

School and Classes as Social Spaces in Current Studies

School usually enhances and reinforces dominant discourses and practices, while it marginalizes and even disables "othered" spaces (Fine & Weis, 2003), such as home and community (Qin, 2007; Leander, 2002; Li, 2006; Moje et al., 2004; Song, 2010). Specifically, school usually excludes family literacy practice (Li, 2006; Pahl & Kelly, 2005), transnational family literacy practice (Song, 2010), community-based knowledge (Moje et al., 2004), and extra-school activities (Leander, 2002), through curriculum, pedagogy, and routine daily practices.

Current studies have addressed the multiplicity of one single class space. Learners in a class are more likely to position themselves, and also be positioned, differently, because of diverse sociocultural and language backgrounds, and more importantly the dynamic relations between majority and minority students, which inevitably enable the production of the multiple social spaces. Hélot and de Mejía's (2008) study showed how a classroom can be evolved into multiple spaces for multilingual students. This study displayed a process of how the learners' common L1 social relations and language practices transformed one English-speaking classroom into multiple language social spaces, i.e., both English language and Spanish language spaces. It is important to point out, however, that although the classroom was successfully transformed into an inclusive space for multiple language users, this journey was initiated by the teacher, and supported by the students. In other words, the students were encouraged by the teacher to start the journey of transforming their class into a space of bilingual practices. While this study provides valuable insights in how bilingual students find their voice in a class, with the assistance from more powerful figures (i.e., adults), more studies are needed to examine how students create an inclusive space of their own.

Late-Arriving Chinese Learners in North American High Schools

The Model Minority label is dangerous since it overlooks the diversity of Chinese learners, and justifies the disinterest in the needs from this group. Scholars have pointed out that Chinese learners can be very different by nature, due to distinct political, historical and sociocultural backgrounds (Eng et al., 2008; Duff, 2001; Roessingh, 2006; Watt & Roessingh, 2001). Among these varieties, one group is under-researched: late-arriving Chinese learners.

Late-arriving learners, also referred to as *late arrivals*, immigrate at or after the age of 12, in contrast to *early arrivals*, arriving at the age of or before elementary education (Roessingh, 2006, 2008). Studies have, although quite insufficiently, investigated the advantages late arrivals have in North American school spaces. Generally, this group is found performing better with comparatively less English vocabulary due to their higher L1 (Cummins & Swain, 1986; Roessingh, 2008).

This group, however, is more likely to be overlooked, since late age on arrival (AOA) is not as apparent as other factors that distinguish them from other groups. Cummins's (1991) study has pointed out the importance of AOA on immigrants' English language proficiency. It takes them 5 years or more to become competent for academic discussions. Cummins (2000) also suggests that late arrivals' higher L1 can enable them to catch up faster. While studies have identified the strengths in school learning, few studies include AOA as one important factor investigating late arrivals' social-temporal relations and social activities on school campus.

Late AOA seems a negative factor in this group's sociocultural integration to dominant school and class spaces (Anderson, 2002; Chuang, 2010; Cummins, 2000; Derwing, DeCorby, Ichikawa, & Jamieson, 1999; Olsen, 2000; Roessingh, 2006; Roessingh & Field, 2000; Zhou, Peverly, Xin, Huang, & Wang, 2003). Late AOA is suggested as a major reason of lower English language proficiency, limited understandings of local sociocultural and historical knowledge, which further constitutes barriers to a smooth social integration. On the other hand, their English-speaking counterparts do not, in some cases do not intend to, develop enough understandings of this group.

Also, this group has stronger ties with their L1 groups (Irving, Chau, Tsang, Benjamin, & Au, 1998; Liang, 2006; Miller, 2003; Minichiello, 2001; Tsang, Irving, Alaggia, Chao, & Benjamin, 2003; Walters, 2003). One interpretation for this strong tie is that their L1 use is used to identify themselves as an insider of Chinese social networks. Another possibility is their settlement plan in the future. Since they are more likely to return to China after their education in North America, using L1 seems an important strategy.

So far, we can find that this group has been attached complex labels. First, they are perceived as Model Minority: quiet, obedient, diligent and academically outstanding. Meanwhile, they are linguistic minority students, a group for which the "first language is a language other than English or a variety of English significantly different from that used for instruction in Ontario schools"

(Ministry of Education, 2005, p. 6), and is in need of extra assistance for "students' success in both their social and academic lives, and to their ability to take their place in society as responsible and productive citizens" (Ministry of Education, 2005, p. 3).

While the labels are incongruous, studies on this group's experiences on school campus have also unfolded a complicated phenomenon. This group has encountered social exclusion in school, yet has somehow successfully completed their high school program (Roessingh, 2006), and entered ideal universities. These impose an interesting yet under-investigated contradiction: Chinese late arrivals have lower English language proficiency, are comparatively isolated in school social interactions, but are more academically successful. A popular interpretation is the Model Minority legacy and Chinese families' high academic expectation. Few studies explore how this group achieves academically despite the language and sociocultural barriers, through the examination of their spatial movement and participation in and across various social spaces at school.

Method

A qualitative case study concentrates on the impacts of social, political, or other contextual facts on focal issues (Stake, 2005), and contemporary events of which researchers usually have no control (Yin, 2009). This approach allows researchers to understand real-life events from a holistic and meaningful perspective, and examine the complexity of a social group or a phenomenon in dynamic social contexts.

Participants

The researcher recruited the participants at an after-school learning center. The center had attracted a large number of Chinese late arrivals for the preparation of international English language tests such as IELTS, because a mandatory language policy requires English language learners of less than 4 years' residence in an English-speaking country to produce an ideal English test result in order for a university admission. Using convenience-sampling method, the researcher invited more than 30 participants for the first-stage data collection, mostly on their length of residence (LOR), AOA, general language use, and residential information in Canada. Out of the 30 participants, 10 were selected for the second-stage data collection, based on the following criteria: (a) both the adolescents' and the parents' consent to continue to participate, and (b) LOR is more than 6 months.

The 10 participants (5 male and 5 female) came to Canada at/after the age of 15, and all planned to complete their high school education. Table 7.1 presents the participants' general information at the time of the data collection (the year of 2010). Their names and schools were disguised by pseudonyms in order to

108 Yamin Qian

TABLE 7.1 Participants' Brief

Name	AOA	Arriving Year	LOR (mos.)	Caregivers in Canada	Residential Status	High School in the GTA
Angel	16	Jan. 2009	23	Aunt	International student	A
Amanda	20	Dec. 2008	24	Mother	Immigrant	B
Ivana	17	Aug. 2009	16	Alone	International student	C
Joe	15	Oct. 2008	26	Mother	Canadian citizen	D
Justin	18	May 2009	19	Mother	Immigrant	E
Kira	16	April 2007	44	Parents	Canadian citizen	F
David	17	Oct. 2009	14	Mother	Immigrant	G
Rachel	16	March 2008	33	Mother	Immigrant	H
Tony	19	Aug. 2008	16	Older brother	International student	C
Travis	20	April 2010	7	Alone	International student	A

protect their privacy. At the time of the data collection, they were full-time students from eight different high schools in the Greater Toronto Area (GTA): Two pairs of the participants, Angel and Travis and Ivana and Tony, were from the same school, A and B, respectively. During the data collection, they did not know another student from their school was also in my research project. All participants were informed before the data collection of their rights to withdraw at their free will, and no negative consequences of their decision should occur. All the participants graduated from their high school and continued their undergraduate education in Canada 1 or 2 years after the data collection, which resonated with the stereotype of Model Minority as a group of successful high school graduates.

Data Collection and Analysis

Based on a carefully designed protocol, I held three semi-structured interviews with each participant, visited their home, collected their reflective journals and course-related writings, and writings on social networks such as Facebook, and observed their interactions at home, out of class, with their peers, and in online spaces. I took field notes of nonverbal details in interviews, and unplanned online and phone conversations with participants, and wrote reflective journals of observation and documentation.

The transcription from the interview data was read multiple times in order to develop a deeper understanding. I used content analysis (Smith, 2000) to examine the contents of interviews from which themes (i.e., school and classes) relating to the research questions were identified. I also used structural analysis to identify patterns and themes emerging from the interviews regarding the participants' discourse, events, and activities in school and class settings. The data from observation, field notes, and other resources were used to triangulate themes and patterns from the interview data. Afterwards, the patterns and themes were used to identify causal and effectual connections to the research focus. In presentation of the findings, I used the participants' words in order to best present the social reality they lived in.

Results

School as "Their" Space of Spatial and Temporal Relations

The participants regarded their school as a space of "theirs," constituted by English social-temporal relations (i.e., the teachers, administrators, and English-speaking counterparts), in which the dominant language, English, was the social language. Different from traditional categorization of Chinese learners by race and ethnicity, the participants categorized people by preferred language use for social communications. In this study, the participants regarded Canadian-born Chinese and early-arriving Chinese as a non-Chinese group, since this group preferred to use English at school for social purposes. In this part, the participants referred to Chinese students in their interviews as students who used Mandarin at school.

The participants looked at their school as an ideal English social space, in which teachers, administrators and English-speaking counterparts were more dominant. They all felt socially distant from school space, yet they took it as their full responsibilities for the sense of aloofness, an inevitable consequence of their limited English language proficiency and late AOA.

Dominant English Social Relations

The 10 participants were first asked to introduce their school. All participants identified the number of Chinese students from mainland China in school as a significant indicator to an ideal school. They all regarded their school ideal because of its significantly smaller number of Chinese students. To them, an ideal school should have a dominant percentage of English-speaking students and staff, which they believed was representative of a space of English-speaking social relations and language practices.

The participants felt satisfied with their school. David introduced his school, "XXX high school is not bad. This school has a smaller number of Chinese students. It is better if the school uses English, because English is mainstream language (of this society)."

The participants believed that a school having a larger number of Chinese students was not an ideal social space. In order to study at an ideal high school, some participants moved residential places, and switched several schools. Two

110 Yamin Qian

participants switched to the current school for this reason. Amanda had switched in total five schools since her landing on Toronto in December 2008, under the category of the Investor Immigrant program, a program attracting experienced business people with a required sum of net income. When I met her in September 2010, she was making a decision of switching from the fourth to the fifth school, both of which were conveniently accessible from her residence. Eventually, Amanda chose the school with a smaller population of Chinese students, "[The previous school] has too many Chinese people. This is why I did not choose that school. They Chinese people don't like to speak English. [They] speak too much Chinese."

Interestingly, Amanda referred to Chinese students as a third person, "They Chinese people," while she is also Chinese. This deliberate distance between herself and other Chinese students suggests her stronger investment in English language, since this distance seems an effective strategy to enhance English language use. Like Amanda, some participants also preferred to distance themselves from Chinese language use. As Angel said,

> In that kind of environment, you are forced to speak English. No matter how poor your English is, at least you are speaking in English. The more you use English [language], the more likely you will be accustomed to English. Gradually, maybe you can renounce your desire for speaking Chinese.

Angel used a strong word, *renounce*, to show her determination of restricting herself from Chinese language use, and becoming an English-only language user in Canada. However, it is important to point out, first, that the participants' preference toward an English-dominant school does not indicate their permanent preference of English to Chinese language. Second, it does not mean that the participants made a choice of language use contradictory to their future plan, some of whom may decide to go back to China. On the contrary, this deliberate distance can further suggest the differences between late arrivals and other groups (e.g., early arrivals). To late arrivals, Chinese language is an obtained symbolic capital, while English language is a to-be-obtained but an essential tool in English social spaces at the present time. The distance can be understood as a strategy at this place for the time being, to compensate for the setbacks due to their late arriving time to English-dominant society.

Temporal Distance: Late Age on Arrival

Although the participants preferred a school with a significantly larger number of English-speaking counterparts, eight out of 10 participants felt foreign at school. The other two participants, Angel and Travis, did not feel isolated since Chinese languages (i.e., Mandarin and Cantonese) and culture were dominantly practiced in their school. Other participants concluded that the sense of foreignness was mainly due to their late AOA, causing the sense at many different levels. David and Joe explained that at the first level, the foreignness was because of their unfamiliarity with the school geographical environment. David explained, "Because I am not very familiar with this school."

Other than the geographical unfamiliarity, all the eight participants believed that the late AOA caused the social disconnection between them and the school. The first cause, they believed, was their lower English proficiency. As Justin explained:

RESEARCHER (R): Do you think your English language proficiency is a factor impacting your school life?
JUSTIN: I think so. If your English is better, you can integrate into their English-dominant space, a broader space.
R: So can I say you did not feel you have yet entered into their broader space?
JUSTIN: Yes, you can. I haven't entered into their broader space.

Another consequence, the participants believed, was their lack of the knowledge of youth pop culture in North America, a phenomenon also discussed by Duff (2001). In this study, the participants also expressed their frustration of not understanding jokes, movies or cartoons discussed by their teachers and classmates. Yet their interpretation reveals their perception of late AOA as an insurmountable gap. The pop culture in this regard is not merely a body of knowledge, it is common lived experiences which have shaped who they are. As David said, "It is too hard to change one's thoughts, one's deeper thoughts. Especially I am not a small kid any more. It is easier for a very young child to change. When you grow up, it is unlikely to change." The temporal distance results in not only the lack of common lived experiences with the language within a set of social relations in the space but, more importantly, it leads to the fundamental difference manifested through local pop culture, through which the youth establish bonds.

David's perception is not rare. Nine participants, i.e. all except Ivana, believed that late AOA was too significant to an extent that they revealed levels of self-suspicion of their L1 background, hoping that they could have come earlier. In this regard, this study suggests that an L1-dominant social network is not merely a consequence of English-language deficiency and future plan, as found by current studies. It actually shows an inevitable solution to the perceived overwhelming temporal distance between two social spaces. When it appears impossible to fix the temporal distance, staying with L1 networks seems a reasonable choice.

Ivana, however, showed a more complicated attitude toward late AOA. In her interview, she explained why she could always have a top mark for her writings:

I felt the education I received in China helps. My Chinese is better, compared to other students. In terms of writing, it helps. You will be more logical, and clear-minded. You won't just talk about this or that. You know how to connect those points. I feel that learning Chinese language does help.

Her perception toward her higher L1 proficiency is supported by current studies on bilingual learners (Cummins, 2000; Roessingh, 2008). Bilingual learners with higher L1 transfer the cognitive skills they learned from L1 to L2 learning. Ivana used her knowledge of an effective academic writing in her English writing, and was always rewarded a top mark. With enough confidence in her outstanding academic performance, Ivana seemed disinterested in constructing social networks with English-speaking counterparts, since *"they don't necessarily like us."* Interestingly, 1 year later after her graduation from the high school, I asked her why she chose the university out of the seven top universities she was admitted to, and she explained, *"This university has a smaller number of Chinese students."* I asked why the number mattered, she further explained:

IVANA: I can naturally become friends with White people.
RESEARCHER: To speak freely?
IVANA: Yes.

While all participants preferred a "their" school in order to speak English freely in an English-dominant society, they believed that late AOA caused significant social distance.

Classes as a Collection of Sub-Spaces with Contradictory Practices

Unlike feeling foreign to the school, the participants positioned themselves differently in varied classes: insiders in some classes, and outsiders in other classes. Generally, they referred to those classes as "their" classes, which required stronger English proficiency and North American dominant sociocultural and historical knowledge. Opposite to "their" classes, "our" classes were more content-based such as Math, Physics and Chemistry, in which they felt more competent. In "their" and "our" classes, they positioned themselves differently in accordance with their perceived connections with the course contents.

"Their" Classes

Silence in "their" classes. All participants said they were quiet in "their" classes. What is significant is their explanations of their silence in these classes. Some explanations resonated with current studies: silence is usually a result of limited English proficiency, Asian cultural influences, and Western teaching pedagogy (Hu & Fell-Eisenkraft, 2003; Zhou, Knoke, & Sakamoto, 2005). This study, however, wishes to highlight the data supporting Ha and Li's (2012) findings.

The silence was their deliberate choice, when they felt excluded from group discussions and course contents. It is an active choice responsive to dominant discourses and practices.

The data suggests that the participants did not view their silence as submissive. The participants chose silence when they felt uninvited, as a silent resistance. Ivana explained her silence as follows:

> Most of students were native, White. In group discussions, they did not want me to talk, so they kept talking... . I felt okay... . Their writing is not as good as mine... . Actually in this course I may not be as verbally eloquent as the natives are, but I am careful in writing. I am careful and I know how to find key points.

Secondly, the participants believed that having a different opinion implies a more significant difference from the dominant. Thus, they chose silence to avoid confrontation. Kira described her silence in one of her history classes:

KIRA: Sometimes ... they think differently from mine. Then, I am afraid to speak [in the class]. When they said their answers, which were always different from mine, I was afraid to tell them my answer.
RESEARCHER: Why don't you think that your answer may be right?
KIRA: But they are the majority.

Kira's explanation articulated another reason of silence: "*But they are the majority.*" Her silence is not necessarily a Chinese cultural practice toward forthcoming conflicts, nor a result of limited English proficiency. It can be the participants' perception of themselves as the marginalized in a class space.

Being late as always late. In "their" classes, both the participants and their teachers perceived the late AOA as a significant setback. Amanda's story efficiently showed both the participants' and the teachers' perceptions.

In order to "catch up" the missed time, Amanda avoided to socialize with her Chinese friends, and explored more chances to use more English at school. She believed that her English should soon become proficient enough for school life. "I felt very accomplished, since after each day, I felt closer to my goal." Yet, one incident in her English class seriously questioned her belief.

Her Grade 12 English teacher was an early-arriving Asian immigrant from Hong Kong. He was concerned with Amanda's and other ESL students' English academic writing abilities, after reading their class assignments. Amanda said, "He came to Canada at a younger age. And he still had some difficulties in dealing with some courses. He had encountered all those difficulties [at the university]. Not to mention us." The teacher encouraged Amanda and other students to spend more time in high school to become more competent for further education.

This teacher's perception reveals two major opinions toward time and immigrant learners' English proficiency. First, it usually takes at least 5 years for immigrant children after the age of 6 to develop academic English proficiency (Cummins, 1991). Another opinion is that ESL students with higher L1 proficiency have more potential in academic learning (Cummins, 2000). Both of the studies have unfolded the cognitive development features of different groups of learners. This teacher, as an early arrival, failed to realize the great distinction between early arrivals and late arrivals. Different L1 proficiency levels do influence learners' academic studies in L2 spaces, as elaborated by Cummins (2000). This teacher's perception suggests that he did not differentiate late arrivals from early arrivals in terms of language learning, a significant distinction proposed and advocated by many scholars (Cummins, 2000; Roessingh, 2008).

Amanda obviously felt distraught. She was convinced that time is significant and that she came "too late." When retelling this story, she cried so uncontrollably that I had to stop the interview. In the end, she said,

> At the beginning I was very confident of myself. But I constantly got marks like this, and really felt discouraged. Do you know [how it feels] when you put into efforts but receive no effects. Again and again, I really felt upset, and hopeless... . I thought about his words. I knew I need to look ahead, because I will live here. But I really have no other options... . He said it is okay. It [my English] will be improved, but I don't think my English will be any better.

"Coming late" is not merely a metaphor of physical appearance in a social space; it completely overrides late arrivals' prior learning experiences in L1 spaces including learners' L1 proficiency. In this study, both the teacher and participants, except Ivana, looked at their lateness disadvantageously: their advanced L1 background is totally ignored in class spaces.

Interestingly, the participants revealed more complex responses, although they took it as their responsibility as a group coming too late to "their" classes. They did not just either struggle for social integration, or stay in their L1 comfort zone. Different from remaining silent in "their" classes, they appeared a different group in "our" classes.

"Our" Classes

While late AOA was a setback in "their" classes, it actually became an advantage in "our" classes. "Our" classes referred to subject content such as Math, Physics, and Chemistry. Because of different curriculum between China and Canada, students from China usually excelled at these courses. In these courses, the participants described themselves as more participatory.

L1 use in "our" class. In "our" classes, the participants felt more confident with the course contents and their English proficiency. They were not silent, and they felt more comfortable and more willing to participate. Tony explained,

> Your answer can be a number, and then about how to do it. To explain how to do it, if you use English language, you don't need metaphoric strategies. You don't need to present it with beautiful words. Just a simple sentence, as long as you make it clear.

Not only the participants positioned themselves as the majority in "our" classes, they were also positioned differently by their English-speaking counterparts. Almost all participants claimed being approached by their English-speaking counterparts for Math questions, to which they were very willing to answer. Some participants even used this chance to construct their English social networks. This casts a significant contrast to their position in "their" classes. For example, Amanda said in Art class nobody talked to her, since *"they knew you came to learn English."*

Probably the most significant finding is, through the use of L1, the participants transformed these classes into a space of "ours." They used L1 in class discussions with their Chinese peers. They explained that it was convenient for them to use L1 since they were communicating with other Chinese students. When asked why not use the English language, Ivana explained: "White guys cannot anyway follow us. Their Math is not at the same level as ours. It is our class. We use Chinese [language] since it is for us," while Liang (2006) suggested the use of L1 in a class was a result of limited English proficiency and peer pressure from L1 groups. This study proposes a new perspective: L1 is used to claim dominance of a social space.

Outstanding yet frustrated. In "our" classes, although they felt more competent with the contents, the participants were still uncertain with the writing of reports. Taking Joe as an example, when he received a lower mark in his Chemistry lab report, he was not sure whether "it was because the experiment I did, or it is because the way I wrote the report." Although they knew the contents, the writing was still an issue. As David said, "I knew what I should write, but the expressions [I used] are probably not very precise."

In the case of having received a top mark, the participants also expressed frustrations. They had to spend at least three or four times longer than their English-speaking counterparts reviewing the course materials and writing up the reports. Rachel effectively expressed the sense of frustration: "They did not know how many times I have read [the course materials], and looked up new words from dictionary, and [think about] how to write. Other people do not know how frustrated I felt. Only I know." This group excelled in "our" classes, yet it did not mean that their English proficiency was not an issue any more. They were still uncertain, and frustrated.

116 Yamin Qian

Discussion: Time, Spaces, and Languages

Through the data, this article has presented the participants' views of school and classes as discrete products of social-temporal relations and social activities. The most significant is the participants' justification of the disconnection at school level yet resistance toward the disconnection at class level, manifested through their doubts of prior lived experiences, silence and L1 use in classes. Time (i.e., late AOA) is a significant factor in the conflicting views toward school, classes, and their prior learning experiences.

While school seems a distant, vague, and ideally "their" space, the late arrivals react and interact differently in "their" classes and "our" classes. The creation of "our" classes is a response to social exclusion in "their" classes, yet none of the participants intended to move to an "our" school. This shows the learners' general desire to integrate into, and obtain dominant social relations in, an English-dominant society. Yet in their day-to-day life, they refuse to conform to the dominance, which in essence denies their previous spatial-temporal relations with L1 and L1 educational spaces.

Classes, as one segment of school, are not all and always "their" sub-spaces. In those classes, silence is in actuality resistance; L1 use is to construct an "our" space; hard work is an inevitable and frustrating choice of a late AOA. The findings provide a new interpretation toward what is traditionally regarded as Model Minority learners' dispositions: quiet, submissive, and hard working. Moreover, L1 use in classes is not always evidence of English deficiency. L1 can be used to show dominance in "our" classes. The use of L1 is a statement of "our" space in contrast to "their" space.

The findings urge teachers and school administrators to look at the late AOA as a positive factor in order to create a genuine inclusive school space. First, while late AOA may result in lack of local practices and limited English proficiency, it can also become an advantage. For example, late arrivals can excel at subject contents, and can take advantage of their higher L1 in English written communications. More specific suggestions are the recognition of this group's strengths as late arrivals in different class spaces. Usually, this group of learners tends to outperform in content areas, in particular Physics, Chemistry and Math, which can become an effective platform for them to first be socially included in class and school spaces, and also to improve their English language. We should also realize that late arrivals' knowledge in subject contents is also very crucial for their successful academic performance. Those late arrivals are more likely to struggle, and even fail their high school program, if they do not excel at those subject content courses.

Second, late AOA should not be regarded as a setback in multicultural and multilingual school spaces. In fact, the deficient view of late AOA reveals a monolingual ideology advantaging North American educational experiences and disadvantaging that of other societies. Through this qualitative case study, it is urgent to adopt a multilingual view toward late arrivals: their L1 background and experiences should be regarded as precious assets, not a deficiency, in North American curriculum and pedagogy.

References

Anderson, J. L. (2002). *Different paths to a shared future: A phenomenological journey* (Doctoral dissertation, Simon Fraser University). (ProQuest Document ID 764796131).

Baynham, M., & Simpson, J. (2010). Placement, and liminality in adult ESOL classes. *TESOL Quarterly, 44*(3), 420–440.

Benson, S. (2010). "I don't know if that'd be English or not": Third space theory and literacy instruction. *Journal of Adolescent & Adult Literacy, 53*(7), 555–563.

Blackledge, A., & Creese, A. (2010). *Multilingualism: A critical perspective*. New York, NY: Continuum.

Blommaert, J., Collins, J., & Slembrouck, S. (2005). Spaces of multilingualism. *Language & Communication, 25*(3), 197–216.

Bourdieu, P. (1989). Social space and symbolic power. *Sociological Theory, 7*(1), 14–25.

Chuang, S. (2010, February). *Perspectives of newcomer adolescent: Language and social exclusion.* Paper presented at 2010 LINC Administrator Conference, Toronto, Canada.

Cummins, J. (1991). Conversational and academic language proficiency in bilingual contexts. In J. H. Hulstijn & J. F. Matter (Eds.), *Reading in two languages* (pp. 75–89). Amsterdam, NLD: AILA.

Cummins, J. (2000). *Language, power and pedagogy: Bilingual children in the crossfire*. Clevedon, UK: Multilingual Matters.

Cummins, J., & Swain, M. (1986). *Bilingualism in education: Aspects of theory, research and practice*. London, UK: Longman.

Derwing, T. M., DeCorby, E., Ichikawa, J., & Jamieson, K. (1999). Some factors that affect the success of ELL high school students. *Canadian Modern Language Review, 55*(4), 532–547.

Duff, P. A. (2001). Language, literacy, content and (pop) culture: Challenges for ELL students in mainstream courses. *The Canadian Modern Language Review, 58*(1), 103–133.

Eng, S., Kanitkar, K., Cleveland, H. H., Herbert, R., Fischer, J., & Wiersma, J. D. (2008). School achievement differences among Chinese and Filipino American students: Acculturation and the family. *Educational Psychology, 28*(5), 535–550.

Fine, M., & Weis, L. (2003). *Silenced voices and extraordinary conversations: Re-imagining schools*. New York, NY: Teachers College Press.

Gutiérrez, K. D. (2008). Developing a sociocritical literacy in the third space. *Reading Research Quarterly, 43*(2), 148–164.

Ha, P. L., & Li, B. (2012). Silence as right, choice, resistance and strategy among Chinese 'me generation' students: Implications for pedagogy. *Discourse: Studies in the Cultural Politics of Education,* 1–16.

Hélot, C., & de Mejĺa, A.-M. (2008). (Eds.). *Forging multilingual spaces: Integrated perspectives on majority and minority bilingual education*. Bristol, UK: Multilingual Matters.

Hu, Y., & Fell-Eisenkraft, S. (2003). Immigrant Chinese students' use of silence in the language arts classroom: Perceptions, reflections, and actions. *Teaching & Learning, 17*(2), 55–65.

Irving, H. H., Chau, S., Tsang, A. K. T., Benjamin, M., & Au, P. (1998). *Satellite children: An exploratory study of their experience and perception: Final report*. Retrieved from http://ceris.metropolis.net/Virtual%20Library/RFPReports/Irving1997.pdf

Leander, K. M. (2002). Polycontextual construction zones: Mapping the expansion of schooled space and identity. *Mind, Culture, and Activity, 9*(3), 211–237.

Leander, K. M., & Sheehy, M. (2004). Spatializing literacy research in research and practice. New York, NY: Peter Lang.

Lee, Y. (2009). *Chinese immigrant students: Negotiating a globalized identity, language, culture and education within multiple contexts* (Doctoral dissertation). University of Washington, Seattle.

Lefebvre, H. (1991). *The production of space*. Oxford, UK: Blackwell.

Li, G. (2006). What do parents think? Middle-class Chinese immigrant parents' perspectives on literacy learning, homework, and school-home communication. *The School Community Journal, 16*(2), 27–46.

Li, G., & Wang, L. (2008). *Model Minority myths revisited: An interdisciplinary approach to demystifying Asian American education*. Charlotte, NC: Information Age.

Li, X., & Giran, A. (2004). The "third place": Investigating an ESL classroom interculture. *TESL Canada Journal, 22*(1), 1–15.

Liang, X. (2006). Identity and language function: High school Chinese immigrant students' code-switching dilemmas in ELL class. *Journal of Language, Identity, and Education, 5*(2), 143–167.

Liaw, M.-J. (2007). Constructing a 'third space' for EFL learners: Where language and cultures meet. *ReCALL, 19*(2), 224–241.

Miller, J. (2003). *Audible difference: ELL and social identity in schools*. Clevedon, UK: Multilingual Matters.

Minichiello, D. (2001). Chinese voices in a Canadian secondary school landscape. *Canadian Journal of Education, 26*(1), 77–96.

Ministry of Education. (2005). *Many roots, many voices: Supporting English language learners in every classroom: A practical guide for Ontario educators*. Retrieved from www.edu.gov.on.ca/eng/document/manyroots/manyroots.pdf

Moje, E. B. (2008). Foregrounding the disciplines in secondary literacy teaching and learning: A call for change. *Journal of Adolescent and Adult Literacy, 52*(2), 96–107.

Moje, E. B., Ciechanowski, K. M., Kramer, K., Ellis, L., Carrillo, R., & Collazo, T. (2004). Working toward third space in content area literacy: An examination of everyday funds of knowledge and discourse. *Reading Research Quarterly, 39*(1), 38–70.

Moje, E. B., Overby, M., Tysvaer, N., & Morris, K. (2008). The complex world of adolescent literacy: Myths, motivations, and mysteries. *Harvard Educational Review*, 107–154.

Olsen, L. (2000). Learning English and learning America: Immigrants in the center of a storm. *Theory into Practice, 39*(4), 196–202.

Pahl, K., & Kelly, S. (2005). Family literacy as a third space between home and school: Some case studies of practice. *Literacy, 39*, 91–96.

Qin, D. B. (2007). Doing well vs. feeling well: Understanding family dynamics and the psychological adjustment of Chinese immigrant adolescents. *Adolescent Adolescence, 37*(1), 22–35.

Robertson, S. L. (2010). "Spatialising" the sociology of education: Stand-points, entry-points, vantage-points. In S. Ball, M. Apple, & L. Gandin (Eds.), *Handbook of sociology of education* (pp. 15–26). London, UK: Routledge.

Roessingh, H. (2006). The teacher is the key: Building trust in ELL high school programs. *The Canadian Modern Language Review, 62*(4), 563–590.

Roessingh, H. (2008). Variability in ELL outcomes: The influence of age on arrival and length of residence on achievement in high school. *TESOL Canada Journal, 26*(1), 87–107.

Roessingh, H., & Field, D. (2000). Time, timing, timetabling: Critical elements of successful graduation of high school ELL learners. *TESOL Canada Journal, 18*(1), 17–31.

Smith, C. P. (2000). Content analysis and narrative analysis. In H. T. Reis & C. M. Judd (Eds.), *Handbook of research methods in social and personality psychology* (pp. 313–335). New York, NY: Cambridge University Press.

Soja, E. W. (1996). *Third space: Journeys to Los Angeles and other real-and-imagined places.* Oxford, UK: Blackwell.

Song, J. (2010). Language ideology and identity in transnational space: Globalization, migration, and bilingualism among Korean families in the USA. *International Journal of Bilingual Education and Bilingualism, 13*(1), 23–42.

Stake, R. E. (2005). Case studies. In N. K. Denzin & Y. S. Lincoln (Eds.), *Handbook of qualitative research* (2nd ed., pp. 443–466). Thousand Oaks, CA: Sage.

Tsang, A. K. T., Irving, H., Alaggia, R., Chao, S. B. Y., & Benjamin, M. (2003). Negotiating ethnic identity in Canada: The case of the "satellite children." *Adolescent and Society, 34*(3), 359–384.

Wallace, C. S. (2004). Framing new research in science literacy and language use: Authenticity, multiple discourses, and the "third space." *Science Education, 88*(6), 901–914.

Walters, J. (2003). Flexible citizens? Transnationalism and citizenship amongst economic immigrants in Vancouver. *The Canadian Geographer, 47*(3), 219–234.

Watt, D., & Roessingh, H. (2001). The dynamics of ELL drop-out. *The Canadian Modern Language Review, 58*(2), 203–223.

Yin, R. K. (2009). *Case study research: Design and methods* (4th ed.). Thousand Oaks, CA: Sage.

Zhou, Y., Knoke, D., & Sakamoto, I. (2005). Rethinking silence in the classroom: Chinese students' experiences of sharing indigenous knowledge. *International Journal of Inclusive Education, 9*(3), 287–311.

Zhou, Z., Peverly, S., Xin, T., Huang, A. S., & Wang, W. (2003). School adjustment of first-generation Chinese-American adolescents. *Psychology in the Schools, 40*(1), 71–84.

8

OPPORTUNITIES TO LEARN AT HOME AND CHINESE-AMERICAN HIGH SCHOOL STUDENTS' MATHEMATICS ACHIEVEMENT

Keqiao Liu and Xiufeng Liu

It has been consistently documented over the past 4 decades that there exist wide gaps, i.e., difference in achievement scores, among students of different racial and ethnic groups, with White and Asian-American students consistently outperforming Black and Hispanic students (Coleman et al., 1966; Haile & Nguyen, 2008; Lee, 2002; Jencks & Phillips, 1998; Peng & Hill, 1995; Rodriguez, 1998). Between White and Asian-American students, research has shown that Asian Americans, in general, are regarded as even higher achievers academically (Wong, Lai, Nagasawa, & Lin, 1998; Wong & Halgin, 2006; Zhao & Qiu, 2009), particularly in mathematics (Aldous, 2006; Kao, 1995; Yan & Lin, 2005).

Various studies have identified determinants of achievement gaps, and one consistent finding is that there are differential opportunities to learn at home of different racial groups/ethnicities (Liu, 2009). While much is known about differential learning opportunities at homes of different racial/ethnic groups, there is much need to understand differential learning opportunities within individual racial/ethnic groups, because within any racial and ethnic group, there is more heterogeneity than homogeneity in opportunities to learn among students at home. Such need is particularly acute for Chinese Americans because often this group is lumped under a broader category of Asian Americans in large national achievement surveys (e.g., National Assessment of Educational Progress [NAEP]) and the Chinese Americans are particularly diverse in cultural heritage, economic status, educational beliefs and values, to name a few (Liu & Li, 2008).

Chinese Americans form the largest subgroup of Asian Americans (The Asian Population, 2010), and this population is increasing rapidly. In 2000, 2,564,190 people constituted Chinese Americans; 10 years later, in 2010, with a 37.9% increase, 3,535,382 people made up the Chinese-American population. With the noticeable presence and the increasing population of Chinese Americans among all Asian Americans, few studies have identified differential learning opportunities in homes of Chinese Americans. The present study intends to make a contribution to the literature in this regard.

Theoretical Framework and Research Hypotheses

There exists various cultural capital at their homes that may facilitate student learning at home (Bourdieu, 1977, 1986). Cultural capital validates individual positions in the social structure, and in turn guides the social mobility, social interaction, and accumulation of social capital. Coleman (1988, 1990) differentiated three types of family capital: economic, human, and social. Researchers have shown that family capital needs to be activated in order to influence student achievement (Lareau & Horvat, 1999). The amount and quality of academically oriented interaction between parents and children at home provides children with access to parents' human capital (Coleman, 1990). The present study aims to understand—among Chinese-American students, what kinds of student and family variables relate to students' twelfth-grade math achievement, and whether the pattern is consistent for students from two different time cohorts.

The research questions are: (a) How do Chinese-American high school students differ in variables related to home? and (b) What are predictors of high school mathematics achievements related to home?

Literature Review

Parental Involvement

Parental involvement plays a positive role in students' academic achievement (Anderson & Minke, 2007; Jeynes, 2007; Zhan, 2005). That is, with higher levels of parental involvement, students tend to academically perform better.

Byfield's (2012) study on African-American fourth- and fifth-grade students found that parental involvement is positively related to academic achievement. The researcher measured parental involvement by surveying parents about habits like "talk to my child about school," "help my child with homework," and "check to see that my child has done his/her homework." Similarly, using the National Education Longitudinal Study of 1988 (NELS: 88), Fan (2001) found that parental involvement and students' achievement is positively related. Fan included component variables such as "discuss programs at school with parents," "discuss school activities with parents," "discuss things studied in class with parents," "how often parents check on R's homework," and "how often help child with homework" to form the parental involvement variable. Zhan (2005), using National Longitudinal Survey of Youth 1997 (NLSY79), reported similar results on the relationship between parental involvement and academic achievement. Finally, Jeynes (2007) conducted a meta-analysis on the relationship between parental involvement and urban secondary school student academic achievement and concluded that there exists a positive relationship.

In general, the positive relationship between parental involvement and academic achievement has been reported in various studies, but it is hard to find any quantitative study that focuses on Chinese Americans. Therefore, this study intends to fill the gap.

Other Home-Related Variables

In this study, we consider a broad range of home-related variables. For example, studies (Blair & Qian, 1998; Fuligni, 1997) show that students' socioeconomic status (SES) has an impact on their academic performance, with higher SES relating to higher academic performance. Mouw and Xie (1999) claimed that the English-dominant group is more likely to perform better than the other language ability subgroups in math and GPA. There are studies that indicate the positive effect of academic engagement (e.g., time spent on homework) on students' academic performance (Chen & Stevenson, 1995; Keith & Benson, 1992). Moreover, it is worthwhile to notice that parental involvement does not equal parental expectation (Fan, 2001; Zhan, 2005). The former is the behavior that is carried out by parents, while the latter is the attitude of the parents. Parents may bear high expectations for their children, while they may not actually engage in their children's education. Students' gender can also have some impact on their academic performance, with Asian-American female students performing better than males (Fuligni, 1997).

Generational Status

Another variable commonly identified as being related to student achievement is generation status. U.S. Census Bureau (2013) data categorizes people into three generational groups: first, second, and third-or-higher generations. The first generation is defined as people "who are foreign born," the second generation as people "with at least one foreign-born parent," and the third-or-higher generation as people "with two U.S. native parents."

There are different theories about how generational status may be related to student achievement. In relatively earlier years, researchers such as Gordon (1964) believed that immigrants would eventually blend into the host society over time. This inevitable assimilation idea can be described as *straight-line assimilation* (Alba & Nee, 1997; Kao & Tienda, 1995). However, more recent publications promote two alternative theories—*accommodation without assimilation* (or *segmented assimilation*) and *immigrant optimism* (Hirschman, 2001; Kao & Tienda, 1995).

Accommodation without assimilation suggests that immigrants become more disadvantaged in relation to the time they stay in the host country (Hirschman,

2001; Kao & Tienda, 1995). This theory proposes a completely opposite effect to *straight-line assimilation*. Therefore, the first generation should be the most advantaged one, followed by second and then third generations.

Immigrant optimism implies that immigrants have greater motivation and expectation for success in the U.S. than non-immigrants (Hirschman, 2001; Kao & Tienda, 1995; Tran & Birman, 2010). Additionally, people of second generation have better English proficiency and a fair amount of knowledge about education in the host country. Thus, the second generation should be the most advantaged one, followed by first and then third generations.

From all the above theories, the third generation is the least advantageous in education. Due to the limitation of the sample size and results from preliminary analysis, this study only differentiates students into first versus second/higher generation students.

Method

Data Sources

Two U.S. national longitudinal large-scale databases were analyzed. The first one is the National Education Longitudinal Study of 1988 (NELS: 88), which first surveyed eighth-graders in 1988 and later followed those students in 1990, 1992, 1994, and 2000. The second one is the Education Longitudinal Study of 2002 (ELS: 2002), which first surveyed tenth-graders in 2002 and later followed those students in 2002, 2004, 2006, and 2012. NELS: 88 and ELS: 2002 are two comparable databases collected by the National Center for Education Statistics (NCES); therefore, it is reasonable to use these two databases to understand possible change in Chinese-American high school students' opportunities to learn at home over time.

In this study, students in NELS: 88 are regarded as Cohort 1 students, while students in ELS: 2002 are regarded as Cohort 2 students. To limit the data sets to Chinese Americans, variables that provide detailed ethnicity information of Asian Americans are utilized. Considering both NELS: 88 and ELS: 2002 are U.S. data sets and students of interest are high school students, if those students identified themselves as Chinese, they are regarded as the Chinese Americans in this study.

Variables

In order to make results from the two data sets comparable, variables from ELS: 2002 and NELS: 88 were matched. That is, based on the codebooks and manuals of the data sets, the descriptions of the items were matched. Further, the coding of the variables was matched. Nevertheless, due to the limitation of the databases, not all independent variables come from the same grade level in high school. For

124 Keqiao Liu and Xiufeng Liu

instance, parental involvement variables in NELS: 88 came from twelfth grade, while in ELS: 2002 they came from tenth grade. The following variables were used:

Twelfth-grade math achievement. This is the dependent variable. It is a continuous variable for twelfth-graders' math test scores.

Parental involvement. This construct consists of three composite variables. That is, parental school involvement, parental life involvement, and family rules.

Parental school involvement is a composite variable based on the sum of three items, the variables being: (a) parent contacted school about school program for year, (b) parent contacted school about plans after high school, and (c) parent contacted school about course selection. For each item, the coding is 1 = none, 2 = once or twice, 3 = three or four times, 4 = more than four times. Reliabilities of this variable were 0.71 and 0.78 for ELS: 2002 and NELS: 88 respectively.

Parental life involvement is a composite variable based on the sum of 12 items, such as (a) parents attended school activities with children, (b) parents worked on homework/school project with children, and the like. For each item, the coding is 1 = never, 2 = rarely, 3 = sometimes, 4 = frequently. The selection of the items was based on results of factor analysis, reliability (ELS: 2002: 0.80 versus NELS: 88: 0.82), and examination of the item content.

Family rule is a composite variable based on two items; that is, family rules for children about maintaining grade average, and family rules for children about doing homework. For each item, the coding is 0 = no, 1 = yes. The selection of the items was mainly based on examination of the item content.

Parental expectation. This dummy coded variable is recorded from how far in school parents expect children to go in education. In this study, parents with expectations that are lower than 4-year degree completion are coded as 0, while parents with expectations that are equal to or higher than 4-year degree completion are coded as 1.

English as the native language. This is a dummy coded variable, which shows whether students' native language is English. Students whose native language is not English are coded as 0, while students whose native language is English are coded as 1. This variable is not included in the analyses that are limited to White students. The aim is to use this variable as a way to signal students' English proficiency.

Female. This is a dummy variable, which indicates students' gender. 0 is coded as male, while 1 is coded as female.

Tenth-grade math achievement. This is a continuous variable, which presents students' standardized math test scores from tenth grade.

SES. This is a continuous variable, which indicates students' socioeconomic status. It is a composite variable that already existed in the databases. More specifically, this variable originates from five items—father's education, mother's education, family income, father's occupation, and mother's occupation.

Number of siblings. This variable indicates the number of siblings that students have, which includes 0 = 0, 1 = 1, 2 = 2, 3 = 3, 4 = 4, 5 = 5, 6 = 6 or more. When doing inferential analyses, this variable is regarded as a continuous variable.

Late for school. This variable indicates how many times a student was late for school, with 0 = never, 1 = 1–2 times, 2 = 3–6 times, 3 = 7–9 times, 4 = over 10 times. This variable is regarded as a continuous variable.

Cut/skip classes. This variable indicates how many times a student cut or skipped classes, with 0 = never, 1 = 1–2 times, 2 = 3–6 times, 3 = 7–9 times, 4 = over 10 times. This variable is regarded as a continuous variable.

Got in trouble. This variable indicates how many times a student got in trouble, with 0 = never, 1 = 1–2 times, 2 = 3–6 times, 3 = 7–9 times, 4 = over 10 times. This variable is regarded as a continuous variable.

In-school suspension. This variable indicates how many times a student was put on in-school suspension, with 0 = never, 1 = 1–2 times, 2 = 3–6 times, 3 = 7–9 times, 4 = over 10 times. This variable is regarded as a continuous variable.

Suspended from school. This variable indicates how many times a student was suspended from school, with 0 = never, 1 = 1–2 times, 2 = 3–6 times, 3 = 7–9 times, 4 = over 10 times. This variable is regarded as a continuous variable.

Remedial math class. This dummy coded variable shows whether a tenth-grader has ever been in a remedial math class, 0 = no, 1 = yes.

Time on math homework. This is a composite variable based on the mean of two items; that is, shows how much time a student spent on math homework in school and how much time a student spent on math homework out of school. For each item, the coding is 1 = none, 2 = less than 1 hour, 3 = 1–3 hours, 4 = 4–6 hours, 5 = 7–9 hours, 6 = 10–12 hours, 7 = 13–15 hours, 8 = over 15 hours. This variable is regarded as a continuous variable.

Generational status. This dummy coded variable indicates the generational status of students, with 0 = second- or third-generation students, 1 = first-generation students.

Marital status. This dummy coded variable indicates the current marital status of the parent respondent, with 0 = not married, 1 = married.

Involvement in neighborhood. This dummy coded variable shows how involved parents feel in their neighborhood, with 0 = just a place to live, 1 = feel a part of neighborhood/community.

Neighborhood safety. This variable indicates parents' view about how safe their neighborhoods were, with 1 = very unsafe, 2 = somewhat unsafe, 3 = somewhat safe, 4 = very safe. This variable is regarded as a continuous variable.

School location. This variable indicates a high school's location, which includes urban, suburban, and rural, with urban as the reference category.

Private. This dummy coded variable shows whether a high school is a private or a public school, with 0 = public school, 1 = private school.

126 Keqiao Liu and Xiufeng Liu

Data Analysis

Since the NELS: 88 and ELS: 2002 employed complex sample designs (i.e., multistage stratified cluster random sampling), the nested structure of these two databases was considered. The software AM was used to deal with this by specifying cluster, strata, and weight rather than weight alone when doing the analysis.

The collinearity between predictors was firstly examined by running the simple correlations. If there was any collinearity, that is any correlation had a value larger than 0.7, the deletion of variable would be considered. Next, the normality of residuals, the outliers, the nonlinearity, and equal variance of residuals were examined. If there were problems with the normality of residuals and outliers, data deletion would be considered; meanwhile, if there were problems with the linearity and equal variance of residuals, data transformation would be considered.

Both descriptive and inferential analyses were conducted. The descriptive analysis included weighted means and correlations. For the inferential analysis, weighted multiple regressions were run for two cohorts of students, respectively. The tested model is shown as below.

Model:

$$Y = \beta_0 + \beta_1 X_1 + \beta_2 X_2 + \beta_3 X_3 + \beta_4 X_4 + \beta_5 X_5 + \beta_6 X_6 + \beta_7 X_7 + \beta_8 X_8 + \beta_9 X_9 + \beta_{10} X_{10} + \beta_{11} X_{11} + e$$

Where,

Y = twelfth-grade math achievement,
X_1 = parental life involvement,
X_2 = parental expectation,
X_3 = tenth-grade math test scores,
X_4 = SES,
X_5 = number of siblings,
X_6 = got in trouble,
X_7 = math remedial class,
X_8 = time on math homework,
X_9 = first generation (versus other),
X_{10} = married (versus not),
X_{11} = neighborhood safety.

Results

Descriptive Analysis

Table 8.1 presents descriptive statistics of all the variables by students' generational status for Cohort 1 and Cohort 2 students.

TABLE 8.1 Descriptive Statistics by Generational Status for Cohort 1 and Cohort 2 Students

Variable Name	First Generation				Second Generation			
	Mean	SD	Min	Max	Mean	SD	Min	Max
				Cohort 1 (NELS: 88)				
Parental school involvement	25.77	6.18	11	48	34.14	6.74	12	46
Parental life involvement	3.43	1.08	1	10	4.14	1.55	2	11
Family rules	1.74	0.63	0	2	1.31	0.89	0	2
Female (versus male)	0.34	0.47	0	1	0.48	0.50	0	1
English as the native language	0.02	0.14	0	1	0.57	0.50	0	1
10th-grade math test score	57.40	7.70	34.88	71.93	60.37	10.94	32.86	71.93
12th-grade math test scores	57.95	7.09	33.06	70.83	61.30	9.15	36.47	71.37
SES	−0.17	0.75	−1.96	1.89	0.55	0.74	−1.46	1.86
Parental expectation	0.96	0.20	0	1	0.95	0.21	0	1
Number of siblings	3.30	2.17	0	6	1.77	1.28	0	6
Late for school	1.06	0.86	0	4	1.33	1.03	0	4
Cut classes	0.29	0.69	0	4	0.41	0.76	0	4
Got in trouble	0.09	0.29	0	2	0.23	0.56	0	3
In-school suspension	0.03	0.18	0	1	0.08	0.30	0	2
Suspended from school	0.01	0.09	0	1	0.04	0.19	0	1
Math remedial class	0.08	0.27	0	1	0.05	0.21	0	1
Time on math homework	1.80	1.85	0	6	2.28	1.44	0	6
Married (versus not)	0.97	0.18	0	1	0.90	0.31	0	1
Involved in neighborhood	0.27	0.45	0	1	0.65	0.48	0	1
Neighborhood safety	3.21	0.51	2	4	3.70	0.50	1	4
Suburban (versus urban)	0.37	0.48	0	1	0.53	0.50	0	1
Rural (versus urban)	0.01	0.10	0	1	0.09	0.28	0	1
Private (versus public)	0.01	0.08	0	1	0.11	0.31	0	1

TABLE 8.1 continued

Variable Name	First Generation				Second Generation			
	Mean	SD	Min	Max	Mean	SD	Min	Max
				Cohort 2 (ELS: 2002)				
Parental school involvement	30.17	7.29	9	44	34.39	7.92	6	48
Parental life involvement	3.55	1.37	2	9	4.04	1.53	1	12
Family rules	1.48	0.75	0	2	1.74	0.50	0	2
Female (versus male)	0.52	0.50	0	1	0.37	0.48	0	1
English as the native language	0.11	0.32	0	1	0.56	0.50	0	1
10th-grade math test score	58.48	10.60	25.71	78.46	54.25	14.82	23.36	84.85
12th-grade math test scores	60.37	10.09	29.72	74.97	57.38	12.18	24.05	76.52
SES	0.19	0.75	−0.99	1.55	0.41	0.78	−0.96	1.79
Parental expectation	0.95	0.21	0	1	0.80	0.40	0	1
Number of siblings	1.28	1.21	0	6	2.06	1.52	0	6
Late for school	1.16	1.09	0	4	1.11	1.15	0	4
Cut classes	0.40	0.73	0	4	0.43	0.97	0	4
Got in trouble	0.26	0.54	0	3	0.48	0.85	0	4
In-school suspension	0	0	0	2	0.15	0.49	0	4
Suspended from school	0	0	0	1	0.06	0.27	0	4
Math remedial class	0.14	0.35	0	1	0.16	0.36	0	1
Time on math homework	3.21	2.2	1	8	3.63	2.68	0.50	8
Married (versus not)	0.82	0.38	0	1	0.82	0.38	0	1
Involved in neighborhood	0.39	0.49	0	1	0.78	0.41	0	1
Neighborhood safety	3.54	0.62	1	4	3.61	0.52	2	4
Suburban (versus urban)	0.51	0.50	0	1	0.53	0.50	0	1
Rural (versus urban)	0.04	0.19	0	1	0.11	0.31	0	1
Private (versus public)	0.07	0.25	0	1	0.11	0.31	0	1

Note: Pairwise deletion was used.

From Table 8.1, we see a few major findings. First, among Cohort 1 students, first-generation students faced a higher level of family rules than second-/higher-generation students. In contrast, among Cohort 2 students, first-generation students faced a lower level of family rules than second-/higher-generation students. Second, among Cohort 1 students, regardless of students' generational status, their parents shared a similar level of expectation. More specifically, nearly all of those parents expected their children to obtain a 4-year university degree. In comparison, for the more recent students (Cohort 2), parents of first-generation students still had high expectation in university completion, but parents of second-/higher-generation students possessed lower expectation than their earlier peers. Third, among Cohort 1 students, first-generation students performed worse than second-/higher-generation students, while for Cohort 2 students, first-generation students performed better than second-/higher-generation students. Fourth, among Cohort 1 students, first-generation students attended more urban than suburban high schools. Among Cohort 2 students, first-generation student attended more suburban high schools than urban high schools, though first-generation students were still more likely than second-/higher-generation students to attend urban high schools. Fifth, among Cohort 1 students, there was a lower proportion of first-generation female students than second-/higher-generation females, but among Cohort 2 students, there was a higher proportion of first-generation female students than second-/higher-generation females. Sixth, among Cohort 1 students, first-generation students had more siblings than second-/higher-generation students. Nevertheless, among Cohort 2 students, first-generation students had fewer siblings than second-/higher-generation students. Seventh, even though the relative status of first- versus second-/higher-generation students did not change for some variables, the change in the actual values can be observed. For instance, among Cohort 1 students, the average value of parental school involvement for first-generation students was 25.77 and for second-/higher-generation students was 34.14. Among Cohort 2 students, the average value of parental school involvement for first-generation students was 30.17 and for second-/higher-generation students was 34.39. Thus, the gap between first-generation and second-/higher-generation students reduced from 8.37 to 4.22. Similarly, among Cohort 1 students, the average value of parental life involvement for first-generation students was 3.43 and for second-/higher-generation students was 4.14. Among Cohort 2 students, the average value of parental life involvement for first-generation students was 3.55 and for second-/higher-generation students was 4.04. Therefore, the gap between first- and second-/higher-generation students reduced from 0.71 to 0.49.

In summary, Table 8.1 suggests the existence of the great variation in various variables related to home and the changes in the patterns of Chinese-American high school students from the aspects of time and generational status.

Multiple Linear Regression

After running simple correlations of all predictors for ELS: 2002 and NELS: 88, respectively, no simple correlation had a value larger than 0.70, which indicated no co-linearity among these variables. Therefore, all predictors were kept.

After running histograms of residuals, which were obtained through multiple regressions, normality of the residuals was met for both Cohort 1 and Cohort 2 students.

After running plots of predicted values against residuals, which were obtained through multiple regressions, the assumptions of equal variance and linearity were met for both Cohort 1 and Cohort 2 in that the scatterplots were basically symmetric along the regression lines (the horizontal line at residual = 0).

Based on preliminary simple correlation results, 11 variables were selected, according to the magnitude of correlations, for regression analysis. According to Table 8.2, the 11 variables in total explained 92% of the variation in twelfth-grade math test performance for Cohort 1 students, while they explained 84% of the variation in twelfth-grade test performance for Cohort 2 students. Therefore, more variance in twelfth-grade math test performance was explained by the 11 variables for Cohort 1 students than for Cohort 2 students.

After controlling for all the other variables, tenth-grade math test scores was the only one that was significantly associated with twelfth-grade math test scores for both Cohort 1 and Cohort 2 students. More specifically, a 1-point increase in tenth-grade math test scores was associated with a 0.78-point increase in twelfth-grade math test scores for Cohort 1 students. In the meantime, a 1-point increase

TABLE 8.2 Weighted Multiple Regression Results for Predicting 12th-Grade Math Performance

Variable Name	NELS: 88 (Cohort 1)		ELS: 2002 (Cohort 2)	
	Coefficient	s.e.	Coefficient	s.e.
Parental life involvement	−0.17	0.23	0.30	0.25
Parental expectation	1.01	1.24	4.96	3.39
10th-grade math test scores	0.78★★★	0.05	0.75★★★	0.06
SES	1.76★★	0.52	0.46	0.60
Number of siblings	0.37★	0.16	−0.48	0.35
Got in trouble	0.39	0.69	−0.74	0.57
Math remedial class	−4.70★★	1.27	−0.04	1.73
Time on math homework	0.14	0.16	−0.19	0.19
First generation (versus other)	0.89	0.91	2.80★★	1.03
Married (versus not)	3.62★	1.56	2.88	1.62
Neighborhood safety	0.75	0.69	−1.15	0.74
R square	92%		84%	

Note: ★ $p < 0.05$, ★★ $p < 0.01$, ★★★ $p < 0.001$

in tenth-grade math test scores was associated with a 0.75-point increase in twelfth-grade math test scores for Cohort 2 students. Therefore, considering both the direction and magnitude of the relationship, Cohort 1 and Cohort 2 students shared a similar tenth-grade math performance and twelfth-grade math performance relationship. In comparison, a 1-unit increase in SES was associated with a 1.76-points increase in twelfth-grade math test scores for Cohort 1 students, while SES was not related to twelfth-grade math test scores for Cohort 2 students. The number of siblings increased by 1 was associated with a 0.37 increase in twelfth-grade math test scores for Cohort 1 students, while number of siblings was not related to twelfth-grade math test scores for Cohort 2 students. Being in math remedial class was associated with a 4.70-points decrease in twelfth-grade math test scores for Cohort 1 students, but it was not associated with twelfth-grade math test scores for Cohort 2 students. Being first-generation students was not related to twelfth-grade math performance among Cohort 1 students, but it was associated with a 2.8-points increase in twelfth-grade math test scores for Cohort 2 students. Moreover, having a currently married parent was associated with a 3.62-points increase in twelfth-grade math test scores for Cohort 1 students; nevertheless, it was not related to twelfth-grade math test scores for Cohort 2 students.

In sum, results from the multiple regression analysis suggest three main findings. First, the 11 selected variables explained most of the variations in twelfth-grade math test performance for both Cohort 1 and Cohort 2 students. Second, tenth-grade math test performance was the sole variable that was significantly associated with twelfth-grade math test scores for both Cohort 1 and Cohort 2 students. Third, difference existed between Cohort 1 and Cohort 2 students in terms of the kinds of home variables showing significant effects. Specifically, SES, number of siblings, remedial math class, and parent married status were significant predictors for Cohort 1 but not for Cohort 2; first generation was a significant predictor for Cohort 2 but not for Cohort 1.

Discussion and Conclusion

According to the results of this study, among Chinese Americans who were high school students back in the beginning of the 1990s, better tenth-grade math test performance, higher SES, more siblings people have, never being in a math remedial class until tenth grade, and having married parents are all associated with better twelfth-grade math performance. In comparison, among Chinese Americans who were high school students in the early 2000s, fewer variables contribute to the variations of twelfth-grade math performance. More specifically, better tenth-grade math performance and being first-generation students are associated with better twelfth-grade math performance. Therefore, Chinese Americans who were high school students back in the early 1990s and who were high school students back in the early 2000s do not share exactly the same home-related education experiences. This finding suggests that Chinese-American students are not a static group; they change over time.

An examination of the descriptive results reveals much variation within Chinese Americans as demonstrated by large ranges of values of home variables. Beside of the existence of disparities between Chinese Americans who were high school students in the early 1990s and who were high school students in the early 2000s, Chinese Americans of different generational subgroups (e.g., first-, second-, or third-or-higher generation subgroups) are also different in their home-related educational experiences. Future research that examines the possible moderation effects of generation status can add more understanding to Chinese Americans' educational experiences. This within group variation is consistent with the previous calls for more attention to within group differences (Liu & Li, 2008).

While prior literature indicates that higher level of parental involvement is associated with students' better academic performance (Anderson & Minke, 2007; Byfield, 2012; Jeynes, 2007; Zhan, 2005), this study does not find any significant relationship between parental involvement (i.e., parental school involvement and parental life involvement) and twelfth-grade math test performance when controlling for variables such as tenth-grade math test performance. On the other hand, results about Chinese-American high school students in the early 2000s seem to agree with the accommodation without assimilation effect as referred to by Hirschman (2001) and Kao and Tienda (1995). That is, first-generation Chinese-American students performed better than second-or-higher generation Chinese-American students in twelfth-grade math tests. Unlike many of the prior research studies such as Mouw and Xie's (1999) research about English proficiency, other student, family, neighborhood, and school variables included in this study either do not significantly correlate with Chinese-American students' twelfth-grade math test performance (e.g., time on math homework) nor show significant patterns for the more recent cohort of Chinese-American students (i.e., students who were high school students in the early 2000s). In comparison, among those variables that have significant effects, the directions of them are as expected based on prior literature. For instance, this study finds higher SES is associated with better twelfth-grade math test performance, which concurs with the study findings of Blair and Qian (1998) and Fuligni (1997).

This study used quantitative methods to examine home variables of Chinese-American high school students in terms of their math test performance across two time periods, which fills the gap of current research about Chinese Americans. Despite some limitations such as small sample sizes, this study offers an in-depth analysis of home-related educational experiences of Chinese Americans from two time cohorts. It can serve as a start point for conducting more quantitative research about Chinese Americans; it can also complement relevant qualitative research.

References

Alba, R., & Nee, V. (1997). Rethinking assimilation theory for a new era of immigration. *International Migration Review, 31*(4), 4, 826–874.

Aldous, J. (2006). Family, ethnicity, and immigrant youths' educational achievements. *Journal of Family Issues, 27*(12), 1633–1667.

Anderson, K. J., & Minke, K. M. (2007). Parental involvement in education: Toward an understanding of parents' decision making. *Journal of Educational Research, 100*, 311–323.

Blair, S. L., & Qian, Z. (1998). Family and Asian students' educational performance: A consideration of diversity. *Journal of Family Issues, 19*(4), 355–374.

Bourdieu, P. (1977). *Outline of a theory of practice*. London, UK: Cambridge University Press.

Bourdieu, P. (1986). Forms of capital. In J. G. Richardson (Ed.), *Handbook of theory and research for the sociology of education* (pp. 241–258). New York, NY: Greenwood Press.

Byfield, P. (2012). Parental involvement and the academic achievement for African American students. *ProQuest Dissertations and Theses*.

Chen, C., & Stevenson, H. W. (1995). Motivation and mathematics achievement: A comparative study of Asian-American, Caucasian-American, and East Asian high school students. *Child Development, 66*(4), 1215–1234.

Coleman J. S. (1988). Social capital in the creation of human capital. *American Journal of Sociology, 94*, 95–120.

Coleman, J. S. (1990). *Foundations of social theory*. Cambridge, MA: Harvard University Press.

Coleman, J. S., Campbell, E. Q., Hobson, C. J., McPartland, J., Mood, A. M., Weinfeld, F. D., & York, R. L. (1966). *Equality of educational opportunity*. Washington, DC: US Government Printing Office.

Fan, X. (2001). Parental involvement and students' academic achievement: A growth modeling analysis. *Journal of Experimental Education, 70*, 27–61.

Fuligni, A. J. (1997). The academic achievement of adolescents from immigrant families: The roles of family background, attitudes, and behavior. *Child Development, 68*(2), 351–363.

Gordon, M. (1964). *Assimilation in American life*. New York, NY: Oxford University Press.

Haile, G. A., & Nguyen, A. N. (2008). Determinants of academic attainment in the United States: A quantile regression analysis of test scores. *Education Economics, 16*(1), 29–57.

Hirschman, C. (2001). The educational enrollment of immigrant youth: A test of the segmented-assimilation hypothesis. *Demography, 38*(3), 317–336.

Jencks, C., & Phillips, M. (Eds.). (1998). *The black-white test score gap*. Washington, DC: Brookings Institution Press.

Jeynes, W. H. (2007). The relationship between parental involvement and urban secondary school student academic achievement. *Urban Education, 42*(1), 82–110.

Kao, G. (1995). Asian Americans as model minorities? A look at their academic performance. *American Journal of Education, 103*(2), 121–159.

Kao, G., & Tienda, M. (1995). Optimism and achievement: The educational performance of immigrant youth. *Social Science Quarterly, 76*(1), 1–19.

Keith, T. Z., & Benson, M. J. (1992). Effects of manipulable influences on high school grades across five ethnic groups. *Journal of Educational Research, 86*(2), 85–93.

Lareau, A., & Horvat, E. M. (1999). Moments of social inclusion and exclusion: Race, class, and cultural capital in family-school relationships. *Sociology of Education, 72*, 37–53.

Lee, J. (2002). Racial and ethnic achievement gap trends: Reversing the progress toward equity? *Educational Researcher, 31*(1), 3–12.

Liu, X. (2009). *Linking competence to opportunities to learn: Models of competence and data mining.* New York, NY: Springer.

Liu, X., & Li, G. (2008). Diversity and equity in science education for Asians in North America: Unpacking the model minority myth. In M.-W. Roth & K. Tobin (Eds.), *The world of science education: Handbook of research in North American* (pp. 369–388). Rotterdam, NLD: Sense.

Mouw, T., & Xie, Y. (1999). Bilingualism and the academic achievement of first- and second-generation Asian Americans: Accommodation with or without assimilation? *American Sociological Review, 64*(2), 232–252.

Peng, S. S., & Hill, S. T. (1995). *Understanding racial-ethnic differences in secondary school science and mathematics achievement* (NCES Publication No. 85-710). Washington, DC: National Center for Education Statistics.

Rodriguez, A. (1998). Busting open the meritocracy myth: Rethinking equity and student achievement in science education. *Journal of Women and Minorities in Science and Engineering, 4*(2–3), 195–216.

The Asian Population. (2010). Retrieved from www.census.gov/prod/cen2010/briefs/c2010br-11.pdf

Tran, N., & Birman, D. (2010). Questioning the model minority: Studies of Asian American performance. *Asian American Journal of Psychology, 1*(2), 106–118.

U.S. Census Bureau. (2013). *Generational Status.* Retrieved from www.census.gov/population/foreign/about/faq.html#4

Wong, F., & Halgin, R. (2006). The model minority: Bane or blessing for Asian Americans. *Journal of Multicultural Counseling and Development, 34*, 38–49.

Wong, P., Lai, C. F., Nagasawa, R., & Lin, T. (1998). Asian Americans as a model minority: Self-perceptions and perceptions by other racial groups. *Sociology Perspectives, 41*(1), 95–118.

Yan, W., & Lin, Q. (2005). Parent involvement and mathematics achievement: Contrast across racial and ethnic groups. *Journal of Educational Research, 99*(2), 116–127.

Zhan, M. (2005). Assets, parental expectations and involvement, and children's educational performance. *Children and Youth Services Review, 28*(8), 961–975.

Zhao, Y., & Qiu, W. (2009). How good are the Asians? Refuting for myths about Asian-American academic achievement. *Phi Delta Kappan, 90*(5), 338–334.

PART III

Chinese-Heritage Students' Cultures and Identities

9

(RE)POSITIONING THE "CHINATOWN" DEFAULT

Constructing Hybrid Identities in Elementary Classrooms

Joseph C. Rumenapp

Students are often stereotyped by their biological races as well as their geographical locations. Asian students in the United States, for example, are often referred to as the *model minority* or *perpetual foreigner* (Lee, 2009; Ng, Lee, & Pak, 2007), though they have a variety of educational experiences. While stereotypes are addressed in discussions of race in education, the diversity among Asian students merits more consideration. In fact, the "model minority" stereotype indexes the cultural notion that Asian American students are all academically high achieving despite evidence that some may struggle academically (Lew, 2004; Vang, 2005; Yang, 2004). While test scores may seem to confirm that Asian students are relatively high performing, they do not explicate the diversity of experiences of Asian Americans as a whole, or Chinese Americans specifically. Furthermore, language and literacy learning cannot be abstracted from students' use of language to position themselves in relation to ethnic, racial, or cultural identities.

While the diverse experiences of Asian Americans have been discussed in many education circles (Kumashiro, 2006; Park, Endo, Lee, & Rong, 2007; Ma & Wang, 2014; Teranishi, 2002), cultural and racial ideologies continue to reify the picture of Asian-American students as a homogeneous group in society. Researchers must always struggle with the broad experiences of sociological groups and with the specific experiences of the individual. Even the construct of "Chinese" itself is problematic when considering learners' experiences in U.S. schools. It erases the diversity within students from Chinese backgrounds. Socioeconomic differences, linguistic differences, differences in immigration histories, and generational differences contribute to a variety of educational experiences that students face. Learners in Chinatowns are a special case because they may be dually stereotyped as "Chinese" and as members of a specific ethnic

138 Joseph C. Rumenapp

enclave. Chinatown communities worldwide are often seen as foreign by tourists within their respective countries and also by travelers from China and Taiwan, facing a dual foreignness. Thus, their educational experiences are wrought with an image of what a Chinese learner should be like.

Student identities, however, are multifaceted and complex, as are their experiences in schools. Teachers need to understand the complexities of communities such as Chinatowns, broadly, and how learners position themselves in relation to "Chinatown." The present study investigates how students accept and reject dominant assumptions about what it means to be Chinese in a Chinatown classroom through discourse, thereby creating hybrid identities. During these language and literacy learning opportunities, students may align with different identities and experience classrooms in a variety of ways.

The Case of So-Called "Chinatowns"

The notion of "Chinatown" means different things, invoking mental concepts, memories, or experiences. Worldwide, Chinatowns look from the outside to be homogeneous communities. They appear to share similar visual styles and are marked by linguistic signs. They have even been called a "Western landscape type" (Anderson, 1987, p. 581) because of these similarities. The term *Chinatown* itself indexes a nation-state, that is China, as well as a local political jurisdiction, namely "town." This model is quite efficient since the name appears on tourist maps, in newspapers, on public transportation, in media and entertainment, as well as in many other textual resources, building a figured world, or a cultural model (Gee, 2011). Cultural models tell us what students *should be like* in a given context. They tell us how students should experience education despite the variety of experiences students actually have in classrooms.

Chinatown provides a particularly interesting site for this study because of the wider ecological context learners may experience, even in classrooms. In tourism literature, Chinatown has become a commodity, presented as distinct and even exotic in order to attract tourists to frequent the area. Santos, Belhassen, and Caton (2008) noted that through increased tourism, the public discourse about Chinatown is being revised from one of negative stigmatization to a celebratory role of multiculturalism while still maintaining the label "Other." Wong (1995) argued that representations of Chinatown construe the locality as homogeneous, rather than recognizing diverse populations. Newer immigrants often feel "foreign" in these enclaves where children have been born and raised. Rather than a community separate from the city, Chinatowns need to be viewed as embedded in and vital to the ecology of the city at large.

However, what one may view as a consistent community type from the outside, indeed demonstrates highly complex differences both among Chinatowns and within any given Chinatown. Benton and Gomez (2001) found that the residents of Chinatowns in Great Britain and Southeast Asia gradually realigned their loyalties to host nations, thereby debunking the notion that there is a cohesion across Chinatowns. In most Chinatowns in the U.S., the earliest immigrants were working-class people from Canton although more recent immigrants may come from many different socioeconomic statuses and regions (Kwong, 1996). Although China has tended, historically, to have an ideology of homogeneity, upon arrival, immigrants may also find that their new home is completely different from the one they left. Chinatown is often a gateway community with newer immigrants moving out when given the opportunity (Kwong & Miščević, 2005). There is a distinct duality in immigration patterns between the "Downtown Chinese," generally lower socioeconomic status immigrants settling in or around Chinatown, and the "Uptown Chinese," the professionals often living in the suburbs or more affluent urban communities (Kwong & Miščević, 2005). Lu (2001) also noted this distinction among newer immigrants to Chicago, most of whom spoke Mandarin, and their perceptions of Chinatown as being for earlier, Cantonese-speaking immigrants. The latter frequent Chinatown for food, shopping, and certain cultural events, though choose education to take place elsewhere supplemented by heritage Chinese schools.

Chinese immigrants throughout U.S. history have met racism, blatant discrimination, poor living conditions, abuses in sweatshops, sex trade, manual labor, exclusion from immigration policies, and a number of other evils that still stereotype and otherwise affect the communities (Chang, 2003). Therefore, while the very notion of Chinatown is assumed to be a monolithic space in which the identity of "Chinese immigrant" is enacted, the lived experiences of residents in Chinatowns may be very different. Schools play an interesting role because students come from a variety of experiences but are assumed to be a homogeneous population, often taught by people from outside of the community. Unlike Chinese schools, which intentionally serve as a cultural community space (Lu, 2001), the public school, in Chinatown, does not necessarily have this function as an explicit goal.

Context of a Chinatown School

Warner is a public elementary school located in a geographically defined Chinatown. The linguistic landscape of the community includes signage in traditional Chinese characters, simplified Chinese characters, Pinyin, and English. The large Chinatown Gate spans over the old section reading "The world belongs to the commonwealth" in Chinese characters while the twelve statues of the zodiac mark the plaza in the relatively new "Chinatown Square." The area is viewed as a tourist destination in the city and even has public transportation nearby with a stop that is called "Chinatown," the only ethnic marker on any public transportation stop in the city. Thus, the community around Warner is iconically identified and marked as Chinese.

140 Joseph C. Rumenapp

The school itself, unlike two other elementary schools in the area, does not include iconic Chinese architecture, though there is some art that identifies the school as ethnically Chinese. While Chinese print is used for the communication of information, it seems to stand more as an emblem and marker than for communication of information. In 2011 Warner had 704 students. Approximately 93% of the students were Asian (mostly Cantonese Chinese), 6% African American, and 1% other. About 26% were reported as bilingual and 95% on free and reduced lunch. The school's webpage has the name written in Chinese characters. The school's voicemail is recorded in both Cantonese and English. Several members of the staff and administration spoke Cantonese, Mandarin, or another Chinese language. The classrooms included in this study were first-, third-, fourth-, and sixth-grade monolingual English classrooms with bilingual support. Two teachers in this study identified as Chinese American, and the other two as African American. Only the first-grade teacher identified as bilingual, being able to speak and understand conversational Taishan and, at a basic level of proficiency, Cantonese.

The Study

As part of a larger professional development project that took place during the 2010–2011 school year, I videotaped 10 class periods in four classrooms, focusing on small groups of students and classroom instruction. I took field notes more frequently and student work was also collected. In total, data included 40 videotaped lessons, 60 field notes, student work, and focus groups and meetings with the teachers. The larger project included teachers performing action research to reflect on instruction; however, the data used for this paper focus on classroom interaction to investigate how students positioned themselves in relation to Chinatown.

Positioning theory was adopted to take into account that language is used to situate the self in relation to others in social discourse. Interactions in the classroom are filled with these moments of establishing and negotiating rights, duties, and obligations (Harré & Moghaddam, 2003). To understand the positions students took up in the classroom, all videos were reviewed to identify situations in which constructs of race, language, or identity were being discussed. Through an iterative coding process, these events were coded to understand how students positioned themselves in alignment or in counter-alignment to the Chinatown identity. For example, if the notion of Chinatown emerged in the event, I viewed it as a sign that was used as a positioning device. That is, because the sign "Chinatown" was used in discourse, the utterances around this sign can be observed to see the positions taken up by social agents.

Classroom discourse has been analyzed to understand the relationship between social actors and the context such as identity (Wortham, 2000) and power (van Dijk, 2001). People are located socially through a variety of semiotic means, including language. Other signs and symbols such as race, ethnicity, age, and gender are used to fit a dominant cultural model positioning one into a particular narrative default. Within talk, students and teachers may make social moves, contesting normative social positions. Classroom discourse becomes important to understand not only how students are positioned but also how they actively contest dominant positions and construct multiple positions, or hybrid identities. Furthermore, discourse analysis may lend insight into how students experience the learning context and how they appropriate the use of language in social contexts.

Discourse analysis was used in this study to understand how students took up positions in relation to Chinatown and rejected the monolithic view that they were, by default, identified as part of the stereotypes of Chinatown. Wortham (2005) warned us of the danger of focusing on the speech event alone, and that we need to establish trajectories of socialization; therefore, I triangulated the data to look for this theme of contesting the Chinatown stereotype across timescales, types of data, classrooms, and students. Below, three of these events will be presented for further analysis and were chosen because they were referenced in multiple pieces of data.

Evidence of Positioning in a Chinatown School

The notion of Chinatown emerged frequently at Warner. However, the ways that students associated with the term were varied. The four teachers in this study occasionally talked about their students as "well behaved" and "smart," in comparison to other schools in which they had worked, mimicking the "model minority" stereotype. Teachers also associated the students with "foreignness" and "immigration," though this was not true for many of them. Students in this school, though predominantly of Chinese descent, had a variety of backgrounds and many students were not Chinese. The complex ways students positioned themselves in talk, on the other hand, demonstrated that students are aware of how they are assumed to be "Chinese" and openly contest this view to align with a hybrid set of identities.

The data used for this study come from three elementary classrooms. After coding for moments when ethnicity was a salient marker in interaction, I conducted a more thorough analysis of the student positioning in relation to this sign. Below I will present three examples that emerged in the data to suggest that students were aware of being defaulted into an identity marked by the idea of Chinatown and demonstrate that they contested these monolithic defaults to express hybrid identities. I chose these three examples because in each example students contest an assumption of assumed ethnic normality. Additionally, these three moments all occurred when students were involved in an instructional conversation oriented toward developing language and literacy skills. These include a moment when (1) an African American girl, Rena, rejected the

142 Joseph C. Rumenapp

implication that she is Chinese (by default of attending the school); (2) a first-grader rejected the notion that he fits the model of antiquated China; and (3) a teacher and students negotiated a foreign/U.S. dichotomy.

Challenging Erasures: I'm Here in this Class; I'm not Chinese

By default, the students at Warner were considered to be of Chinese descent. Teachers, students, and administration talked about the students and the community as Chinese, thereby erasing the possibility for hybrid identities to be expressed. Even more interesting was the dominant categorization of students as Chinese when, in fact, there were several African American students in the classes. Teachers and students in Warner drew on wider semiotic resources from the community to construct a "Chinese" ethnic identity. When the discussion turned to talking about Chinese parents, one African American girl rejected being grouped in with the class under the pretense that "all Chinese parents either watch the news or read the newspaper."

Ms. S recognized the example presented here as an instance of students engaging in critical literacy. She had been studying classroom discourse and intentionally setting up the classroom to facilitate discussion among students. Through the intentional organization of classroom discourse, she hoped to enhance students' language and literacy learning. During this lesson, students were talking about different problems in the world. One problem that came up was global warming, and some students expressed questions as to whether their parents knew what that was or not due to the dominant language in the community being Cantonese and not English. Some students commented that all of their parents should know the word "environment" because they watch the news in English or read the newspaper. The critiques that ensued centered not only on literacy and scientific discourse, but rather on the assumptions their peers were making about cultural practices and identity.

The transcript below demonstrates a close affiliation to being Asian by some of the students in Ms. S's third-grade classroom (transcript conventions are presented in the Appendix at the end of the chapter). All of the students in the classroom, with the exception of Rena, who identified as African American, identified as either Chinese or Asian (one girl was identified by the teacher as biracial but identified herself as Asian). They seemed to use the terms *Asian* and *Chinese* interchangeably in the majority of classroom talk, but in the example below it seems Jia made a distinction of *Asian* referring to a wider group and *Chinese* a more specific group. The initial assumption that all of the Chinese parents, and by extension, perhaps, all parents of students in the classroom follow the news, is rejected on two different levels in the following example (see the Appendix for a key to reading the excerpts):

01	JIA:	Ms. S . environment . for Asian families . they will cause in the
02		Chinese like uhm: news . they always say environment as the air
03		that pollutes it.
04	MS. S:	Uh huh …
05	JIA:	So they should understand this question because they watch the
06		news (2 sec) about the air . being polluted.
07	STUDENTS:	((OC: Students begin asking questions)) What if they don't
08		know? What if they don't watch the news?
09	JIA:	EVER/ every adult watch the news.
10	STUDENTS:	((OC: immediately start talking almost at the same time about
11		whether their parents watch the news or not)) yeah, my work.
12	RENA:	I'm here in this class and I'm not Chinese.
13	JIA:	I said Asian.
14	KENNETH:	It is Asian, Jia we are Asian.

That the students were contesting generalizations is important because it demonstrates their awareness of the diverse experiences in the classroom. While Jia argued that all Asian families should understand the word "environment" because it had been recently in the news (lines 1–2), students began to discuss whether that is true or not. Jia specified Asian families in line 1, erasing the diverse experiences in the classroom. Rena challenged this erasure by telling the class that she is "in this class and I'm not Chinese" (line 12). For Rena, the discussion about whether the word "environment" should be used in a survey to be given to parents and community members centered too much on the notion of "Asian families" and did not fully represent her voice. This demonstrates a default in the classroom in which students were assumed to be homogeneously Asian. Other students did not contest this assumption as Rena did. Instead, the other students took up alternative positions in which "Asians" were not identified as a homogeneous group. In line 13 Jia reaffirmed that she was talking about Asian families specifically, positioning Rena as an outsider. However, in line 14 Kenneth used the "we" to group the classroom as a whole as Asian but with varied experiences, and he seemed to include the term "Chinese" under the broader term "Asian." Thus we see the default to a homogeneous ethnic group reified, though diversity within the group being expressed.

The dominant model in this class was the default of all students as "Asian" or "Chinese." Students, however, experience and are aware of being positioned in classroom discourse. The space in Ms. S's classroom allowed for this assumption to be contested by both Rena and Kenneth. These two stances ("I'm not Chinese" and "we are Asian") index opposition to a dominant ideology that the classroom, like Chinatown, is homogeneous.

144 Joseph C. Rumenapp

Distancing "Old China": We Have Pencils Now

In the first-grade classroom, students distanced themselves from the identity associated with "China" in the sense of antiquity and tradition. Since Chinatown is a sort of museum of historical China (Ko, 2011), this seemed to be a resource in the construction of ethnicity as something historic and not always something lived out or practiced. The representations of China within Warner are not those of the ultramodern east-coast cities of China such as Beijing and Shanghai, nor of Hong Kong and Taiwan, to which many Chinatown students could trace their ancestry. In fact, the classroom discourse seems very much to mirror or reify dominant positions of Chinatown as antiquated China, but with self-positioning away from such a place.

For the young students in a first-grade class, talk about China was fairly common. In one lesson, the teacher, Lee, asked the students to organize some pictures of technology and put them into the past, present, or future sections on a graphic organizer. Things that belonged in the future category were things that the students had never seen before. Things they see or use would be present. Things they may never have seen, but perhaps saw a picture of or they knew about but didn't use would be from the past. This gave students the opportunity to apply critical thinking skills as well as to develop their oral language skills in discussion. As I walked around the classroom, I noted that one group seemed to associate things that were from China as part of the past as seen in the following field note from November 30, 2010:

> One boy had a picture of a feather pen and a girl put it in present. He said "no" it was something from China, so it was from the past. One African American girl said "maybe they still use it in China," so it would be present. He said that "we have pencils now."

The girl, perhaps, had really seen a feather pen, or maybe seen a movie or picture in which she thought the feather pen was in present use. The boy's response, however, was that if it was from China, it was in the past; though the intent was to use the pen as an iconic representation of a relic from Euro-American roots. The boy's association with the pen from China and from the past is the important indexical feature (China indexes *past*). The African American girl suggests it is possibly still being used as a form of technology in China, but the boy responds "we have pencils now." We should note the difference between the girl's "they" and the boy's "we"; it seems that the boy was speaking as someone who has shifted from the "historical" Chinese and is associated with a different group who uses "pencils." He contrasted the framing of his identity versus that of the historical feather pen users from China.

As an entrenched Chinatown ideology, the ethnicity that is portrayed is one of unassimilated, non-modern Chinese. For the students in Lee's class, they "have pencils now." The students rejected a certain type of identity associated with "Old China," that is, the pervasive view of China in the Chinatown stereotype of ethnicity perpetuated, in part, by the tourism business of the exotic Orient (Santos et al., 2008) and proposed by their peer. By implication, they positioned themselves into a different social position than that which is indexed by Chinatown as a symbolic whole, consistent with the findings of Ko (2011) regarding responses of and resistance to mainstream stereotypes of Chinese Americans. This activity, intended to let students organize items into chronological categories, also opened up a space for students to talk about and challenge assumptions about ethnicity and history. Multiple interpretations of the items (i.e., feather pen) were possible, requiring students to negotiate meaning.

Challenging Foreignness: Negotiating the Dichotomy

In a sixth-grade science classroom, the teacher Allison constructed a foreign/U.S. dichotomy in one science lesson by discussing technologies that are made in the United States and those made in Asia (e.g., Japanese cars). Allison is of Chinese descent. She does not speak the languages of her parents and does not live in the same community as her students. During an interview she explained that she was called *jook sing*, which she understood to be a derogatory term similar to "hillbilly" by members of the community; therefore, she considered herself to exist solely on the U.S. side of the dichotomy constructed in class. Students generally had to fall on one side of the dichotomy or the other, in part due to the discourse structure of the class in which the teacher mediated talk by interjecting almost every other utterance. The following example occurred about a half of an hour into a lesson:

> ABSOLUTELY ... The United States wants to be number one ... not JUST (1.0 pause) foreign countries want to be number one but the United States. Did you ev:er see: a bumper sticker on somebody's car that said BUY: AMERICAN? (3.0 pause) That mea:ns don't buy foreign products. (2.0 pause) WELL HOW DO YOU FEEL ABOUT THAT? YOU'RE FROM CHI:NA MOST of you (1.0 pause). Do you want them to buy things from the United States or do you want them to buy things from your native country CHINA? Think about the things that are made in Chi:na. Who can name things that are made in CHINA? (4.0 pause) PETER stand up, face them. What are some things made in China?

As the teacher positioned her students, they were obliged to answer with stereotypical items made in China. This is consistent with the folk view/myth that China is a manufacturing nation (e.g., "Made in China") while the United States is a consumer. The hegemonic positioning of the U.S. over China instills a sense of otherness and superiority, as pointed out by Santos and her colleagues

146 Joseph C. Rumenapp

(2008) and is consistent with the historical operation of Chinatowns (Anderson, 1987).

The teacher in this example also took an active role in positioning her students, most of them, as "from China." While the majority of the students were indeed of Chinese descent, the teacher associated them as being from their "native country China" whether or not they had been born in China or identified with it as a country of origin. The implication is that they should have a certain allegiance and affiliation with China. Throughout the class, however, students experienced the positioning possibilities in classroom discourse differently and took up stances in which they align with the U.S. side of the dichotomy, as evidenced below:

> Because in the United States our cars are made in Japan. They might have some new things since their cars are made better, but the cars in the United States may be made better than cars from Toyota.

While in this example Erica identified as from the United States through the use of the plural possessive "our cars," in other examples students took up the position of being "from China." Later in this same lesson, for example, students oscillate between the two sides in classroom discourse. Below the pronouns are underlined to demonstrate the speaker's orientation toward others. Allison asked the class the following question:

```
01   ALLISON:   HOW do you think your parents will feel about that? Not
02              made in China anymore everything has to be made in America?
03              What do you (pl.) think? Mei?
```

By referring to "your" parents, Allison linked the students' families to a sense of foreignness. Mei took this up with the use of the third-person plural "they," presumably understanding the linking between the parents and foreignness (or China).

```
04   MEI:   I think they will be sad because mostly they have foreign
05          things and then they won't have them.
```

Mei repositioned Allison's "your parents" to "they," a third-person plural rather than a possible first-person possessive construction (my parents). Perhaps Mei was responding about her parents specifically; however, it is more likely that the general "they" was a response on behalf of the class, as she had been identified to respond to the question posed in line 1 which was a general "they" to the audience "you" (line 3). Allison then asked Lynn to respond to Mei.

```
06   ALLISON:   Why not LYNN? (2 sec) tell me why . speak up give me
```

07		evidence . turn around. Don't FACE ME . face them.
08	LYNN:	Just because they want people to buy their things doesn't
09		mean they have to cancel um: supplies from other countries.

Lynn, rather than linking to the previous comment by Mei, used the pronoun "they" to point to the United States rather than back to the parents. She distanced herself from Allison's imposition of "foreignness" above and erasure of alternative ethnic identities. This can be most clearly seen when Allison asked Andrea, an African American girl to respond:

10	ALLISON:	ANDREA? Stand up and face your colleagues.
11	ANDREA:	I think that if they don't have foreign things then their
12		culture . they have culture then they cannot buy any of
13		them things .. then it will be bad for them.
14	ALLISON:	You mean the foreign people or from American people?
15	ANDREA:	The foreign people.
16	ALLISON:	So they won't have anything from their culture? Is that
17		what you are saying? Why is it bad for them?
18	ANDREA:	Because if you don't have anything you can't celebrate—

Andrea took "they" (line 11) up as a more general "they" (foreign people), mirroring Lynn's distant "they" (line 8) (United States people). Allison clarified she is talking about "foreign people" (line 14), now imposing the name of foreignness for the first time in this segment and formalizing the link between the pronouns (lines 01–05 and 11–18) and the idea of "foreignness," which perhaps may not have been Andrea's intention at all. Allison framed the issue as a generational issue by saying, "How do you think your parents would feel?" She configures the idea of "foreignness" through the parents, thereby making the alignment to foreignness indirect. One must align with parents, who in turn are aligned as foreign.

Up until this point, it is possible that the students were talking about people who have foreign things or cultures that are foreign, but Allison's comment projected "foreignness" as dichotomized with "American" (a dichotomy which, no doubt, had surfaced prior in the conversation about car and cell phone manufacturers), to people. People can be "foreign." Andrea responded to Allison's question with the second-person pronoun rather than the third-person pronoun (line 18). By doing so she began to break down the dichotomy by using the general rhetorical "you." Allison interrupts Andrea:

19	ALLISON:	—NO MORE CHINESE DRAGON. NO MORE RED
20		ENVELOPES FOR YOU. Those are made in China not the
21		United States. How do you feel about that? Min Hin?
22	MIN HIN:	Because if you … I will have no more envelopes with money in
23		them

148 Joseph C. Rumenapp

Allison also used the second-person "you," but instead of a rhetorical "you" she specified the Chinese and Chinese-American students in the class (line 20) and thereby reoriented Andrea's comment to be "you" referring to the other students, not the "you" in the rhetorical sense. This is confirmed by Min Hin's uptake by use of the first-person pronoun, consenting to the position of foreignness (line 22). The students became the foreign "you" linked to the "foreignness" throughout this interaction. Min Hin began first by using a rhetorical "you," but instead cuts herself off by switching to "I" in regards to the red envelopes, positioning toward the foreignness Allison had projected upon the iconic dragons and envelopes. Andrea was completely cut off and silenced as Allison presumes upon the class a sense of foreignness (of which Andrea is not a part but is now aligned with Allison on the U.S. side of the dichotomy).

While Allison's lesson was intended to move forward an agenda of multiculturalism by bringing to the forefront the backgrounds of students, she erases the possibility of hybrid ethnic identities as well as the ethnicity of the African American students. In fact, the positioning of the students as markedly "Chinese" and "foreign" remakes an ethnic identity. Particularly, this happens because Allison draws on semiotic resources with which she is familiar (i.e., Chinese envelopes and dragons). Thus, the classroom incorporates the same semiotic cohesion found in Warner and in the wider Chinatown that assumes a homogeneous ethnic identity. Due to the limiting positions constructed via the foreign/U.S. dichotomy that the teacher sets up, students are unable to express a sense of hybrid identity.

Discussion and Implications

The three examples presented above come from elementary students in classrooms in a U.S. Chinatown. Students were positioned into default categories that extend the metaphors and functions of the community into the classrooms. Students were seen as part of the Chinatown model; however, they took up positions to complicate this dominant model. Rena, for example, overtly expressed that she is not Chinese and, by implication, recognized that the dominant discourse of the classroom centers on the assumption that all of the students are Chinese. Meanwhile, Kenneth challenged the assumption that all "Asians" have the same home experiences. Similarly, in the sixth-grade classroom, the instructional discourse was used to set up a dichotomy between U.S. and foreign students. Instead, however, students oscillated back and forth, at times challenging the teacher's imposed dichotomy. Finally, the example from first grade in which students discussed whether an antique fountain pen is from modern China demonstrates the awareness that, in Chinatown at least, China is considered old and the present situation of the students in the United States is more advanced or modern.

This study, in line with Ma and Wang (2014), seeks to complicate assumed hegemonic and homogeneous views of Chinese-background learners. Huska (2012) noted that Chinese immigrants studying in an adult ESL class considered Chinatown non-diverse while mainstream America was diverse. However, as they interacted in an ESL class, they saw English as a way to move beyond Chinatown and inhabit other social (and spatial) trajectories. Both Huska's study and the present study indicate that students desire to be perceived as more than the homogeneous members of Chinatown, trapped into narrowly defined social positions, using language education to do so. As was also attested at Warner in younger classrooms, students refused to communicate in languages other than English or explicitly told peers to use English. Implications for research include a renewed sense of examination of local contexts, specifically focusing on the semiotic tools used to mark people, communities, and ethnicities. As opposed to focusing on narrow concepts of culture, ethnicity, and race, expanded notions of these constructs as social practices must be maintained. The students in this study took up agentive roles to practice their ethnicities through social positioning in classroom discourse. Further investigation into the complexities of students in Chinatown schools is warranted, and research in schools in other North American Chinatowns would help to understand whether these findings are consistent in other contexts.

These examples, as a whole, demonstrate that assumed homogeneity in a particular North American Chinatown can be, and often is, contested in classroom discourse. We can find examples of students who contest dominant cultural models and take up more complex identities than the ethnicity that is often presented and practiced by Chinatown as a commodity to be traded in the tourism and museum marketplaces. As Santos and Yan (2008) pointed out, ethnicity can be repurposed, "Chicago's Chinatown is redesigning and remarketing itself through its conscious and concerted use and maneuvering of the ethnic Other" (p. 895). Students, aware of this dominant position, demonstrate a more complex sense of identities and social values.

This research also calls on teachers to understand the complexities of any given community. Communities are places with people but are oftentimes marked from the outside as a particular type of place, and teachers who enter schools but are not from the community bring in dominant stereotypes. In this case, teachers often carry in the assumptions that the students affiliate with China. They have stereotypes both from national/ideological assumptions of Chinatowns as well as from the local expressions. Students and their parents also may have little affiliation with China as such, but rather with the China that is imagined. China as a nation and China as an imagined nation codified by North American Chinatowns differ greatly. While a default to an imagined ethnicity is dominant, students make sense of their identities through social practice in classrooms. Teachers should attend to the positions students take up in the classroom to allow for expressions of multiple and hybrid identities.

Attending to the way students interact in social practice can yield helpful information for teachers who genuinely try to understand their students and develop their academics as well as their sense of self.

In Warner Elementary there was a bilingual program. While this study focused on English medium classes, other students were receiving instruction in Cantonese or services in Mandarin. However, during my fieldwork I saw an "othering" and stereotyping of the bilingual students. In the younger grades, students who had been transitioned out of the bilingual classrooms did not speak Cantonese or Mandarin in the classroom, despite the fact that they had teachers who not only allowed but encouraged it. This may be preliminary evidence for a recursive nature to the "othering" that takes place in Chinatown and has implications for teachers. Students in Warner were in a stereotyped place, affecting the way language and learning occurred in the classroom. The teachers, though not actively endorsing the stigmatization of the Chinese language, could play a role in subverting this system and repositioning Chinese in the classrooms as a positive.

Finally, this study was conducted as part of a larger study (Razfar et al., 2015) in which the teachers were learning to use discourse analysis as an action research tool to understand their students' identities as well as their own instruction. As was the case with Ms. S, teachers can attend to the positioning of students in interaction and can open up opportunities for allowing students to reposition themselves. The conversation about ethnic identity was possible because Ms. S intentionally studied the role discourse plays in the classroom and allowed space in her classrooms for students to solve problems and engage in critique (see Rumenapp, 2013). Teachers working in communities in which students are stereotyped should actively study classroom interaction to allow for students to interact with one another and to challenge the very stereotypes that may mark them.

Conclusion

This study attempted to reveal the complex identity work students do in classrooms in connection to literacy and language learning. While this can be extrapolated to all students everywhere, the particular context yields rich insight into the complex identities and social values experienced in classrooms. Chinese-background students in U.S. schools, particularly those in Chinatowns, express hybrid identities. This diversity is played out in the discursive identities of students in classrooms who experience classroom discourse in varied ways and used classroom discourse to take up varied social identities. Students of Chinese descent exist not as leftover immigrants from China, nor as iconic tokens in Chinatowns. They exist in a hybrid space, transcending reductionist views of ethnicity and immigration history.

Acknowledgments

Data collection for this study was funded by the Department of Education's Office of English Language Acquisition through a training grant focused on improving instruction for English Language Learners under the direction of Dr. Aria Razfar at the University of Illinois at Chicago. I would also like to thank Valerie Cawley for her insights and feedback.

Appendix

ALL CAPS	Emphasized speech
. .. ...	Micro pauses
[ ]	Overlapping speech
—	Cut off or interruption
/	Self-correction
: ::	Vowel elongation
(( ))	Observer notes

References

Anderson, K. J. (1987). The idea of Chinatown: The power of place and institutional practice in the making of a racial category. *Annals of the Association of American Geographers, 77*(4), 580–598. doi:10.1111/j.1467-8306.1987.tb00182.x

Benton, G., & Gomez, E. T. (2001). *Chinatown and transnationalism: Ethnic Chinese in Europe and Southeast Asia.* Canberra, AU: Australian National University.

Chang, I. (2003). *The Chinese in America: A narrative history.* New York, NY: Viking Adult.

Gee, J. P. (2011). *An introduction to discourse analysis: Theory and method* (3rd ed.). New York, NY: Routledge.

Harré, R., & Moghaddam, F. M. (2003). *The self and others.* Westport, CT: Praeger.

Huska, L. C. (2012). *Destinations in flux: English and spatial imaginaries in Chicago's Chinatown* (Unpublished master's thesis). University of Chicago, Chicago.

Ko, J. L. (2011). *Cultural representations and museums: The construction of ethnicity in Chicago's Chinatown* (Doctoral dissertation). Available from Pro-Quest Dissertation and Thesis database. (UMI No. 3462810)

Kumashiro, K. K. (2006). Toward an anti-oppressive theory of Asian Americans and Pacific Islanders in education. *Race, Ethnicity and Education, 9*(1), 129–135. doi: 10.1080/13613320500490879

Kwong, P. (1996). *The new Chinatown.* New York, NY: Hill & Wang.

Kwong, P., & Miščević, D. (2005). *Chinese America: The untold story of America's oldest new community.* New York, NY: The New Press.

Lee, S. J. (2009). *Unraveling the "model minority" stereotype: Listening to Asian American youth* (2nd ed.). New York, NY: Teachers College Press.

Lew, J. (2004). The "other" story of model minorities: Korean American high school dropouts in an urban context. *Anthropology and Education Quarterly, 35*(3), 303–323. doi: 10.1525/aeq.2004.35.3.303

Lu, X. (2001). Bicultural identity development and Chinese community formation: An ethnographic study of Chinese schools in Chicago. *Howard Journal of Communications, 12*(4), 203–220. doi: 10.1080/106461701753287723

Ma, W., & Wang, C. (Eds.). (2014). *Learner's privilege and responsibility: A critical examination of the experiences and perspectives of learners from Chinese backgrounds in the United States.* Charlotte, NC: Information Age.

Ng, J. C., Lee, S. S., & Pak, Y. K. (2007). Contesting the model minority and perpetual foreigner stereotypes: A critical review of literature on Asian Americans in education. *Review of Research in Education, 31*(1), 95–130. doi:10.3102/0091732X07300046095

Park, C. C., Endo, R., Lee, S. J., & Rong, X. L. (2007). *Asian American education: Acculturation, literacy development, and learning. Research on the education of Asian Pacific Americans.* Charlotte, NC: Information Age.

Razfar, A., Troiano, B., Nasir, A., Yang, E., Rumenapp, J. C., & Torres, Z. (2015). Teachers' language ideologies in classroom practices: Using English learners' linguistic capital to socially re-organize learning. In P. Smith (Ed.), *Handbook of research on cross-cultural approaches to language and literacy development* (pp. 261–298). Hershey, PA: IGI Global.

Rumenapp, J. C. (2013). *RE-positioning English learners in teacher development: A language ideologies approach to urban education* (Doctoral dissertation). Retrieved from http://gradworks.umi.com/36/04/3604079.html

Santos, C. A., Belhassen, Y., & Caton, K. (2008). Reimagining Chinatown: An analysis of tourism discourse. *Tourism Management, 29*(5), 1002–1012. doi:10.1016/j.tourman.2008.01.002

Santos, C. A., & Yan, G. (2008). Representational politics in Chinatown: The ethnic other. *Annals of Tourism Research, 35*(4), 879–899. doi:10.1016/j.annals.2008.06.006

Teranishi, R. T. (2002). Asian Pacific Americans and critical race theory: An examination of school racial climate. *Equity and Excellence in Education, 35*(2), 144–154. doi:10.1080/713845281

van Dijk, T. A. (2001). Critical discourse analysis. In D. Schiffrin, D. Tannen, & H. E. Hamilton (Eds.), *The handbook of discourse analysis* (pp. 352–371). Malden, MA: Blackwell.

Vang, C. T. (2005). Hmong-American students still face multiple challenges in public schools. *Multicultural Education, 13*(1), 27–35.

Wong, K. S. (1995). Chinatown: Conflicting images, contested terrain. *MELUS, 20*(1), 3–15.

Wortham, S. (2000). Interactional positioning and narrative self-construction. *Narrative Inquiry, 10*(1), 157–184. doi:10.1075/ni.10.1.11wor

Wortham, S. (2005). Socialization beyond the speech event. *Journal of Linguistic Anthropology, 15*(1), 95–112. doi:10.1525/jlin.2005.15.1.95

Yang, K. (2004). Southeast Asian American children: Not the "model minority." *The Future of Children, 14*(2), 127–132.

10

HETEROGENEITY AND DIFFERENTIATION BEHIND MODEL MINORITY DISCOURSE

Struggles of Chinese Students in Canadian Schools

Dan Cui

Chinese students are usually represented as a model minority in the North American context (Cui & Kelly, 2013; Lee, 1996; Li & Wang, 2008). The model minority discourse depicts Chinese students as a homogenous group of high-academic achievers and trouble-free learners. They excel in math and science but lack interest in social activities and sports. They are smart and hardworking but quiet and non-assertive when facing unfair treatment. Within the model minority discourse, Chinese students' academic performance is overemphasized while the other aspects of their school life, such as their struggles as under-achievers and racialized minorities, are often ignored. As a consequence, their divergent social positions based on race, class, and academic performance have not been adequately researched. In this context, this chapter examines the struggles of Chinese students in Canadian schools, with a particular focus on the issues of heterogeneity and differentiation behind a model minority discourse.

Chinese Immigrant Youth in Canada

In Canada, research on Chinese immigrant youth, particularly the second generation, has yet to be fully developed. Despite the immigration policy change in the 1960s in which applicants were assessed on their education levels and skills rather than racial and ethnic origin, it is only in the last decades that Canada has received a large number of non-European immigrants from Asia, Caribbean, Latin America, and Africa (Jantzen, 2008). Chinese immigrants account for 3.7% (1.1 million) of the total Canadian population with the majority of them being foreign born, only 26.7% Canadian born, and 2.8% being third generation or more (Statistics Canada, 2011). In comparison, European descendants, particularly those from British and French groups, are from third-plus generations (Jantzen,

2008). This demographic phenomenon, which is further compounded with the model minority discourse, contributes to the lack of academic attention on Chinese immigrant descendants, particularly the second generation.

The existing studies tend to focus on their academic performance or labor market transition by comparing Chinese students with other ethnic groups (Boyd, 2008; Kunz, 2003). However, as McDonald and Quell (2008) indicated, in a pluralistic society a focus on identity and developing a sense of connectedness to the larger society are as important as socioeconomic inclusion—without a sense of civic inclusion and cohesion, people may still regard themselves as outsiders even if they are socioeconomically included. Drawing on the 2002 Ethnic Diversity Survey, Reitz and Banerjee (2007) found that 33% of children of Chinese immigrants reported experiencing racial discrimination, and this figure ranked second highest after those of African Canadians. Little is known about how racism affects Chinese students' school experiences, their daily interaction with teachers and peers, and their identity construction as racialized minorities.

The Study

This study draws on data from a larger research project that examines the identity construction and belonging negotiation among first- and second-generation Chinese Canadian youth in Alberta, Canada. About 9.5 percent (644,100) of the Albertan population is foreign born with Chinese as its second largest racialized minority group (Statistics Canada, 2011). Grounded theory was employed as the main research methodology for its bottom-up approach in theory construction (Charmaz, 2006). Maximum variation sampling and snowball sampling was first used to recruit a diverse group of participants that varies in terms of their socioeconomic background, gender, place of origin, generation status, and length of stay in Canada. Recruitment flyers were distributed to several local immigrant service organizations, Chinese bilingual schools, the main campuses of the University of Alberta and the University of Calgary, Chinese professional associations, and the local Chinese websites in Edmonton and Calgary. After initial contact, 36 Chinese youth agreed to participate in a 1.5–2-hour semi-structured interview. Prior to their interviews, participants were required to fill out a survey questionnaire that was used to collect their demographic information. The survey data was then organized in an Excel database. Data analysis began simultaneously with data collection. After initial data analysis, further data was collected through theoretical sampling to refine tentative categories. Three coding strategies were employed in this process, including initial coding and focused coding as well as axial coding, which was used to identify relationships between codes and categories (Charmaz, 2006). All the interview documents, codes, and memos were organized and managed through qualitative data analysis software, Atlas-Ti.

In this way, the final sample consisted of 36 Chinese Canadian youth with 19 males and 17 females. Among them, 21 were second generation who were either born in Canada or came to Canada by the age of 6, while 15 were first generation who immigrated to Canada after they were 6 years old. Of these, 25 youth had immigrant parents from mainland China, 10 from Hong Kong, and only one from Taiwan. Their ages ranged between 15–25 years, which fit the universal youth definition by the United Nations (UNESCO, n.d.). Except for a few participants who were still in senior high school, the majority of research participants were university students. Their average age was 19.2 years. These youth came from diverse family backgrounds. Their parents' occupations range from university professors, businessmen, engineers, and technicians, to housekeepers, restaurant cooks, bus drivers, and the unemployed.

During the interview, participants were asked to talk about factors that affect their identity construction and sense of belonging negotiation at school, within the family, and through their formative contact with Canadian mainstream media. This chapter focuses on their school experiences and some related discussion of how Chinese youth perceive media representation of Asian students as model minorities.

Heterogeneity behind a Model Minority Representation

The model minority discourse represents Chinese students in a stereotypical image, that is, they are smart and hard-working academic achievers but having little interest in social activities. Compared with children from other ethnic groups, they receive more family support, thus belonging to a group of privileged and advantaged students in academic competition. However, interview data from my study with first- and second-generation Chinese Canadian youth revealed a different story.

Are They All Academic Achievers?

Participants in the study included not only high achievers who were accepted by those very academically competitive schools or programs such as the Academic Challenge (AC) program and International Baccalaureate (IB) program, but also under-achievers whose struggle with schooling was often silenced by the model minority discourse. On the one extreme end of the continuum in terms of academic performance, there were some Chinese students who proudly called themselves "IB students." Students in the IB program enjoyed the benefits of small class size and teachers' favorable attitudes and treatment. They had their own social group which was distinguished from those in the regular track. They perceived themselves as being cool, special, and goal-oriented winners in the academic competition. As described by Catherine, who was a former IB student and a university student during the time of interview:

> In X [school], people group. I was in the IB program so I pretty stuck with all the kids [in that program] … As an IB kid, we pretty much stuck together from Grade 10 to 12 because unlike the regular stream, you got stuck with them. Another thing with IB is everyone is going for a goal and doing well in school. On that sense, you get along for sure.

However, on the other extreme end, there were Chinese students who had no interest in schoolwork, or had poor school performance due to many interrelated factors such as language barriers. Sam was a case in point. At the age of 14, he immigrated with his mother to Canada while his father stayed in mainland China running the family business. During the time of interview, Sam was a senior high student who had stayed in Canada for 2.5 years, but still struggled with English proficiency. Unlike his other Chinese peers, he was not in the IB program but streamed to English 20-2 with an English score below 50. Although being pushed by his mother to work hard, he acknowledged that he had no interest in study. Instead, he enjoyed spending his day hanging out with older boys, playing cards, and eating hot-pot. He scornfully laughed at his school peers who competed for marks which he believed were meaningless. Rather than being a shy and obedient Chinese boy as represented in the model minority discourse, Sam also believed he was unique and "cool," in talking back to school teachers in class.

The above two contrasting examples indicate that not all the Chinese students are highly motivated learners with great interest and passion in study. Sam is such a case. Coming from a wealthy family background, he acknowledged that he had no worries about his future. In addition to this family factor, his low motivation in learning also resulted from his struggle with English fluency and lack of necessary guidance and school support. Being disappointed by his academic performance, Sam began to develop a resistant attitude towards schoolwork and teachers, which would further entrench him in the malicious cycle of low-achievers. Similarly, drawing on the data from the National Assessment of Educational Progress Reading Report Card between 1998 and 2003, Li (2008) revealed that in some American states Asian students have lower achievement levels than other minority groups. She cautioned that the model minority discourse which highlighted Asian students' academic success may deny the struggles of under-achievers, thereby preventing school administrators, teachers, and policymakers from helping out these disadvantaged students (Cui & Kelly, 2013).

Having Little Interest in Social Activities and Privileged with Parental Support?

In November 2010, Canada's leading news magazine, *Maclean's*, published an article entitled "Too Asian?" which best manifested a variety of racial stereotypes about Asian students (Cui & Kelly, 2013). More specifically, the "Too Asian?"

article argued that Asian students' academic achievements were closely associated with an incomplete and one-dimensional lifestyle—an unbalanced focus on academic work at the sacrifice of social activities. This article said:

> The focus on academics was often to the exclusion of social interaction. 'The kids were getting 98 per cent but they didn't have other skills,' she [a guidance counselor] says. 'Their parents would come in and write in the résumé letters that they were in clubs. But the kids weren't able to do anything in those clubs because they were academically focused.
>
> *(Findlay & Köhler, 2010, p. 78)*

The publication of this "Too Asian?" article coincidentally happened during the later stage of my data collection. Therefore, I asked participants to read this article and voice their opinions during the interview. Monica's comments represented the majority of the participants' responses. As she said: "When I first read this, my feeling was that a lot of the comments are stereotypical Asian, not all of us are like that, like not all of us just study and have no social life at all." As well, Joe recalled his social activities as a member of stage crew in high school:

> I was in that crew where we would set up lights, sound system and all that... . Lots of time commitment ... sometimes the auditorium gets used on the weekend. You have to make it to school and then set everything up 30 minutes before start-up. So that's what I was involved in.

Against the stereotypical image that Chinese students are only academically focused, participants indicated their active involvement in the school basketball team, music band, student organizations such as debate club and church activities. Apart from problematizing Chinese students as "anti-social" type of people, the "Too Asian?" article also depicted them as spoiled children who were privileged with unequal parental support in the academic competition with their White peers. It is worthwhile to note that such discourse totally ignored the divergent socioeconomic backgrounds that Chinese students come from (Cui & Kelly, 2013). Not every Chinese parent has the linguistic and cultural capital as well as time and energy to help their children in the way as indicated by the "Too Asian?" article. In fact, existing research reported that racialized minority immigrants might have encountered many institutional and systemic barriers in entering into the Canadian labor market, such as language barriers, and non-recognition or devaluation of their foreign credentials (Guo, 2013). Some participants indicated their immigrant parents took several lower-paid part-time jobs in the service industries in order to make ends meet, thus having limited involvement and time commitment in their schoolwork. Not to mention those parents who themselves also struggled with language barriers. Jerry, a top student

158 Dan Cui

from an academically competitive school, noted that he seldom saw his father at home during the school year, because his father was a cook at a local Chinese restaurant who had to work very late every day. Jerry's mother was a housewife with little knowledge of English. Nobody in his family could help him with schoolwork, except himself. Attributing Chinese students' academic achievement to the extra parental support they were claimed to receive, as one participant sharply critiqued, aims to "deny your efforts."

Differentiation in Social Interaction with Teachers and Peers

Another issue with model minority discourse is that by highlighting the academic achievement of Chinese students, it silences their various struggles at school. One of the major difficulties that many Chinese students experience is the differentiation and exclusion along the racial line, particularly during their social interaction with teachers and peers (Cui, 2011, 2015).

Hidden Curriculum in Class

Henry, Tator, Mattis, and Rees (2006) indicated that "one of the most difficult aspects of racism to isolate and identify is hidden curriculum" (p. 204). *Hidden curriculum* refers to the unintended outcomes of the schooling process in which students learn in a tacit way about school norms, values, and their places (McLaren, 2003; Wotherspoon, 2009). It is manifested in the hidden message that teachers deliver to students through their eye contact, body language, expectation, grade marking, and the like. The model minority discourse highlights Chinese students' academic strength in science while the flip side of such stereotypes is the assumption that they are problematic English learners. Some teachers may draw on such a racial stereotype to form their expectation of Chinese students' academic performance in English class. Barbara, a Canadian-born Chinese student noted that she was disappointed at her English teacher's low expectation of her. As she relayed:

> I don't know if they [teachers] did it consciously but I guess they did make a distinction between the different races, I guess kind of by expectation. Like they expect the Chinese students to do well but they also expect them to be bad in English and stuff. I'm pretty sure like in Social and Humanities, I think they kind of come in with the perception that you're going to do bad because you don't really speak the language.... I think White teachers are probably the worst for it. They can be a little more prejudiced especially for classes like English and Social and World Literature and everything. They kind of pick on the people that they don't think are as good too. I think a lot of people don't like those kinds of classes. The teacher has a lot of control and they can pick on you.

Similarly, Andrew shared his observation of how the racial stereotype that Chinese students are not good at sports affected teachers' expectation of Chinese students' performance in physical education class:

> A lot of students weren't expected to reach the same level as a lot of the White kids just like for resistance training, they were pushed further than we were. The teacher was basically like their expectation of you wasn't as great.

As Fleras and Elliott (2007) noted, "racism is so naturalized in history and society that it constantly finds new and complex forms of expression by making itself more invisible" (p. 54). The two examples on hidden curriculum reveal that racism can be as invisible as teachers' expectation in affecting Chinese students' self-esteem and confidence in English and physical education class (Cui, 2011).

Peer Exclusion along the Racial Line

Canada's multiculturalism policy has been implemented over 40 years; however, racial discrimination that was deeply rooted in Canadian history does not disappear with the initiation of multiculturalism policy; rather, it has been continually reproduced in the contemporary Canadian society, particularly in major social institutions such as school. Participants in my study revealed the difficult time for them to be accepted by local students at school (Cui, 2011).

Michael once moved with his immigrant parents to a small town in Alberta and spent his junior high school year there. As the only Chinese student in that school, he recalled being excluded from team projects in social studies class, and being addressed with racial slurs, such as "Chinaman" and "Chink."

> There was one time in the social studies class we all had to assemble into groups. Basically all the White kids got into groups and I was basically forced to be excluded from any of the groups … eventually I got into a group and then they started piling all the work to me.

Similarly, Catherine described the teasing that bothered her in an urban school.

> There were always teasing from students. The low chances are like, *Me Chinese Me no Dumb*. I cannot remember what other part of the teasing was but that always bugs me. They do actions. It really, really bugs me because it made fun of Chinese people.

The exclusion and discrimination that Chinese students encountered at school is not a recent phenomenon but has a long history in Canadian society (Cui, 2011). During the early decades of the twentieth century, Chinese children experienced

160 Dan Cui

school segregation in British Columbia in the name of the so-called health and moral threat that they presumably posed to White students (Stanley, 2011). Chinese people were viewed as an uncivilized and heathen population, thus inferior to Europeans (Anderson, 1991). The ideology of White supremacy was not simply a popular discourse that was prevalent in local media, but more importantly, it was constructed as school knowledge that was used to educate the younger generations of Canadians. Stanley (2011) argued that for the British Columbia students, that the "Chinese had different characters and qualities than whites was something that they learned at the same time that they learned how to read. That 'the Chinese' were aliens and not 'Canadian' was shown to be natural and obvious" (p. 112). Nearly 100 years has passed; however, the legacy of White supremacy did not disappear in history. The narratives by Michael and Catherine clearly showed that racism has been discursively maintained and reproduced in the school field and has continually affected the social interactions between Chinese students and students from the White dominant group, no matter how well they have achieved academically.

Intragroup Differentiation

Notably, racial discrimination not only manifests as a differentiation between the dominant White group and racialized minorities, but also exists as an intragroup distinction among Chinese students themselves (Cui, 2015). More specifically, it functions via the identity label of *FOB (fresh off the boat)*. This term is particularly used by those more culturally assimilated second-generation people to refer to their newcomer Chinese peers who may still maintain their ethnic cultural characteristics in terms of ways of dressing, talking, and doing. For Jessica, a Canadian-born Chinese (CBC), a FOB is a person who speaks Mandarin with other Chinese students rather than English, who eats Chinese food and watches Chinese movies, and who is dressed and acts in a more Asian way and cares about what happens in his or her home country. Briefly speaking, compared with those who are more "Canadianized" (quotes from participants), a FOB is viewed as culturally aberrant from the so-called Canadian norms. As a result, participants, especially CBC, indicated that they would maintain a distance from FOBs. As Angela said, "I'm not very good friends with many FOBs... . Naturally there's a stigma with FOBs being not that cool or I don't know how to describe it, culturally not with it." Barbara noted that the identity label of FOB pushed her away from associating with Chinese cultural practices such as Chinese television and music. She explained that although FOB peers she met were generally very nice people, they were not welcomed or accepted by the dominant White group. As she revealed, "if you talked to the White society, they are just like, oh, they are really *weird*. So because of that, I kind of push myself away from that kind of identity."

Drawing on Bourdieu's theoretical concepts of habitus (1994), I argue that the identity label of FOB demonstrates an intragroup differentiation and a form of

Model Minority Discourse: Students' Struggles **161**

"racialized habitus" of social agents (Cui, 2015). *Habitus*, for Bourdieu, refers to a system of durable dispositions that generate perceptions and practices. To build on Bourdieu, I raised a concept of racialized habitus, which functions as social agents' schemes of perception that ensure the active presence and constancy of racism over time. More specifically, the intragroup differentiation that some CBC students called their newcomer peers as FOB best demonstrated the function of racialized habitus of the former group. As Bourdieu (1984) argued, "social identity lies in difference, and difference is asserted against what is closest, which represents the greatest threat" (p. 479). By making a distinction from FOB, CBC used this identity label to strategically mobilize their social positions in the field of racial hierarchy. In so doing, they unwittingly accepted the legitimacy of devalued Chinese cultural heritage and its associated Chinese identity based on the criteria imposed by the White dominant group. In seeking their membership in the dominant group, they have discursively reinforced a belief of their own racial inferiority via the identity label of FOB.

Conclusion

This chapter critically examines the issues of heterogeneity and differentiation among Chinese students in Canada against a stereotypical model minority representation. Central to the model minority discourse is the essentialist view that treats Chinese students as a group of academic achievers who are hardworking, quiet, obedient, and excel in science but lack interest in social interaction (Lee, 1996; Li & Wang, 2008). My study with first- and second-generation Chinese immigrant youth in Canada reveals that the model minority discourse obfuscates the needs of under-achievers, ignores a variety of social activities and interests in which Chinese students engage, and disguises their struggles as racialized minorities at school. Particularly, my study calls for academic attention that racism does not disappear in history but has been continually maintained, reinforced, and reproduced in contemporary Canadian society. It may be manifested in the pathological media representation that derides Chinese students as socially deficient and deviant but academically privileged with extra parental support. What is made absent from such discourse is a variety of institutional and systemic barriers that Chinese immigrant parents faced in making a living in a new environment as well as their divergent capacities and resources in helping their children with schoolwork. Also, Chinese students as a heterogeneous group have divergent interests in school subjects, social activities, and hobbies. By "essentializing" them as "working-machine" type of people with undesirable personalities and lifestyles, Canadian mainstream media tends to reinforce racial stereotypes and legitimate dominance and naturalize unequal power relations between the White dominant group and racialized minorities. The purpose of such media discourse as shown in the "Too Asian?" article is not simply to construct an undesirable social identity for Asian students; more importantly, it is to attack their hard-earned educational opportunities and to prevent them from accessing postsecondary institutions (Cui & Kelly, 2013). The function of media as an ideological status apparatus (Althusser, 1971) which is used by the dominant group to protect their privilege and domination cannot be ignored.

Furthermore, the contemporary forms of racism may be manifested as hidden curriculum and racialized habitus in the educational field. Teachers' low expectation of Chinese students' academic potentials in subjects such as English and physical education, may affect their self-confidence and, accordingly, their actual performance in these classes as a result of self-fulfilling prophecy. The differentiation along the racial line not only exists in the social interaction between students and teachers but also among students themselves. Theoretically, I raised a concept of "racialized habitus" which could better explain how students internalize racist social structures as a kind of acquired social dispositions that inform their present and future actions towards racialized minorities. The racialized habitus may function as an inter-group exclusion of White students against their Chinese peers as well as an intra-group distinction among the Chinese students themselves, as shown in the identity label of FOB. The term *FOB* assumes that there is only one legitimate Canadian culture and Canadian identity, against which other cultural identities are deemed as deviant and inferior. In derogatively labeling those whose ways of doing and speaking are different from the alleged Canadian norms as FOB, some Chinese students, especially CBC, strategically seek their membership in the domain cultural group at the expense of perpetuating racial hierarchy in the long run (Cui, 2015; Pyke & Dang, 2003). My study with first- and second-generation Chinese youth in Canada highlights their silenced struggles at school behind a model minority discourse. It calls for more academic attention on the reproduction of racism in the educational field.

References

Althusser, L. (1971). Ideology and ideological state apparatuses. In L. Althusser (Ed.), *Lenin and philosophy and other essays* (pp. 121–173). London, UK: New Left.

Anderson, K. J. (1991). *Vancouver's Chinatown: Racial discourse in Canada, 1875-1980*. Montreal and Kingston, CAN: McGill-Queen's University Press.

Bourdieu, P. (1984). *Distinction: A social critique of the judgment of taste*. Cambridge, MA: Harvard University Press.

Bourdieu, P. (1994). *In other words: Essays towards a reflexive sociology*. Cambridge, UK: Polity Press.

Boyd, M. (2008). Variations in socioeconomic outcomes of second generation young adults. *Canadian Diversity, 6*(2), 20–24.

Charmaz, K. (2006). *Constructing grounded theory: A practical guide through qualitative analysis*. London, UK: Sage.

Cui, D. (2011). Two multicultural debates and the lived experiences of Chinese-Canadian youth. *Canadian Ethnic Studies, 43/44*(3-1), 123–143.

Cui, D. (2015). Capital, distinction and racialized habitus: Immigrant youth in the fields of Canadian schools. *Journal of Youth Studies*. doi:10.1080/13676261.2015.1020932

Cui, D., & Kelly, J. (2013). "Too Asian?" or the invisible citizen on the other side of the nation? *Journal of International Migration and Integration, 14*(1), 157–174.

Findlay, S., & Köhler, N. (2010, November 22). "Too Asian". *Maclean's, 123*(45), 76–81. Retrieved from www2.macleans.ca/2010/11/10/too-asian/

Fleras, A., & Elliott, J. L. (2007). *Unequal relations: An introduction to race, ethnic, and aboriginal dynamics in Canada* (5th ed.). Toronto, CAN: Pearson/Prentice Hall.

Guo, S. (2013). Economic integration of recent Chinese immigrants in Canada's second-tier cities: The triple glass effect and immigrants' downward social mobility. *Canadian Ethnic Studies, 45*(3), 95–115.

Henry, F., Tator, C., Mattis, W., & Rees, T. (2006). *The color of democracy: Racism in Canadian society* (3rd ed.). Toronto, CAN: Thomson Nelson.

Jantzen, L. (2008). Who is the second generation? A description of their ethnic origins and visible minority composition by age. *Canadian Diversity, 6*(2), 7–12.

Kunz, J. L. (2003). *Being young and visible: Labour market access among immigrant and visible minority youth. Final report* (SP-581-08-03E). Ottawa, CAN: Human Resources Development Canada. Retrieved from http://files.eric.ed.gov/fulltext/ED505319.pdf

Lee, S. (1996). *Unraveling the "model minority" stereotype: Listening to Asian American youth.* New York, NY: Teachers College Press.

Li, G. (2008). Other people's success: Impact of the "model minority" myth on underachieving Asian students in North America. In G. Li & L. Wang (Eds.), *Model minority myth revisited: An interdisciplinary approach to demystifying Asian American educational experiences* (pp. 213–231). Charlotte, NC: Information Age.

Li, G., & Wang, L. (Eds.). (2008). *Model minority myth revisited: An interdisciplinary approach to demystifying Asian American educational experiences.* Charlotte, NC: Information Age.

McDonald, M., & Quell, C. (2008). Bridging the common divide: The importance of both "cohesion" and "inclusion." *Canadian Diversity, 6*(2), 35–38.

McLaren, P. (2003). Critical pedagogy: A look at the major concepts. In A. Darder, M. Baltodano, & R. D. Torres (Eds.), *The critical pedagogy reader* (pp. 69–96). New York, NY: RoutledgeFalmer.

Pyke, K., & Dang, T. (2003). "FOB" and "Whitewashed": Identity and internalized racism among second generation Asian Americans. *Qualitative Sociology, 26*(2), 147–172.

Reitz, J. G., & Banerjee, R. (2007). Racial inequality, social cohesion and policy issues in Canada. In K. Banting, T. J. Courchene, & E. L. Seidle (Eds.), *Belonging? Diversity, recognition and shared citizenship in Canada* (pp. 489–545). Montreal, CAN: Institute for Research on Public Policy.

Stanley, T. (2011). *Contesting white supremacy: School segregation, anti-racism, and the making of Chinese Canadians.* Vancouver, CAN: UBC Press.

Statistics Canada. (2011). *Immigration and ethnocultural diversity in Canada: National household survey, 2011* (Catalogue no. 99-010-x2011001). Ottawa, ON: Statistics Canada. Retrieved from www12.statcan.gc.ca/nhs-enm/2011/as-sa/99-010-x/99-010-x2011001-eng.cfm

UNESCO. (n.d.). What do we mean by "youth"? Retrieved from www.unesco.org/new/en/social-and-human-sciences/themes/youth/youth-definition/

Wotherspoon, T. (2009). *The sociology of education in Canada* (3rd ed.). Oxford, UK: Oxford University Press.

11

"I FEEL PROUD TO BE AN IMMIGRANT"

How a Youth Program Supports *Ibasho* Creation for Chinese Immigrant Students in the U.S.

Tomoko Tokunaga and Chu Huang

> My *Ibasho* have two different parts. One part is in China, and other part is in America. I always sat on the ground in the garden when I was in China. I like to talk and share my experience to the plants and my pet dog. Even though it did not understand what I was talking about but it still stayed with me and would not be far away from me. The plants and wind can blow away my sadness, and bring more happiness to me. When I just moved to America, I felt bored, depressed and I also wanted to go back to China because everything was strange and nothing was familiar. Such as the language the life and people.

This is an excerpt from an essay that Hua,[1] a 17-year-old first-generation Chinese immigrant girl, wrote about her *Ibasho* in China and the United States. *Ibasho* is a Japanese concept of places where one feels a sense of comfort, safety, and acceptance. She learned about this concept from the Ibasho workshop we conducted, and reflected on her experiences of Ibasho in two of her homes. Like other participants of this study, Hua was born and raised in China and recently immigrated to the United States with her family in search of a better education and future opportunities. Upon migration, she struggled to adjust to a new language, tradition, and culture in an unfamiliar environment and desired to move back to her homeland where she had ample Ibasho in her daily life.

Her experience is not unique. Given the statistics that show a 46% increase of Asian American population from 2000 to 2010 (Hoeffel, Rastogi, Kim, & Shahid, 2012), there is a growing number of newly arrived students from Asian countries, including China, who are entering the American education system. Thrust in an unfamiliar country as a racial and linguistic minority, recent Chinese immigrant students, specifically from low-income families, struggle with cultural, linguistic, and social adjustments (Louie, 2004; Wong, 2010). While they are expected to be a "model minority" with high academic and educational attainment (Lee, 2009), many struggle academically due to the low socioeconomic status of their families which impacts the schools these youth attend (Lew, 2006; Louie, 2004), a lack of social capital (Lee, 2005; Um, 2003), and low expectations by teachers and counselors (Ngo & Lee, 2007; Um, 2003). It is crucial to understand their linguistic and cultural challenges and support the development of spaces where they could thrive and feel accepted, affirmed, and comfortable.

In this chapter, we focus on the possibilities of a community-based organization (CBO) in supporting the creation of Ibasho for recent Chinese immigrant youth. In doing so, we purposefully use a Japanese concept of Ibasho, as it offers a powerful lens in understanding the lived experiences of minority students and exploring the role of CBOs to heal, affirm, and empower these youth. CBOs are important sites that value and integrate the knowledge, ability, and strength that young people bring into their programs (Fine, Weis, Centrie, & Roberts, 2000; Heath, 2001; Reyes, 2007; Weis & Dimitriadis, 2008; Wong, 2010). They have played a critical role in providing academic, emotional, and social support to underserved Asian American youth (Wong, 2010). We believe that CBOs have enormous potential to facilitate their linguistic, cultural, and social-emotional adjustment, and ultimately supporting a more promising future for this population.

This chapter, co-authored by a researcher and a practitioner, examines the ways in which the Chinese Youth Leadership Program (CYLP), run jointly by a CBO and high school, supports Ibasho creation for 18 first-generation Chinese immigrant high school students in the United States. It begins with an exploration of the concept of Ibasho and then it presents the methodology including the description of the field site, participants, and data collection. The main section first documents the students' negotiation of Ibasho in China and the U.S. and then explores the role of CYLP in supporting their Ibasho creation. It concludes by emphasizing the potential of CBOs in developing Ibasho and suggesting the possibilities of the concept of Ibasho in creating caring and affirming spaces for minority youth in North American countries and beyond.

Japanese Concept of Ibasho

This study purposefully uses a Japanese indigenous concept of Ibasho (居場所), which relates to understanding the well-being of people, specifically children and youth in Japan (Bamba & Haight, 2007). The word *Ibasho* literally means "a place to be" in Japanese, but in recent years it has attached emotional meaning of "security, safety, and comfort, or acceptance and recognition from others" (Sumida, 2003, p. 3) to a place. The change in the meaning occurred due to the problem of *Futoko* (school non-attendance) in Japanese education which started in the mid-1980s. There was an increase in the number of students who did not or could not attend school because of the rigidness, regulation, and strong control at school and difficulty in developing relationships (Sumida, 2003). Policy makers, educators, and media discussed how to create Ibasho outside of school (e.g., an alternative school which is free from traditional school rules, cultures, and values) where non-attendant students could be accepted, included, and feel a sense of self (Sumida, 2003). Today, the concept of Ibasho is used more commonly and broadly in Japanese society, which has diversified and complicated its meaning.

Abiru (2012) mentioned that common understanding of Ibasho contains the following criteria: (a) *Tojisha*'s ("person concerned") subjectivity, (b) relationships with others, and (c) physical space (pp. 36–37). Furthermore, Sumida (2003) explored conditions of Ibasho for children and argued: (a) children themselves need to acknowledge the place as their Ibasho (subjective condition) and (b) Ibasho is a physical space where children have stable relationships with others (objective condition) (pp. 5–7). It is where children "feel relaxed and comfortable, have calm and stable mind, and feel accepted by people around them" (p. 5). One of the important aspects of this concept is that it is a self-defined and self-acclaimed place. One needs to acknowledge the place as Ibasho rather than others defining or providing Ibasho for one (Bamba & Haight, 2007, p. 406).

The concept of Ibasho is unique and there is no equivalent meaning in the Western concepts. The notion of home is similar to Ibasho but it commonly refers to "'family,' 'community' or 'homeland/nation'" (Al-Ali & Koser, 2002, p. 6). Specifically for immigrants, home is often discussed in relation to the structures of nation-states such as ancestral home, nation of origin, or a new settlement country. On the contrary, Ibasho captures various physical spaces in people's everyday lives and focuses more on the psychological and emotional aspect (e.g., feel included or not). For example, Ibasho for a student could be his or her room, dinner table, a park, a mall, a community center, a street, or a school hallway where he or she enjoys spending time and feels relaxed and comfortable. In addition, *Ibasho* is a practice-oriented term and emphasizes the process of creation rather than seeing it as unchangeable. As the Japanese phrase *Ibasho dukuri* (creation of Ibasho) reveals, this concept is often used when adults discuss the ways to create supportive and inclusive spaces (e.g., community centers, clubs, alternative schools) for children and youth, including *Futoko* students (Tanaka & Hagiwara, 2012). It is a robust concept to understand the struggles of minority students and to create affirming and welcoming spaces for them.

The Study

Sites of the Study

The main participants of this study are 18 first-generation Chinese immigrant high school students (ages 15 to 20) who regularly participated in CYLP, a program for Chinese immigrant students. CYLP is provided jointly by Central High School and Community Center for Families (CCFF), a community-based organization located in Chinatown on the East Coast of the United States. CCFF has more than 40 years of history serving the Asian immigrant and Asian American community, specifically low-income Chinese immigrants in the larger metropolitan area. The roots of CCFF in Chinatown includes a history of providing family centered services and advocating for many rights for the local residents in the community.

Central High is a racially/ethnically diverse school and has a student population that is approximately 39% African American, 35% Hispanic, 19% Asian, and 6% White, among others (2014–2015). The school offers specific programs that meet the needs of students such as Sheltered English Instruction (SEI) for Chinese native speakers. CYLP was developed from a partnership between Central High and CCFF in 2011. CYLP is offered as an elective course at the school with the intentions of engaging Chinese immigrant students in developing their leadership skills with a strengths-based approach in recognizing the skills that students have in contributing to the community as a leader. The teacher leader of the Chinese SEI strongly suggested for CYLP to be offered at school to keep student consistency and student retention as CYLP was in forming stages. The mission of CYLP is to: (a) provide the tools to navigate social institutions, (b) create and nurture leadership development skills, and (c) empower students to create positive social changes in their communities. Chu Huang who works for the youth center department of CCFF is the CYLP coordinator. During the school year of 2013–2014, she ran the program for 50 minutes for 4 days using one of the Chinese SEI classrooms at Central High. CYLP is treated as an elective course where students receive credits by participating in the program. The instruction of the program is in both English and Chinese. CYLP focuses on a range of content from community centered issues like gentrification to create projects for the community and sharing and discussing about identity self-exploration.

CYLP was initially developed to meet the needs of Chinese immigrant students at Central High who did not have many opportunities for extracurricular activities at school and local community organizations to develop leadership skills. The students often experienced racial discrimination and did not have much voice at school so the teacher leader of Chinese SEI requested a specific program for this population. In addition, there was a need to increase opportunities for students, including Chinese immigrant youth to engage and learn across cultural and identity differences and encourage more collaboration and learning across the diverse student body. In the first year, CYLP curriculum was developed closely between both the CYLP program coordinator and the teacher leader of the Chinese SEI in order to meet the shared goals in supporting the students. It took 3 years for CYLP to build a momentum for students and Central High staff to be familiar with CCFF and see the outcome of former students in CYLP. CYLP eventually became a pipeline for students to continue with their involvement throughout their high school years through upperclassmen being a peer mentor and then an advisory group member.

Among the 18 students who participated in this study, 11 were female and seven were male. All the students were born and raised in China and immigrated to the U.S. between 2011 and 2013. Except for one student who is from Fuzhou, Fujian Province, all other students are from Guangdong Province, cities including Taishan, Guangzhou, Kaiping, and Huizhou. They speak various languages including Mandarin, Cantonese, Taishanese, Kaipingese, Hakka, and Fujianese. They are all identified as English Language Learners (ELLs) given their length of time in the U.S., primary language at home, and level of proficiency based off their English comprehension skills (oral, written, and listening). Their ages range from 15 to 20 years old and there are 10 freshmen, seven sophomores, and one junior (school year of 2013–2014). Many of them are older than the grade they are supposed to be in because of the language barrier or a fragmented education. Most of the students' families immigrated to the U.S. to search for better economic and academic opportunities. As new arrivals, many live in Chinatown in a city on the East Coast. Some students entered the U.S. without their parents and live with their relatives. They come from low-income family backgrounds and their parents often work in low-wage service jobs such as at restaurants, grocery stores, and hotels. Many of the students have the pressure to provide financial support, be responsible for domestic work, and serve as the primary interpreter for their family.

Data Collection

Data collection consisted of the Ibasho workshop, individual and group interviews, "informal ethnographic interviews" (Agar, 1996), and participant observations which took place at Central High and CCFF from March to August 2014. The Ibasho workshop was developed collaboratively between Tomoko, a Visiting Scholar from Japan, and Chu, the CYLP coordinator. The initial contact was facilitated through existing individual and programmatic relationships between organization staff and faculty from the city's public university. The trust building is critical in the collaboration because there needs to be a mutual understanding where everyone is working towards the same goal and have credibility towards each other's efforts and approaches in meeting the goal together. Tomoko, who had completed graduate training in both Japan and the U.S. and conducted longitudinal ethnographic fieldwork with Asian immigrant youth in Japan and the U.S. (Tokunaga, 2011, 2012), had an interest in introducing the Japanese concept of Ibasho to Chinese immigrant students. She also wanted to make her research more applied and practical. Chu thought that learning about Ibasho was interconnected with the efforts of CYLP and inviting a concept that was beyond the American context could be beneficial for her students in acknowledging diverse tools and lenses from Asian countries, which led to our collaboration.

We conducted the workshop in June 2014 using three CYLP class times (50 minutes each) at Central High. The first session was composed of Tomoko's lecture on the meaning of Ibasho and an activity in which the students reflected and wrote about their Ibasho using the guided questions and shared with their classmates. During the second and third sessions, the students created a poster of their Ibasho. We asked the students to draw Ibasho in China, Ibasho in the U.S., and Ibasho in the future. They used stickers, markers, and colored construction papers to create their own poster. The students shared their posters with the group and asked questions to each other towards the end of the third session. In August 2014, three CYLP students visited the Asian American course at the city's public university and presented their Ibasho in front of college students, graduate students, professors, and staff. Prior to the visit, we held a practice session (2 hours). Nine students participated and wrote a short essay in English (about a page) that described their poster.

After the Ibasho workshop sessions, Tomoko conducted one to three semi-structured interviews with all the students in English between June and August 2014. Tomoko gave preference to the students to be interviewed alone or with a group (two to three students that they preferred) based on their comfort level and availability. The average interview time was about an hour. Using the Ibasho poster the students created, she asked them about their childhood days in China, family relationships, school experiences, future dream, among others.

Besides the workshops and interviews, Tomoko visited CYLP programs at school and CCFF on multiple occasions. She observed the programs and had informal conversations with the students, teachers, and staff to further understand the experiences of CYLP students. Based on 3 years of her experiences as CYLP program coordinator, Chu has provided various insights and thoughts on working with the students. We had multiple conversations, both informal and formal, and shared our thoughts, feelings, and experiences on working with the students from our initial contact. Specifically, during the workshops, we supported each other through open and consistent communication and feedback on lesson plans. Our continuous collaboration allowed us to make the foreign concept more relevant to and useful for the students.

"I Have More Ibasho in China": Struggling to Search for Ibasho in the U.S.

The students often expressed that they had more Ibasho in China than in the U.S., including daily dinners, family gatherings, and time spent outside with their friends. Due to systematic and structural barriers and linguistic and cultural differences, the students struggled to create Ibasho in a new country where they could feel a sense of community and freedom.

Sense of Community in China and Loneliness in the U.S.

The students often happily expressed their memories of their Ibasho in China where they were surrounded by many family members, neighbors, and friends.

They felt a sense of community, comfort, and relaxation. Their parents usually did not work long hours (many of their mothers stayed at home) so they had daily dinners and many family gatherings. As Xiao Yu stated, "They [my parents] are usually at home. We have lunch and dinner together. We sometimes go to travels." She explained that in the U.S. her parents work until late at night so it was rare to have dinner together or go on a family trip. Similarly, Qing Yi reminisced about her warm memories with her family, specifically with her grandmother in China. "In China, I lived with my family every day. Because my grandmother always cooking for me... . We always eat together. Because we don't eat lunch with my family in the U.S." The students often reminisced about their experiences of homemade food, grandmothers' cooking, and family dinners. In Xin Xin's Ibasho poster, she drew herself (facing backwards) watching TV alone in the U.S. (with the word *ME*) while she is watching TV with her family in China (with the word *FAMILY*). Her poster showed a stark contrast between her solitary life in the U.S. and her life in China where she was surrounded by caring family.

They also yearned for fond memories with their friends, relatives, and neighbors in China. They often gathered with like-minded people and went for shopping, had BBQs, and participated in various events. Surrounded by many people who spoke the same language and shared the culture, the students felt a strong sense of community and acceptance, which are important components of Ibasho. Ai Qing, Xiao Yu's sister, stated, "Go shopping... . When we have vacation we always do BBQ with my friends. When winter coming we also have hotpot... . And so many friends. And my grandparents... . My father's family, my mother's family, I had two grandparents ... [in China]." Similarly, Phung cherished warm memories of doing BBQs with his close friends and relatives in the countryside in China. He drew a bonfire and explained that they used rice straws to make fire and grilled potatoes and chicken.

These experiences differed in the U.S. where many of the parents held multiple jobs and worked long hours with an inflexible work condition so family time was not common. Ming wrote on her Ibasho poster that her parents needed to work every day so she only had a few hours or less each day to spend time with her family in the U.S. Their family home sometimes did not provide a sense of Ibasho for them. The students often stayed at home by themselves, occupied their time on the Internet, watched movies and TV shows, and played videogames, which led to feelings of sadness and solitude. It was apparent from how Li Min sadly explained that he was usually at home playing online games because "there is no place to go."

Freedom in China and a Lack of Mobility in the U.S.

The students also felt that they have freedom in China to visit many places and are able to create many Ibasho, which was profoundly different from how they felt with having restrictions in the U.S. Qing Yi described, "In China, my Ibasho is to go to the market with my friend…. Sometimes we go to park and swing with my friends. And we go to eat food and drink bubble tea." Qing Yi drew an Ibasho poster where she enjoyed her time outside with her friends and family in China while she drew herself sleeping in her bed in the U.S. She said, "[I drew] My bed…. Because when I come to America, I always get tired, and I just want to eat and sleep. A lot…. In weekend, I sleep a lot. I get up around 12 or 1 o'clock." Perhaps she often felt exhausted because of the struggles of speaking in English and navigating a new and alienating environment. Similarly, Xi Hao said, "I think my Ibasho is in the morning I went running with my father … we lived near the ocean … in Guanzhou…. It is beautiful!" He explained how he often went outside to play badminton and went running with his father in China but did not have similar experiences in the U.S.

Their feelings of confinement and restriction were partially related to an unfamiliar environment, safety concerns, and limited English ability. Upon migration, they were thrust in an unfamiliar environment where they experienced different traditions, cultures, and languages. Phung emphasized that he did not have to express everything to communicate with people in China but in the U.S. he had to, which added more stress. In addition, due to safety concerns, the students did not feel safe to travel and expand their social spheres in the U.S. They spent most of their time at school, home, and their neighborhood, including parks, gym, and CCFF. Even in Chinatown where many of the students lived, they did not feel safe. The girls specifically talked about the fear and anxiety of walking alone in their neighborhood and some parents were protective of their daughters. Importantly, they were not confident in their English ability, which limited them to visit new places. Qing Yi articulated, "I think in China the language is easier for me to communicate so I have a lot of places to go with my friends and family but in the U.S. I can't because of language. I don't have as many activity as I had in China. I had a lot of activities with my friends in China." They have fear and concerns of not being able to communicate with people in the U.S. and feeling stranded in a strange environment.

The Role of CYLP in Supporting Ibasho Creation and Cultural Adjustment

While the students struggled to search for Ibasho in a new country, CYLP became an important Ibasho for them and assisted them in building more Ibasho in a foreign environment.

CYLP as an Important Ibasho for Students

Around noon on a school day, 18 CYLP students gather at one of the Chinese SEI classrooms on the second floor of Central High. It is a fairly small room with six long tables lined up in two rows. Many student projects are displayed on the wall of the classroom. One of them is a timeline of Asian American history which includes the date of arrival to the U.S. for the CYLP students. The students greet their friends and talk loudly and excitingly in a mix of Mandarin, Taishanese, and Cantonese. As they sit on their chairs, they watch Chu write down the agenda and the goal of the class on the white board in front of the classroom and soon ask questions on how they are going to spend the time together.

This room, one of the Chinese SEI classrooms, was an important physical space for the students at school. It was apparent from how four of the students drew a picture of this classroom in their Ibasho posters. In Xiao Yu's poster, she drew colorfully a classroom in her school in China on the left side of the poster and this CYLP classroom on the right side, which were both Ibasho for her. She wrote "enjoy it" in the picture of CYLP classroom and talked about fun moments with her classmates and warm support she received from the teachers. While she often struggled with learning English and other subjects at school, this classroom was where she could feel joy and pleasure with her friends. Li Min, one of the CYLP peer mentors, drew the CYLP classroom and also the room at CCFF where CYLP peer mentors had regular meetings (with words "CYLP youth" and "CYLP peer mentor" underneath the pictures) in his Ibasho poster. He added that he enjoyed the time together during CYLP programs and meetings and the fact that he was able to talk a lot. Ai Qing drew a map of the Chinese SEI unit (classrooms, hallways, etc.) on the second floor of the school in one section of her poster. She said that this part of the school is her Ibasho because she is surrounded by Chinese students who share similar backgrounds and can use Chinese language with them. She felt comfortable being in this space, having "close feeling" to the students and supportive teachers in Chinese SEI, so she rarely went to different floors.

CYLP itself served as one of the essential Ibasho for Chinese immigrant students through providing a sense of community, comfort, and support. Long wrote in his essay, "When I got in CYLP... I started feeling comfortable and relaxed in CYLP." As Ai Qing said, "I think just have CYLP members together to join the activities then that is Ibasho." The students treasured the time together during the CYLP program, doing various activities, going on fieldtrips, and having meetings at CCFF. It was where they could speak their own languages, share the struggles with their friends from similar culture and language, and support each other. CYLP was a safe space where these students were encouraged to talk, not be blamed for making mistakes, and express their opinions. Lili, another peer mentor, wrote in her Ibasho essay, "As an immigrant student, I feel like I am being understood when I am at CCFF.... CCFF also introduced me to CYLP which is a life changing experience for me. I could find myself when I am participating in CYLP." Hagiwara (2001) explained that feeling a sense of self in Ibasho is extremely crucial. In CYLP, Lili did not have to perform to be an "ideal" student but could be herself and felt accepted by others.

The students were encouraged to use a "border tongue" (Anzaldúa, 2007, p. 77), a mix of Chinese and English, during the CYLP program. Chu articulated, "I understand that there is the pressure of speaking in English 24/7 during school hours, but I want to create a safe space where students are able to be who they are by sharing their thoughts and asking questions. I encourage students to express themselves in the language that they feel is the best way to articulate their thoughts and feelings. This was a unique space where students are able to switch between both languages freely." Understanding the students' bilingual and bicultural backgrounds allowed them to feel accepted at CYLP as well as eased their adjustment to their school lives.

Bridging and Expanding Ibasho for Chinese Immigrant Youth

CYLP connected the students to the school, community and the society, and assisted them to expand their Ibasho in the U.S. Abiru (2012) mentioned that Ibasho has a potential in bridging and connecting people to the society. She argued that Ibasho becomes an opportunity for a person to facilitate participation and build relationships, which leads to an expansion of Ibasho in the public sphere (pp. 46–47). CYLP provided many opportunities for the students to participate in activities, meet people, and make connections, among others. Long stated, "Because in this program there are many opportunities to go to other events … how to communicate with other people." Similarly, Xiao Yu said, "CYLP gave us many chance to meet new friends … many activities and supports you to learn English and talking your thinking and ideas with another… . Especially Ms. Chu taught me many many things how to learn English, how to face people, Americans, gave me many many things. Very nice …"

Chu was a transcultural informant who attempted to transform often foreign and alienating spaces into spaces where students can create multiple Ibasho. Chu lived and worked in Chinatown with personal accounts in the community as she was raised in an immigrant household and saw the development of this community throughout the decades. Even though Chu did not share similar experiences as recent immigrant students, she gained insight on the challenges of newcomers. Chu became the cultural bridge between the community and the school. Since the CYLP program took place during school hours at the school space rather than in the community, Chu was able to observe the students at school and connect with the Central High staff and teachers. Chu argued, "I believe by integrating CYLP helped redefine the classroom and learning space."

Contrary to a deficit view towards immigrant students, CYLP acknowledged the students as "cultural brokers" who have the knowledge, ability, and skills to straddle multiple cultures, traditions, and languages. Their view was similar to what Yosso (2005) termed "community cultural wealth," a perspective which focused on cultural strength and assets of Communities of Color (p. 82). CYLP taught the students to feel confident of their language, culture, and immigrant backgrounds, and value their transcultural experiences. Hua argued, "I am proud of being an immigrant. Because even though your local language is your second language but you can learn this and you know more than one language than who was born in America... . If you did not join CYLP, you just feel my English is not good, I don't want to talk to you, and just always be alone, just talk to someone who can speak the same language with you, in that way you cannot improve your language." As implied in Hua's statement, CYLP continuously sent encouraging and empowering messages of being an immigrant rather than perceived them as a vulnerable group that needed assistance. These messages allowed the students to hold multiple languages and cultures simultaneously and gave courage for them to approach people, build relationships, and create more Ibasho where they are accepted and can be themselves.

The curriculum of CYLP had a social justice lens and centered on the lived experiences of Chinese immigrant students. It focused on the content that was not taught in the school curriculum and allowed youth to take action to become agents of change. For example, the students learned about the history of Chinatown where they live now, including the problem of gentrification, and participated in some protests and activism to fight for preservation of the physical space where Chinese local residents have resided for a long period of time. Hua states, "She [Chu] always shared new things about community to us. The society. I learned a lot about neighborhood... . Chinatown has a lot of hotels. Houses are expensive and [CYLP] just protest in the street." While most of the students lived in Chinatown, they rarely knew about the historical backgrounds and the current situation of the neighborhood. They seemed to live in a small bubble in Chinatown without seeing the connection between their family's recent immigration history and the Chinese immigrant pioneers to this neighborhood. CYLP played a significant role in providing relevant knowledge to the students, helping them contextualize their lives in the history, and connecting them to the local residents and the community. It allowed the students to feel a sense of roots and belonging to the Chinatown community, and perceive it as a potential Ibasho for them.

In addition, in May 2014, the CYLP students organized and led a school event that celebrated the Asian American Pacific Islander heritage month. The theme was "embracing our diversity" that featured diversity, contributions, and struggles of Asians in the U.S. This school-wide event was significant as students, teachers, and staff were able to collaborate across units through performance and participation. Students from the Special Education unit performed skits, Vietnamese students performed dances to Korean pop music, and Central High staff and students across units participated in the fashion show. Teachers from their respective units participated in wearing traditional clothes and the headmaster was a highlight in appearing in the fashion show. Aside from this event, CYLP students also created workshops around the history of Asian Americans to teach their peers and identified school areas to display about the diversity, contributions, and struggles of Asians in the U.S. and abroad. They also made morning announcements through the school intercom to share historical facts and pioneers in honor and recognition of the Asian American Pacific Islander heritage month.

While the CYLP students were very nervous about performing and speaking in English in front of a large audience, this opportunity gave them confidence and courage to voice their opinions in public as apparent from how the students repeatedly mentioned about this event afterwards. Through this event, many of the students at Central High learned about CYLP students and were informed of the cultural backgrounds of these recent Chinese immigrant students. Creating more Ibasho for these students at school is not easy, especially given the history of racial tensions and segregation at Central High. The teacher leader of Chinese SEI expressed that Chinese immigrant students were often invisible and their educational problems were not taken seriously by some teachers due to the prevalent model minority stereotypes. These events, however small and minute, could make positive change to the awareness of other students, staff and teachers, which could lead to creating a more welcoming and affirming school atmosphere. Transforming the mainstream is essential in building more Ibasho for minority students.

The CYLP students often explained how they became more "brave," "confident," and outspoken after they joined CYLP. Looking back at the time they immigrated, the students often expressed their feelings of shyness, fear, and anxiety due to their English ability and minority status in the U.S., which shows a contrast. Long expressed, "If I didn't get into this program [CYLP], I am still a shy person.... They changed my personality a little bit. Before I would not talk to the people even in Chinese maybe." He appreciated how CYLP pushed him to communicate and connect with people and express his thoughts to others, and encouraged him to become a peer mentor for younger CYLP students. Similarly, Hua mentioned, "I feel very brave now.... When I first time joined CYLP, I was very shy and I don't like to talk. And now I would like to talk. Now I always translate a lot in CYLP.... It is good for immigrant.... I know how to improve myself and to be more confident and not shy. I think Ms. Chu worked very hard for us."

Chu argued, "Due to the struggles that the youth have to confront in their daily lives, it is important for them to have an adult ally that understood where they were coming from and is aware of their strengths and capabilities.... I push students to focus on their strengths. I try to empower youth through resources and recognizing their intersectionality of identities and the complexities of it." While the students shared many similarities such as race, ethnicity, class, and immigration generation, they were diverse in terms of gender, language, family composition, educational background, and age, among other ways, which impacted the ways they created Ibasho. It was vital for CYLP to acknowledge the "intragroup differences" (Dill & Zambrana, 2009, p. 7) and facilitate Ibasho creation tailored to each student.

We also acknowledge that there were constraints of CYLP in creating Ibasho for the students. Sometimes, it was difficult to balance academic tasks and leisure time for the students. Giving assignments to students was a way to improve their English skills and develop academic skills but sometimes the students felt stressed and overwhelmed from it. In addition, it was challenging to keep all the youth engaged and committed to the program throughout the entire year. Partially given the limited resources in funding, there were constraints in assisting each student to expand their own Ibasho in a meaningful way. However, CYLP attempted to be flexible and creative in supporting youth develop multiple Ibasho in a new environment.

Conclusion and Implications

The Chinese immigrant students acknowledged that they have many Ibasho in China where they felt a sense of community and acceptance by caring family, friends, and neighbors as well as having freedom to visit many places. However, as they migrated to an unknown and alienating country, the place they felt a sense of Ibasho changed. Due to structural inequalities and cultural and linguistic differences, they spent much time at home and their social world became limited to family home, school, and online space. Their Ibasho was often associated with a sense of confinement, isolation, and exhaustion. The short amount of time spent in a new environment also added to the difficulties in expanding their Ibasho. In the midst of the struggles, CYLP served as an important Ibasho and assisted the students to transform alienating spaces such as schools and neighborhoods into Ibasho. CYLP acknowledged the students as cultural brokers who had strength to navigate multiple cultures and languages, and empowered them as potential leaders who have valuable experiences and voices to make a change in the society.

While the notion of Ibasho originated in Japan, this concept could be useful for scholars, policy makers, teachers, and practitioners in North American countries and beyond who work with minority students, including Chinese immigrant students. Schools and CBOs could incorporate this notion in developing their educational programs. For example, a workshop using this concept could be an effective way to learn about the students' lived experiences, including important places and people for them. Educators could use this information and assist youth to bridge and expand their Ibasho in their daily lives. In addition, educators could think of the ways to make a physical space (e.g., a school classroom or a room of CBO) comfortable for the students and consider how to build nurturing and caring relationships among students and adults. Since Ibasho cannot be provided by others, educators should be careful not to impose their values and rules in developing Ibasho. Educators should also consider the ways to transform mainstream spaces into spaces where minority students can feel a sense of Ibasho, which will contribute to well-being for all.

Lastly, we suggest educators teach a foreign concept which could be beneficial for immigrant students, specifically as it relates to cultural adjustment. Researchers and practitioners could collaborate and co-develop and co-lead a workshop. While none of the students in this study were Japanese or understood Japanese language, many of them appreciated learning this Japanese concept. Some showed enthusiasm to learn a Japanese language and culture, in which they already had some interests from watching anime and manga. Others mentioned that it was refreshing and stimulating to learn a foreign concept at an American school where English was the dominant language. While it is beyond the scope of this paper for further analysis, it was empowering to witness students using this Japanese concept to reflect on their experiences and to acknowledge their agency, ability, and skills in expanding Ibasho in a new land. We would like to close this chapter by continuing with Hua's quote shared in the introduction. "However, day after day, I got a new idea that I have to find my own Ibasho and way to integrate into the society rather than people push you to do thing... . I think making Ibasho in our life can help us have a great future."

Acknowledgments

We appreciate Professor Peter Kiang and the Asian American Studies Program at University of Massachusetts Boston for connecting us through strong community partnership and continuously supporting our research and practice with Chinese immigrant students. We would like to thank the CYLP students, CCFF, teacher leader of Chinese SEI from Central High, and Central High for cooperating with our project and sharing their important perspectives and experiences with us. This research was supported by Grants-in-Aid for Japan Society for the Promotion of Science (JSPS) Fellows (#25-4932) awarded to the first author.

Note

1 To protect anonymity, we used pseudonyms for names of the students, the staff, the organization, and the youth program.

References

Abiru, K. (2012). Ibasho no hihanteki kento [Critical analysis of Ibasho]. In H. Tanaka & K. Hagiwara (Eds.), *Wakamono no ibasho to sanka: Yu-su wa-ku ga kiduku aratana shakai. [Ibasho for youth and youth participation: New society developed through youth work]* (pp. 35–51). Tokyo, Japan: Toyokan.

Agar, M. (1996). *The professional stranger: An informal introduction to ethnography* (2nd ed.). San Diego, CA: Academic Press.

Al-Ali, N. S., & Koser, K. (2002). *New approaches to migration?: Transnational communities and the transformation of home.* New York, NY: Routledge.

178 Tomoko Tokunaga and Chu Huang

Anzaldúa, G. (2007). *Borderlands la frontera: The new mestiza* (3rd ed.). San Francisco, CA: Aunt Lute Books.

Bamba, S., & Haight, W. L. (2007). Helping maltreated children to find their Ibasho: Japanese perspectives on supporting the well-being of children in state care. *Children and Youth Services Review, 29*(4), 405–427.

Dill, B. T., & Zambrana, R. E. (2009). Critical thinking about inequality: An emerging lens. In B. T. Dill & R. E. Zambrana (Eds.), *Emerging intersections: Race, class, and gender in theory, policy, and practice* (pp. 1–21). New Brunswick, NJ: Rutgers University Press.

Fine, M., Weis, L., Centrie, C., & Roberts, R. (2000). Educating beyond the borders of schooling. *Anthropology & Education Quarterly*, 31, 131–151.

Hagiwara, K. (2001). Kodomo wakamono no Ibasho no jouken [Conditions for children's and youth's Ibasho]. In H. Tanaka (Ed.), *Kodomo wakamono no Ibasho no kousou: "Kyoiku" kara "kakawarinoba" e [Ibasho for children and youth: From "education" to "a place for interaction"]* (pp. 51–65). Japan: Gakuyou shobou.

Heath, S. B. (2001). Three's not a crowd: Plans, roles, and focus in the arts. *Educational Researcher, 30*(7), 10–17.

Hoeffel, E. M., Rastogi, S., Kim, M. O., & Shahid, H. (2012). *The Asian population: 2010.* U.S. Census Bureau. Retrieved from www.census.gov/prod/cen2010/briefs/c2010br-11.pdf

Lee, S. J. (2005). *Up against whiteness: Race, school, and immigrant youth.* New York, NY: Teachers College Press.

Lee, S. J. (2009). *Unraveling the "model minority" stereotype: Listening to Asian American youth* (2nd ed.). New York, NY: Teachers College Press.

Lew, J. (2006). *Asian Americans in class: Charting the achievement gap among Korean American youth.* New York, NY: Teachers College Press.

Louie, V. S. (2004). *Compelled to excel: Immigration, education, and opportunity among Chinese Americans.* Stanford, CA: Stanford University Press.

Ngo, B., & Lee, S. J. (2007). Complicating the image of model minority success: A review of Southeast Asian American education. *Review of Educational Research, 77*(4), 415–453.

Reyes, A. (2007). *Language, identity, and stereotype among Southeast Asian American youth: The other Asian.* Mahwah, NJ: Lawrence Erlbaum Associates.

Sumida, M. (2003). Kodomotachi no Ibasho to taijinsekai [Children's Ibasho and interpersonal world]. In M. Sumida & H. Minami (Eds.), *Kodomotachi no Ibasho to taijinsekai no gendai [Children's Ibasho and interpersonal world today]* (pp. 3–20). Fukuoka, Japan: Kyushu University Press.

Tanaka, H. & Hagiwara, K. (2012). *Wakamono no ibasho to sanka: Yu-su wa-ku ga kiduku aratana shakai. [Ibasho for youth and youth participation: New society developed through youth work].* Tokyo, Japan: Toyokan.

Tokunaga, T. (2011). 'I'm not going to be in Japan forever': How Filipina immigrant youth in Japan construct the meaning of home. *Ethnography and Education, 6*(2), 179–193.

Tokunaga, T. (2012). *Sites of belonging, sites of empowerment: How Asian American girls construct "home" in a borderland world* (Doctoral dissertation). University of Maryland, College Park, MD.

Um, K. (2003). *A dream denied: Educational experiences of Southeast Asian American youth.* Washington, DC: Southeast Asian Resource Action Center. Retrieved from www.ocf.berkeley.edu/~sasc/wp-content/uploads/2012/01/A-Dream-Denied.pdf

Weis, L., & Dimitriadis, G. (2008). Dueling banjos: Shifting economic and cultural contexts in the lives of youth. *Teachers College Record, 110*(10), 2290–2316.

Wong, N. W. A. (2010). "Cuz they care about the people who goes there": The multiple roles of a community-based youth center in providing "Youth (Comm)Unity" for low-income Chinese American youth. *Urban Education, 45*(5), 708–739.

Yosso, T. J. (2005). Whose culture has capital? A critical race theory discussion of community cultural wealth. *Race Ethnicity and Education, 8*(1), 69–91.

12

OF COWBOYS AND COMMUNISTS

A Phenomenological Narrative Case Study of a Biracial Chinese-White Adolescent

Mary B. McVee and Zachary C. M. Zhang

It was a fall evening and Mary (first author) and Jian sat at the dinner table with their children, Jaden, 16, and Lillianna, 11. The family was discussing Zachary (second author), 18, who had just had his first major college exam and called back home:

> *Mary*: Zach called and said he got a 95, an A, on his Calculus test.
> *Jaden*: Yeah, now he's an A-sian and not just a B-sian!

The family laughed a lot at the comment and later shared it with Zach. In addition to the levity, the comment provoked family talk and reflection on the layers of meaning in this one phrase. The statement, like much humor, trades on knowledge of text and subtext. Not all humor is benign or happy; humor sometimes has more to do with derision, humiliation, or stereotyping (Howitt & Owusu-Bempah, 2005) than an aesthetic experience (Morreall, 1987). The humor in the above statement relies upon knowledge of several tropes. One is that of Asians as a model minority (Lee, 1994, 2009), suggesting that all Asians get "A's" in their academic work. But the saying also belies a painful element of dark humor—"real Asians" get A's, and those who do not get A's are not real Asians, or in this case, are not "real Chinese." This raises the question of what it means to be a "successful" Asian or Chinese student in the U.S. educational system.

The context above is also layered with another identity struggle. Zachary, Jaden, and their sister Lillianna are not only Chinese; they are biracial children of a Chinese father (Jian) and a White American mother (Mary) whose extended family proudly holds to its Norwegian and Scotch-Irish identities. Regardless of what the children Zach, Jaden, and Lillianna (also known as Zhang Jie, Meng Meng, and Lan Lan) may think about themselves, the American mainstream—still largely dominated by White, Euro-American tropes—typically perceives them as Chinese, and Chinese world perceives of the three children as American. Though they have not chosen this space themselves, the children inhabit a unique cultural space of "betweeness" (Bhabha, 2004) where they perform identities related to being "Chinese," "being Norwegian-Chinese-American," or "being American" and so on.

This observation that minority youth perform identity in hybrid or in-between spaces is not a new one. Scholars from multiple disciplines such as sociology, education, and anthropology have written about the performative identities of minority youth in the U.S. in relation to education. Scholars have extended Lee's original critique, pushing back against the model minority myth (e.g., Chou & Feagin, 2014; Li & Wang, 2008). However, relatively few studies address biracial children even though multiracial families are becoming increasingly more common in the U.S. (Funderburg, 2013; Lee & Bean, 2004). This chapter makes a significant contribution to the literature by exploring issues of biracial (Chinese/Euro-American) identity and literacy in relation to schooling, particularly as seen through Zach's narratives.

We frame the chapter as a phenomenological case study using narrative (Creswell, 2013).[1] As such, our purpose is to understand the lived experience of a biracial child, Zach, from his own perspective. Narrative methods of inquiry are used to establish storylines and positions (Moghaddam & Harré, 2010; McVee, 2013) across time and space. Zachary's early narratives were reconstructed with help from Mary and rewritten for this chapter. We also consulted journals Mary kept to record Zach's language development and school experiences. We analyzed for crosscutting themes that addressed issues of identity related to ethnicity, culture, and schooling. To refine analysis, we consulted literature on biracial identity and schooling. The chapter is structured around four storylines of identities performed and enacted by Zach across time and space: preschool, early elementary school, middle school, and high school. We have woven the literature framing the study into our analysis that appears after each narrative storyline. We have foregrounded analysis related to Zachary's Chinese identity more so than his White identity, although readers will clearly see elements of White identity portrayed throughout the narratives. We conclude by considering issues related to biracial children and youth and point to ways to extend the work already undertaken in this area (e.g., Li & Wang, 2008; Ma & Wang, 2014).

Narrative 1 Pre-School: *"My Other Dad Has a Motorcycle"*

Zachary/Zhang Jie was born in Michigan where his parents Jian and Mary had moved after leaving China so Zachary's mom could pursue a doctorate at Michigan State University (MSU). Living in graduate student housing in University Village Apartments, Zachary's life was filled with people who knew him as Zhang Jie, Zachary, or by both names. At home, he was called by his

Chinese name Zhang Jie. His earliest caregivers were Chinese neighbors who were the parents of fellow university students. These surrogate grandparents spoke little or no English and were excellent babysitters. They made special meals of *jiaozi* (dumplings) for Zhang Jie. And later for brother Zhang Meng ("Meng Meng" or Jaden) who was born when Zhang Jie was 2. At church, there were many Chinese and Asian families. Zhang Jie's closest playmate Chris was also biracial Chinese-Euro American. Because Zhang Jie had spent a significant amount of time with Chinese speakers, he was fairly bilingual, and spoke many words and phrases only in Chinese, a few of these were: *baba* (daddy), *chi wan fan* (eat dinner), *yue liang* (moon), *xishou* (wash hands), *didi* (little brother), *tiao wu* (dance), *tuzi* (rabbit), *wode* (mine). When Mary completed her doctorate, the family packed up, left MSU, and moved to Nevada where Mary had taken a job at the University of Nevada, Reno.

The move to Reno seemed stressful on Zhang Jie. As a smaller city and university, Reno did not have a large Chinese community, and although the family would have preferred homecare for the boys, they were enrolled in a daycare. They were the only Chinese speakers where most children were monolingual English speakers. Both Zach and his brother Jaden went by their English names. Eventually, Zachary started acting out at daycare. Each day Mary dropped him off with his lunch, a Chinese-style box filled with rice and leftovers from dinner the night before—tofu and pork, beef and green beans, or the occasional "American" dinner of spaghetti. During lunchtime, the teachers at the daycare would warm Zach's lunch releasing the wonderful aromas of Chinese flavors into the air. Sitting at the tables with the other 4-year-olds, Zach would watch his classmates eat peanut butter and jelly or ham on white bread with no crust. One day, Zach's teacher reported to his mom: "Today during lunch Zach took his lunchbox and threw it straight down at the floor. Rice went everywhere!" Zach could be strong willed and stubborn, but he seldom was defiant in such a disruptive manner. The teacher then added, "And he yelled: 'I wanna samwich!'" The teacher was understanding about this situation noting that it was not the first 4-year-old tantrum she had experienced. The next day Zach took a sandwich to daycare for lunch just like all the other kids.

Around this time, Zach started saying some unusual things. One day he said, "My dad has a motorcycle." Mary replied, "Baba doesn't have a motorcycle." (*Baba* is Chinese for "daddy" and was the only thing Zachary had ever called his father). Zachary replied, "Not Baba, my other dad. My other dad has a motorcycle." This went on for many weeks as Zach insisted that he had another dad. This other dad was usually riding motorcycles or doing something very exciting, but he was also only described as a "dad" and never as *Baba*.

In analyzing Zachary's narrative it is important to consider that Zachary's move to a new environment coincided developmentally with the time when children begin to become aware of race and ethnicity. For example, Maldonado (2013) reviewed research that found that at the age of 3 children "could not

Of Cowboys and Communists **183**

correctly self-identify [race or ethnicity].... Yet, by the age of four, children could accurately identify themselves and others in racial and ethnic terms" (p. 38). While children are more self-aware at the age of 4, Maldonado cautiously reminds us that identity is malleable and not fixed. Maldonado found that the young children in his study were aware of race and made comments about race, but teachers were often uncomfortable discussing differences based on race, ethnicity, or gender, even if they overheard what children were saying. Furthermore, Husband (2012) contended that this colorblind approach is common among early childhood educators indicating that even if Zachary's teachers were aware that this was a racial/ethnic identity issue and not just a lunch issue, they may not have wanted to address it.

At the age of 4 Zachary was becoming aware of racial and ethnic categories, but cognitively and developmentally he did not have the tools to understand or explain the cultural and linguistic shifts he was experiencing or his emotional response to these changes. Naming practices can be particularly identity driven (see Keegan, Abdallah, & McVee, 2011). Although he was too young to process these shifts metacognitively or to articulate them through language, it was clear that Zachary's embodied understanding included a growing awareness of racial and ethnic difference. He compensated for felt or embodied differences by adjusting the outward markers of appearance to resolve incongruities. The issues that Zachary was grappling with were cultural differences (eating rice and meat dishes for lunch) and linguistic and ethnic differences (having a "dad" vs. a "*baba*" and having a Chinese father and not a White father like other children at the daycare). To resolve these issues, Zach would bring a sandwich to school to be like everyone else. Inventing a "dad" to talk about put Zach on equal footing linguistically and socially; Zach could talk about this "dad" at school without having to call Baba (who was not a "dad") by the wrong name. These events demonstrate the beginning of Zachary's understandings of biracial and bicultural identity and his emerging awareness of in-between spaces of identity and culture (Bhabha, 2004). Zach's experiences are also representative of situational identity in which identity is fluid, shifting to meet variation of contexts (Suzuki-Crumly & Hyers, 2004).

Narrative 2 Elementary School: *"What Is the Point?"*

After a year in Nevada, the family moved to Buffalo, NY. This story took place in first grade: after only a year in a monolingual daycare, Zhang Jie was now Zachary, the boy who spoke little Chinese and almost all English. After starting school, Zachary shortened his name to Zach.

When Zach was in elementary school, he came home one day with a work sheet with a list of comprehension questions about the story *Grandfather's Journey* (Say, 1993). Zach had read *Grandfather's Journey* many times with his mom, seated side by side with brother Jaden who pointed his pudgy fingers at the evocative

184 Mary B. McVee and Zachary C. M. Zhang

watercolor illustrations of steam trains, ships, mountains, and a boy and his grandfather. When the family read, they talked about their own journeys, not between Japan and America as in *Grandfather's Journey*, but between New York and China and New York and Montana. These were the homes that Zachary knew—the places where his grandfathers lived. Even though the story is about a young man's journey from his home in Japan and out into the world, the story resonated with Zach's world, with China and Montana, with grandfathers and travel and wanting to be in more than one place at a time. On this day Zachary resisted completing the comprehension worksheet. Worksheets were never an easy chore for him, but this day, he seemed unusually agitated. When asked why he replied in succinct, factual sentences, "Mom, we read the story at school. The teacher asked us the questions. We answered them. She *knooows* we know the answers." Then he paused for dramatic effect, looked directly at his mom and asked, "What … is … the … point?"

In our analysis we noted that Zach inferred that the worksheet activity was more about doing school than authentic, engaged learning. He correctly analyzed and supported with evidence that his teacher already knew that he knew the answers on the worksheet. While the worksheet was labeled as a comprehension exercise, it had more to do with the skill of following directions, learning the norms of responding to questions, and completing homework— all tasks associated with traditional views of reading and school that are disembodied literacy practices (Gee, 2004). Overall, Zach's elementary school experiences seldom called for authentic or engaged learning or meaning making. In this regard, Zach's experiences were likely not so different from some of his mainstream peers. Children of any ethnicity, for example, could also easily lose interest or motivation for schooling when it focused on narrowly defined skills and high-stakes assessments. They might also ask, as Zach did: What is the point?

Reading into this activity, we also posit that Zach's frustration was not merely that he had to write answers to questions his teacher already knew he had answered orally. Although he had not expressed it, his understanding of the book was not just the events that took place in it. The story, as discussed at home, was an embodied representation of Zach's experiences. At home he discussed the images, the colors, the words, and the events. These different modalities worked together with Zach's own lived or embodied experiences to evoke meaning that was also tied to places, sounds, smells, sights, and people that Zach knew. Zach's own understanding of the text and his identity connection to it, were not important. Zach carried with him "funds of knowledge" (Moll, Armanti, Neff, & Gonzalez, 1992) that were overlooked by his teacher. Unlike many of his classmates, Zach had traveled widely. He had been to China twice and to Montana many times. The idea of traveling the world was not an abstract concept. Additionally, the text represented explorations of identity and ethnicity that Zach could already relate to. The story tapped into "cultural maps," "cultural resources," and "social allegiances" that Zachary had a growing awareness of (Enciso, 1994, pp. 532–533).

Narrative 3 Middle School: *"I'm a Civilian"*

One night in middle school while going through the regular routine of reading stories, picking up toys, and chatting about the day, Zachary started telling his mom about his views of the social groupings in his school. Seeing an opportunity to record the insights of a child from his own perspective, and having been trained as a researcher, Zach's mom quickly grabbed a pen and began writing. Mary still uses these notes with students learning qualitative research methods because Zach's description is a good example of an analysis of "cultural domains" whereby ethnographers identify different types of relationships (Spradley, 1980, p. 93).

Zach's story about his fifth-grade middle school experience identified three main groups of students: Pops (the popular students); Outcasts (very unpopular students or social outcasts); and Civilians (students who aren't popular and who are not outcasts). Zach used some words frequently when describing the groups: *greed, power, follow, kicked out, vengeance,* and *disputes*. His storied analysis of the social groupings of middle school incorporated several metaphors. Popular students were like "People who have bread to leave a trail. Others eat the crumbs." Outcasts were like "Mafia—you leave them alone, they leave you alone." Civilians were in between these two groups and included sub-groups like "gossips, trouble makers, class clowns, athletes, and non–athletes." Civilians could "sometimes go in and out of other groups."

According to Zachary, he was a "Civilian," meaning that he wasn't popular, but he wasn't an outcast, so he was not bullied or picked on. However, near the end of fifth grade Zachary alluded to someone saying "mean" things to him. During sixth grade he mentioned that the same boy was still "bugging" him. With much additional cajoling and prodding, he eventually revealed this was a boy who had begun teasing him in fourth grade. In fourth grade the bully continually referred to Zach as Japanese, even though he knew Zach was Chinese. As is the case with much bullying, this behavior escalated across time until the boy, who was White, called Zachary a "Chinese Nigger." This culminating event took what the boy knew about Zach's ethnic Chinese heritage and Zach's outward appearance as Asian and combined this knowledge with the N-word—a word that the boy knew to be powerful, derogatory, racist, and forbidden. Zachary heard the message loud and clear: "You are different, strange, weird, and not one of us."

Yet at the same time that Zach was experiencing the ups and downs of middle school social groupings and bullying, he would involve his brother and friends in playful banter around race. Words that could be associated with racial markers (e.g., "I don't like black licorice," or "I only like white chocolate") would be met with a question: "Why? Are you racist?" Because Zachary's American grandmother strongly identified as Norwegian, Zach borrowed this notion and began to tell people: "I'm Norwegian" because he liked seeing their reaction. Zach used humor to surface issues of racial tension and to indirectly mock those individuals who might dislike particular racial or ethnic groups because of color or other physical characteristics.

Middle school is when bullying occurs with the greatest frequency (Eslea & Rees, 2001), and boys are more likely to be involved in verbal bullying (Wang, Iannotti, & Nansel, 2009). Humor is one of the ways that Zach dealt with these challenges. Shao-Kobayashi (2013) also observed humor in the ways that Jun, a Japanese-Columbian transnational student, positioned himself when others inquired about his ethnic heritage. Humor is important because it is often a way for those who lack power to try to find power in a situation where they may feel powerless (Palmer, 2005). Such talk is also reminiscent of Bakhtinian notions of carnival (Bakhtin, 1984). In carnivalesque interactions, norms are turned upside down; painful labels or words can be twisted and used as a counter-weight against the forces of prejudice.

We do not mean to suggest that this made everything all right for Zach at school all the time, but it was one of the ways he learned to combat prejudice and to deal with issues of difference. He was also gaining awareness that as a biracial individual, he would face different experiences than his monoracial peers (Brackett et al., 2006). After the name-calling incident above, Zachary did finally mention the incident to his mom who reported it to the school principal. The principal took the reported incident very seriously, addressed it with the other boy and his parents, and the bullying stopped.

In early adolescence many children, regardless of ethnicity, struggle with identity. An important point to remember is that identity is not static, but fluid. Biracial youth may consider their own identities as multifaceted (Greer, 2001). This is particularly important for biracial or multiracial children who may feel they are forced to accept a particular identity. For example, immigrant Michael Vaughn, who was actually biracial Korean and White, recalled the devastating impact that the intentional mislabeling of his ethnicity caused (Davis, 2009) when he was bullied in school and referred to as "Chinese." Even as an adult Vaughn still recalled the powerful emotions. In addition, fluid identities are not always embraced by others. Consider how professional golfer Tiger Woods stirred controversy with his objection to being called "African American" referring to himself as "Cablinasian" to include all of his identities as African American, Asian American, Caucasian American, and Native American (see Hall, 2001, p. 334).

Furthermore, Rockquemore (1998) noted that physical appearance is "critical in understanding how individuals develop and maintain racial identities" (p. 204). She refers to not only physical appearance but also language use and clothing. Khanna (2004) found that while the research related to appearance and multiracial individuals is divided, multiracial individuals in her study reported incidents of inclusion and exclusion based on their physical features. As an educator who conducts research in multicultural concerns, Mary was not surprised to learn that a White student had used a racial epithet. Over time Mary has talked with Zach about how people have or will perceive him. Because of his multiethnic features in particular contexts, he could easily be perceived to be Hispanic or Native American. While this could be a positive experience, it may not always be so. When developmentally appropriate, parents should talk to their children about race and perceptions and how to respond to these appropriately (O'Donoghue, 2005; Rollins & Hunter, 2013).

Narrative 4 High School: *"The Communist and the Cowboy"*

Zach wrote the following narrative for his college admissions essay:

> The first time my grandfathers met, a communist and a cowboy made peace. Grandpa Charles McVee, the all-American cattle rancher, who was the grandson of Irish homesteaders, came to my home in New York with my grandmother from Montana. When they arrived, they met yéyé (grandfather) Zhang, who survived the Chinese civil war as a pro-communist anti-aircraft gunner and started a family of nine. When he arrived at the Buffalo Niagara National Airport in late August of 2012, he was only visiting the United States for the third time. Before their visit, I admit to being a bit conflicted about my cultural backgrounds, but now completely embrace who I am and the intricate cultures that formed me.
>
> My ethnicity is one half Han Chinese on my father's side and one half Irish/Norwegian on my mother's side. Before my grandfathers arrived I had shied away from my Chinese side. I refused to speak Chinese at home. I avoided the Chinese holiday parties given by my parents, and in elementary school, I even threw away homemade meals of savory beef and moist rice in favor of the blander, but more American style school lunch. Looking back I had a gargantuan fear of rejection because of a few insults and harsh words hurled at me. I think everyone knows that when you are young, having your differences pointed out can be emotionally debilitating. I had subconsciously decided to appear and act more "American" and began to disregard important lessons I had learned from my Chinese side.
>
> In 2012, seeing two great men representing two utterly different societies, cultures, ideologies and languages spend time together as family changed me forever. I have come to respect what each culture had to teach me. I realized that the knowledge they each passed down is worth honoring and remembering. If it were not for their mutual love of shooting I might have never seen that two completely different people can have something in common.
>
> Seeing my grandfathers shoot my air rifle at targets in the back yard made me have a revelation. I finally began to understand that no matter how different my cultural backgrounds are the similarities and the things that

they have in common are far more important. In a flash I was flooded with memories and lessons that I could finally accept. I thought back to my visit to yéyé's sod-clay brick home, which was no larger than twice the size of my kitchen. I now understood his contentedness and the priority he placed on people over material goods. I thought back to branding cattle and doing farm work with Grandpa Charles. In the summers I had spent with him on his land I learned how to work hard, as well as how that hard work leads to great rewards. However, I had never been able to accept the lessons of my past until I saw my grandfathers sitting and smiling together in the humid heat of that late August sun.

Since that late August experience much has changed. Grandpa Charles died and a greying yéyé decided that due to his poor health and old age he will not leave China again. With the state of things as they are, I feel a new sense of responsibility welling up within me. I am determined to grow their legacy, to accentuate all of them that is within me. Whether it be college, a career, or a family of my own, the Communist war vet and the American cowboy will be my spirit guides through life. They have given me a sense of self-confidence and determination that will hold steadfast for the rest of my life.

Zach's final narrative encapsulates the idea that "Multiracial persons are 'both and neither' of their heritages, and this provides a unique standpoint or life experience" (Brackett et al., 2006, p. 439). As Zach has framed this narrative, it has a clear resolution: Zach once rejected his Chinese heritage and did not wish to identify with it, but now he embraces all of his identities (Labov & Waletzky, 1967). This is not to say that Zach's identity is now fixed. Indeed, as narrators revisit an experience and retell it, they can change their interpretation of dramatic events, even introducing doubt where a first telling may have demonstrated a clear resolution (McVee, 2005). Furthermore, sometimes we may even change our remembrance of the events themselves, shifting both their emplotment and our interpretation of the events (Draaisma, 2004). As an adult Zach may come to understand these stories of youth, ethnicity, and heritage in different ways or with additional meanings (see Florio-Ruane, 1997).

While Zach's final story comprises one structural narrative, the meaning of that narrative actually stems from the myriad social-historical-cultural interactions that Zach had across his life. The day-to-day discourse interactions and multiple positionings that occur through those interactions are what ultimately construct a sense of self, including Zach's ethnic, racial, and cultural identities. Bamberg (2011) noted that it is in the "way stories surface in everyday conversation (small stories)" that "identities are continuously practiced and tested out" (p. 15). This means that while Zach is now able to form one coherent story to comprise his identity, all the smaller day-to-day interactions, some of which were described above, played a part in his identity construction and the phenomena of being biracial and bicultural.

Discussion and Conclusion

There is often a tension that exists for multiracial individuals. Suzanne, a biracial Chinese-White woman spoke of how she received the message that minorities should be validated and celebrated, but this stirred conflict: "But you know it's like, well, what about me?... . I'm not like Chinese, but I'm not like American. Well, I mean I look Chinese, or whatever, there's something, you know different ..." (Shin, 2010, p. 203). Counter examples can be found in other biracial individuals. Veronica, a biracial Japanese-White woman described how she wore minority status as a kind of multicultural badge. "If I had a dollar for every time I was told I looked 'exotic' [because of my biracial features] I would be a millionaire... . Throughout my academic career I had been celebrated as a student who came from a 'culturally diverse background' and could supply something other than a White homogenous perspective, and I was comfortable talking about culture; it was essentially my comfort zone... . Because I had lived my entire life being told that I was culturally diverse and exotic looking compared to my Caucasian classmates, I had developed some kind of superiority complex about my cultural knowledge. I was on a cultural power trip ..." (McVee & Boyd, 2016, pp. 96–97). There is an in-betweeness about Zach's narrative and ethnic identity when compared with these particular narratives.

Based on in-depth interviews with Black-White biracials, Rockquemore (1998) identified four different categories that typified how individuals understood their identities. One of these, based on Anzaldua (1987), is that of border-identity. In the *border-identity*, biracial individuals see their perspective as a unique one, based not in one race/culture or another but as two parts that create a unique additional dimension. This is the type of in-between cultural space that Bhabha (2004) writes about. Zach's final narrative reflects this recognition that one does not have to choose to reject one half, but in embracing both sides of one's heritage something greater than the sum of one's parts is created. However, major works published on biracial identity around practical advice, conceptual models, and research tend to focus on Black-White identity (e.g., Khanna, 2011; Rockquemore, 2002; Rockquemore & Laszloffy, 2005; Wright, 2000), although there are exceptions. Davis (2009) published a guide for educators that addresses biracial and multiracial identity issues across multiple groups. Asian heritage is typically addressed from a monoracial perspective (e.g., Wu, 2002). Notable exceptions here are research by Williams-León and Nakashima (2001a) and literature such as *Half and Half* (O'Hearn, 1998).

It is clear that much more research is needed on biracial children of Chinese and Asian heritage, and there are very limited studies of biracial children of Asian heritage in general. This is surprising because official documents such as U.S. Census data now allow individuals to report identity in multiple categories making it easier to identify multiracial individuals. Asians are one of the fastest growing minority groups in the U.S. with one of the highest rates of intermarriage with other ethnic/racial groups, but overall there is little research on biracial or multiracial Asian populations (Hall & Turner, 2001; Khanna, 2004; Shao-Kobayashi, 2013; Standen, 1996).

In particular when researching biracial youth, there are few ethnographic studies (Shao-Kobayashi, 2013), and those few studies that exist are often limited to survey research. Khanna (2004) calls for studies using methods such as in-depth interviewing. Her study of multiracial Asians contained Korean-White, Chinese-White, Japanese-White, and Indian-White, Filipino-White, and Thai-White participants. In many studies these Asian groups are all referred to under one category of "biracial" or "multiracial." However, not all Asians are the same. Even for those who identify as Chinese, the social, political, and historical divisions shape identities and what it means to be Chinese. For example, one can be Taiwanese Chinese or mainland Chinese (Yu & Kwan, 2008). Additionally, biracial individuals may have strong ethnic identifications (e.g., Chinese, Japanese, etc.) (Xie & Goyette, 1997).

Whether one's birthparents immigrated several generations ago or recently also influences identity. Chang's (2013) exploration of a biracial student of Chinese/Mexican heritage typifies the complexity inherent in many explorations of biracial children where issues of class and community also influence identity formation and school success. Many factors influence biracial identity including appearance, social status, and community interactions (Rockquemore, 1998; Hall & Turner, 2001). Additional factors also play a role in identity development: gender of multiracial child in relation to gender of parents, exposure to non-White cultural heritage, generational influences, and patterns of immigration (Khanna, 2004).

O'Donoghue (2005) found that there is very little research on the perspectives of White mothers raising biracial children; her study addressed White mothers raising biracial, Black-White, adolescents. In reviewing the literature for this chapter almost all of the studies we identified as relating to biracial adolescents or parents addressed Black-White biracial children; this confirms what many other authors have also noted: that there are few studies of non-Black/White children and families (Rollins & Hunter, 2013). We found no studies addressing large numbers of biracial Asian-White or Chinese-White heritage, although we found one study of biracial Polynesian-White individuals (Allen, Garriott, Reyes, & Hsieh, 2013). The studies we reviewed focused on U.S. populations but mirror trends in other Western countries. Studies in a British context have paid the most attention to children with one White parent and one parent of African/Caribbean origin. Britton (2013) writes that this focus of study "reflects the centrality of the binary division of Black and White to the historical development of racism" (p. 1311).

Prior to the turn of the century—just as the U.S. 2000 Census allowed individuals to check multiple racial categories—there was a surge of studies examining biracial and multiracial identity. In contrast, it is surprising to note the relative lack of research since that time, particularly in education where there has been much attention focused on race, but comparatively little research focused on multiracial or biracial students. Additionally, across the literature, it was disturbing to find that when researchers do focus on racial or ethnic identity, at times there is a tendency to pathologize biracial or multiracial youth by emphasizing the maladaptive and deleterious effects of biracial identity by exploring markers of anxiety, depression, self-esteem, or at-risk indicators. The lack of studies is especially surprising when considering that the numbers of biracial and multiracial individuals in the U.S. is increasing (Funderburg, 2013) particularly amongst Asian-American communities (Williams-León & Nakashima, 2001b).

In this chapter we have presented a representation of biracial identity through the narratives of Zach's lived experiences. Clearly, this is a partial representation. We have not addressed the issues of Zach's heritage language that plays a powerful role in identity development (Shin, 2010). In addition, we have only minimally addressed parental involvement in identity construction. We have foregrounded the development of Zach's ethnic and racial Chinese identity but have not fully discussed the development of his White or Euro-American identity. These omissions point to stories yet to be told and identities yet to be constructed. However, the power of phenomenological research combined with narrative is that it gives voice to the individual and his perceptions about his own racial identities. This provides additional insights that go beyond survey research and may serve as an impetus for other studies conducted in a phenomenological and narrative frame.

Note

1   Creswell (2013) distinguishes between phenomenology and narrative as two separate forms of inquiry, but they are complementary, and we draw from both traditions for this chapter.

References

Allen, G. E. K., Garriott, P. O., Reyes, C. J., & Hsieh, C. (2013). Racial identity, phenotype, and self-esteem among biracial Polynesian/White individuals. *Family Relations, 62*(1), 82–91.

Anzaldua, G. (1987). *Borderlands/La Frontera: The new Mestiza.* San Francisco, CA: Aunt Lute Books.

Bakhtin, M. M. (1984). *Rabelais and his world.* Bloomington, IN: Indiana University Press.

Bamberg, M. (2011). Who am I? Narration and its contribution to self and identity. *Theory & Psychology, 21*(3), 3–24.

Bhabha, H. (2004). *The location of culture* (2nd ed.). New York, NY: Routledge.

Brackett, K. P., Mracus, A., McKenzie, N., Mullins, L. C., Tang, Z., & Allen, A. M. (2006). The effects of multiracial identification on students' perceptions of racism. *The Social Science Journal, 43*, 437–444. doi:10.1016/j.soscij.2006.04.016

Britton, J. (2013). Researching white mothers of mixed-parentage children: The significance of investigating whiteness. *Ethnic and Racial Studies, 36*(8), 1311–1322, doi: 10.1080/01419870.2013.752101

Chang, B. (2013). Voice of the voiceless? Multiethnic student voices in critical approaches to race, pedagogy, literacy, and agency. *Linguistics and Education, 24*(3), 348–360.

Chou, R. S., & Feagin, J. R. (2014). *The myth of the model minority: Asian Americans facing racism* (2nd ed.). Boulder, CO: Paradigm.

Creswell, J. W. (2013). *Qualitative inquiry and research design: Choosing among five approaches* (3rd ed.). Thousand Oaks, CA: Sage.

Davis, B. M. (2009). *The biracial and multiracial student experience: A journey to racial literacy.* Thousand Oaks, CA: Corwin.

Draaisma, D. (2004). *Why life speeds up as you get older: How memory shapes our past.* Cambridge, UK: Cambridge University Press.

Enciso, P. (1994). Cultural identity and response to literature: Running lessons from Maniac Magee. *Language Arts, 71*(7), 524–533.

Eslea, M., & Rees, J. (2001). At what age are children most likely to be bullied at school? *Aggressive Behavior, 27*(6), 419–429.

Florio-Ruane, S. (1997). To tell a new story: Reinventing narratives of culture, identity, and education. *Anthropology & Education Quarterly, 28*(2), 152–162.

Funderburg, L. (2013). The changing face of America. *National Geographic*, October. Retrieved from http://ngm.nationalgeographic.com/2013/10/changing-faces/funderburg-text

Gee, J. P. (2004). *Situated language and learning: A critique of traditional schooling.* New York, NY: Routledge.

Greer, T. (2001). Half, double or somewhere in-between? Multi-faceted identities among biracial Japanese. *Japan Journal of Multilingualism and Multiculturalism, 7*(1), 1–17.

Hall, C. C. I., & Turner, T. I. C. (2001). The diversity of biracial individuals: Asian-White and Asian-minority biracial identity. In T. Williams-León & C. L. Nakashima (Eds.), *The sum of our parts: Mixed-heritage Asian Americans* (pp. 81–92). Philadelphia, PA: Temple University Press.

Hall, R. E. (2001). The Tiger Woods phenomenon: A note on biracial identity. *The Social Science Journal, 38*(2), 333–336.

Howitt, D., & Owusu-Bempah, K. (2005). Race and ethnicity in popular humor. In S. Lockyer & M. Pickering (Eds.), *Beyond a joke: The limits of humour* (pp. 47–64). New York, NY: Palgrave Macmillan.

Husband, T. (2012). "I don't see color": Challenging assumptions about discussing race with young children. *Early Childhood Education Journal, 39*, 365–371. doi:10.1007/s10643-011-0458-9

Keegan, K. M., Abdallah, F., & McVee, M. B. (2011). Names and nationalities: Positioning and hybrid identity in the narrated experiences of a Palestinian-American teacher's experience. In M. B. McVee, C. H. Brock, & J. A. Glazier (Eds.), *Sociocultural positioning in literacy: Exploring culture, discourse, narrative, and power in diverse educational contexts* (pp. 27–48). Cresskill, NJ: Hampton Press.

Khanna, N. (2004). The role of appraisals in racial identity: The case of multiracial Asians. *Social Psychology Quarterly, 67*(2), 115–131. doi:10.1177/019027250406700201

Khanna, N. (2011). *Biracial in America: Forming and performing racial identity.* Lanham, MD: Lexington.

Labov, W., & Waletzky, J. (1967). Narrative analysis: Oral versions of personal experience. In J. Helm (Ed.), *Essays on the verbal and visual arts* (pp. 12–44). Seattle, WA: University of Washington Press.

Lee, S. J. (1994). Behind the model-minority stereotype: Voices of high- and low-achieving Asian American students. *Anthropology & Education Quarterly, 25,* 413–429. doi:10.1525/aeq.1994.25.4.04x0530j

Lee, S. J. (2009). *Unraveling the "model minority" stereotype: Listening to Asian American youth* (2nd ed.). New York, NY: Teachers College Press.

Lee, J., & Bean, F. D. (2004). America's changing color lines: Immigration, race/ethnicity and multiracial identification. *Annual Review of Sociology, 30,* 221–242.

Li, G. F., & Wang, L. (2008). *Model minority myth revisited.* Charlotte, NC: Information Age.

Ma, W., & Wang, C. (Eds.). (2014). *Learner's privilege and responsibility: A critical examination of the experiences and perspectives of learners from Chinese backgrounds in the United States.* Charlotte, NC: Information Age.

McVee, M. B. (2005). Revisiting the Black Jesus: Re-emplotting a narrative through multiple retellings. *Narrative Inquiry, 15*(1), 161–195.

McVee, M. B. (2013). Interracial friendship and enmity between teachers and students: Lessons of urban schooling from a 'cracker girl.' In R. Harré & F. M. Moghaddam (Eds.), *The psychology of friendship and enmity* (Vol. 2, pp. 205–218). Santa Barbara, CA: Praeger.

McVee, M. B., & Boyd, F. (2016). *Exploring diversity through multimodality, narrative, and dialogue: A framework for teacher reflection.* New York, NY: Routledge.

Maldonado, C. (2013). *Classes within a class: The discourses of race, ethnicity, gender, and socioeconomic status in a preschool classroom* (Unpublished doctoral dissertation). University at Buffalo, SUNY, Buffalo, NY.

Moghaddam, F. M., & Harré, R. (2010). *Words of conflict, words of war.* Santa Barbara, CA: Praeger.

Moll, L. C., Armanti, C., Neff, D., & Gonzalez, N. (1992). Funds of knowledge for teaching using a qualitative approach to connect homes and classrooms. *Theory Into Practice, 31*(2), 132–141.

Morreall, J. (1987). Funny ha-ha, funny strange, and other reactions to incongruity. In J. Morreall (Ed.), *The philosophy of laughter and humor* (pp. 188–207). Albany, NY: State University of New York Press.

O'Donoghue, M. (2005). White mothers negotiating race and ethnicity in the mothering of biracial, Black-White adolescents. *Journal of Ethnic and Cultural Diversity in Social Work, 14*(3/4), 125–156.

O'Hearn, C. C. (Ed.). (1998). *Half and half: Writers on growing up biracial and bicultural.* New York, NY: Pantheon Books.

Palmer, J. (2005). Parody and decorum: Permission to mock. In S. Lockyer & M. Pickering (Eds.), *Beyond a joke: The limits of humour* (pp. 81–99). New York, NY: Palgrave Macmillan.

Rockquemore, K. A. (1998). Between black and white: Exploring the 'biracial' experience. *Race and Society, 1*(2), 197–212.

Rockquemore, K. A. (2002) *Beyond Black: Biracial identity in America.* Thousand Oaks, CA: Sage.

Rockquemore, K. A., & Laszloffy, T. (2005). *Raising biracial children.* Lanham, MD: AltaMira Press.

Rollins, A., & Hunter, A. G. (2013). Racial socialization of biracial youth: Maternal messages and approaches to address discrimination. *Family Relations, 62*(1), 140–153.

Say, A. (1993). *Grandfather's journey.* New York, NY: Houghton Mifflin.

Shao-Kobayashi, S. (2013). 'My dad is a Samurai': Positioning of race and ethnicity surrounding a transnational Colombian Japanese high school student. *Linguistics and Education, 24*(3), 361–372.

Shin, S. J. (2010). 'What about me? I'm not like Chinese but I'm not like American': Heritage-language learning and identity of mixed-heritage adults. *Journal of Language, Identity, and Education, 9,* 203–2010.

Spradley, J. P. (1980). *Participant observation.* Belmont, CA: Wadsworth.

Standen, B. C. S. (1996). Without a template: The biracial Korean/White experience. In M. P. P. Root (Ed.), *The multiracial experience: Racial borders as the new frontier* (pp. 245–260). Thousand Oaks, CA: Sage.

Suzuki-Crumly, J., & Hyers, L. L. (2004). The relationship among ethnic identity, psychological well-being, and intergroup competence: An investigation of two biracial groups. *Cultural Diversity and Ethnic Minority Psychology, 10*(2), 137–150.

Wang, J., Iannotti, R. J., & Nansel, T. R. (2009). School bullying among adolescents in the United States: Physical, verbal, relational, and cyber. *Journal of Adolescent Health, 45*(4), 368–375.

Williams-León, T., & Nakashima, C. L. (Eds.). (2001a). *The sum of our parts: Mixed-heritage Asian Americans.* Philadelphia, PA: Temple University Press.

Williams-León, T., & Nakashima, C. L. (2001b). Reconfiguring race, rearticulating ethnicity. In T. Williams-León & C. L. Nakashima (Eds.), *The sum of our parts: Mixed-heritage Asian Americans* (pp. 3–10). Philadelphia, PA: Temple University Press.

Wright, M. (2000). *I'm chocolate, you're vanilla: Raising healthy Black and biracial children in a race-conscious world.* San Francisco, CA: Jossey-Bass.

Wu, F. H. (2002). *Yellow: Race in America beyond black and white.* New York, NY: Basic Books.

Xie, Y., & Goyette, K. (1997). The racial identification of biracial children with one Asian parent: Evidence from the 1990 census. *Social Forces, 76*(2), 547–570.

Yu, F. L. T., & Kwan, D. S. M. (2008). Social construction of national identity: Taiwanese versus Chinese Consciousness. *Social Identities, 14*(1), 33–52. doi: 10.1080/13504630701848515

PART IV

Other Sociocultural Variables Confronting Chinese-Heritage Learners

13

A BIOECOLOGICAL MODEL OF CHINESE AMERICAN CHILDREN'S SOCIO-EMOTIONAL AND BEHAVIORAL ADJUSTMENT

Stephen H. Chen, Jennifer Ly, and Qing Zhou

The Chinese American population in the United States is marked by contrasts. On the one hand, Chinese Americans are "old" Americans, with distinct waves of large-scale immigration to the United States beginning as early as the mid-1800s, and again after 1965 (Pew Research Center, 2012). By contrast, the current Chinese American population is comprised primarily of "new" Americans: 2010 Census estimates indicate that over 75% of Chinese Americans are foreign born (Pew Research Center, 2012).

Chinese Americans are also distinguished by contrasts in socioeconomic status and cultural orientation. Despite longstanding perceptions as a uniformly well-educated, high-achieving "model minority," in reality, Chinese Americans inhabit the extremes of the socioeconomic spectrum. Chinese American adults exceed national averages in obtaining bachelor's degrees (51.1% vs. 28.2%), but also exceed national averages in failures to complete high school (18.0% vs. 14.4%). Likewise, although Chinese Americans report annual household incomes that are higher than the national median ($65,060 vs. $49,800), a higher percentage of Chinese Americans also fall below poverty lines (13.7% of Chinese Americans vs. 12.8% of the U.S. population) (Pew Research Center, 2012). In addition, although Chinese Americans are frequently grouped under a single ethnic label, immigrants in the United States identifying as "Chinese" or "Chinese American" may in fact represent a host of different cultures, countries, and regions of origin (e.g., China, Hong Kong, Taiwan, Vietnam, Singapore), each with their own unique cultural heritage. Finally, Chinese Americans may vary in the degree to which they are oriented to Chinese and American cultures. As one indicator, among adults in the United States who spoke Chinese at home, nearly half (44.3%) also spoke English "very well," whereas nearly one-third (29.6%) spoke English "not well" or "not at all" (Ryan, 2013).

The diversity and complexity of this population raise a host of considerations for educators and practitioners working with Chinese American students and their families. For example, a Chinese American student may be a monolingual English speaker, an English language learner, or relatively balanced in his or her Chinese and English proficiencies. Likewise, while Chinese American parents may be broadly stereotyped in the popular media as "tiger parents," the diversity of cultural orientations in this population may also contribute to striking variations in parenting styles and family emotional climates, all of which may influence a student's performance in the classroom. Variables outside of the immediate family context should also be weighed accordingly: is the family living in a low-income or a high-crime neighborhood? Does the family have access to community services offered in their preferred language? Finally, at the core of these variables are considerations of important individual-level factors, including the child's temperament and stage of development.

Considering all of the variables "beyond the classroom" that can influence a child's development and school performance is a complex task for any educator. This task is even more challenging for educators working with a group as diverse as Chinese American immigrants. Thus, the aims of this chapter are twofold: (a) to provide a conceptual framework for organizing the myriad factors that may influence the development of Chinese American children from immigrant families, and (b) to present findings from our longitudinal study of Chinese American immigrant families in the San Francisco Bay Area, with a specific focus on the socio-emotional and behavioral processes that may influence children's performance in the classroom.

The Bioecological Model of Development

Bronfenbrenner's theoretical models (Bronfenbrenner, 1977; Bronfenbrenner & Morris, 2006) are among the most widely cited and influential conceptualizations of influences on human development (Rosa & Tudge, 2013; Tudge, Mokrova, Hatfield, & Karnik, 2009). Most relevant to the present volume, Bronfenbrenner's theories have been extended to examine cultural influences on development (Causadias, 2013) and have also been applied to educational settings (Swick & Wiliams, 2006), most notably in the development of the federal Head Start program in the United States (Bronfenbrenner, 1974; Zigler & Muenchow, 1992).

In its most mature form, Bronfenbrenner's bioecological model considers the interactions between four components: individual-environmental *processes*, characteristics of the individual *person*, environmental *contexts*, as well as the *time* periods in which these interactions took place (Bronfenbrenner & Morris, 2006). In this chapter, we use these four components as an organizational framework and consider how mechanisms from each of these areas (i.e., process, person, context, and time) play a role in the development of Chinese American children.

The present chapter applies the bioecological model to examine the social, emotional, and behavioral development of Chinese American immigrant children. Previous research with Chinese American children has emphasized academic and educational outcomes, while neglecting closer investigation of children's behavioral and socio-emotional adjustment (Qin & Han, 2011). Indeed, while the literature examining the behavioral and mental health adjustment of Asian American youth is limited, a growing body of research highlights risks for behavioral and psychological maladjustment in Asian American youth (Choi & Lahey, 2006; Huang, Calzada, Cheng, & Brotman, 2012; Rhee, Chang, & Rhee, 2003; Song, Ziegler, Arsenault, Fried, & Hacker, 2011). Furthermore, even less research has examined the socio-emotional and behavioral adjustment of Chinese American immigrant children in early elementary school, a critical developmental period that may be especially influential for immigrant or ethnic minority children (García Coll & Szalacha, 2004).

The Kids and Family Project

This chapter presents findings from the U.C. Berkeley Kids and Family Project, a longitudinal investigation of 258 Chinese American immigrant families in Northern California. Through support from the Foundation for Child Development, the Kids and Family Project aimed to identify risk and protective factors contributing to the development of Chinese American children who were either first-generation immigrants (born outside of the United States) or second-generation immigrants (born in the United States to at least one foreign-born parent). Recognizing the lack of longitudinal research with Chinese American children in early elementary school, we collected data at two time points: first, when children were in first and second grades, and again approximately two years later.

Consistent with the theme of this volume, we also recognized the need to look beyond children's academic outcomes and examine the mechanisms that could contribute to aspects of Chinese American children's socio-emotional and behavioral adjustment. Thus, at both time points, the child and one participating parent completed a 2-hour laboratory assessment that included parent-reported measures of children's behavioral and socio-emotional functioning, family relationships and interactions, and school and neighborhood environments; behavioral and computerized measures of children's self-regulation; interactive tasks between parents and children; and standardized tests of children's academic achievement. In addition, children's teachers also completed ratings of teacher–child relationship quality and children's behavioral adjustment. Given the broad scope of the assessment, this chapter focuses on the process, person, context, and time variables that were found to be most salient for children's socio-emotional and behavioral adjustment.

Process

From the classroom to the playground to the dinner table, much of a child's day is spent in social interactions. As such, it is little wonder that *proximal processes*—the enduring, direct interactions between a human and his or her environment—are theorized to be the chief mechanisms influencing human development (Bronfenbrenner & Morris, 2006). Our research with Chinese American children suggests that two proximal processes, children's interactions with their parents and their teachers, are closely linked to their socio-emotional and behavioral adjustment.

Child–Parent Relationships

Of the proximal processes influencing Chinese American children's development, parenting styles and parent–child relationships have received the most scholarly attention. Indeed, investigations of parenting styles in Chinese American families and their effects on children's development are among the most frequently cited psychology papers on Chinese Americans (Chao, 1994, 2001) and the topic continues to generate both scholarly and popular interest (e.g., Chua, 2011; Kim, Wang, Orozco-Lapray, Shen, & Murtuza, 2013). Much of the research on this topic has focused on two parenting styles—*authoritarian* parenting, characterized by low warmth and high levels of control or demandingness, and *authoritative* parenting, characterized by high warmth and high control—and has examined the validity of these two constructs in Chinese American families (Chao, 1994, 2001).

Much of the existing research examining effects of parenting styles on Chinese American children in immigrant families has focused primarily on academic outcomes. Furthermore, few investigations have examined how the proximal processes of parenting styles may be influenced by broader contexts, such as cultural values. To address this gap, we examined the effects of Chinese American parenting styles on children's social and behavioral adjustment and examined how these parenting styles were influenced by children's and parents' orientation to Chinese and American culture. Consistent with prior research with families in mainland China (Chen, Zhou, Eisenberg, Valiente, & Wang, 2011), our findings with Chinese American immigrant families indicated that parents' authoritarian parenting styles were associated with poorer social and behavioral adjustment in children, including lower social competence, higher internalizing problems, and higher externalizing problems (Chen et al., 2014). Our research also found that "culture gaps"—specifically, discrepancies between parents' and children's orientations to Chinese culture—were associated with lower authoritative parenting practices, and in turn, higher externalizing behavior problems.

Child–Teacher Relationships

The child–teacher relationship is another process-level factor that can play a central role in children's development. In applying the bioecological model to the child–teacher relationship, Pianta and Walsh (1996) conceptualized development as a reciprocal process, such that children's relational models may guide their interactions with teachers, while teachers can also reshape children's relational models, subsequent behaviors, and future relationships (Sabol & Pianta, 2012). Indeed, positive teacher–child relationships have been linked to children's well-being in areas of achievement, behavioral adjustment, and socio-emotional functioning (e.g., Hamre & Pianta, 2001; Hughes, Wu, Kwok, Villarreal, & Johnson, 2012; O'Connor, Dearing, & Collins, 2011).

The child–teacher relationship may be particularly important for Chinese American immigrant students. In traditional Chinese society, teachers are viewed as educators and models of morality, and thus play an instrumental role in socializing Chinese youth (Altbach, 1991; Stevenson & Stigler, 1992). Moreover, Chinese Americans share a high value of education and a high regard for teachers (Ly, Zhou, Chu, & Chen, 2012). Consistent with these views, some research examining child–teacher relationships in Chinese American populations indicates that students' ratings of attachment to teachers and attachment to school predict lower levels of internalizing problems. In addition, school supportive factors moderated the association between peer victimization and children's internalizing problems (Yeh et al., 2013).

To our knowledge, our research with Chinese American children was the first to examine the associations between positive teacher–child relationships and children's development in a heterogeneous sample of elementary school-aged children. Recognizing that relationships are reciprocal, this project was unique because it examined the quality of the teacher–child relationship from both teachers' and students' perspectives. In a cross-sectional study examining children's academic achievement, we found that teacher-rated warmth was positively associated with children's reading achievement, teacher-rated conflict was negatively associated with girls' math achievement, and child-rated relationship quality was positively related with boys' reading achievement (Ly et al., 2012).

In a later study (Ly & Zhou, in review), we examined the role of teacher–child relationship quality in predicting children's behavior problems, controlling for demographic variables and prior levels of behavior problems. The teacher–child relationship quality at the first time of assessment (when children were in first and second grades) was not significantly related to teacher-rated behavior problems at the second time of assessment (when children were in third and fourth grades). However, teachers' ratings of conflict at the first assessment predicted higher levels of parent-rated behavior problems at the time of the second assessment.

This particular study also underscored the importance of child characteristics (i.e., behavior problems) in the teacher–child relationship. Similar to findings with other American children, results indicated that Chinese American children with higher levels of teacher-rated externalizing problems at the first assessment reported lower levels of closeness in their relationships with their teachers at the second assessment. Importantly, although some research has suggested that the prevalence of externalizing problems is lower in Chinese American youth (e.g., Chang, Morrissey, & Koplewicz, 1995), our findings suggest that externalizing problems in Chinese American youth have similar negative implications for children's social and behavioral adjustment.

In addition, our study found that internalizing problems predicted subsequent behavior problems and lower teacher–child relationship quality in this sample, which underscores the vulnerability that Chinese American children may experience with regard to internalizing behavior problems. Although few school-based interventions focus on strengthening the quality of relationships between teachers and children, some research suggests that classroom-based interventions are effective at decreasing children's externalizing problems (Driscoll, Wang, Mashburn, & Pianta, 2011). Given that teachers' views about students and their home cultures shape their engagement with children (Lareau, 2003; Yamamoto & Li, 2012), it is also important for school-based interventions to consider how teachers' expectations regarding Asian immigrant youth may impact their interactions with students.

Person

Both parents and teachers can attest that a child's temperament plays an instrumental role in their respective relationships. Within the bioecological model, a child's temperament is conceptualized as an individual, or *person* characteristic: these can include *force characteristics*, such as temperament or dispositions; *resource characteristics*, such as individual abilities or skills; and *demand characteristics*, such as individual characteristics that either elicit or discourage reactions from the social environment (Bronfenbrenner & Morris, 2006). Much of our research on person characteristics in Chinese American children has focused on children's *self-regulation*, or the internal or transactional processes that enable an individual to guide goal-directed activities over time and across changing contexts (Karoly, 1993). Most relevant to this volume, a well-established body of research has linked children's self-regulatory capacities to their learning and academic performance (Eisenberg, Valiente, & Eggum, 2010; Ursache, Blair, & Raver, 2012).

Studies examining the links between children's self-regulation skills and their academic performance have conceptualized and measured self-regulation in a variety of ways. For example, *effortful control* refers to temperamentally based differences in individuals' reactivity and regulation (Rothbart & Bates, 2006), and thus can reflect force or demand characteristics in the bioecological model. Another widely studied self-regulatory construct, *executive function*, has been broadly defined as referring to "top down" or "higher order" skills that involve planning, coordination, and control over attention, cognition, and behavioral tendencies (Blair, Zelazo, & Greenberg, 2005). Thus, within the bioecological model, executive functioning skills can be conceptualized as constituting a child's resource characteristics. Finally, aspects of self-regulation can also serve as demand characteristics that elicit responses from a child's environment. In our previous research with Chinese children in families in mainland China, higher levels of effortful control were found to predict lower levels of authoritarian parenting across time points (Lee, Zhou, Eisenberg, & Wang, 2013).

A growing body of research has linked different self-regulatory processes to a variety of outcomes among Chinese American children and adolescents, including leadership and communication skills (Liew, Kwok, Chang, Chang, & Yeh, 2014). In the Kids and Family Project, we have sought to identify different factors that may shape the development of Chinese American children's self-regulatory processes. One factor highlighted by our research is parenting styles: Chinese American children's self-regulation skills were negatively associated with authoritarian parenting practices, and in turn, mediated the negative association between authoritarian parenting and children's poorer performance on standardized math and reading assessments (Chen et al., 2015). Another study examining children's self-regulatory skills utilized teachers' ratings of children's effortful control in the classroom setting. In this analysis, children whose parents were observed to express higher levels of anger or frustration during an interactive puzzle activity were rated by their teachers as presenting with lower levels of effortful control (Chen, Zhou, Main, & Lee, in press).

Taken together, these studies highlight Chinese American children's self-regulatory skills as a person-level characteristic that is integral to their performance in the classroom. Likewise, by highlighting the interactive relationships between person (self-regulation) and process components (parenting styles and parental expression of emotion), our results also suggest that a child's behaviors and emotions in the classroom may not reflect his or her individual temperament or family processes, but an interaction between these two components.

Context

Perhaps the most well-known aspect of the bioecological model is the concept of *contexts*, which consists of an individual's nested network of both proximal and remote systems. Proximal systems include the *microsystem*, which refers to the context in which the individual is most directly and consistently engaged, and the *mesosystem*, which refers to the interactions among an individual's microsystems, such as communications between parents and teachers. More remote systems include the *exosystem*, which refers to a context in which an individual is not directly engaged, yet influences the individual. For example, while a child may not be directly exposed to a parent's stressful or hostile work environment, this exosystem may compromise the quality of parent–child interactions at home. Finally, at the broadest level, the *macrosystem* refers to the individual's larger cultural context, and may include groups of individuals who share values, belief systems, or behavioral practices.

This conceptualization of nested contextual systems suggests that research needs to take into account the interactions and interrelations among these systems. However, previous research with immigrant families has focused on examining each of these contexts in isolation, and perhaps as a result, has yielded mixed findings. For example, previous research examining the effects of neighborhood characteristics on immigrant children has found lower behavioral and emotional problems among immigrant children living in communities with a higher ethnic density (the number of same-ethnicity members in one's neighborhood) (Georgiades, Boyle, & Duku, 2007). By contrast, other studies have found higher ethnic density to be associated with poorer child outcomes, such as higher perceptions of discrimination (Juang & Alvarez, 2011). Furthermore, although a substantial body of research suggests that neighborhood economic disadvantage adversely affects children's psychological well-being (Leventhal & Brooks-Gunn, 2000), few studies have examined these effects within a sample of Chinese American children in immigrant families. Similarly, although some studies with Chinese immigrant families have examined the associations between acculturation and gaps in parent–child acculturations on children's outcomes (Costigan & Dokis, 2006; Liu, Benner, Lau, & Kim, 2009), relatively few studies have tested how the macrosystem-level effects of culture and acculturation might be mediated by mechanisms at the microsystem level, such as parent–child interactions (see Kim, Chen, Li, Huang, & Moon, 2009, for an exception).

Recognizing the importance of examining multiple levels of influence and their interactions on children's development and outcomes, the Kids and Family Project aimed to capture the indirect and direct effects of three different contextual systems—families, neighborhoods, and cultures—on children's socio-emotional and behavioral adjustment. In one study examining the effects of neighborhood characteristics and parenting styles on children's behavioral problems, a higher neighborhood concentration of Asian residents was positively associated with higher levels of authoritarian parenting, which in turn was associated with higher levels of internalizing and externalizing problems (Lee et al., 2014). Additionally, in an alternative model, neighborhood economic disadvantage was positively associated with children's externalizing problems, which in turn was associated with lower authoritative parenting (Lee et al., 2014).

Our research also examined the relations between macrosystem- and microsystem-level contexts by focusing specifically on parents' and children's emotion-related interactions. In one study, we found that mothers' orientations to Chinese and American cultures were associated with their use of emotion-related language during a storytelling activity with their children. Consistent with hypotheses, mothers' higher orientation to Chinese culture was associated with lower quality of emotion discussion and lower use of emotion-related language (Tao, Zhou, Lau, & Liu, 2013). In another study, we examined the associations between Chinese American parents' cultural orientations and two types of emotional expression: self-reported patterns of emotional expressivity in the family, and observations of non-verbal expressions of emotion during an interactive parent-child task. Results from this study indicated that parents' cultural orientations were most consistently associated with their self-reported, rather than their observed emotion (Chen et al., in press).

Time

In contrast to the effects of parents or teachers, or even neighborhoods, the effects of time on a child's development seem more abstract. Yet Bronfenbrenner conceptualized time as a defining property of the bioecological model, and rightly so. First, the respective influences of parents, teachers, and peers may ebb and flow across different periods of a child's development. More broadly, the timing of historical events and government policies can also play a key role in children's development, particularly among children from immigrant or ethnic minority families. As one tragic example, during World War II, Executive Order 9066 and the resulting relocation and internment of Japanese American families drastically upended school, neighborhood, and peer contexts for thousands of Japanese American children.

We have integrated two considerations of time in our research with Chinese American children. First, we have focused on students in the early stages of their formal education. Previous research has shown grade- or age-related changes in teacher–child relationship quality during the early elementary school years, with average levels of teacher-reported conflict increasing between kindergarten and the fifth grade, and with the greatest increases between kindergarten and the first grade (Jerome, Hamre, & Pianta, 2009). Furthermore, as children entered the later elementary school and middle school grades, teacher-rated closeness was lower than in earlier grades (Jerome et al., 2009). Second, given that middle childhood is a critical developmental period in which ethnic minority and/or immigrant children are likely to experience exclusion, devaluation, invisibility, discrimination, and racism for the first time (García Coll & Szalacha, 2004), it is important to explore the behavioral adjustment and socialization experiences of Chinese American immigrant children in this stage of development.

Time also plays a crucial role in the development of immigrant families as they adjust to life in the United States. By focusing specifically on families in which at least one parent or child was born outside of the United States, we have captured a glimpse of immigrant families in a specific generational window and through the processes of acculturation and cultural maintenance. Our project considers how each successive generation may impact different components of the bioecological model and raises new questions for researchers and educators. Based on the bioecological model of development, it is important to consider how different aspects of time (e.g., stages of academic and ethnic development, immigrant generational status) might play a role in the academic achievement and school engagement of Chinese American children.

Conclusion

Throughout this chapter, we have provided a detailed conceptual framework for organizing the myriad of factors that contribute to the development and psychological adjustment of Chinese American children from immigrant families. Indeed, results from the Kids and Family Project underscore the importance of examining the direct and indirect influences of process (e.g., child–parent and child-teacher relationships), person (e.g., self-regulation skills), context (e.g., ethnic density, cultural orientation), and time (e.g., developmental stage, immigration status) on Chinese American children's behavioral and socio-emotional functioning. Despite the image of Asian Americans as a model minority of high achievers, a growing body of work suggests that Asian children in immigrant families experience a host of obstacles at school, including discrimination, peer harassment, and feeling ignored by teachers and other school staff members (Kao, 1999; Qin, Way, & Mukherjee, 2008). In addition, focusing on the high academic performance of Asian American children is problematic because it neglects the needs of underachieving children and overshadows the difficulties and challenges experienced by children in this group (Yamamoto & Li, 2012).

Given that the academic school year provides teachers with a relatively small window of time to develop a comprehensive understanding of each student's unique needs and strengths, it is important for teachers to recognize that various levels of the child's system can interact to impact a child's development and engagement in school. For example, our research suggests that teacher–child relationships marked by high levels of teacher-rated conflict predict higher levels of behavior problems over time. When taking into consideration the different factors that can influence the engagement and socio-emotional adjustment of Chinese American immigrant students, it is also important to consider the child's stage of development (e.g., age/grade level) as well as the timeline of his or her family's immigration. Based on the research reviewed in this chapter, we encourage educators and practitioners working with Chinese American children from immigrant families to identify and consider how potential variables of process, person, context, and time may play a role in their students' classroom performance.

References

Altbach, P. G. (1991). *Introduction: The uses of a comparative perspective.* In D. C. Smith (Ed.), *The Confucian continuum.* New York, NY: Praeger.

Blair, C., Zelazo, P., & Greenberg, M. (2005). The measurement of executive function in early childhood. *Developmental Neuropsychology, 28,* 561–571. doi:10.1207/s15326942dn2802_1

Bronfenbrenner, U. (1974). Is early intervention effective? *Early Childhood Education Journal, 2*(2), 14–18.

Bronfenbrenner, U. (1977). Toward an experimental ecology of human development. *American Psychologist, 32,* 513–531.

Bronfenbrenner, U., & Morris, P. A. (2006). The bioecological model of human development. In R. M. Lerner (Ed.), *Handbook of child development: Vol. 1. Theoretical models of human development* (6th ed., pp. 793–828). Hoboken, NJ: Wiley.

Causadias, J. M. (2013). A roadmap for the integration of culture into developmental psychopathology. *Development and Psychopathology, 25,* 1375–1398.

Chang, L., Morrissey, R. F., & Koplewicz, H. S. (1995). Prevalence of psychiatric symptoms and their relation to adjustment among Chinese-American youth. *Journal of the American Academy of Child & Adolescent Psychiatry, 34*(1), 91–99.

Chao, R. K. (1994). Beyond parental control and authoritarian parenting style: Understanding Chinese parenting through the cultural notion of training. *Child Development, 65,* 1111–1119. http://dx.doi.org/10.2307/1131308

Chao, R. K. (2001). Extending research on the consequences of parenting style for Chinese Americans and European Americans. *Child Development, 72,* 1832–1843. doi:10.1111/1467-8624.00381

Chen, S. H., Hua, M., Zhou, Q., Tao, A., Lee, E. H., Ly, J., & Main, A. (2014). Parent-child cultural orientations and child adjustment in Chinese American immigrant families. *Developmental Psychology, 50*(1), 189–201. doi:10.1037/a0032473

Chen, S. H., Main, A., Zhou, Q., Bunge, S. A., Lau, N., & Chu, K. (2015). Effortful control and early academic achievement of Chinese American children in immigrant families. *Early Childhood Research Quarterly, 30,* 45–56. doi:10.1016/j.ecresq.2014.08.004

Chen, S. H., Zhou, Q., Eisenberg, N., Valiente, C., & Wang, Y. (2011). Parental expressivity in Chinese families: Relations to parenting styles and children's psychological adjustment. *Parenting: Science and Practice, 11,* 288–307.

Chen, S. H., Zhou, Q., Main, A., & Lee, E. H. (in press). Chinese American immigrant parents' emotional expression in the family: Relations with parents' cultural orientations and children's regulation. *Cultural Diversity and Ethnic Minority Psychology.* Advance online publication: http://dx.doi.org/10.1037/cdp0000013

Choi, Y., & Lahey, B. B. (2006). Testing the model minority stereotype: Youth behaviors across racial and ethnic groups. *The Social Service Review, 80,* 419–452. doi:10.1086/505288

Chua, A. (2011) *Battle hymn of the tiger mother.* New York, NY: Penguin Press.

Costigan, C. L., & Dokis, D. P. (2006). Relations between parent–child acculturation differences and adjustment within immigrant Chinese families. *Child Development, 77,* 1252–1267. doi:10.1111/j.1467-8624.2006 .00932.x

Driscoll, K. C., Wang, L., Mashburn, A. J., & Pianta, R. C. (2011). Fostering supportive teacher–child relationships: Intervention implementation in a state-funded preschool program. *Early Education and Development, 22,* 593–619. doi:10.1080/10409289.2010.502015

Eisenberg, N., Valiente, C., & Eggum, N. D. (2010). Self-regulation and school readiness. *Early Education and Development, 21*, 681–698. http://dx.doi.org/10.1080/10409289.2010.497451

García Coll, C., & Szalacha, L. A. (2004). The multiple contexts of middle childhood. *The Future of Children, 14*, 80–97. Retrieved from http://futureofchildren.org/futureofchildren/publications/docs/14_02_FullJournal.pdf#page=79

Georgiades, K., Boyle, M. H., & Duku, E. (2007). Contextual influences on children's mental health and school performance: The moderating effects of family immigrant status. *Child Development, 78*, 1572–1591. doi:10.1111/j.1467-8624.2007.01084.x

Hamre, B. K., & Pianta, R. C. (2001). Early teacher–child relationships and the trajectory of children's school outcomes through eighth grade. *Child Development, 72*, 625–638. doi:10.1111/1467-8624.00301

Huang, K.-Y., Calzada, E., Cheng, S., & Brotman, L. M. (2012). Physical and mental health disparities among young children of Asian immigrants. *The Journal of Pediatrics, 160*, 331–336. doi:10.1016/j.jpeds.2011.08.005

Hughes, J. N., Wu, J.-Y., Kwok, O., Villarreal, V., & Johnson, A. Y. (2012). Indirect effects of child reports of teacher–student relationship on achievement. *Journal of Educational Psychology, 104*, 350–365. doi:10.1037/a0026339

Jerome, E. M., Hamre, B. K., & Pianta, R. C. (2009). Teacher–child relationships from kindergarten to sixth grade: Early childhood predictors of teacher-perceived conflict and closeness. *Social Development, 18*, 915–945. doi:10.1111/j.1467-9507.2008.000508.x

Juang, L. P., & Alvarez, A. N. (2011). Family, school, and neighborhood: Links to Chinese American adolescent perceptions of racial/ethnic discrimination. *Asian American Journal of Psychology, 2*, 1–12. doi:10.1037/a0023107

Kao, G. (1999). Psychological well-being and educational achievement among immigrant youth. In D. J. Hernandez (Ed.), *Children of immigrants: Health, adjustment, and public assistance* (pp. 410–477). Washington, DC: National Academies Press.

Karoly, P. (1993). Mechanisms of self-regulation: A systems view. *Annual Review of Psychology, 44*, 23–52.

Kim, S. Y., Chen, Q., Li, J., Huang, X., & Moon, U. J. (2009). Parent–child acculturation, parenting, and adolescent depressive symptoms in Chinese immigrant families. *Journal of Family Psychology, 23*, 426–437. doi:10.1037/a0016019

Kim, S. Y., Wang, Y., Orozco-Lapray, D., Shen, Y., & Murtuza, M. (2013). Does "tiger parenting" exist? Parenting profiles of Chinese Americans and adolescent developmental outcomes. *Asian American Journal of Psychology, 4*(1), 7.

Lareau, A. (2003). *Unequal childhoods: Class, race and family life*. Berkeley, CA: University of California Press.

Lee, E. H., Zhou, Q., Eisenberg, N., & Wang, Y. (2013). Bidirectional relations between temperament and parenting styles in Chinese children. *International Journal of Behavioral Development, 37*(1), 57–67.

Lee, E. H., Zhou, Q., Ly, J., Main, A., Tao, A., & Chen, S. H. (2014). Neighborhood characteristics, parenting styles, and children's behavioral problems in Chinese American immigrant families. *Cultural Diversity and Ethnic Minority Psychology, 20*(2), 202–212.

Leventhal, T., & Brooks-Gunn, J. (2000). The neighborhoods they live in: The effects of neighborhood residence on child and adolescent outcomes. *Psychological Bulletin, 126*, 309–337. doi:10.1037/0033-2909.126.2.309

Liew, J., Kwok, O., Chang, Y. P., Chang, B. W., & Yeh, Y. C. (2014). Parental autonomy support predicts academic achievement through emotion-related self-regulation and adaptive skills in Chinese American adolescents. *Asian American Journal of Psychology, 5*(3), 214.

Liu, L. L., Benner, A. D., Lau, A. S., & Kim, S. Y. (2009). Mother–adolescent language proficiency and adolescent academic and emotional adjustment among Chinese American families. *Journal of Youth and Adolescence, 38*, 572–586. doi:10.1007/s10964-008-9358-8

Ly, J., & Zhou, Q. (in review). *Bidirectional associations between teacher–child relationship quality and behavior problems in Chinese American immigrant children.*

Ly, J., Zhou, Q., Chu, K., & Chen, S. H. (2012). Teacher–child relationship quality and academic achievement of Chinese American children in immigrant families. *Journal of School Psychology, 50*, 535–553. doi:10.1016/j.jsp.2012.03.003

O'Connor, E., Dearing, E., & Collins, B. A. (2011). Teacher–child relationship and behavior problem trajectories in elementary school. *American Educational Research Journal, 48*, 120–162. doi:10.3102/0002831210365008

Pew Research Center. (2012). *The rise of Asian Americans.* Washington, DC: Pew Social & Demographic Trends. (June 19, 2012 publication).

Pianta, R. C., & Walsh, D. J. (1996). *High-risk children in schools: Constructing sustaining relationships.* New York: NY: Routledge.

Qin, D. B., & Han, E.-J. (2011). The achievement/adjustment paradox: Understanding the psychosocial struggles of Asian American children and adolescents. In S. S. Chuang & R. P. Moreno (Eds.), *Immigrant children: Change, adaptation, and cultural transformation* (pp. 51–74). Lanham, MD: Lexington Books.

Qin, D. B., Way, N., & Mukherjee, P. (2008). The other side of the model minority story: The familial and peer challenges faced by Chinese American adolescents. *Youth & Society, 39*(4), 480–506. doi:10.1177/0044118X08314233

Rhee, S., Chang, J., & Rhee, J. (2003). Acculturation, communication patterns, and self-esteem among Asian and Caucasian American adolescents. *Adolescence, 38*, 749–768.

Rosa, E. M., & Tudge, J. (2013). Urie Bronfenbrenner's theory of human development: Its evolution from ecology to bioecology. *Journal of Family Theory & Review, 5*(4), 243–258.

Rothbart, M. K., & Bates, J. E. (2006). Temperament. In N. Eisenberg, W. Damon, & R. M. Lerner (Eds.), *Handbook of child psychology: Vol. 3. Social, emotional, and personality development* (6th ed., pp. 99–166). Hoboken, NJ: Wiley.

Ryan, C. (2013). *Language use in the United States: 2011.* Washington, DC: U.S. Census Bureau, August.

Sabol, T. J., & Pianta, P. C. (2012). Recent trends in research on teacher–child relationships. *Attachment and Human Development, 14*, 213–231. doi:10.1080/1461673 4.2012.672262

Song, S. J., Ziegler, R., Arsenault, L., Fried, L. E., & Hacker, K. (2011). Asian student depression in American high schools: Differences in risk factors. *The Journal of School Nursing, 27*, 455–462. doi:10.1177/1059840511418670

Stevenson, H., & Stigler, J. (1992). *The learning gap: Why our schools are failing and what we can learn from Japanese and Chinese education.* New York, NY: Simon and Schuster.

Swick, K. J., & Williams, R. D. (2006). An analysis of Bronfenbrenner's bio-ecological perspective for early childhood educators: Implications for working with families experiencing stress. *Early Childhood Education Journal, 33*(5), 371–378.

Tao, A., Zhou, Q., Lau, N., & Liu, H. (2013). Chinese American immigrant mothers' discussion of emotion with children: Relations to cultural orientations. *Journal of Cross-Cultural Psychology, 44*(3), 478–501.

Tudge, J. R., Mokrova, I., Hatfield, B. E., & Karnik, R. B. (2009). Uses and misuses of Bronfenbrenner's bioecological theory of human development. *Journal of Family Theory & Review, 1*(4), 198–210.

Ursache, A., Blair, C., & Raver, C. C. (2012). The promotion of self-regulation as a means of enhancing school readiness and early achievement in children at risk for school failure. *Child Development Perspectives, 6,* 122–128. http://dx.doi.org/10.1111/j.1750-8606.2011.00209.x

Yamamoto, Y., & Li, J. (2012). Quiet in the eye of the beholder: Teacher perceptions of Asian immigrant children. In C. García Coll (Ed.), *The impact of immigrant on children's development* (pp. 1–16). Berkeley, CA: Karger. doi:10.1159/000331021

Yeh, C. J., Liao, H.-Y., Ma, P.-W., Shea, M., Okubo, Y., Kim, A. B., & Atkins, M. S. (2013). Ecological risk and protective factors of depressive and anxiety symptoms among low-income, Chinese immigrant youth. *Asian American Journal of Psychology.* Advance online publication. doi:10.1037/a0034105

Zigler, E., & Muenchow, S. (1992). *Head Start: The inside story of America's most successful educational experiment.* New York, NY: Basic Books.

14

CULTIVATING CREATIVITY AMONG CHINESE-HERITAGE STUDENTS IN NORTH AMERICA

Cecilia S. Cheung

> You can't invent Google, Facebook or the iPod unless you've mastered the basics, are willing to put in long hours and can pick yourself up from the floor when life knocks you down the first 10 times.
>
> *Amy Chua,* Battle Hymn of the Tiger Mother

A laudable goal in education is to foster creativity among students. The ability to generate *novel* and *useful* solutions to problems appears to be essential in enhancing the quality of students' learning (e.g., Feldman, Csikszentmihalyi, & Gardner, 1994; Simonton, 2012). Despite the value of creativity in students' education, cultivating such a quality among students is notably challenging (e.g., Sternberg & Williams, 1996; Sternberg, 2001; Williams, Markle, Brigockas, & Sternberg, 2001). This concern may be particularly pronounced among Chinese-heritage students residing in North America, given the potential discord around learning that may exist between their heritage and host cultures (Fuligni, 1997; Fuligni & Yoshikawa, 2004). While North America entails ethnically and culturally diverse geographical regions across the United States and Canada, Chinese-heritage students are often exposed to similar cultural norms that guide their experiences in school (Chen, 2012; Chen & Tse, 2008; Markus & Kitayama, 1991); hence, without dismissing the possibility of within-group variation, Chinese-heritage students in North America are considered herein as a whole. This chapter reviews empirical research in the past 2 decades focusing on the experiences of native Chinese as well as Chinese-heritage students, in relation to the challenges and prospects of creativity development among them. Articles included in the review are based on a literature search on PsycINFO, with a focus on studies published in the last 2 decades (i.e., between 1995 to 2015). Consideration is given to the

212 Cecilia S. Cheung

unique challenges and opportunities for distinct pathways of creativity development among Chinese-heritage students in North America.

Creativity: Novel and Practical Ideas

Despite the pluralistic definitions of creativity, researchers have identified two qualities—*novelty* and *practicality* as essential markers of creativity (e.g., Cattell & Butcher, 1968; Plucker & Makel, 2010). Creative ideas are novel in that they diverge from well-established manners and approaches to solving problems. Individuals' engagement in divergent thinking, or the process of exploring a variety of possible solutions, is central to generating novel ideas (e.g., Guilford, 1950; Kozbelt, Beghetto, & Runco, 2010). Besides novelty, creative ideas are also qualified by their usefulness (e.g., Albert & Runco, 1999; Kozbelt et al., 2010). Creative solutions to problems should be relevant to the problem at hand, feasible, as well as realistic. This chapter considers creative experiences—known as "little-c"—that are evident in a wide range of domains and activities both within and without the classroom (e.g., coming up with a new way to train a puppy and solving math equations in a non-routine fashion). These experiences may not necessarily result in substantive contributions to a particular field (cf. paradigm-shifting contributions of genius or eminent individuals; see Kozbelt et al., 2010), but are nonetheless largely accessible by many students.

Models of Learning: Chinese vs. The West

A myriad of research indicates that Chinese students differ from their Western counterparts in their conceptions about learning and its purpose (Li, 2004, 2005, 2009; Watkins, 2010); such differences may have implications for Chinese-heritage students' development of creativity in the North American context. Although a seemingly universal goal of learning is to acquire knowledge, the Chinese model of learning—as exemplified in the Confucian doctrines—views that learning serves a unique function in the moral development of individuals. Beyond knowledge acquisition, the learning process is often seen as an avenue toward self-perfection (Li, 2012). Through learning, students are not only expected to acquire thorough understanding of the subject matter, but also develop desirable personal qualities, known as *ren*—a highly regarded moral standard which entails the virtues of benevolence, humanity, and kindness (Hwang, 2011; Li, 2003).

According to the Confucian philosophy, observing and adhering one's thoughts and acts to the standards of *ren* are essential in the learning process. As a consequence, a key goal in education is to instill in students the ability to observe, contemplate, and reflect on oneself (Lau, Hui, & Ng, 2004; Li, 2004; Watkins & Biggs, 1996). In the classroom, teachers often serve as the virtuoso in their respective fields, and students are expected to observe and imitate the exemplary work of their teachers (Mok & Morris, 2001; Paine, 1990). Although explicit teaching of *ren* has become increasingly obsolete in contemporary China, the core values about learning and education outlined in the Confucian doctrines remain influential (Mok & Morris, 2001; Li, 2012; Paine, 1990). Notably, while the Chinese model of learning does not downplay the importance of innovation and originality, these qualities may be emphasized to a lesser extent than observing and imitating exemplary work.

The Western model of learning, in contrast, regards learning as an inquisitive process that leads to innovative discovery and creation of new ideas (Russell, 1975). Given its focus on active inquiry and discovery, a key goal in education is to instill in students heightened interest and curiosity (Li, 2012). To this end, ideas and acts that deviate from old traditions or routines are often encouraged in the classroom. Moreover, students' ability to generate original thoughts and new solutions to problems are often seen as markers of success in the learning process. Although the Western model of learning does not dismiss the importance of personal and moral qualities, a primary goal in education revolves around cultivating innovative and creative mindsets in students (e.g., Biggs, 1998; Li, 2012).

For a majority of Chinese-heritage students who are exposed to both the Chinese and North American models of learning, their navigation through the two seemingly distinct approaches may be challenging. In North American classrooms with a pedagogic emphasis on innovative discovery and active inquiry (e.g., Alfieri, Brooks, Aldrich, & Tenenbaum, 2011; Klahr & Nigam, 2004), Chinese-heritage students may find their learning style at odds with the expectations prized in such classrooms. For one, observations conducted in classrooms in Asia and the United States reveal that Asian students are less accustomed to the inquisitive style of learning (Markus & Kitayama, 1991; Givvin, Hiebert, Jacobs, Hollingsworth, & Gallimore, 2005; Tobin, Wu, & Davidson, 1989). Students in the Chinese and Japanese classrooms are relatively more reticent and receptive, compared to their North American counterparts (Li, 2012). Coupled with the possibility that Chinese-heritage students may have distinct understanding of the core attributes of creativity (discussed in the next section), the pathways leading to developing innovative ideas among Chinese-heritage students may be vastly distinct from their European American counterparts.

Conceptions of Creativity

Beyond cultural models of learning, differences in individuals' conception of creativity may play a role in how Chinese-heritage students come to appreciate creative endeavors and activities in the classroom. Students' differential views on the attributes of creativity can in turn have implications for the development of meaningful instructional approaches and evaluative criteria to optimize learning.

214 Cecilia S. Cheung

To date, studies converge in documenting that attributes, traits, and behaviors that are typically considered creative in the West are not necessarily ubiquitous across cultural milieus. Although several creative acts are considered largely "universal" across cultures, conceptions of fine aspects of creativity often vary widely among individuals from Eastern and Western cultural heritages (Lim & Plucker, 2001; Niu & Sternberg, 2002).

Using open-ended questions to solicit individuals' views about creativity, research has shed light on both the similarities and disparities in individuals' conceptions of creativity across cultures. There is growing evidence that individuals largely agreed upon a finite set of attributes characterizing creative acts, regardless of their cultural orientations. For example, focusing on individuals residing in East Asia (including China, Japan, and India) and the United States, research indicates that "originality" and "innovation" are commonly nominated as attributes of creativity, regardless of culture (Niu & Sternberg, 2002). However, disparities are also evident: While "aesthetic tastes" and "sense of humor" are considered traits of creativity among European Americans, they are rarely nominated by individuals of East Asian descent as essential qualities characterizing creativity (Paletz & Peng, 2008; Yue & Rudowicz, 2002). Conversely, East Asian individuals nominated "independence" and "high levels of activities" as attributes indicative of creativity; however, such descriptions are less prevalent among Western individuals' repertoire of attributes (Chan & Chan, 1999; Niu & Sternberg, 2002).

Focusing specifically on China, research reveals interesting disparities between Chinese and Western individuals' understanding of creativity. In one study, Chinese individuals consider qualities including "inspirational" and "contribution to the society" as markers of creativity (Rudowicz & Hui, 1997). These qualities were minimally, if at all, nominated by their Western counterparts when prompted to offer a list attributes of characterizing creative individuals (Niu & Sternberg, 2002; Rudowicz & Hui, 1997). Hence, while creativity is seen as a personal quality in the West, Chinese individuals consider creativity as acts that can be accompanied with social significance: Creative acts are innovative but can also be benevolent to others and generative in the society.

Despite of a lack of empirical research on the conceptions of creativity among Chinese-heritage students, it is conceivable that their understanding of the core components of creativity is at least in part colored by their heritage culture. Given their exposure to and contact with their heritage culture, Chinese-heritage students may acquire understanding of a set of traits and attributes that are typically considered creative based on their heritage culture's view. However, given their exposure to both the Chinese and Western cultures, it appears possible that Chinese-heritage students' conceptions of creativity can have some resemblance, but are qualitatively distinct from those characterizing their native (Chinese) counterparts. Through constant assimilation and accommodation of information in their heritage and host cultures, new conceptions characteristic of Chinese-heritage students may be instantiated.

Given the potential for diverse conceptions of creativity, devising evaluative criteria in the classroom with sensitivity to culture appears to be particularly beneficial. To this end, teachers' receptiveness to the various forms of creative expressions appears critical. While a finite set of attributes about creativity may constitute the core evaluative component (e.g., aesthetic ability), incorporating additional traits and attributes indicative of creativity (e.g., assisting others using non-traditional means) may allow for the identification of creative acts and expressions among Chinese-heritage students. The enriched evaluative criteria can also allow students of diverse cultural backgrounds to recognize, appreciate, and learn from distinct approaches to creative ideas and acts.

The Role of Parents

Students' learning experiences are not limited to the school front. Family, especially parents, can play a pivotal role in students' education. Although parents of Chinese-heritage students vary with regard to their socioeconomic background as well as the extent of acculturation, various aspects characterizing their parents' practices often share similarities (Chao & Tseng, 2002). Research indicates that Chinese parents, compared to their Western counterparts, tend to place heightened emphasis on their children's educational endeavors (Chao, 1994, 1996). Because of the value they place on children's success in school, many Chinese parents consider their children's grades—a concrete indicator of performance—of importance in the learning process. Notably, while Chinese parents do not repudiate the importance of creativity (see Chao, 1996), children's performance in standardized tests and examinations tends to be the center of attention for many parents of Chinese descent.

The heightened emphasis Chinese parents place on their children's academic success is in part reflected in their enthusiastic involvement in their children's learning (Chao, 1994; Cheung & Pomerantz, 2011; Huntsinger, Jose, Larson, Balsink Krieg, & Shaligram, 2000). Compared to their Western counterparts, parents of Chinese descent tend to view children's educational success as crucial to children's upward mobility along the social and economic ladders (Chao, 2000; Pomerantz, Ng, & Wang, 2008). Consequently, Chinese parents are often willing to devote much time and effort to ensure their children's success in school. At times, Chinese parents' emphasis on the significance of school grades can come at the expense of creativity. For example, to enhance children's performance in schools, Chinese parents may encourage children to partake in extra classes that focus on drills and practices (e.g., exam preparation schools). Engagement in these academically oriented activities may curtail children's time and opportunity to take part in other non-academic activities for developing creativity.

Beyond parents' involvement in children's learning, the interactive style between parents and children may also contribute to children's creativity. Indeed,

216 Cecilia S. Cheung

the parenting style of Chinese-heritage parents in North America has been a topic of much interest in the past few decades, with a majority of research focusing on the implications of Chinese parenting style for children's school engagement and achievement (e.g., Chao & Tseng, 2002; Huntsinger, Jose, Liaw, & Ching, 1997). Research focusing on native Chinese as well as Chinese immigrant families in the United States indicates that Chinese parents often employ heightened control compared to their Western counterparts—especially when children's learning is of concern (e.g., Chao, 1994; Cheung & Pomerantz, 2011; Huntsinger et al., 2000; Ng, Pomerantz, & Deng, 2014). Although parents' controlling strategies in the context of learning are often motivated by love and care to ensure children do not fall short of standards, the possibility that heightened levels of parental control can stifle children's creative expressions warrants attention (see Koestner, Ryan, Bernieri, & Holt, 1984).

Research in the West indicates that parents' control places restraints on children's experience of autonomy, which may undermine children's creativity (Deci & Ryan, 2000; Koestner et al., 1984). Indeed, parents' use of controlling strategies may interfere with children's cognitive resources, thereby limiting children's capacity to generate innovative ideas and new solutions to problems. Furthermore, parents' heightened emphasis on academic achievement, coupled with their controlling practices, may lead children to feel particularly apprehensive of failures in their academic pursuit. As such, children may resort to using conservative, yet success-proof, approaches to minimize the risk of failure.

Stereotypes about Chinese-Heritage Students

Stereotypes are omnipresent in many societies. Views about specific groups of individuals can have powerful influence on how individuals think, feel, and act (e.g., Vescio, Gervais, Snyder, & Hoover, 2005). Chinese-heritage students in North America are often seen as hardworking and academically successful. As a consequence, Chinese-heritage students have been traditionally regarded as one of the "model" minority groups in North America (Kim & Yeh, 2002; Lee, 1994). However, Chinese-heritage students have not been typically viewed as outstanding in the creative realm, with some evidence indicating that Chinese teachers view certain traits of creativity as undesirable in the classroom (Chan & Chan, 2010).

Chinese-heritage students' success in the academic arena is often credited to the value they place on education as well as the time and effort they devote to their studies (Schneider & Lee, 1990; Sue & Okazaki, 1990); however, their success is seldom attributed to their originality in learning (Kauffman, 2006). Chinese teachers also appear to favor students who are hardworking, rather than creative in the classroom. For example, in a study focusing on Chinese teachers in Hong Kong, several traits characterizing creative Chinese students, including "always questioning" and "active," are often perceived as undesirable, in part because such qualities can be disruptive to the teachers' pedagogical plans (Chan & Chan, 2010). An ideal Chinese-heritage student, portrayed stereotypically, is one who is diligent, excellent in their academic performance, and reserved in their verbal and creative expressiveness (Wong, Lai, Nagasawa, & Tieming, 1998). While stereotypes are often misguided beliefs without strong basis, they can have a powerful effect on individuals (Vescio et al., 2005). Indeed, students who abide firmly by stereotypic views may dismiss the importance to engage in creative endeavors, which in turn may undermine the quality of their learning in the long run.

Stereotypes may not only influence Chinese-heritage students, but also teachers in classrooms with students from diverse backgrounds. Research indicates that teachers' biased preconceptions about students' academic prowess can influence their pedagogical strategies and expectations (Rosenthal, 1995). For example, teachers who are given erroneous information that their students are faltering tend to provide fewer challenging activities in the classroom (Rosenthal & Jacobson, 1992). In a similar vein, stereotypes about Chinese-heritage students can have an impact on teachers' practices: teachers may adjust their pedagogical approach based on misguided views about their students' propensity to succeed in the creative realm. A teacher under the influence of such biases may dedicate less effort to nurture creativity in the classroom. Over time, a vicious cycle may be instantiated such that students' lowered creative outputs potentiate the perpetuation of the stereotypic views.

Challenges and Prospects

Given the personal, familial, and societal contributions to Chinese-heritage students' learning experiences, utilizing a single approach to foster creativity (e.g., solely focusing on inquisitive learning) in diverse classrooms may be suboptimal. Taking into consideration the confluence of the school and home environments characterizing Chinese-heritage students' experience may be particularly important to understanding the mechanisms underlying creativity development. The following discussion focuses on the key challenges and prospects to developing creativity among Chinese-heritage students, with attention to the unique pathways of creativity development among these students.

Challenges

Student level. In contrast to the Western model of learning which places strong emphasis on discovery and innovation, the Chinese model of learning places substantial focus on self-improvement through contemplation and reflection. Given their exposure to both models of learning, Chinese-heritage students may find it difficult to strike a balance between the rather inconsistent goals in learning. Means to elicit creativity in the classrooms may also be differentially received by

218 Cecilia S. Cheung

students from diverse cultural origins. For example, the encouragement of inquiry and active exploration in the classroom can be seen as threatening for students who are inclined to remain reticent and reflective in the learning process. Simply imposing approaches advocated by the Western model of learning may not be entirely beneficial for the Chinese-heritage students. Beyond the distinct models of learning, Chinese-heritage students' conceptions about creativity can pose challenges to devising meaningful criteria for evaluating students' creative work. Specifically, a heavy reliance on evaluative approaches biased toward Western attributes and traits (e.g., sense of humor) can limit Chinese-heritage students' potential to express creativity in ways that may not be typical in the Western cultural context.

Familial level. Parents of Chinese-heritage students often place heightened emphasis on their children's academic achievement, sometimes even at the expense of creativity. Given the investment parents devote to their learning endeavors, Chinese-heritage students may resort to utilizing practiced and success-proof methods, so as to minimize the plausibility of disappointing their parents. Simply encouraging students to attempt new ways to solving problems may be met with apathy. Indeed, when prompted to complete an academic task, Chinese-heritage students may be more inclined to using well-practiced methods, rather than attempting innovative solutions, to ensure success. Chinese parents' heightened control may also undermine children's feelings of autonomy, thereby potentially limiting children's creative expression.

Societal level. Stereotypes about Chinese-heritage students can confer significant impact on their thoughts and behaviors. Shared, albeit sometimes erroneous, views about Chinese students' underwhelming quest for creative activities in the classroom can impact both students and teachers. Students who abide firmly by the stereotypic views may see themselves as lacking the ability to succeed in the creative realm. Misguided by the same stereotypes, teachers may likewise alter their teaching approaches and expectations for Chinese-heritage students, which may in turn undermine these students' creative potential.

Prospects

Despite challenges in cultivating creativity among Chinese-heritage students in North America, their experiences afford unique opportunities to develop their creative potentials. In particular, given their exposure to the Western and Eastern cultures, Chinese-heritage students can reap the benefits of "both worlds." The constant exercise of assimilating and accommodating cultural experiences, as practiced by many Chinese-heritage students given their enriched cultural experiences, can be conducive to creativity (Cheng & Leung, 2013; Leung, Maddux, Galinsky, & Chiu, 2008). Desirable qualities of the Chinese learner (e.g., an emphasis on hard work) may also provide unique bases on which creativity can be nurtured.

The impact of multicultural experience. Chinese students residing in North America, as with their counterparts exposed to rich multicultural experiences, are advantageous with regard to their potential to achieve high levels of creativity. Research indicates that exposure to distinct cultures and cultural practices are essential ingredients for innovation (Leung et al., 2008). For many Chinese-heritage students in North America, the home and school environments often represent two distinct environments in which they spend substantial amount of time engaging. These contexts can provide them with enriched, albeit sometimes conflicting, cultural experiences. The rich cultural experiences afford Chinese-heritage students in North America with plentiful opportunities to exercise their creative minds.

Cultural basis for creativity. Qualities of the ideal Chinese learner, such as tenacity and hard work, may provide a basis for developing creativity. Given the importance of both the novelty and utility aspects of creativity, the mastery of basic skills and knowledge may be a force behind the successful generation of useful ideas. It is conceivable that when the utility aspect of creativity is taken into consideration, solid mastery of basic skills can be a basis for the creation of meaningful breakthroughs, as well as useful deviations from old paradigms and traditions. Amy Chua's quote included in the beginning of the chapter, albeit seemingly anecdotal, highlights the importance of perseverance in recent innovations in technology. In order to foster creativity, solid mastery of knowledge and heightened tenacity in the face of challenge—two notable qualities of the ideal Chinese learner—may provide necessary foundations for developing students' creative potential.

Conclusions

Given the distinct emphases on creativity in China and the West, Chinese-heritage students in North America are faced with challenges and opportunities to develop creativity in the classroom and beyond. Personal, familial, and sociocultural factors join forces to shape the unique experience of Chinese-heritage students. These experiences can gravitate students toward curtailed opportunities for creative expression, especially when they possess little desire to develop their creative potential. However, their enriched multicultural experiences can nonetheless afford unique possibility for developing creativity. Research effort focusing specifically on Chinese-heritage students in North America, beyond cross-national research, will provide much needed insight on the necessary conditions to foster creativity in diverse classrooms in North America.

Acknowledgments

The author would like to thank Dr. Jenny Yau of Azusa Pacific University for her valuable comments on an earlier version of the manuscript.

References

Albert, R. S., & Runco, M. A. (1999). A history of research on creativity. In R. J. Sternberg (Ed.), *Handbook of creativity* (pp. 16–31). New York, NY: Cambridge University Press.

Alfieri, L., Brooks, P. J., Aldrich, N. J., & Tenenbaum, H. R. (2011). Does discovery-based instruction enhance learning? *Journal of Educational Psychology, 103,* 1–18. doi:10.1037/a0021017

Biggs, J. (1998). Learning from the Confucian heritage: So size doesn't matter? *International Journal of Educational Research, 29,* 723–738.

Cattell, R. B., & Butcher, H. J. (1968). *The prediction of achievement and creativity.* Indianapolis, IN: Bobbs-Merrill.

Chan, D. W., & Chan, L. (1999). Implicit theories of creativity: Teachers' perception of student characteristics in Hong Kong. *Creativity Research Journal, 12,* 185–195. doi:10.1207/s15326934crj1203_3

Chan, D. W., & Chan, L. (2010). Implicit theories of creativity: Teachers' perceptions of student characteristics in Hong Kong. *Creativity Research Journal, 12,* 185–195.

Chao, R. K. (1994). Beyond parental control and authoritarian parenting style: Understanding Chinese parenting through the cultural notion of training. *Child Development, 65,* 1111–1119.

Chao, R. K. (1996). Chinese and European American mothers' beliefs about the role of parenting in children's school success. *Journal of Cross-Cultural Psychology, 27,* 403–423.

Chao, R. K. (2000). The parenting of immigrant Chinese and European American mothers: Relations between parenting styles, socialization goals, and parental practices. *Journal of Applied Developmental Psychology, 21,* 233–248.

Chao, R., & Tseng, V. (2002). Parenting of Asians. In M. H. Bornstein (Series Ed.), *Handbook of parenting: Vol. 4 Social conditions and applied parenting* (2nd ed., pp. 59–93). Mahwah, NJ: Lawrence Erlbaum.

Chen, X. (2012). Culture, peer interaction, and socioemotional development. *Child Development Perspectives, 6,* 27–34.

Chen, X., & Tse, H. C. (2008). Social functioning and adjustment in Canadian-born children with Chinese and European backgrounds. *Developmental Psychology, 44,* 1184–1189.

Cheng, C.-Y., & Leung, A. K.-Y. (2013). Revisiting the multicultural experience—creativity link: The effects of perceived cultural distance and comparison mindset. *Social and Personality Psychological Science, 4,* 475–482.

Cheung, C. S., & Pomerantz, E. M. (2011). Parents' involvement in children's learning in the United States and China: Implications for children's academic and emotional adjustment. *Child Development, 82,* 932–950.

Chua, A. (2011). *Battle Hymn of the Tiger Mother.* New York, NY: Bloomsbury.

Deci, E. L., & Ryan, R. M. (2000). The "what" and "why" of goal pursuits: Human needs and the self-determination of behavior. *Psychological Inquiry, 11,* 227–268.

Feldman, D., Csikszentmihalyi, M., & Gardner, H. (1994) *Changing the world: A framework for the study of creativity.* Westport, CT: Praeger.

Fuligni, A. J. (1997). The academic achievement of adolescents from immigrant families: The roles of family background, attitudes, and behavior. *Child Development, 68,* 261–273.

Fuligni, A. J., & Yoshikawa, H. (2004). Parental investments in children in immigrant families. In A. Kalil & T. DeLeire (Eds.), *Parent investments in children: Resources and behaviors that promote success* (pp. 139–161). Mahwah, NJ: Lawrence Erlbaum.

Givvin, K. B., Hiebert, J., Jacobs, J. K., Hollingsworth, H., & Gallimore, R. (2005). Are there national patterns of teaching? Evidence from the TIMSS 1999 Video Study. *Comparative Education Review, 49*, 311–343.

Guilford, J. P. (1950). Creativity. *American Psychologist, 5*, 444–454.

Huntsinger, C. S., Jose, P. E., Larson, S. L., Balsink Krieg, D., & Shaligram, C. (2000). Mathematics, vocabulary, and reading development in Chinese American and European American children over the primary school years. *Journal of Educational Psychology, 92*, 745–760.

Huntsinger, C. S., Jose, P. E., Liaw, F., & Ching, D. (1997). Cultural differences in early mathematics learning: A comparison of Euro-American, Chinese-American, and Taiwanese-Chinese Families. *International Journal of Behavioral Development, 21*, 371–388.

Hwang, K. K. (2011). *Foundations of Chinese psychology: Confucian social relations* (Vol. 1). New York, NY: Springer.

Kauffman, J. C. (2006). Self-reported differences in creativity by ethnicity and gender. *Applied Cognitive Psychology, 20*, 1065–1082.

Kim, A., & Yeh, C. (2002). *Stereotypes of Asian American students*. New York, NY: ERIC Clearing House on Urban Education. (ERIC Document Reproduction Service No. ED462510). Retrieved from http://eric. ed.gov/ERICDocs/data/ericdocs2/content_storage_01/0000000b/80/2a/ 35/2c.pdf

Klahr, D., & Nigam, M. (2004). The equivalence of learning paths in early science instruction: Effects of direct instruction and discovery learning. *Psychological Science, 15*, 661–667.

Koestner, R., Ryan, R. M., Bernieri, F., & Holt, K. (1984). Setting limits on children's behavior: The differential effects of controlling versus informational styles on children's intrinsic motivation and creativity. *Journal of Personality, 54*, 233–248.

Kozbelt, A., Beghetto, R. A., & Runco, M. A. (2010). Theories of creativity. In J. C. Kaufman & R. J. Sternberg (Eds.), *Cambridge handbook of creativity* (pp. 20–47). New York, NY: Cambridge University Press.

Lau, S., Hui, A. H. H., & Ng, G. Y. C. (2004). *Creativity: When East meets West*. New Jersey, NJ: World Scientific.

Lee, S. J. (1994). Behind the model-minority stereotype: Voices of high- and low-achieving Asian American students. *Anthropology and Education Quarterly, 25*, 413–429.

Leung, A. K., Maddux, W. W., Galinsky, A. D., & Chiu, C. (2008). Multicultural experience enhances creativity: The when and how. *American Psychologist, 63*, 169–181.

Li, J. (2003). The core of Confucian learning. *American Psychologist, 58*, 146–147.

Li, J. (2004). Learning as a task or virtue: U.S. and Chinese children explain learning. *Developmental Psychology, 40*(4), 595–605.

Li, J. (2005). Mind or virtue: Western and Chinese beliefs about learning. *Current Directions in Psychological Science, 14*(4), 190–194.

Li, J. (2009). Learning to self-perfect: Chinese beliefs about learning. In C. Chan & N. Rao (Eds.), *Revisiting the Chinese learner: Psychological and pedagogical perspectives* (pp. 35–70). Comparative Education Research Centre (CERC), University of Hong Kong and Springer Press.

Li, J. (2012). *Cultural foundations of learning: East and West*. New York, NY: Cambridge University Press.

Lim, W., & Plucker, J. A. (2001). Creativity through a lens of social responsibility: Implicit theories of creativity with Korean samples. *Journal of Creativity Behavior, 35*, 115–130.

Markus, H. R., & Kitayama, S. (1991). Culture and the self: Implications for cognition, emotion, and motivation. *Psychological Review, 98*, 224–253.

Mok, I., & Morris, P. (2001). The metamorphosis of the 'virtuoso': Pedagogic patterns in Hong Kong primary mathematics classrooms. *Teaching and Teacher Education, 17*, 455–468.

Ng, F. F., Pomerantz, E. M., & Deng, C. (2014). Why are Chinese parents more psychologically controlling than American parents? "My child is my report card". *Child Development, 85*, 355–369.

Niu, W., & Sternberg, R. J. (2002). Contemporary studies on the concept of creativity: The East and the West. *Journal of Creative Behavior, 36*, 269–288.

Paine, L. (1990). The teacher as virtuoso: A Chinese model for teaching. *Teachers College Record, 92*, 49–81.

Paletz, S., & Peng, K. (2008). Implicit theories of creativity across cultures: Novelty and appropriateness in two product domains. *Journal of Cross-Cultural Psychology, 29*, 286–302.

Plucker, J. A., & Makel, M. C. (2010). Assessment of creativity. In J. C. Kaufman & R. J. Sternberg (Eds.), *Cambridge handbook of creativity* (pp. 48–73). New York, NY: Cambridge University Press.

Pomerantz, E. M., Ng, F. F., & Wang, Q. (2008). Culture, parenting, and motivation: The case of East Asia and the US. In M. L. Maehr, S. A. Karabenick, & T. C. Urdan (Eds.), *Advances in motivation and achievement: Social psychological perspectives* (Vol. 15, pp. 209–240). Bingley, United Kingdom: Emerald Group.

Rosenthal, R. (1995) Critiquing Pygmalion: A 25-year perspective. *Current Directions in Psychological Science, 4*, 171–172.

Rosenthal, R., & Jacobson, L. (1992). *Pygmalion in the classroom* (Expanded ed.). New York, NY: Irvington.

Rudowicz, E., & Hui, A. (1997). The creative personality: Hong Kong perspective. *Journal of Social Behavior & Personality, 12*, 139–157.

Russell, B. (1975). *A history of western philosophy and its connection with political and social circumstances from the earliest times to the present day*. New York, NY: Simon & Schuster.

Schneider, B., & Lee, Y. (1990). A model for academic success: The school and home environment of East Asian students. *Anthropology and Education Quarterly, 21*, 358–377.

Simonton, D. K. (2012). Teaching creativity: Current findings, trends, and controversies in the psychology of creativity. *Teaching of Psychology, 39*, 217–222.

Sternberg, R. J. (2001). Teaching psychology students that creativity is a decision. *The General Psychologist, 36*(1), 8–11.

Sternberg, R. J., & Williams, W. M. (1996). *How to develop student creativity*. Alexandria, VA: Association for Supervision and Curriculum Development.

Sue, S., & Okazaki, S. (1990). Asian-American educational achievements: A phenomenon in search of an explanation. *American Psychologist, 45*, 913–920.

Tobin, J. J., Wu, D. Y. H., & Davidson, D. H. (1989). *Preschool in three cultures*. New Haven, CT: Yale University Press.

Vescio, T. K., Gervais, S. J., Snyder, M., & Hoover, A. (2005). Power and the creation of patronizing environments: The stereotype-based behaviors of the powerful and their effects on female performance in masculine domains. *Journal of Personality and Social Psychology, 88*, 658–672.

Watkins, D. A. (2010). Learning and teaching: A cross-cultural perspective. *School Leadership & Management, 20*, 161–173. doi:10.1080/13632430050011407

Watkins, D., & Biggs, J. (1996). *The Chinese learner: Cultural, psychological and contextual influences*. Hong Kong, China: Comparative Education Research Centre, University of Hong Kong.

Williams, W. M., Markle, F., Brigockas, M., & Sternberg, R. J. (2001). *Creative intelligence for school (CIFS): 21 lessons to enhance creativity in middle and high school students*. Needham Heights, MA: Allyn & Bacon.

Wong, P., Lai, C. F., Nagasawa, R., & Tieming, L. (1998). Asian Americans as a model minority: Self-perceptions and perceptions by other racial groups. *Sociological Perspectives, 41*, 95–108.

Yue, X. D., & Rudowicz, E. (2002). Perception of the most creative Chinese by undergraduates in Beijing, Guangzhou, Hong Kong, and Taipei. *Journal of Creative Behavior, 36*, 88–104.

15

WHO ARE THEIR PARENTS?

A Case Study of the Second-Generation Chinese American Students' Middle-Class Parents and Their Parenting Styles

Xuan Jiang and Gwyn W. Senokossoff

Historically and culturally, Chinese parents and their parenting styles have had a great impact on their children's educational values and academic performance (Chen & Lan, 1998). Often, Asian American students have been labeled as the "model minority" because of their higher academic achievements over other groups (Cooc & Gee, 2014; Zhao & Qiu, 2009). In the past, Chinese parents' parenting styles have differed greatly from mainstream American parents in several ways (Gorman, 1998). First, Chinese mothers encourage their children to focus on interpersonal relationships with others rather than their own individual traits and talents (Hsu in Gorman, 1998). Second, Chinese parents maintain the expectation of parental respect and obedience. Third, many Chinese parents stress education as the path to social mobility (Chao in Gorman, 1998). Fourth, Chinese parents "emphasize psychological discipline" (Fivush & Wang, 2005, p. 490). Under such parenting styles, Chinese students, including Chinese Americans, are more willing to accept their parents' advice and fulfill parents' academic expectations, compared to other ethnic groups in the United States (Chen & Lan, 1998). However, does this mean that Chinese American families never experience any parent–child conflict and are always portrayed with harmony? How do Chinese parents guide their children today? Parenting styles and family dynamics regarding parenting need to be explored and examined as one of the vital factors in Chinese American students' academic performance. In this chapter, we will examine the parenting styles of second-generation Chinese Americans' parents based on a case study of five Chinese professional middle-class families in the United States. This case study will illuminate the similarities and differences of the parenting styles among these parents, which may help educators to develop a deeper understanding of this ethnic socioeconomic group.

Theoretical Framework

Parenting Styles

Permissive. Baumrind (1966) proposed "three prototypes of adult control that have influenced the child-rearing [and teaching] practices of educators, parents, and child-development experts" (p. 889). These prototypes have been used in several research studies to compare the parenting styles of Chinese, Chinese American, and European American parents. The first parenting style is "permissive." Permissive parents tend to behave in a nonpunitive way. They consult their children about policy decisions, provide explanations for family rules, and demand little household responsibility (Baumrind, 1966). They serve as a resource for their children and allow them to regulate their own behavior as much as possible. Further, they use reason and manipulation to guide their children.

Authoritarian. Authoritarian parents attempt to control and evaluate their children's behaviors by a standard set of conduct rules (Baumrind, 1966). They prize obedience and use punitive measures to curb self-will. In addition, they restrict their children's autonomy and assign household chores to promote a respect for work.

Authoritative. Authoritative parents try to direct their children's activities in a reasonable manner (Baumrind, 1966). They encourage discussion, explain the reasoning behind their rules, and ask the child what his or her objections are when he or she refuses to conform. Both autonomy and conformity are valued. While these parents enforce their perspectives, they value their children's perspectives and desires.

Chinese American Parenting Styles

Authoritarian. Of the three parenting styles that Baumrind (1966) described, several researchers have identified Chinese American parents' style as authoritarian (Gorman, 1998; Lee et al., 2014; Wu, 2008). However, in traditional Chinese culture, this parenting style is viewed as loving and concerned rather than punitive and controlling (Wu, 2008). The extensive involvement of Chinese parents in their children's lives is meant to foster more effort and hard work and appears to boost Chinese children's confidence levels (Wu, 2008).

Authoritative. Other researchers, Cheah, Leung, Tahseen, and Schultz (2009), examined the parenting styles of 85 immigrant Chinese mothers of preschoolers and found that they endorsed an authoritative parenting style. These mothers valued high levels of warmth, reasoning, and autonomy. In addition, the children in the study showed more self-control and fewer problems in school according to their teachers. However, one limitation for this study was that most of the mothers were educated and from middle to high socioeconomic backgrounds.

Other parenting profiles. More recently, Kim, Wang, Orozco-Lapray, Shen, and Murtuza (2013) conducted a three-wave longitudinal study of 444 Chinese American families to identify parenting profiles and explore their effects on the adjustment of adolescent children. Based on eight parenting dimensions, four parenting profiles emerged: supportive parenting, tiger parenting, easygoing parenting, and harsh parenting. Supportive parenting is considered very similar to Baumrind's (1966) authoritative parenting style while harsh parenting is thought to be like Baumrind's authoritarian style (Kim et al., 2013). Easygoing parenting is akin to Baumrind's permissive parenting style. Tiger parenting is believed to be a combination of Baumrind's authoritarian and authoritative parenting styles along with high academic pressure. Though Kim et al.'s (2013) parenting profiles might resemble Baumrind's prototypes, they found one additional parenting dimension—shaming. Kim et al. (2013) discovered that the use of shaming was an important aspect of Chinese culture and parenting. In each of the four parenting profiles, shaming was used to some extent. The harsher and more restrictive the parenting style was, the more shaming was employed. However, the largest proportion of parents in this study fell into the supportive parenting category which utilized only small amounts of shaming.

Parenting Style Effects on Children

Of the parenting styles described, the authoritative and supportive parenting styles appear to produce the best outcomes for children. Children of the parents in these categories experience low academic pressure, high GPAs, high educational attainment, low parent–child alienation, few depressive symptoms, and high family obligation (Kim et al., 2013; Lee et al., 2014). Tiger parenting, authoritarian, and harsh parenting seem to have the opposite effects (Kim et al., 2013; Lee et al., 2014).

Professional Middle-Class Parents' Parenting

Social class and educational background may also strongly determine parenting strategies and styles (Keller & Abels, 2005; Keller et al., 2004). For example, middle-class professional immigrant parents who are exposed to European American culture in their work and community may develop slightly different parenting styles (Yamamoto & Li, 2012). In a study by Mau (1997), parenting styles, socioeconomic status, and educational expectations all positively correlated with students' academic achievements in school. Chinese middle-class immigrant parents, who value education and have high academic expectations, tend to produce successful children (Kao, 1995).

This Study

Research shows that parenting styles and family dynamics regarding parenting may affect students' academic performance. In an effort to understand and support second-generation Chinese American children in school, the researchers chose to implement this study. Many first-generation Chinese Americans were born and raised outside the United States (Sua´rez-Orozco & Sua´rez-Orozco, 2001) and their children were born and raised in the United States. These second-generation children appear to have higher levels of conflict and lower levels of family cohesion than other generational groups of Chinese Americans (Qin, Rak, Rana, & Donnellan, 2012, p. 870).

Further, both of the researchers are parents as well. The second author is a third-generation immigrant from Finland and mother of two sons, and the first author is a mother of a 2-year-old daughter who is a second-generation Chinese American. The first author believes that her parents' parenting style was vital to her academic performance throughout her life. Her experiences led to her interest in the role of parents and parenting styles in second-generation Chinese Americans' academic performance in the United States where Chinese children are confronted with the differences between their native culture and American culture.

Methodology

The primary goal of the study was to explore the parenting styles of second-generation Chinese Americans' parents in the United States. An exploratory case study design was used. Case study is an "intensive, holistic description and analysis of a single entity" (Merriam, 1998, p. 27). In this study, "a single entity" (Merriam, 1998, p. 27) refers to the second-generation Chinese American students' parents. They share the same cultural and educational background, having been taught by their parents and been educated in school in a similar way—in a "bounded system" (Stake, 2005, p. 444). Since each of the participant's native language was Chinese, the first author whose native language was also Chinese conducted the interviews. Each participant was given the opportunity to be interviewed in either Chinese or English. The interviews provided rich description (Creswell, 2007).

Participants

A purposive sampling through oral exchanges was employed to select participants for this study. The eligible participants most likely to give "information about the phenomenon of interest" (Merriam, 2002, p. 20) were the Chinese parents of second-generation Chinese American K–12 students. The first researcher recruited the participants by talking to her friends who had social connections in the local community and professional connections through work. She sent emails to her friends with the research proposal and consent forms attached and asked them to distribute the emails. Her contact information was provided on the consent form for any potential participant who had questions. Further, she also recruited participants from a local park where many Chinese men play soccer every Saturday afternoon, the mothers chat, and the children play on a set of three playgrounds. In this particular community, the parents were middle-class professionals.

Demographic information of participants. The five families' parents were well educated with years of higher-education experiences (one with a bachelor's, three with a master's, and six with doctorate degrees). They had all lived in the United States for over 10 years. Their professions were mostly in the academic fields (e.g., professors, researchers). The parents who participated in this research study were the ones who reported themselves as parenting their children more than their spouses (see Table 15.1 for the demographic information of each

TABLE 15.1 Who Are the Parents and Their Children?

	Participants				
Characteristics	*Zhao*	*Qian*	*Sun*	*Li*	*Zhu*
Age	40–49	50–59	30–39	40–49	30–39
Years in the U.S.	14	15	15	16	12
Profession	researcher	researcher	professor	statistician	none
Highest degree	Doctorate	Doctorate	Doctorate	Master's	Master's
Father/Mother	father	mother	father	mother	mother
SES in their childhood	NA	Low	NA	NA	NA
Main parenting person	father	mother	father	mother	mother
Spouse's age	40–49	50–59	30–39	40–49	40–49
Spouse's years in the U.S.	14	14	15	16	12
Spouse's profession	researcher	self-employed	CPA	professor	science researcher
Spouse's highest degree	Bachelor's	Doctorate	Master's	Doctorate	Doctorate
Number of children	2	2	3	1	2
Age of children	21 and 9	25 and 11	8, 6, and 2.5	11	11 and 5
Grade-level (K–12) boy/girl	3 – boy	6 – boy	3 – boy	5 – girl	5 – girl
Gifted program	Yes	Yes	Yes	Yes	Yes
Test grade ever earned	A, B, C	A, B, C, D	A	A, B	A, B

Note: The demographic information of each participant is displayed with their pseudonyms.

participant with their pseudonyms). It can be seen that both fathers and mothers were involved in their children's education, without any gender differences.

Demographic information of participants' children. Most of the children were attending elementary schools and only one (Qian's son) attended middle school at the time of interviews. The children's grade levels ranged from Grade 3 to Grade 6. The three boys and two girls were all in the gifted programs in their schools, but were not necessarily straight "A" students. All of the parents chose public schools, which included one public charter school (Sun) and one public magnet school (Qian), for their children. They did not send their children to private schools, mainly due to economic reasons.

Data Collection

Five families were recruited for the study. The participants' confidentiality during and after the research study was guaranteed, thus each participant was asked to select a pseudonym for him- or herself. After approval from the Institutional Review Board (IRB) and before the participants signed their written consent forms, the first researcher explained the research study to them. She also told the participants that they had the right not to participate in the study or to withdraw from the study at any time.

After the consent forms were signed, this researcher asked each parent to choose a convenient time and place for the data collection. She tried to honor their requests as much as her schedule would allow. She met with them at their homes, the park, their place of work, or a friend's house.

Prior to the interview, the researcher asked each participant to complete a brief set of written questions to collect the parents' demographic information. This took approximately five minutes. She also provided them with a list of counseling resources that they might access if their children did become aware of any of the information regarding the interviews. Next, she interviewed each participant in a private room in the place they chose, where none of their children or their children's friends were present. The parents were also cautioned not to discuss any information regarding the interview in front of their children. The interviews lasted approximately 35 minutes and were audio-recorded.

A semi-structured, responsive conversation format (Rubin & Rubin, 2005) beginning with open-ended questions was used for the interviews. Follow-up questions were also used when needed. Due to the participants' preferences, all of the interviews were conducted in the Mandarin Chinese language.

According to Bogdan and Biklen (2007), "skin color, race and cultural identity sometimes facilitates, sometimes complicates, and sometimes erects barriers in fieldwork" when "researchers are studying people within their same ethnic group" (p. 96). Such was the case in this study. Although the first researcher's insider perspective afforded her a better understanding of the participants' cultural identity, values, parental roles, and immigrant experiences in the United States, the participants may have taken for granted that she already knew certain facts, and therefore, did not mention them or just illustrated them briefly. To minimize this shortcoming, the researcher used probes recommended by Bodgan and Biklen (2007) during the interviews, such as: "Take me through the experience." "Would you explain that?" "Could you please give me an example?" and so on.

Data Analysis

Data analysis in exploratory case study research should be detailed and intensive "for the unit of study" (Flyvbjerg, 2011, p. 301), so that the case study can "represent the case" (Stake, 2005, p. 460). In this study, data analysis began when the first researcher transcribed and translated each of the interviews. Next, both researchers independently read through the transcripts looking for key words and phrases concerning the research questions. Once each researcher completed her initial analysis of the data, they created coding categories based on the patterns and topics they uncovered, and then, combined the data.

Findings

The following findings are displayed to tell each participant's parenting story.

Educational Values

Good education is important. Each parent who was interviewed expressed how important it was to them that their children receive a good education. Zhao, a father of two boys, said: "Chinese, comparatively, care [for] the next generation's education." Qian, a mother of two boys, stated that she bought a house in the best part of the school district that she could afford. Then, when it was time for Qian's son to go to middle school, they participated in the District's lottery to get her son into a better school, because she heard that there were bullying cases in the local middle school. Two other parents, Li and Zhu, also expressed that they chose to buy their homes in a particular neighborhood, so that their children could attend "A" schools. Further, Zhu, a mother of two girls, stated that she had chosen not to work outside the home, so that she could be available for her children.

Home environment with education as a priority. All of the parents mentioned that they had books and rich book resources at home. They either borrowed books from local libraries, or more often, bought various books (fiction, history, literature, exercise books, etc.) to advance their children's knowledge. They read to their children when they were young and now read with them. Those books were mainly in English, except that one parent mentioned he bought many textbooks and exercise books in Chinese from China.

Moreover, study was the permanent priority that helped create an academic atmosphere at home. Parents learned with and for their children. They learned

English terminologies to teach/tutor their children, using their previous content knowledge which was in the Chinese language. In addition to books and tutoring, parents spent a lot of time and money to develop their children's extracurricular interests and hobbies at home and out. They sent their children to private classes with private teachers or coaches to help them become well-rounded students.

Learning virtues over learning outcomes. All the parents shared their high expectations for their children's academic performance, including straight As and being a knowledgeable person. However, they value learning virtues or virtues in general more than good grades. Zhao talked a lot about his expectations that his son be a psychologically healthy, self-disciplined, and autonomous learner. Sun mentioned persistence and routine. Similarly, Li mentioned self-regulation and self-discipline. Zhu mentioned learning habits many times. These parents were all strong believers of developing good thinking processes which can regulate their children's self-learning, and thus, lead to outstanding academic results and a promising future.

Educational Practice

Time management. All the parents agreed that they needed to set up rules to help their children with time management. Time was set aside for academic activities first: mornings before school, after school, weekend mornings, or weekends in general. The written and/or oral rules gave their children an awareness of routine and planning, in terms of hours and even minutes (in Sun's family). During these allocated time periods, Chinese American students followed the schedule to do whatever was assigned.

Academic tasks were a top priority. Homework completion, checking, and explaining came first, and reinforced supplemental practices were second. Some parents also supplemented the school curriculum with advanced activities and more difficult exercises to achieve differentiated instruction for their children.

Extracurricular activities to promote health. Extracurricular activities took up a lot of spare time, which also required time management and persistence. All the children in the participants' families were enrolled in multiple extracurricular classes (see Table 15.2). Most parents believed that these activities promoted emotional and physical health as well as a sense of responsibility and a work ethic.

Rebellious process but fruitful results. No matter whether the activities were academic or extracurricular, the parents confessed that their children were not always willing to follow the routine practice (e.g., one child needed to play tennis or another needed to learn extra knowledge), and they might resist, make a fuss or show their anger. However, once the children developed the habit or routine, they were more likely to enjoy such a learning process and their parents' supervision or company.

The children would totally agree and appreciate such additional learning activities when they experienced success such as: winning a game, receiving

232 Xuan Jiang and Gwyn W. Senokossoff

TABLE 15.2 Children's Extracurricular Activities

Participant	Extracurricular Activities
Zhao's younger son	Tennis, piano, drawing
Qian's younger son	Tennis, piano, drawing
Sun's elder son	Judo, swimming, soccer, ice-skating, ice hockey, table tennis, badminton (in China), and guitar
Li's daughter	Piano, violin, drawing, ice-skating, dancing, tennis
Zhu's elder daughter	Reading, gymnastics, ballet, drawing, piano, cello

Note: The extracurricular activities included all the previous and current activities the participants' children had.

praise from teachers, accepting applause from their classmates, or being selected for an award. Their self-pride was the main incentive that led them to their future efforts.

Parenting in General

Parental support. Even though none of the parents considered homeschooling their children, each of them spent additional time tutoring, guiding, and monitoring their children's studies at home. Zhao checked his son's daily assignments and tutored him in math. Qian had tutored her son in math and reading when he was younger and still worked with him on school projects. Sun provided extra lessons for his son and still spent time teaching him whenever he could. Li taught her daughter routines for completing her homework and reviewing her grades to determine which subjects were most important to work on. Further, Zhu spent time reading with her elder daughter from a very young age.

Sacrifice. Sacrifice was the most obvious theme revealed from these parents' roles: Zhao sacrificed his tennis time for his son's tennis practice; Zhu stayed at home for her daughters instead of working for economic well-being; Sun used every minute of his available time to teach his children, no matter how exhausted he was; Qian gave up preparing for her test to be a medical doctor to focus on her little son; Li sacrificed her one day off to volunteer in her daughter's school.

Awareness and involvement. Policy awareness and school involvement was another strong theme. Li volunteered in her daughter's school from Kindergarten to Grade 2; two other parents (Sun and Zhu) both mentioned the teacher–student ratio to show their educational policy awareness; all the parents spoke in English when discussing academic terms such as: Reading Plus, Accelerated Reader (AR) Test, IQ Test, and clubs which demonstrated their knowledge of what their children were doing at school.

Discussion

Parenting Style

Based on the data we collected, it seems that all of the five participating parents utilized a parenting style with a major component similar to Baumrind's (1966) authoritative style. Zhao identified his parenting style with his older son as harsh, saying that he followed "Chinese traditional education methods and beat [his] son." He compared himself to the "Tiger mom" who said that when her children make mistakes, she tells them they are wrong, asks them to put their hands out and flogs them with rulers. However, with his younger son, Zhao was striving to parent with a more authoritative style. He was using more reasoning and discussion with his younger son.

Parenting Styles Similar or Different from Their Parents'

One of the questions we asked each parent in the interview was whether they thought their parenting styles were closely related to their own parents'. Each parent said that their style was different from their parents'. Zhao said that he and his wife have taken on the responsibility for raising their son whereas if they were still in China, their parents, the grandparents, would have done a large part of the parenting. Li said that her parents did not monitor the children as much as she does, but that she appreciated the freedom her father gave her to buy and read whatever books she liked. Qian felt that she had no role models for parenting and supporting children in school, because her mother was illiterate and her father was away working much of the time. She felt that she did learn to appreciate hard work by watching her father. Finally, Zhu felt that her parents worked very hard and did not have much time to help their children. She stated that she was self-disciplined as a child while her brother was not, and therefore, he was not as successful as she was.

Back and Forth between the U.S. and China

Maintaining cultural identity. The interviewed parents were the first-generation Chinese Americans. First-generation Chinese immigrants tend to have strong bonds to their culture of origin, thus they may retain their cultural heritage in order to maintain a sense of belonging or cultural identity (Kelley & Tseng, 1992). The parents in this study were making a concentrated effort to share their cultural values with their children. Three of the parents spoke of the importance of helping their children maintain their cultural identity. Zhao said that he wanted "to be sure that his son will be a Chinese." He sent his son to a Chinese-language school to maintain his native language. Sun's family only spoke Chinese at home and they required their son to read and write in Chinese. This family also traveled back to China often and they taught their son to recognize himself as both Chinese and American. Further, they taught him about the Chinese festivals and holidays. Li's family moved into their current neighborhood because a lot of Chinese families were living there. In addition, they continued to encourage their daughter to make friends with other Chinese children and to identify herself as both Chinese and American. While these first-generation Chinese parents tried to maintain their cultural beliefs, they were also exposed to American norms and values. They had to negotiate their own beliefs and values within mainstream American culture.

American versus Chinese education. Most parents seem happy with the education their children's schools provide. For instance, Zhao spoke highly of "American Education," because "it is a type of inspiring education, with stimulus to develop children's ability of thinking and judging." He was also fond of the "freedom" the school gave, by saying "teachers here give more chances to students to think independently and do [their] own research" as opposed to schools in China where "teachers just teach knowledge directly without giving chances for students' development.... Students [in the U.S.] are inspired at a very young age to think, get knowledge, review literature, and write." He also mentioned two other important factors which contributed to the merits of public school education in the U.S.—"teachers' responsible disposition and parent involvement chances."

Sun did not give any satisfying examples; instead, he complained that the school did not provide any academic activities in the afternoons, did not give enough homework, was short on teachers and resources, and did not implement any differential instruction for gifted students despite the fact that his son was in the gifted program. This parent supplemented his son's education with textbooks from China in math and Chinese literature. Nevertheless, Qian and her son, a middle-school student, thought that there was so much homework that her son did not have time for extra academic practices and piano practice. There may be a difference between the elementary and middle-school workload.

Factors that Influence Academic Performance

Each of the participants' school-aged children was attending gifted programs in their schools and performing at the top of their classes. As we analyzed the data, we identified several factors that we believed to have influenced their academic performance. First, every interviewed parent was involved in their child's education, supporting him or her when extra tutoring or encouragement was needed. Second, each participant described a gift or talent that their son or daughter exhibited at an early age and each parent responded by providing additional instruction or resources, such as books. Third, each parent described routines they set up for their children at a young age related to homework, additional tutoring, and practice. They also described how they limited television, videogames, and computer time. According to the parents, although the children were not always happy about the routines set for them, they grew accustomed to the routines and appreciated them when they were successful in school or in their extracurricular activities. Finally, the parents also described peer competition with other Chinese American children or their American counterparts. Each of these parents encouraged their children to make friends with other dedicated students who were also excelling in school.

Conclusion

Academic and Practical Implications

Academic success. Several academic and practical implications may be drawn from this study to inform the educational community. First, it may provide insight into the myth that all Chinese American students are gifted. Each parent in this study described how much he or she valued education, how he or she spent concentrated time tutoring the children, and how they set up study routines and taught the children time management. Further, when their children showed interest in a particular area, they provided lessons to develop those skills. In each case, dedication, high expectations, and hard work led to successful students.

Maintaining native culture. Another theme that was very clear in this study was the maintenance of Chinese culture. All the parents shared how important it was that their children know their native culture and home language. Several of the parents spoke of celebrating Chinese festivals and how they supported their children's use of their native language through speaking and writing. Others spoke of trips they were able to take with their children to China. Although this is commendable, we realize that many Chinese immigrants do not have the same opportunities. Often, the second or third generation loses their language and much of their culture as they become Americanized (Fillmore, 2001). When children lose their first language, they often lose "their sense of worth, their cultural identities, and their family connections" (Fillmore, 2001, p. 207). All the families in our study wanted their children to become proficient in oral and written English. They saw English proficiency as a sign of success and acceptance. However, educators need to be aware of the potential for the loss of a child's native language and cultural identity. Teachers need to consciously teach multicultural awareness and help all students develop cultural competence.

Emotional well-being. Another minor theme that was touched on in our study was emotional well-being. One father, Zhao, mentioned that in addition to wanting his child to succeed academically, he wanted his son "to be an outstanding person and psychologically healthy." He was very aware of the pressures children may face in school and at work. He wanted his son to learn to deal with disappointment as well as success. Zhao related the story of a young man that he attended college with. The man was in the top 10 of 400 students and he committed suicide when his girlfriend broke up with him. This experience left a great impression on Zhao. Regardless of the young man's academic achievements, he was not psychologically healthy. Several research studies have dealt with this topic of psychological-emotional stress (Cooc & Gee, 2014). Teachers need to be aware of the difficulties that Chinese American children face when they are trying to navigate American schools and find ways to support these students.

Limitations in the Study

There are some limitations to this study. The sample size of the study was small and limited to one geographic area in South Florida. Further, the socioeconomic and professional backgrounds of the participants were very similar. Generalizability for this study would be limited; however, our findings did support similar findings from earlier studies.

Direction for Future Research

A larger study with Chinese parents from different socioeconomic and professional backgrounds as participants would be stronger. Another interesting aspect of this study that was not explored was the children's perspectives of their parents and their parenting styles. It would be very interesting to see how the children's perspectives aligned with their parents'. It would also be fascinating to follow these children through college and into their adult years in a longitudinal study to see if their success continues and to find out how they choose to parent their own children.

Final Thoughts

This exploratory case study has revealed that the participating parents and their parenting styles have had a great impact on their children's educational values, learning habits and virtues, and academic performance (Chen & Lan, 1998). The participating parents also disclosed that there were occasional parent–child conflicts in the process of academic or extracurricular activities (Qin et al., 2012), along with the fact that their children would appreciate such pressure/pushes on their harvest. The participants' parenting styles, generally, have been greatly influenced by the following factors such as *where, when,* and *by whom* they were raised. Moreover, their parenting styles were also aligned with the new contextual settings where their children lived and received education. Furthermore, due to more exposure to Western parenting styles and increasing time in the United States, the interviewed parents seemed to be wrestling with the idea of how much they should change their parenting styles to meet their children's needs in this environment of native Chinese culture and American culture.

References

Baumrind, D. (1966). Effects of authoritative parental control on child behavior. *Child Development, 37*(4), 887–907. Retrieved from www.jstor.org/stable/1126611

Bogdan, R. C., & Biklen, S. K. (2007). *Qualitative research for education: An introduction to theories and methods* (5th ed.). Boston, MA: Pearson.

Cheah, C., Leung, C., Tahseen, M., & Schultz, D. (2009). Authoritative parenting among immigrant Chinese mothers of preschoolers. *Journal of Family Psychology, 23*(3), 311–320. doi:10.1037/a0015076

Chen, H., & Lan, W. (1998). Adolescents' perceptions of their parents' academic expectations: Comparison of American, Chinese-American, and Chinese high school students. *Adolescence, 33*(130), 385–390.

Cooc, N., & Gee, K. A. (2014). National trends in school victimization among Asian American adolescents. *Journal of Adolescence, 37*, 839–849.

Creswell, J. W. (2007). *Qualitative inquiry and research design: Choosing among five approaches* (2nd ed.). Thousand Oaks, CA: Sage.

Fillmore, L. W. (2001). Loss of family languages: Should educators be concerned? *Theory and Practice, 39*(4), 203–210.

Fivush, R., & Wang, Q. (2005). Emotion talk in mother-child conversations of the shared past: The effects of culture, gender, and event valence. *Journal of Cognition and Development, 6*(4), 489–506.

Flyvbjerg, B. (2011). Case study. In N. Denzin & Y. Lincoln (Eds.), *The sage handbook of qualitative research* (4th ed., pp. 301–316). Thousand Oaks, CA: Sage.

Gorman, J. C. (1998, Jan.) Parenting attitudes and practices of immigrant Chinese mothers of adolescents. *Family Relations, 47*(1), 73–80.

Kao, G. (1995). Asian Americans as model minorities? A look at their academic performance. *American Journal of Education, 103*(2), 121–159.

Keller, H., & Abels, M. (2005). *The culture of parenting: Infants' social experiences in different eco cultural environments.* Paper presented at the Society for Research in Child Development 2005 Biennial meeting in Atlanta, GA, USA.

Keller, H., Lohaus, A., Kuensemueller, P., Abels, M., Yovsi, R. D., Voelker, S., ... Mohite, P. (2004). The bio-culture of parenting: Evidence from five cultural communities. *Parenting: Science and Practice, 4*(1), 25–50.

Kelley, M. L., & Tseng, H. (1992). Cultural differences in child rearing: A comparison of immigrant Chinese and Caucasian American mothers. *Journal of Cross-Cultural Psychology, 23*(4), 444–455.

Kim, S., Wang, Y., Orozco-Lapray, D., Shen, Y., & Murtuza, M. (2013). Does "tiger parenting" exist? Parenting profiles of Chinese Americans and adolescent developmental outcomes. *Asian American Journal of Psychology, 4*(1), 7–18. doi:10.1037/a0030612

Lee, E., Shou, Q., Ly, J., Main, A., Tao, A., & Chen, S. (2014). Neighborhood characteristics, parenting styles, and children's behavioral problems in Chinese American immigrant families. *Cultural Diversity and Ethnic Minority Psychology, 20*(2), 202–212.

Mau, W. C. (1997). Parental influences on the high school students' academic achievement: A comparison of Asian immigrants, Asian Americans, and white Americans. *Psychology in the Schools, 34*(3), 267–277.

Merriam, S. B. (1998). *Qualitative research and case study applications in education.* San Francisco, CA: Jossey-Bass.

Merriam, S. B. (2002). Assessing and evaluating qualitative research. In S. B. Merriam (Ed.), *Qualitative research in practice: Examples for discussion and analysis* (pp. 18–33). New York, NY: John Wiley & Sons.

Rubin, H. J., & Rubin, I. S. (2005). *Qualitative interviewing: The art of hearing data* (2nd ed.). Thousand Oaks, CA: Sage.

Qin, D. B., Rak, E., Rana, M., & Donnellan, B. M. (2012). Parent-child relations and psychological adjustment among high-achieving Chinese and European American adolescents. *Journal of Adolescence, 35*(4), 863–873.

Stake, R. E. (2005). Qualitative case studies. In N. Denzin & Y. Lincoln (Eds.), *The Sage handbook of qualitative research* (3rd ed., pp. 443–466). Thousand Oaks, CA: Sage.

Suárez-Orozco, C., & Suárez-Orozco, M. (2001). *Children of immigration: The developing child*. Cambridge, MA: Harvard University Press.

Wu, E. (2008). Parental influence on children's talent development: A case study with three Chinese American families. *Journal for the Education of the Gifted, 32*(1), 100–129.

Yamamoto, Y., & Li, J. (2012). What makes a high-quality preschool? Similarities and differences between Chinese immigrant and European American parents' views. *Early Childhood Research Quarterly, 27*(2), 306–315.

Zhao, Y., & Qiu, W. (2009). How good are the Asians? Refuting four myths about Asian American academic achievement. *Phi Delta Kappan*. Retrieved from http://pdk.sagepub.com/content/90/5/338.full.pdf+html

16

CANTONESE EMERGENT BILINGUALS IN THE "LATINO/MANDARIN" U.S. EDUCATION LANDSCAPE

A Critical Case Study in Chicago

Jason Goulah

> *Chief Justice Warren E. Burger:* Mr. Steinman, one practical problem that may
> or may not be lurking in this case. I gather that there are at least three and
> perhaps more major Chinese dialects spoken in such form that the person
> from one area of China can barely communicate with another. What is the
> obligation of the state? Must they have classes in the Cantonese dialect and
> then some other dialect?
>
> *Edward H. Steinman:* I think that what has been happening, Your Honor, is
> that the Court is focusing [on] only one possible method that would be a
> bilingual method where the teacher speaks Chinese as well as English …
>
> *Chief Justice Warren E. Burger:* Which Chinese?… . Which Chinese dialect?
>
> *Excerpts from Oral Arguments,* Lau v. Nichols *(December 10, 1973)*

Forty-one years have passed since the U.S. Supreme Court voted unanimously
for Kinney Timmon Lau and roughly 1,800 non-English-speaking Chinese
students against the San Francisco Unified School District, overruling the lower
courts and effecting language education rights for non-native English-speaking
students in U.S. public schools. That arguably the most important legal case for
bilingual education was brought in the name of Lau, a non-native English-
speaking Chinese minor, by and through his mother, Kam Wai Lau, and six
other Chinese and Chinese-American petitioners, cannot be overstated in the
current moment of increased Asian immigration.

Asians—led by Chinese—have overtaken Latinos as the largest group
immigrating into the U.S. (Pew Research Center, 2013). The Asian population
grew 47% between 2000 and 2010 (Asian American Center for Advancing Justice,
2011) and constitutes the largest shift in political influence since 2000 (Nakagawa,
2014). Asians are "the highest-income, best-educated and fastest-growing

240 Jason Goulah

racial group in the United States" (Pew Research Center, 2013, p. v). These statistics, however, perpetuate the Asian "model minority" myth and belie the realities of inter- and intra-Asian groups' success and access in the U.S., particularly with regard to education (Lowe, 2015). One example is the disparity between state and local perspectives, policies, and practices toward Cantonese and Mandarin, and its implications for meeting the needs of Cantonese-speaking Chinese students, even and especially in instances where they constitute a larger portion of the growing Chinese population than Mandarin speakers.

This chapter presents initial findings from an ongoing 3-year critical ethnography (Creswell, 1998; Rogers, 2004) of one "low-performing" public high school's efforts to meet the linguistic, sociocultural, sociopolitical, and academic needs of the growing population of Cantonese-speaking Chinese students in a mostly Spanish-speaking Latino community in Chicago, Illinois, in the United States. Chicago Public Schools (CPS) is the nation's third largest—but most segregated—school district, and provides an important optic for understanding the hearts and minds of Chinese students in the current, demographically shifting U.S. education landscape. This landscape is dominated on one hand by an explicit and now mainstream focus on meeting the linguistic, sociocultural, sociopolitical, and academic needs of the dominant and growing minority Latino population (Palmer & Martínez, 2013). On the other hand, this landscape includes a developing—but still peripheral—focus on addressing similar needs of the emerging "Chinese-immigrant" population (Lao, 2004; Ma & Wang, 2014). Part and parcel with these foci is a parallel focus on sustaining Spanish as the country's most prevalent K–12 foreign and heritage language while increasing K–12 curricular access to Mandarin as a (militarily, politically, and economically critical) foreign/heritage language (Pufahl & Rhodes, 2010).

In the current era of increased content standards and aggressive testing, particularly relative to English language learners (ELLs) (Kibler, Valdés, & Walqui, 2014), the above foci intersect and cohere around students' access—or lack of access—to content-rich bilingual (English-Spanish and English-Mandarin) education (Goulah & Soltero, 2015). Seemingly lost in this landscape, however, is critical consideration of the linguistic, sociocultural, and academic needs of the large population of Cantonese-speaking Chinese immigrant and Chinese-American students in U.S. schools. Cantonese-speaking Chinese students are regularly lumped with their Mandarin-speaking peers (and, more limiting, with all Asians in general [Wu, 2002]) despite differing languages and often differing sociocultural and sociopolitical concerns, and their particular interests are thereby frequently lost or marginalized.

Literature Review

Scholarship on "Chinese"-English bilingual education in the United States is limited. I use "Chinese" because some of the scholarship, implicitly echoing

Chief Justice Burger's question of "Which Chinese?" in the epigraph, considers whether Cantonese or Mandarin should be the variety or dialect of instruction, and which of these has more value, power, and legitimacy socioculturally, politically, and geo-economically (Cheng & Tang, 2014).

Wang (1974), for example, advocated for Mandarin bilingual programs because Mandarin is the official language of China, Taiwan, and the United Nations; is necessary for reading and writing; and "has a simpler sound system and can be studied further at many U.S. universities" (p. 1). Li's study in Britain's Chinese complementary schools, however, illustrated that for British-Chinese students Cantonese, more than Mandarin, "has proved to be particularly useful in the teaching and learning of specific words and phrases, many of which are transliterations of English" (García & Li, 2014, p. 114).

Indeed, there are four tones in Mandarin but up to nine in Cantonese, and there is a noteworthy difference between Cantonese speech and Chinese writing, and an equally noteworthy difference between simplified and traditional orthographies. Cantonese and Mandarin differ in lexicon and grammar, and even though they share much cognate vocabulary with the same source, they are as mutually unintelligible "as French differs from Spanish, or Swedish from German" (Matthews & Yip, 2011, p. 6).

Translanguaging and Chinese Bilingual Education

Li (2014) and Creese and Blackledge (2010) explored both Cantonese and Mandarin from the perspective of learners' *translanguaging*, or the fluid and heteroglossic movement in and across language varieties and proficiencies. They argued that learners' heteroglossia across English, Cantonese, and Mandarin, rather than a traditional division among the three languages in classroom practice, actually leads to (if not represents) richer and more authentic bilingualism. Indeed, translanguaging as dynamic lingualism is theoretically *en vogue* in the field of language education (García & Li, 2014), but empirical studies of its instructional effectiveness for Chinese (Cantonese and/or Mandarin)—or any language—bilingualism remain limited.

Chinese Bilingual Education in the U.S. and the Role of Parents

An early study on Chinese bilingual education conducted in the U.S. is Guthrie's (1985) ethnography of two classrooms in California's "Little Canton." Guthrie found that what began in the 1970s as a maintenance bilingual education program became a transitional program by the 1980s, and she found that disagreement remained about which Chinese variety should be used in the Chinatown school. Guthrie's document-, observation-, and interview-based study also explored immigrant and Chinese-American parents' perspectives of bilingual education in the context of Little Canton's physical, historical, political, sociocultural, linguistic, and demographic complexities. Engaging multiple dialect groups, Guthrie found that Chinese-American parents tend to live in "better" suburban environments, have children who speak English natively, and want their children to learn traditional Chinese social values and Chinese as a heritage language. The immigrant parents, who are comparatively marginalized socioeconomically, politically, and ethnolinguistically, however, tend to live in Little Canton, in the city, and want their children to master English.

Particularly relevant to the present discussion of Cantonese ELLs in a majority Latino Chicago neighborhood are Guthrie's findings that from its inception the school's bilingual program was, as Glaessner (1987) observed, "not grounded in the community's interest in establishing its goals but rather comprised the residue of a politically motivated mandate for bilingual education initiated by the Hispanic community" (p. 110). Glaessner added, "[Guthrie] also points out the impact of this situation on the hiring and firing of staff and the many divisive feelings that emerged in an environment where job security was constantly being threatened" (1987, p. 110).

Echoing Guthrie's (1985) study, Lao (2004), Wang and Phillion (2007), and Wang (2009) examined Chinese in the U.S. context, specifying neither Cantonese nor Mandarin but instead exploring Chinese and Chinese-American parents' beliefs about, and involvement in accessing, Chinese bilingual and heritage language education for their children. Wang and Phillion (2007) asserted that more than 30 years after *Lau v. Nichols*, Chinese Americans still face language inequality, and Lao argued that "[t]he paucity of research on Chinese-English bilingual education and/or Chinese parents' language attitude is troubling. The absence of research has contributed to the 'invisibility' of Chinese Americans as frontline participants in the molding of children and educational policy" (p. 100).

Lao (2004) surveyed 86 Chinese parents in San Francisco about their attitudes and expectations regarding bilingual education for their children. She found that parents strongly support Chinese-English bilingual education and understand the purpose and underlying principles of bilingual education. Lao added that while English- and Chinese-dominant parents differed with regard to certain aspects of their responses, they shared views about the practical advantages of being bilingual and for enrolling their children in Chinese-English bilingual school. These advantages included career opportunities, improved self-image, and integration within the Chinese-speaking community.

Lao (2004), Wang and Phillion (2007), and Wang's (2009) studies echo Guthrie's (1985) ethnography in that they also examined parents' perspectives on bilingual education; however, unlike many of the immigrant parents in Guthrie's study, those chronicled by Lao, Wang and Phillion, and Wang favor Chinese bilingual and heritage language education, and, further, the authors cast these parents' views and efforts to access Chinese language for their children as a social justice movement. The parents' views in these authors' studies are consistent with those of Cantonese parents referenced in California's, now dated, *A Handbook for*

Teaching Cantonese-Speaking Students (California State Department of Education, 1984). Parents referenced in the handbook placed a high value on California's Chinese-language schools as a way of maintaining their children's Cantonese language and culture.

Cantonese Bilingual Education in the U.S. and the Role of Parents

Empirical studies on specifically Cantonese bilingual programs in the U.S. are limited. Leung and Uchikoshi (2012), as one example, examined Cantonese-speaking parents' language ideologies and family language policies relative to their Cantonese-English bilingual children's achievement scores in Cantonese and English. They found that elementary school children in bilingual classrooms scored higher than children in English-only classrooms on Cantonese tasks. However, they also found that significantly more children in bilingual programs than in the mainstream classrooms used Cantonese as a home language. Their findings stress "the integral component of the family ... in children's bilingual development and bring up timely issues relating to family language planning and policy" (Leung & Uchikoshi, 2012, p. 294).

Uchikoshi (2014) examined vocabulary growth rates in first and second languages for Spanish- and Cantonese-speaking ELLs across kindergarten through second grade in six schools. Her results indicate a within-language effect of concepts about print on vocabulary and suggest that language exposure had an effect on English vocabulary. Specifically, earlier exposure to English led to increased English vocabulary in kindergarten, but it did not interfere with native-language vocabulary acquisition.

Uchikoshi (2014) also found that the Cantonese-speaking children had higher English expressive vocabulary scores than the Spanish-speaking children, a difference that remained across the 3 years. However, she also found that the Spanish-speaking children had steeper growth rates in first-language vocabulary than the Cantonese-speaking children, after controlling for language of instruction.

According to Leung and Uchikoshi (2012), the limited literature on Cantonese-language education focuses on linguistic areas of verb acquisition, classifiers, morphological and phonological awareness, and longitudinal language studies. Moreover, this literature occurs mainly in non-U.S. contexts and centers on primary grades. None of it examines Cantonese emergent bilinguals in high schools or scrutinizes the sociocultural issues and school-wide practices facilitating or preventing home language maintenance. In addition, Leung and Uchikoshi (2012) asserted that the overwhelming majority of studies on "Chinese children's language" or "Chinese as a heritage language" are "densely focused on Mandarin language research" (p. 297). And as more socioeconomically established Mandarin-speaking Chinese immigrate to the U.S. and inform the educational landscape (Ma, 2014; Ma & Wang, 2014), and as Mandarin remains tied to

China's growing political, military, and economic power, the demand for Mandarin, for researching Mandarin acquisition, and for meeting Mandarin speakers' concerns has increased (Cheng & Tang, 2014; He, 2009; Tollefson & Tsui, 2014).

The overwhelming majority of the aforementioned (limited) literature on Cantonese bilingual education in the U.S. context occurred in California. Consideration of Cantonese learners in other states is exceedingly limited. Further, although the extant literature provides a triangulated understanding of parents' views about bilingual education, none of it specifically examines school-wide initiatives—irrespective of or in conjunction with parents' views—to meet Cantonese-speaking Chinese students' linguistic and cultural needs in the context of increased education policies and standards, or of the demographically shifting, "Latino/Mandarin" U.S. education landscape. Uchikoshi's (2014) study of Spanish- and Cantonese-speaking students offers some insight, but it is limited by grade level (K–2) and its specifically linguistic scope. The ongoing study presented here aims to begin to bridge some of the gaps in the literature by looking at how one Chicago public high school, located in a predominantly Spanish-speaking Latino community, has endeavored to meet the linguistic, sociocultural, and academic needs of its growing population of Cantonese-speaking emergent bilinguals.

Theoretical Framework

This chapter is framed on one hand by the above-mentioned extant scholarship on "Chinese"-English bilingual education in the U.S. and abroad. On the other hand, it is framed by theories of language policy and planning (LPP), *local* language ecology, and language choice as value creation (Hatano, 2009, 2013; Kubota & McKay, 2009).

The current, postmodernist and critical phase of LPP evidences approaches that are "fluid (vs. systematic), contextualized (vs. universal), diverse (vs. unitary), and relative (vs. absolute)" (Hatano, 2013, p. 51). This phase centers on the issues of power between speech communities that were ignored or marginalized in LPP's early push toward standardization. Ricento (2000) contended that in LPP's current phase macro-sociopolitical events such as "massive population migrations," "the reemergence of national identities," "the globalization of capitalism," and "the penetration of Western culture and technology in the developing world" have engendered an awareness of issues such as language loss and linguistic human rights (p. 203). Hatano (2013) ascribed the cause of language loss to monolingual ideologies of dominant groups and, instead, advocated "multilingualism and linguistic diversity in which all mother tongues or native languages are given equal status" (p. 51). This tension between dominant and nondominant language ideologies is at play in Chicago, where Cantonese-speaking ELLs have limited access to bilingual education and, further, where Cantonese is limited as a K–12

"Latino/Mandarin" U.S. Education Landscape **245**

world language—even though the American Council on the Teaching of Foreign Languages (ACTFL) supports Cantonese and the Illinois State Board of Education (ISBE) licenses teachers in Cantonese as a foreign and heritage language.

Hatano (2009, 2013) and Kubota and McKay (2009) examined the realities of the dominant-nondominant ideological tension in a Japanese context, where national policies require English as a foreign language instead of the locally present—and individually more desirable—immigrant and diasporic languages of the community. Hatano (2009) used Bakhtinian (1981) heteroglossia and Makiguchian (1981–1988) value creation to theorize this tension between the "authoritative discourse" of administrated language policies and students' "internally persuasive" preferences and practices as dialogic value creation. Bakhtinian heteroglossia is well established in language education. Makiguchi's notion of value creation, or *soka* in Japanese, is perhaps less so (see Goulah, 2013). Value creation theory envisions human agency and authentic happiness enacted through the creation of values of aesthetic beauty, individual gain, and social good. Hatano argued that learners create such value through bottom-up language choice. Here, I examine language policy and local school-wide practices around Cantonese, Mandarin, Spanish, and English through this theoretical lens of the dialogic tension between authoritative discourse (what I call "value *prescription*") and internally persuasive discourse—of students, families, and school personnel— as a means of local value creation.

Methods and Data Analysis

I used a case study design (Creswell, 1998) for this ongoing 3-year ethnographic inquiry. The case is one high school in a predominantly Spanish-speaking, Latino neighborhood in Chicago that is experiencing an increase in Cantonese- and, to a much lesser extent, Mandarin-speaking students. I began collecting data in 2014, observing 30 teachers' classrooms, meeting with administrators and program chairs, and interviewing teachers multiple times each month. I keep an ethnographic journal and analyze data using an ongoing, recursive two-stage process of inductive-deductive thematic critical analysis (Boyatzis, 1998; Rogers, 2004).

In the first stage of analysis, I annotated ethnographic data relative to content and a priori themes based on the reviewed scholarship, my theoretical framework, and emerging themes (Boyatzis, 1998). In the second stage, I analyzed data inductively regarding repeated patterns and emergent themes, then deductively to consider emergent themes relative to pertinent literature and the guiding research question about how the school meets Cantonese-speaking students' various needs (Boyatzis, 1998). I developed codes by systematizing different colored ink and highlighting for each theme. This created a visual model of convergent themes, which I developed into a narrative of initial findings (Emerson, Fretz, & Shaw, 2011). I present this narrative below as a "holistic

246 Jason Goulah

cultural portrait of the social group that incorporates both the views of the actors in the group (emic) and the researcher's [etic] interpretation" (Creswell, 1998, p. 60). I frame this narrative with "interpretive commentary" (Davis, 1995), which provides triangulation, credibility, transferability, and dependability (Mackey & Gass, 2015).

Cantonese Emergent Bilinguals in the "Latino/Mandarin" U.S. Education Landscape: A Case in Chicago

The demographically shifting, "Latino/Mandarin" U.S. education landscape is present at Hough High School [pseudonym] in Chicago. A historically White, working-class, English-dominant public high school, Hough now contains 1,600 native-Spanish-speaking Latinos, 360 native-English-speaking Whites, and 340 native-Chinese-speaking students, the overwhelming majority of whom speak Cantonese natively. As Hough High has struggled unsuccessfully to meet the needs of its quickly growing Latino population, teachers and administrators now struggle to embrace and meet similar needs of the school's growing Cantonese-speaking population. Hough is a "low-performing school" and has been officially visited and reprimanded by the U.S. Department of Education, ISBE, and the CPS Office of Language and Cultural Education. As just one example why, Hough struggled in 2013 to test even 65% of its ELL population with the WIDA proficiency test for assessing comprehension and communication in English state-to-state (ACCESS) to determine accurate proficiency levels and assign students to appropriate classes. Given such results Hough was noncompliant with state policies; but the school was noncompliant with regard to ELLs for other reasons too. Thus, also in 2013, Hough secured a federal *School Improvement Grant* (through the state) to professionally develop and hire administrators and teachers, particularly with regard to ELLs.

Until 2014, bilingually endorsed teachers at Hough were endorsed only in Spanish-English, and the three Chinese-speaking teachers—only one of whom speaks Cantonese—are licensed only in Mandarin as a foreign language. According to Skorton and Altshuler (2012), "There have been some positive recent developments: Over the past decade, the Chicago Public Schools have expanded instruction in [Mandarin] Chinese to include 43 schools and serve 12,000 students. Many of these students are Hispanic and will be trilingual." Thus, Chicago now claims the nation's largest K–12 Mandarin foreign language program (Skorton & Altshuler, 2012).

The increased presence of Mandarin programs in Chicago is important, necessary, and commendable; however, it has contributed to a lack of access to, and even a pejorative view of, Cantonese. For example, whenever I ask Mandarin licensure candidates about Cantonese, the usual response is either that Cantonese is not the language of mainland China or that it is not an official language, and therefore it should not be taught as a foreign language. Seemingly lost on them is any understanding of local language ecology (Hatano, 2013; Kubota & McKay, 2009) in light of Chicago's large Cantonese-speaking population, not to mention the facts that the United Nations recognizes Cantonese as a language, it is the *de facto* official language of Hong Kong (Cheng & Tang, 2014), and ACTFL and ISBE recognize Cantonese as a licensure area.

Exacerbating the situation is the dearth of Cantonese-speaking, bilingually endorsed, secondary-level content teachers in Chicago. Therefore, even though Hough hired a Cantonese-English bilingually endorsed teacher for the 2014–2015 academic year, the disparity of appropriately credentialed teachers has resulted—and still largely results—in Hough assigning Mandarin-speaking foreign language faculty to meet the linguistic needs of Cantonese-speaking emergent bilinguals, while Spanish-speaking students' similar needs are met (at least procedurally) by Spanish-English bilingually endorsed teachers, and Mandarin-speaking students' needs are met (again, at least procedurally) by Mandarin-speaking teachers licensed in Mandarin as a foreign and heritage language. Thus, despite best intentions, Hough remains noncompliant with state and federal laws, and Hough's Cantonese-speaking Chinese students are no longer just "up against Whiteness" (Lee, 2005); they are also "up against" Latinos and Mandarin.

Since data collection began, initial findings suggest marked improvements in Hough's conscious actions to meet the needs of all ELLs, in general, and of the Cantonese-speaking emergent bilinguals, in particular. These early initiatives can be characterized as school-wide administrative actions and teacher practices.

Administrative Actions and Teacher Practices

The administration now explicitly promotes Hough as a "trilingual-tricultural" school and has begun posting signs, albeit in limited number, in the main entry in all three of its major languages—Spanish, English, and (simplified) Chinese. The administration has indicated that it also intends to post signs outside the building in all three languages. When data collection began, signage appeared in English only. The school's website now contains the school motto in all three languages and has more information in each language, though Chinese is still noticeably the least present. Some school-produced t-shirts contain the school motto in all three languages, and there has been discussion of printing the school name in English, Spanish, and Chinese on the athletic and extracurricular club uniforms.

The above actions are important and necessary to shift Hough's expressed identity from being (just) "a high school" to being a Spanish, English, and Chinese (Cantonese *and* Mandarin) "trilingual-tricultural" high school. Such actions not only represent the realities of the entire Hough community, but they also work to foster stronger and sustained school–parent–community networks, engender pride among *all* Hough students, further teachers' understanding and practice, and help to develop *all* ELLs' bilingual and bicultural achievement (Goulah & Soltero, 2015). These seemingly simple actions are inspired by and reach out to the hearts and minds of Cantonese emergent bilinguals and their parents, and in this the Hough administration has begun to create values of beauty, gain, and good (Goulah, 2013; Makiguchi, 1981–1988, Vols. 5 & 6).

As important and commendable as these initiatives are, Hough can make even greater efforts to embrace its identity and cultivate an active culture as a trilingual-tricultural school. Indeed, *all* signage and murals in hallways and classrooms, as well as all signage outside and *on* the building, should appear equally in English, Spanish, and Chinese, in both simplified and traditional characters as both represent the Hough community. In addition, all school policies and practices, anything on the school website, and the school's discipline code should likewise appear equally in Spanish, English, and Chinese; and daily announcements should be made in all three languages.

Administration also took steps to recruit and hire Cantonese-speaking, credentialed faculty. In fact, because of Hough's dramatically decreasing budget, the principal elected to dismiss some monolingual content faculty so that faculty, an administrator, and staff with credentials, experience, and abilities in Cantonese, Mandarin, and/or ELL issues could be hired instead. This is similar to findings in Guthrie's (1985) study. Specifically, the principal hired a Cantonese-speaking bilingual language arts teacher; a credentialed Mandarin-speaking teacher; an assistant principal experienced in Spanish and ELL issues; and a Cantonese-English bilingual office staff to liaise with the community and foster relationships with, and input from, Cantonese-speaking parents and community partners.

Much like the principal in Guthrie's (1985) study, the newly hired administrator at Hough parlayed Spanish specialization and previous administrative experiences with ELLs into steps to foster and coach inexperienced teachers, and to enact ACCESS administration preparation for tens of teachers, allowing Hough to reach 100% testing compliance in early 2015. This not only meets state compliance, but it also identified students' actual proficiency levels for appropriate class placement.

In addition, under the new administrator's initiatives with the bilingual liaison, Hough has begun hosting Cantonese-speaking parent meetings, ESL classes for the Chinese parents, and monthly Cantonese and Mandarin parent–principal meetings (all things that have existed for the Spanish-speaking parents). In light of the number of studies that show the importance Cantonese parents play in working with schools to foster their children's bilingualism and academic achievement (Guthrie, 1985; Lao, 2004; Wang, 2009; Wang & Phillion, 2007), such efforts by the school are important and necessary. Moreover, as with the example above, such efforts create values of individual gain for the school and social good for the Chinese community, and this good further allows members of the Chinese community to create their own personal and social value moving forward (Goulah, 2013; Makiguchi, 1981–1988, Vols. 5 & 6).

Finally, the administration began sponsoring multiple whole-faculty and department-specific professional development sessions on sociocultural, linguistic, and academic aspects of educating ELLs. When data collection began, few teachers at Hough seemed to understand or account for such issues, and very few observed classes evidenced accommodations for the ELL population, particularly as they relate to Cantonese or Mandarin speakers. In short, Hough illustrated Menken's (2013) critique that high schools typically maintain steadfast monolingual (English) instruction.

In certain instances, some Spanish-speaking content teachers were observed translating instruction for Spanish-speaking ELLs. Although translation is not recommended in certain approaches to bilingual education (Cummins, 2008), Cantonese students did not receive this same instructional accommodation, which not only potentially disadvantaged them academically but also established inequality and possibly perceived teacher preference publically in the classroom. Assuredly the teachers translated with the best intention to help whomever they could by whatever means possible, but Hough needs to recruit and hire more Cantonese-English bilingual content teachers to provide the Cantonese-speaking students equal access to rigorous education.

The overwhelming majority of teachers and department chairs at Hough expressed a sincere desire to meet the needs of all ELLs, but especially of the Cantonese-speaking Chinese students, who they said do not get the same instructional support because so few teachers speak Cantonese or have experience with Cantonese culture. Whereas some teachers speak Spanish, they felt they could at least speak to the Spanish-speaking ELLs and help clarify information, if not meet their needs through bilingual education. Certain teachers and department chairs have created a monthly group to discuss and ameliorate ELL issues, and to resolve noncompliance issues. They also created a newsletter about ELL issues, services, and accomplishments, which they periodically disseminate to foster a shared school-wide understanding.

Linked to teachers' concerns is an observed lack of comprehensive program design and standards-based curricula for all ELLs, in general, and Cantonese emergent bilinguals, in particular. As Hough's student population becomes increasingly diverse ethnolinguistically, measures must be taken to establish clear bilingual programs and curricula that account for the large number of Cantonese speakers and their sociocultural, ethnolinguistic, geographic, and academic needs (Guthrie, 1985; Lao, 2004; Leung & Uchikoshi, 2012; Wang, 2009; Wang & Phillion, 2007). Whether through an *en vogue* "translanguaging" approach that seeks to accentuate the local ecology of multiple languages (Spanish, Cantonese, English, and Mandarin) in a single school or classroom context (García & Li, 2014; Li, 2014), or something more traditionally divided (Cummins, 2008), steps must be taken to avail all ELLs, including and especially the currently underserved

Cantonese-speaking students, pathways to maintain and improve their home languages, and obtain the newly established Illinois *Seal of Biliteracy* (Public Act 98-0560) on their academic transcripts.

Conclusion

This chapter examined one "low-performing" public high school's initial efforts to meet the linguistic, sociocultural, and academic needs of the growing population of Cantonese-speaking Chinese students in a Spanish-speaking Latino community in Chicago. Situated in what I call the demographically shifting, "Latino/Mandarin" U.S. education landscape, this chapter examined the disparity between state and local perspectives, policies, and practices toward Cantonese and Mandarin, and identified significant insufficiencies Cantonese emergent bilinguals face that even their Mandarin-speaking and Spanish-speaking Latino ELL peers do not. Thus, more than 40 years after *Lau v. Nichols* and in the context of dramatically increased Asian (and Latino) immigration in the U.S., Cantonese-speaking Chinese students are no longer just "up against Whiteness" (Lee, 2005), but they are also up against Latinos and Mandarin.

The observed school has taken substantive, important, and commendable steps in just one year to begin meeting Cantonese-speaking students' needs, but more work is necessary. Also necessary is more scholarship among the research community to inform the successful implementation of Chinese (Cantonese and Mandarin) bilingual programs. There is a dearth of research on Chinese (especially Cantonese) instruction, adequate teacher and administrator preparation, program evaluation, and professional development to help teachers apply general and specific research theories in language acquisition to Cantonese and Mandarin bilingual classes.

As this is a longitudinal ethnography, future inquiry will more closely examine cross-linguistic/cross-ethnic interactions among students at Hough. Early observations indicate a number of Chinese-Latino student couples, trilingual students (English, Spanish, and Chinese; Cantonese, Mandarin, and English), Latino students enrolling in Mandarin, Cantonese-speaking students enrolling in Spanish and Mandarin, and both Latino and Cantonese-speaking students seeking programs in Cantonese. Future data collection will also examine Hough's success in fostering relationships with parents and community partners to change the school culture and improve students' standards-based academic achievement. These and other emerging findings will be reported in future scholarship.

References

Asian American Center for Advancing Justice. (2011). *A community of contrasts: Asian-Americans in the United States: 2011*. Los Angeles, CA: Author.

Bakhtin, M. M. (1981). Discourse in the novel. In M. Holquist (Ed.), *The dialogic imagination: Four essays by M. M. Bakhtin* (pp. 259–422). Austin, TX: University of Texas Press.

Boyatzis, R. E. (1998). *Transforming qualitative information: Thematic analysis and code development*. Thousand Oaks, CA: Sage.

California State Department of Education. (1984). *A handbook for teaching Cantonese-speaking students*. Sacramento, CA: Author.

Cheng, S. P., & Tang, S. W. (2014). Languagehood of Cantonese: A renewed front in an old debate. *Open Journal of Modern Linguistics, 4*, 389–398. doi:10.4236/ojml.2014.43032

Creese, A., & Blackledge, A. (2010). Translanguaging in the bilingual classroom: A pedagogy for learning and teaching? *The Modern Language Journal, 94*(1), 103–115. doi:10.1111/j.1540-4781.2009.00986.x

Creswell, J. W. (1998). *Qualitative inquiry and research design: Choosing among five traditions*. Thousand Oaks, CA: Sage.

Cummins, J. (2008). Teaching for transfer: Challenging the two solitudes assumption in bilingual education. In J. Cummins & N. H. Hornberger (Eds.), *Encyclopedia of language and education* (2nd ed., Vol. 5; pp. 65–75). New York, NY: Springer.

Davis, K. A. (1995). Qualitative theory and methods in applied linguistics research. *TESOL Quarterly, 29*, 427–453. doi:10.2307/3588070

Emerson, R. M., Fretz, R. I., & Shaw, L. L. (2011). *Writing ethnographic fieldnotes* (2nd ed.). Chicago, IL: University of Chicago Press.

García, O., & Li, W. (2014). *Translanguaging: Language, bilingualism and education*. New York, NY: Palgrave Macmillan.

Glaessner, B. (1987). Review of a school divided: An ethnography of bilingual education in a Chinese community, by Grace Pung Guthrie. *American Journal of Education, 96*(1), 108–112.

Goulah, J. (Ed.). (2013). Special issue: Makiguchi Tsunesaburo in the context of language, identity, and education. *Journal of Language, Identity & Education, 12*(1), 1–73.

Goulah, J., & Soltero, S. W. (2015). Reshaping the mainstream education climate through bilingual-bicultural education. In Y. Freeman & D. Freeman (Eds.), *Research on preparing inservice teachers to work effectively with emergent bilinguals* (Advances in research in teaching series) (pp. 177–203). London, UK: Emerald Books.

Guthrie, G. P. (1985). *School dividend: An ethnography of bilingual education in a Chinese community*. Mahwah, NJ: Lawrence Erlbaum.

Hatano, K. (2009). Voice in EFL education in a Japanese context: Makiguchi's perspectives in the concept of "voice." *Educational Studies, 45*, 165–180. doi:10.1080/00131940902762219

Hatano, K. (2013). Makiguchian perspectives in language policy and planning. *Journal of Language, Identity & Education, 12*(1), 50–60. doi:10.1080/15348458.2013.748429

He, A. E. (2009). Educational decentralization: A review of popular discourse on Chinese-English bilingual education. *Asia Pacific Journal of Education, 31*(1), 91–105. doi:10.108 0/02188791.2011.544245

Kibler, A., Valdés, G., & Walqui, A. (Eds.). (2014). Special Issue: K–12 standards-based educational reform: Implications for English language learner populations. *TESOL Quarterly, 48*(3), 433–650.

Kubota, R., & McKay, S. (2009). Globalization and language learning in rural Japan: The role of English in the local linguistic ecology. *TESOL Quarterly, 43*(4), 593–619. doi:10.1002/j.1545-7249.2009.tb00188.x

Lao, C. (2004). Parents' attitudes toward Chinese-English bilingual education and Chinese-language use. *Bilingual Research Journal, 28*(1), 99–121. doi:10.1080/1523588 2.2004.10162614

Lee, S. J. (2005). *Up against whiteness: Race, school and immigrant youth.* New York, NY: Teachers College Press.

Leung, G., & Uchikoshi, Y. (2012). Relationships among language ideologies, family language policies, and children's language achievement: A look at Cantonese-English bilinguals in the U.S. *Bilingual Research Journal, 35*, 294–313. doi:10.1080/15235882.2 012.731588

Li, W. (2014). Who's teaching whom? Co-learning in multilingual classrooms. In S. May (Ed.), *The multilingual turn: Implications for SLA, TESOL, and bilingual education* (pp. 167–190). New York, NY: Routledge.

Lowe, G. (2015). The model minority narrative and its effect on Asian American identity and social status. In N. D. Hartlep (Ed.), *Modern societal impacts of the model minority stereotype* (pp. 323–350). Hershey, PA: IGI Global.

Ma, W. (Ed.). (2014). *East meets West in teacher preparation: Crossing Chinese and American borders.* New York, NY: Teachers College Press.

Ma, W., & Wang, C. (Eds.). (2014). *Learner's privilege and responsibility: A critical examination of the experiences and perspectives of learners from Chinese backgrounds in the United States.* Charlotte, NC: Information Age.

Mackey, A., & Gass, S. M. (2015). *Second language research: Methodology and* design (2nd ed.). New York, NY: Routledge.

Makiguchi, T. (1981–1988). *Makiguchi Tsunesaburo zenshu* [*The complete works of Tsunesaburo Makiguchi*] 10 vols. Tokyo, Japan: Daisan Bunmeisha.

Matthews, S., & Yip, V. (2011). *Cantonese: A comprehensive grammar.* London, UK: Routledge.

Menken, K. (2013). Emergent bilingual students in secondary school: Along the academic language and literacy continuum. *Language Teaching, 46*(4), 438–476. doi:10.1017/S0261444813000281

Nakagawa, S. (2014). *Asian Americans on the Sunday shows: What they talk about when they talk about us.* Oakland, CA: ChangeLab.

Palmer, D., & Martínez, R. A. (2013). Teacher agency in bilingual spaces: A fresh look at preparing teachers to educate Latina/o bilingual children. *Review of Research in Education, 37*, 269–298. doi:10.3102/0091732X12463556

Pew Research Center. (2013, April 4). *The rise of Asian Americans (updated edition).* Washington, DC: Author.

Pufahl, I., & Rhodes, N. C. (2010). *Foreign language teaching in U.S. schools: Results of a national survey.* Washington, DC: Center for Applied Linguistics.

Ricento, T. (2000). Historical and theoretical perspectives in language policy and planning. *Journal of Sociolinguistics, 4*(2), 196–213.

Rogers, R. (Ed.). (2004). *An introduction to critical discourse analysis in education.* Mahwah, NJ: Lawrence Erlbaum Associates.

Skorton, D., & Altschuler, G. (2012, August 27). America's foreign language deficit. *Forbes.* Retrieved from www.forbes.com/sites/collegeprose/2012/08/27/americas-foreign-language-deficit/

Tollefson, J. W., & Tsui, A. B. M. (2014). Language diversity and language policy in educational access and equity. *Review of Research in Education, 38*(1), 189–214. doi:10.3102/0091732X13506846

Uchikoshi, Y. (2014). Development of vocabulary in Spanish-speaking and Cantonese-speaking English language learners. *Applied Psycholinguistics, 35*(1), 119–153. doi:10.1017/S0142716412000264

Wang, P. C. (1974). Some extra problems that the bilingual teachers of Chinese children should consider. ERIC Documents 107112, 1–14.

Wang, Y. (2009). Language, parents' involvement, and social justice: The fight for maintaining minority home language, a Chinese-language case study. *Multicultural Education, 16*(4), 13–18.

Wang, Y., & Phillion, J. (2007). Chinese American students fight for their rights. *Educational Foundations, 21*(1-2), 91–106.

Wu, F. H. (2002). *Yellow: Race in America beyond black and white.* New York, NY: Basic Books.

CONCLUSION

Looking beyond the Stereotypes and Moving Forward: Cultivating the Hearts and Minds of Chinese-Heritage Learners

Wen Ma and Guofang Li

This book features research on Chinese-heritage students in North American K–12 schools by an international interdisciplinary team of educators. As you have read, the chapters include both theoretical reviews and empirical studies on Chinese-heritage students' learning of English as a new language and Chinese as a heritage language, their learning across the curriculum, their hybrid experiences and identities, and various sociocultural and familial variables affecting their academic, emotional, and psychological well-being. Collectively, these chapters showcase how these young students' educational journeys have been; why their experiences and perspectives are similar to but also noticeably different from those of their peers from other cultural, ethnic, and linguistic backgrounds; and what their minds and hearts are longing for. Their educational experiences in the new globalized era not only have theoretical importance about K–12 Chinese-heritage students' schooling, identities, and cultures beyond report cards and test scores but also have pedagogical and practical relevance to help their North American teachers better teach them, for their families and communities to better support them, as well as for other students to learn about and with this increasingly significant cohort of students across the educational spectrum.

Ma (2014) argued that the Chinese and North American educational perspectives evolved as a product of their own sociocultural circumstances, and both can be strengthened with complementary elements from the other. Therefore, a "middle-ground" approach may be especially relevant for Chinese-heritage learners who are simultaneously influenced by their prior cultural backgrounds and present North American realities. The case-after-case explorations of Chinese-heritage students' experiences in and outside of schools not only shed light on how they handle schooling and navigate across inter-cultural, cross-lingual, and multi-racial spaces, but also offer alternative conceptual

Looking beyond Stereotypes, Moving Forward **255**

lenses for the educational community to critically reflect on the issue of how we may all benefit by reaching some "middle ground" between the two divergent perspectives. The following themes are particularly worth noting.

Disparity in Educational Achievement among Chinese-Heritage Learners

Chinese education is rooted in a Confucian tradition, which was tied with the over 1000-year-old civil service examination system (*Keju*). Back then, successful candidates had to learn classic texts by heart, master foundational literary knowledge and skills, and use strong discipline and self-discipline to work hard and persistently throughout the long years of preparation. Today Keju is of course no longer practiced, but its influence is still widely felt since the country relies on the National Entrance Examinations (Gaokao) to select any students for college education. As Ma (2010) suggested, this has resulted in a pervasive test-oriented school culture: tests are built into core subject areas and each grade level, and getting high scores becomes the only measure, even the ultimate goal, of learning by students in Chinese schools.

Such a test-smart culture has also explicitly or implicitly impacted the mentality and behavior of Chinese-heritage students (and their parents, too) in North America. For example, some of them focus narrowly on school subjects that are tested, and some also spend more time studying or go to special test-prep classes just to raise their scores (Spencer, 2012). Inarguably, working hard to pursue academic goals through personal efforts ought to be promoted amongst all learners, but such pursuits would be more meaningful when driven by genuine interest towards larger goals of acquiring the knowledge and then applying it to solve real-life problems. Cramming just for high scores not only misplaces the priorities, but also may make other students who could not afford such test-prep classes perceive these as unfair academic practices (Baker, 2012), which have added to the stereotypes that Chinese-heritage students (other Asian-American students, too) are single-minded, goal-oriented *learning-machines* or *book worms*. This, in turn, has contributed to what Zhao (2009) categorized as the "high scores but low abilities" (p. 80) phenomenon: Chinese learners are hard working and score high in tests, but some of them do not do as well in applying what was learned to creatively solve problems.

On the other hand, previous research (e.g., Chua, 2011; Li, 2006; Park, Endo, Lee, & Rong, 2007) on students from Chinese backgrounds reveals that many of them attain academic excellence in North American schools, in many instances through almost impeccable personal efforts and unwavering familial support. Besides the large national and state/provincial databases that clearly show their test scores to be comparable to their White counterparts, the high percentage of them among the Intel Science Talent Search winners and finalists and the team members for the U.S. international mathematics and science Olympiads provide further anecdotal evidence about their excellence at the national and international levels. Consequently, many view them as "trouble-free learners."

Nevertheless, the bright success stories may have unintentionally overshadowed many of the real problems and issues faced by other Chinese-heritage students. As underscored in this volume, a great number of them are not high achievers, and quite a few have academic difficulties, even failures, for a variety of reasons. Some of the chapters depict, with fine details, tremendous complexities and nuances in the academic experiences of Chinese-heritage students in authentic K–12 settings. For example, echoing Cui's call to debunk the stereotypical "model minority" discourse that fails to capture the diversity among them, Gunderson and D'Silva and Qian highlight the challenges for diverse Chinese-heritage students (especially those late-arriving students) in Canadian schools. Lan and de Oliveira, and Lao, Lee and Arzate report similar struggles by Chinese-heritage students learning science and academic English in an American context. Additionally, while Zhou, Oxford and Wei demonstrate the power of strong parental support on Chinese-heritage learner's English learning and literacy practices, Lao, Lee, and Arzate, and Tokunaga and Huang reveal the negative impact of the lack of parental support for the "parachute kids" and new immigrants in K–12 schools. Finally, several chapters such as Lao, Lee, and Arzate, Lan and de Oliveira, and Qian expose much about the difficulties of learning English as a second language and learning content areas through the language, whereas Wen and Li unpack the challenges of maintaining Chinese as their first language across the home, weekend language school, and mainstream school contexts. As well, Du, Stooke, and Heydon raise the issue of neglecting Chinese-heritage language learners' spontaneous multimodal literacy practices that are closely linked with their cultural identities.

Permeating through the pages are live examples of numerous students having a wide range of academic experiences, challenges, and difficulties. These findings should give pause to those educators who hold a worry-free, celebrative attitude about Chinese-heritage students' academic performance in K–12 schools. As the chapters demonstrate, while some are succeeding, there are those who are silently struggling to learn English and other subjects (yes, including mathematics and science), and many are feeling isolated from the native-born students and teachers, too. This requires us to search behind the aggregated assessment figures to find the real problems and tackle them as needed. Only then can we help all diverse learners acquire the needed language and literacy skills to pursue sustainable academic excellence as they become intrinsically motivated to discover, to engage in inquiry across the curriculum, and to advance knowledge to benefit others.

Pathways to Well-Rounded Development

Many Chinese-heritage learners (or their parents) often come from a test-oriented educational milieu, in which test scores are taken as the predominant measure of a student's learning (and a teacher's teaching) in the fierce competition for limited educational resources and opportunities. As a result, students are pressured to pursue academic goals relentlessly, and many of them have consequently developed strong academic skills. Unfortunately, this means unbearably long hours to study the content and to prepare for tests, sometimes even at the price of giving up sleep, health, other artistic, music, athletic activities, or personal hobbies.

In the mainstream North American school culture, however, teachers, business leaders, policymakers, and the society at large hold that learning the academics is only one of the key ingredients for success. A young person is believed to need all kinds of extracurricular enrichments to lay a solid foundation necessary for a richer and more fulfilling life, and one cannot be a "lone learning machine" in the twenty-first-century globalized era. Instead, one needs to be well rounded, be able to think critically, communicate and collaborate with others cooperatively, and apply what is learned to solve real-life problems creatively. Few would argue that such a comprehensive skill set is even more important than what has been learned from textbooks.

Against this shifting educational outlook, some of the chapters provide useful conceptual lenses to help us refocus from academics-centeredness to a more comprehensive growth perspective. In particular, the bioecological model presented by Chen, Ly and Zhou pushes us to think beyond learners' academic performance to look at socio-emotional and behavioral aspects by focusing on the process, person, context, and time variables that affect Chinese immigrant children's balanced development across school, career, and life. Cheung's chapter further engages our thinking on how to cultivate creativity in Chinese-heritage students, an area of competence that is commonly thought to be lacking among Chinese learners due to their overwhelming focus on test-taking abilities. While Cheung explains the unique challenges that Chinese-heritage learners face in developing creativity, she also outlines distinct pathways of creativity development among Chinese-heritage students through dispelling stereotypes and capitalizing on their cultural traits and multicultural experience. Moreover, Jiang and Senokossoff examine parenting styles with insight about how a group of well-educated Chinese parents, contrary to the popular perception that they are "tiger" parents who only want academic excellence, also pay attention to their children's sociocultural development and psycho-emotional health.

Finally, one of the most important aspects to develop a "whole person" must address Chinese learners' multiple identity development and their self-image over competing cultural affiliations. While students from only Chinese ethnic background need to make peace with being Chinese and a racial minority in the White majority society, McVee and Zhang retell the complex psychological and spiritual entanglements a student has gone through before coming to terms with his biracial identity of being Chinese and Norwegian American. Since these immigrant students' identities are shaped up by their own lived experiences and circumstances, some have to wrestle with the identities of being Cantonese amongst other racial minorities such as Spanish-speaking Latinos and Mandarin-speaking Chinese in their schools and communities (see Goulah's chapter), and others dwell in what Cui calls a "racialized habitus" to conform to the mainstream and distance themselves from the newer immigrants mocked as "FOB" (*fresh off the boat*).

All these substantive evidences urge educators and parents alike to consider how to simultaneously build Chinese-heritage students' academic strengths and attend to their emotional and psychological needs while remaining mindful of their identities unfolding towards achieving proximal "whole-person" development comprehensively. In a globalized twenty-first-century context, it is vital for them to gain academic knowledge and skills, as well as to grow productive dispositions and sound body and mind for their future lives. In the process, their cross-cultural and multilingual experiences may actually give them an edge to help them see the pros and cons of the Chinese and North American perspectives and maximize the strengths from both. This kind of critical thinking may not only facilitate their transition from just being good students with good scores to productive and responsible adults, but also contribute to the larger goal of building more tolerant multicultural schools and society.

Importance to Attend to Individual Needs and Abilities

The chapters in this volume document diverse Chinese-heritage students' experiences in and outside of K–12 schools. The rich nuances and notable variation across the chapters not only paint a panoramic and dynamic picture about their situations and lives but also speak unequivocally about the need to drop a one-size-fits-all approach for their schooling. Theoretically, this volume extends the literature on Asian-American and Canadian students to showcase the educational conditions of Chinese-heritage K–12 students, a much under-researched area. As explained in the Introduction, we use the term *Chinese-heritage students* to refer to a heterogeneous group of students, who, while sharing some common Chinese cultural and linguistic legacy, are a mix of different backgrounds and origins, including earlier Chinese immigrants, diasporic Chinese from other countries and regions, and the ongoing waves of Chinese from China. With such a diverse population, individuals are bound to have different strengths and accomplishments, but also unique problems and challenges to be worked on. Therefore, indiscriminately labeling all of them as model minority or high achievers, as if they all came out of the same mold, does not capture the tremendous complexity and diversity in their experiences, nor is it conducive to nurturing their proximal personal and social development. They deserve, as all students, to be taught and socialized in accordance with individual abilities, needs, and circumstances.

Gunderson and D'Silva in this volume regard terms such as *Chinese* as "highly questionable" since they obscure obvious differences for such a huge and

Looking beyond Stereotypes, Moving Forward **259**

divergent population. This point is also echoed in the Foreword by Luke who raised the important question, "what is Chineseness?" as well as in Pang, Han, and Pang's (2011) discussion of the achievement gap in seventh-grade reading and mathematics by diverse Asian-American subgroups. Therefore, we need more appropriate and group-specific categories to disaggregate the heterogeneity and complexity among this population (such as those documented in this volume), so that we can consider pedagogical and practical implications of the findings for the educational community, for their teachers and parents, and for themselves in the current standards-based educational context.

The findings in this volume offer us some important lessons about how to better educate Chinese-heritage learners in today's classrooms and beyond. Pedagogically, better understanding the backgrounds and needs of individual students may help teachers differentiate instruction for the individual and other subgroups. Some as described by Gunderson and D'Silva, by Qian, and by Lan and de Oliveira have to cope with the label of being ESL learners, whose competence in their first language, Chinese, was overlooked or deemed as a deficit, while others who, guided by their parents, totally plunge into the sea of English and quickly pick up even stronger literacy skills than their native-born peers (see the chapter by Zhou, Oxford, and Wei). Due to the arrival time difference, some of these students may still lack English-language proficiency to manage all the expected learning tasks across content areas. In class learning processes, teachers ought to allow additional wait time for them to process the content and come up with their responses to reading, writing, and oral questions. Also key to effective teaching is what Lan and de Oliveira refer to as "subject-specific instructional support" to help to close gaps in personal knowledge and everyday experience between immigrant and native-born students. Consistent with Chen, Ly, and Zhou's finding that child–teacher relationships correlate with Chinese immigrant children's reading and mathematics performance, it is important to establish a caring learning environment, in which the teachers patiently listen and observe to understand the learners' needs, and then give situated instructional support. One of the most useful lessons for teachers to draw from this volume is to collaborate with Chinese parents. In keeping with the deep-rooted value placed on education and the respect reserved for educators, a point emphasized in this volume repeatedly (see the chapters by Zhou, Oxford, and Wei, and by Jiang and Senokossoff), classroom teachers will find a lot of Chinese parents willing to do whatever is educationally necessary on the home front.

Classroom teachers also need to critically reflect on their potential prejudice and guard against stereotyping Chinese-heritage learners. Some of them may seem to fit the racialized norm by being hardworking to learn the content fast, some may appear more vulnerable and less focused on the learning tasks, still others may exhibit a host of behavioral and psychological problems, and their English proficiency may span a wide range. All these myriad differences demand teachers to exercise their professional teaching skills to figure out the most appropriate scaffolding based on individual leaners under different situations. Importantly, teachers should not rush to judgment. The newly arrived Chinese student from a disadvantaged family background in a fourth-grade science classroom in Lan and de Oliveira's chapter offers a powerful example: The student simply did not have real-life experience with commonplace mainstream American concepts such as "cereal" and "dryer," but each time she asked for clarification, the science teacher either ignored the questions, or felt the student was deliberately causing trouble. Such dismissive attitudes and lack of responses "unintentionally" encouraged other native-born peers' open ridicule. Examples like this again prove the absolute necessity for teachers to carefully monitor their own beliefs and assumptions, establish an inviting classroom environment, learn and attend to students' nuanced differences, and facilitate each and every student's maximal learning and growth.

It is always helpful for parents to keep in mind the multilayered challenges their children have to handle in adjusting to a new culture and place, ranging from managing literacy and content area learning, coping with peer relations and pressures, adjusting to rapid language and cultural changes, to figuring out the inevitable questions of *who I am* and *where I am going* in learning and life. They may experience all kinds of transitional hardship, stress, confusion, and even pain in the schooling and socialization processes. It is plausible to have community-based Ibashu as a safe haven, but nothing ever replaces the unconditional love, empathy, and support from parents, especially when children are going through "identity wars" as cross-cultural and biracial travelers. Just as Jiang and Senokossoff caution parents to set high yet realistic academic goals for children, without exerting excessive pressure just for the sake of tests scores, Chen, Ly, and Zhou remind parents to be mindful of their children's socio-emotional and psychological health, all aimed at their balanced growth.

Even more important, Chinese-heritage students will be better off if we equip them with critical thinking skills so that they can learn to be cognitively, physically, emotionally, and psychologically strong as newcomers and minority learners. There are occasional reports of tragic occurrences involving these impressionable young students (Lee, 2014). When confronted with seemingly insurmountable problems and pressures, they should know where and how to seek help for their academic, emotional, and psychological needs (American Psychological Association, 2015). From our own lived experiences as former immigrant students, we understand that journey can be full of ups and downs, but it will eventually be very enriching, and rewarding, too.

In conclusion, this volume expands the existing research literature on Chinese-heritage students by providing close-ups of this under-researched, misunderstood population beyond a group profile. We hope the findings will help the educational community reflect on some of the larger sociocultural, theoretical, pedagogical, and practical issues that impact their academic performance and well-rounded development. We trust that the student voices, perspectives, and insights that emerged from this book will help us better understand and work with Chinese-heritage students to maximize their full potential in North American K–12 schools and beyond.

References

American Psychological Association. (2015). Suicide among Asian Americans. Retrieved from www.apa.org/pi/oema/resources/ethnicity-health/asian-american/suicide.aspx

Baker, A. (2012, Sept. 28). Charges of bias in admission test policy at eight elite public high schools. *The New York Times*, p. A28.

Chua, A. (2011). *Battle hymn of the tiger mother*. New York, NY: The Penguin Press.

Lee, J. Y. (2014, Aug. 5). Crushed by parental and societal pressure, Asian students are resorting to suicide. *Alternet*. Retrieved from www.alternet.org/education/crushed-parental-and-societal-pressure-asian-american-students-are-resorting-suicide

Li, G. (2006). *Culturally contested pedagogy: Battles of literacy and schooling between mainstream teachers and Asian immigrant parents*. Albany, NY: SUNY Press.

Ma, W. (2010). Bumpy journeys: A young Chinese adolescent's transitional schooling across sociocultural contexts. *Journal of Language, Identity, and Education, 9*(2), 107–123.

Ma, W. (Ed.). (2014). *East meets West in teacher preparation: Crossing Chinese and American borders*. New York, NY: Teachers College Press.

Pang, V. O., Han, P. P., & Pang, J. M. (2011). Asian American and Pacific Islander students: Equity and the achievement gap. *Educational Researcher, 40*(8), 378–389.

Park, C. C., Endo, R., Lee, S. J., & Rong, X. L. (Eds.). (2007). *Asian American education: Acculturation, literacy development, and learning*. Charlotte, NC: Information Age.

Spencer, K. (2012, Oct. 27). For Asians, school tests are vital steppingstones. *The New York Times*, p. A18.

Zhao, Y. (2009). *Catching up or leading the way: American education in the age of globalization*. Alexandria, VA: ASCD.

AFTERWORD

Redefining Education Outcomes

Yong Zhao

One of the persistent problems in education is the narrow definition of outcomes. For a long time, mainstream educational research, policy, and practice have by and large used academic achievement, mostly indicated by test scores, as the sole outcome of education. As such, test scores have largely defined the success or failure of students, teachers, schools, and education systems. Consequently, improvement in test scores has been the goal of systemic reform efforts, classroom pedagogical improvements, as well efforts of students and parents.

This narrow definition of outcomes has bedeviled education as a field globally. It has misguided the global search for more effective educational practices and policies, institutional arrangements, and parental patterns. Because of the narrow definition, policies and practices associated with better test scores are deemed effective and better, and thus worth emulating. For example, the performance on international assessments such as the Program for International Student Assessment (PISA) and the Trends in International Mathematics and Science Study (TIMSS) has been used as the basis to determine effective education systems globally. A broad range of policy and practice lessons have been drawn from high-performing education systems such as Shanghai, Singapore, Hong Kong, Finland, and Korea (Schmidt, 1999; Tucker, 2011).

The narrow definition of educational outcomes has also distorted educational research at the classroom and school levels. In the search for more effective instructional methods, curriculum designs, school environments, or other educational devices, education researchers have mostly defined *effectiveness* as the capacity to improve test scores (e.g., see Hattie, 2009). Without taking into consideration other valuable human qualities, this research tradition has resulted in a promotion of methods, curricula, and other educational treatments that have positive impact on test scores and dismissing others that may not have an impact on test scores, but may have great impact on other important human qualities such as socio-emotional well-being and physical health. It has also led to mischaracterization of what works in education (What Works Clearinghouse, 2014) and a drastic oversimplification of factors that affect the well-being of the whole child.

As a result, the narrow definition of *education outcomes* has also led to curricular and pedagogical homogenization around the globe (Zhao, 2012, 2015b). The past few decades have witnessed a sharp increase in attempts to align curriculum and pedagogy to high-performing educational systems, defined by their performance on international assessments. There has also been a dramatic increase in accountability policies based on test scores. Nations that did not have the tradition of national curriculum and assessment have begun to develop and implement national curriculum and assessment (Zhao, 2015b). The result is a narrow and homogenized education experience for students (Alexander, 2009; McMurrer, 2007; Tienken & Zhao, 2013), which focus only on improving test scores in a few subjects.

The danger of a homogenous and narrow education experience is grave because we know that education should not be all about good test scores. There is mounting evidence that success in life depends on many human qualities that are not measured by test scores (Cohen, 1999; Duckworth, Peterson, Matthews, & Kelly, 2007; Duckworth & Yeager, 2015; Goleman, 1995; Levin, 2012; Zhao, in press). Test scores have been a poor indicator of life success of individuals and prosperity of nations (Zhao, in press). More important, an exclusive focus on improving test scores can lead to long-term damages to other human qualities that may matter more for life, such as creativity, curiosity, and confidence (Zhao, in press).

Fortunately there is a gradual awakening in the field of education, sort of a renaissance. As the limitations and dangers of the narrow definition of educational outcomes become more apparent, education researchers, policymakers, and educators have gradually begun to see the importance of understanding and educating the whole child. The call for broadening outcome measures has been sounded (Duckworth & Yeager, 2015; Zhao, in press). Even the OECD/PISA program began to expand its assessment beyond math, reading, and science. Starting in 2012, PISA began to assess creative problem solving (OECD, 2014). Nations that have traditionally performed well on international assessments, particularly East Asian nations, have undertaken massive efforts to reform their educational policies and practices to move away from the tradition of excessive focus on testing (Zhao, 2015a).

However, the change is not easy. To shift the traditional paradigm of education that focuses excessively on test scores towards one that cultivates all aspects of human qualities, a lot more work needs to be done. This book, *Chinese-Heritage Students in North American Schools: Understanding Hearts and Minds Beyond Test Scores*, makes an excellent contribution to the much needed paradigm shift.

Drs. Wen Ma and Guofang Li have gathered an impressive collection of scholars to study a broad range of issues concerning one specific group of students—Chinese-heritage students—in a specific context—North America. The selection of the subject is of tremendous insight because this population may have suffered the most from the narrow definition of educational outcomes. The "Chinese" have carried the stereotypical status of being excellent in test taking globally for a long time. Scholarly studies about this group of students beyond their academic supremacy have been rare in mainstream English literature. This rich collection of studies reveals the diversity and complexity of Chinese students in North America. It clearly shows that Chinese students are much more than test scores.

However, I believe the value of this volume goes way beyond demystifying Chinese students. It exemplifies the nature of works necessary for the new paradigm of education. The studies included in this volume clearly demonstrate the power of a broad perspective on education in enhancing our understandings of children and their education. By looking beyond test scores, the scholars included in this book are able to gain deeper understandings and provide fresh perspectives. Coupled with a broad range of methodologies, the researchers are able to present a much more comprehensive picture of the education process and context of a population of students who have been subject to serious misunderstanding and mischaracterization, which in fact has been the fate of almost all students.

I am hopeful this book will serve to inspire similar efforts in the entire field of education and that one day we can move beyond test scores as the only outcome measure in education.

References

Alexander, R. J. (2009). *Towards a new primary curriculum: A report from the Cambridge Primary Review. Part 2: The Future* (Vol. 2009). Cambridge, UK: University of Cambridge Faculty of Education.

Cohen, J. (1999). *Educating minds and hearts: Social emotional learning and the passage into adolescence.* New York, NY: Teachers College Press.

Duckworth, A. L., Peterson, C., Matthews, M. D., & Kelly, D. R. (2007). Grit: Perseverance and passion for long-term goals. *Journal of Personality and Social Psychology, 92*(6), 1087–1101.

Duckworth, A. L., & Yeager, D. S. (2015). Measurement matters: Assessing personal qualities other than cognitive ability for educational purposes. *Educational Researcher, 44*(4), 237–251.

Goleman, D. (1995). *Emotional intelligence.* New York, NY: Bantam Books.

Hattie, J. (2009). *Visible learning: A synthesis of over 800 meta-analyses relating to achievement.* New York, NY: Routledge.

Levin, H. M. (2012). More than just test scores. *Prospects: The Quarterly Review of Comparative Education, 42*(3), 269–284.

McMurrer, J. (2007). *Choices, changes, and challenges: Curriculum and instruction in the NCLB era.* Washington, DC: Center on Education Policy.

OECD. (2014). *PISA 2012 results: Creative problem solving: Students' skills in tackling real-life problems* (Vol. V). Paris, FRA: OECD.

Schmidt, W. H. (1999). *Facing the consequences: Using TIMSS for a closer look at U.S. mathematics and science education.* Boston, MA: Kluwer Academic.

Tienken, C. H., & Zhao, Y. (2013). How common standards and standardized testing widen the opportunity gap. In P. L. Carter & K. G. Welner (Eds.), *Closing the opportunity gap: What America must do to give every child an even chance* (pp. 113–122). New York, NY: Oxford University Press.

Tucker, M. (Ed.). (2011). *Surpassing Shanghai: An agenda for American education built on the world's leading systems.* Boston, MA: Harvard Education Press.

What Works Clearinghouse. (2014). *What works clearinghouse: Procedures and standards handbook, Version 3.0.* Washington, DC: What Works Clearinghouse, Institute of Education Sciences.

Zhao, Y. (2012). *World class learners: Educating creative and entrepreneurial students.* Thousand Oaks, CA: Corwin.

Zhao, Y. (2015a). *Lessons that matter: What we should learn from Asian school systems.* Melbourne, AUS: Mitchell Institute for Health and Education Policy.

Zhao, Y. (2015b). A world at risk: An imperative for a paradigm shift to cultivate 21st century learners. *Society, 52*(2), 129–135.

Zhao, Y. (Ed.). (in press). *Counting what counts: Reframing education outcomes.* Bloomington, IN: Solution Tree.

CONTRIBUTORS

Araceli Arzate was the ELD Department Chair at Mark Keppel High School and is currently a teacher there. She has taught every level offered of ELD and has been an advocate for her students since she started her teaching career.

Stephen H. Chen is an Assistant Professor in the Psychology Department at Wellesley College, where he directs the Culture and Family Development Laboratory. His research examines how culture and family processes influence development and mental health across the lifespan.

Cecilia S. Cheung is an Assistant Professor of Psychology at the University of California, Riverside. Her research aims to understand how children's environment shapes their motivation and achievement in school, with a primary focus on the roles of parents and culture. Her recent research examines children's creativity in the United States and East Asia.

Dan Cui is a SSHRC Postdoctoral Fellow jointly affiliated with the Graduate School of Education, the University of California, Berkeley and the University of British Columbia. Her research interests include immigrant youth, international students, immigration and integration, sociology of education, comparative and international education, and social justice and equity in education.

Luciana C. de Oliveira is Associate Professor in the Department of Teaching and Learning at the University of Miami, Florida. Her research focuses on English language learners (ELLs) at the K–12 level. Most recently, she has examined the linguistic challenges of the Common Core State Standards for ELLs. She can be reached at ludeoliveira@miami.edu.

Contributors **267**

Reginald Arthur D'Silva is the academic director of the UBC-Ritsumeikan international exchange programs at the University of British Columbia where he teaches language and content as well as global citizenship studies courses. His research interests are in TESL, international education, and the integration of technology in language and literacy contexts. He can be contacted at reginald. dsilva@ubc.ca.

Xiaoxiao Du is an internationally trained educator and researcher whose main research area is language, culture, and identity. Her research interests include ESL/EFL learning and teaching, multilingualism, multiculturalism, and multiliteracies as well as culturally and linguistically diverse students' literacy practices and identity constructions across domains.

Jason Goulah is Associate Professor of Bilingual-Bicultural Education and Director of the Institute for Daisaku Ikeda Studies in Education at DePaul University, where he also directs the Bilingual-Bicultural Education and World Languages Education programs.

Lee Gunderson is a Professor in the Department of Language and Literacy Education and Head, pro tem of the Department of Educational and Counseling Psychology and Special Education at the University of British Columbia. He conducts longitudinal research that explores the academic and language development of immigrant and ESL students. He can be contacted at lee. gunderson@ubc.ca.

Rachel M. Heydon is Professor of Curriculum Studies at Western University, Canada. Her work focuses on literacy and identity options across the lifespan. Her publications include numerous journal articles and books, including *Learning at the Ends of Life: Children, Elders and Literacies in Intergenerational Curricula*.

Chu Huang is a youth leadership program coordinator for high school youth, specifically newcomers and second-generation immigrant students in a Community Based Organization in Chinatown. She provides access, opportunities, and support to empower marginalized youth and families through providing tools that are necessary to navigate systems to achieve successes.

Xuan Jiang is an Assistant Professor of Teachers of English to Speakers of Other Languages (TESOL) at Saint Thomas University. Her main research focuses on contextualization and de-contextualization of borrowed curriculum in elementary and middle schools and the use of instructional strategies to English speakers of other languages (ESOL) in science classes.

268 Contributors

Shu-Wen Lan is Assistant Professor in the Department of Modern Languages at National Pingtung University of Science and Technology in Taiwan. Dr. Lan's research focuses on the teaching of English language learners (ELLs) in elementary classrooms, and academic English for non-native English-speaking students. She can be reached at swlan@mail.npust.edu.tw.

Ravy S. Lao is a lecturer in the Charter College of Education at California State University, Los Angeles where she instructs education courses to, and supervises student teaching of, teacher candidates in the Division of Curriculum and Instruction, as well as teaches in the TESOL Master's Program in the Division of Applied and Advanced Studies.

May Y. Lee is a teacher at Mark Keppel High School who has taught subjects ranging from English, ELD, Mandarin, and Student Leadership. Ms. Lee also leads professional development sessions focused on the transition to U.S. Common Core State Standards.

Guofang Li is a Professor and Canada Research Chair (Tier 1) in Transnational/ Global Perspectives of Language and Literacy Education of Children and Youth in the Department of Language and Literacy Education, Faculty of Education, University of British Columbia, Canada. Her recent research interests are longitudinal studies of immigrant children's language and literacy development through the educational systems, immigrant children's new literacy practices in and out of school, and teacher education and professional development for culturally and linguistically diverse children and youth.

Keqiao Liu is a doctoral student, majoring in Educational Psychology and Quantitative Methods, from the State University of New York at Buffalo.

Xiufeng Liu is Professor of Science Education in the Graduate School of Education and Director for Center for Educational Innovation, University at Buffalo/SUNY. He conducts research in closely related areas of technology-enhanced science assessment, applications of Rasch measurement in science education, and public understanding of science.

Allan Luke is Emeritus Professor, Queensland University of Technology, Australia; Adjunct Professor, University of Calgary, Canada; Honorary Professor, Beijing Normal University, PRC. He lives in Brisbane, Australia.

Jennifer Ly is a licensed clinical psychologist at the University of California, San Francisco. Her research and clinical interests include developing, adapting, and implementing evidence-based and culturally sensitive psychosocial treatments for high-risk youth.

Contributors **269**

Wen Ma is Associate Professor of Education at Le Moyne College. His research interests include class discussions across K–12 settings, literacy and content literacy strategies, and English language learners. His most recent research focuses on teacher education and Sino-US comparative educational studies. He can be reached at maw@lemoyne.edu.

Mary B. McVee is Director of CLaRI (Center for Literacy and Reading Instruction) and Associate Professor of Literacy Education at the University at Buffalo/SUNY. Her research focuses on positioning theory, social and embodied learning; digital literacies and multimodality; narrative, and language, literacy, and culture.

Rebecca L. Oxford is a specialist in language and education. She is Professor Emerita and Distinguished Scholar-Teacher, University of Maryland. She currently teaches at two branches of the University of Alabama and has authored or edited 12 books and numerous reference articles.

Yamin Qian is an Assistant Professor in the School of English and Education, Guangdong University of Foreign Studies, China. Her main interests are bilingual and multilingual education, critical sociolinguistics, multiliteracies, and L2 writing education.

Joseph C. Rumenapp is an Assistant Professor of Education at Judson University. He received his Ph.D. from the University of Illinois at Chicago in Literacy, Language, and Culture. His research interests include education in urban contexts, language ideologies in education, and second language and literacy development.

Gwyn W. Senokossoff is an Assistant Professor of Literacy at Coker College. Her research focuses on: early intervention in reading, reading comprehension instruction with delayed readers and children with autism spectrum disorders (ASD), and the use of children's literature to support English language learners and develop cultural competence in native speakers.

Rosamund (Roz) Stooke teaches Curriculum courses at Western University, Canada. Her research explores the translocal organization of literacy curricula in formal and informal settings such as public libraries and playgroups. Her most recent publication is a co-edited book entitled *Negotiating Spaces for Literacy Learning: Multimodality and Governmentality*.

Tomoko Tokunaga is a Project Assistant Professor of the International Center at Keio University. She was a Fulbright scholar and received her Ph.D. in Educational Leadership and Policy Studies at the University of Maryland, College Park. She conducts ethnographic research with Asian immigrant youth in Japan

270 Contributors

and the United States, specifically focusing on notions of identity, agency, belonging, and home.

Michael Wei is Associate Professor and Program Director of TESOL program at University of Missouri—Kansas City. His research interests include learning English to near native-like proficiency, reading/writing English as a second or foreign language, learning environments, early second-language development, and second-language acquisition.

Keying Wen is interested in heritage language education. Her research focuses on Chinese-heritage language teacher preparation in heritage-language schools and teacher quality in Chinese programs in public school.

Zachary C. M. Zhang is a student at the University of Montana, Missoula where he is studying history and political science and where he serves as a proud member of the Montana National Guard.

Yong Zhao currently serves as the Presidential Chair and Director of the Institute for Global and Online Education in the College of Education, University of Oregon, where he is also a Professor in the Department of Educational Measurement, Policy, and Leadership. He is also a professorial fellow at the Mitchell Institute for Health and Education Policy, Victoria University. His works focus on the implications of globalization and technology on education. He has published over 100 articles and 20 books.

Qing Zhou is a faculty member of the Psychology Department at the University of California, Berkeley. She directs the Culture and Family Study Lab and conducts research on cultural, family, and temperament influences on socio-emotional and academic development of children from immigrant and ethnic minority families.

Yalun Zhou is an Assistant Professor at Rensselaer Polytechnic Institute. Her research interests are Applied Linguistics and Second Language Acquisition. Her recent work involves emerging technology uses in language teaching and learning.

INDEX

Note: Locators in **bold** refer to tables; locators in *italic* refer to figures.

A Handbook of Teaching Cantonese-Speaking Students (California State Department of Education) 242–3

A Synthesis of Research on Second Language Writing in English (Leki, Cumming, and Silva) 56

Academic Challenge (AC) program 155

academic essay writing study 4, 55–6, 68–9, 259; assessments 60; Chinese schooling systems 56–7; parachute kids 57, 60; research-based instructional strategies 66–8; student demographics 61–3, **62**; student linguistic profiles **63**; student writing assessments 4, 61, 63–6; study methodology 61–4; study results/discussion **63**, 64–8; study setting/context 58–60; theoretical frameworks 57–8 *see also* scientific education (classroom discourse)

academic outcomes: heritage language learners 16–17; looking beyond 262–4 (*see also* test scores); parenting styles 234–6

accommodation without assimilation (segmented assimilation) 122–3

acculturation 6, 74; bioecological model 199, 204, 205, 206; youth pop culture 111 *see also* socialization

achievement gaps 120, 255–6 *see also* heterogeneity/differences

aesthetic tastes, conceptions of creativity 214

America *see* United States

Asian American Pacific Islander heritage month 174

Asian identity 142–3, 148, 156–7, 161 *see also* Chineseness

Asian immigrants, demography 239–40

attitudes to cultural assimilation: heritage language learning 14, 15, 20, 21, 26; resistant 110, 113, 116, 156, 231

authoritarian parenting styles 200, 203, 225, 226

272 Index

autonomy, parenting styles 216, 218, 225

Baumrind, D. 225–6
betweeness, phenomenological narrative study 181
bilingual education study 6, 239–40, 250; administration and teacher practices 247–50; case study 246–50; data collection/analysis 245–6; literature review 240–4; parental involvement 241–4; study methodology 245–6; theoretical frameworks 244–5; translanguaging 241
bilingualism 12; case study 27– 30, 33, 37– 39; critical spatial theory 105; home language learning 14, 15
bioecological model 6, 197–9, 206, 257; child's temperament 202–3; Kids and Family Project 6, 199, 204; nested contextual systems 203–5; social interaction 200–2; time periods/temporal contexts 198, 205–6
biracial identity 6, 257 *see also* bilingual education study; identity; multiracial identity
'border tongue' 173
Bourdieu, P. 43, 160–1
Bronfenbrenner, U. 6, 198–9, 205 *see also* bioecological model
bullying 185, 186, 230

California English Language Development Test (CELDT) 59, 60
California High School Exit Examination (CAHSEE) 55–6, 63, 67
California Writing Project 58, 61, 63 *see also* academic essay writing study
Canadian schooling systems 45

Canadian studies 88–9, 98–101, 161–2; databases 90–1; demographic data 153–4; grade-point averages **93**, *94*, 97, 98; hidden curriculum 158–9, 162; immigrant study group 91–2, **92**, 98–9; literature review 89–90; model minority stereotype 153, 155–8, 161; parental involvement 156–8; peer exclusion 159–60; primary student group 94–5, 99; secondary interview group 95–8; secondary random sample 92–3, **93**; social relations 156–61; study setting/context 154–5 *see also* multimodal literacy theory
Cantonese 11; academic essay writing 59; bilingual programs 239–50; Chinatown communities 139–40; heterogeneity/differences 90, 91–2, **92**, **93**, *94*, 95, 96–100 *see also* bilingual education study
caring learning environments 259
case studies: Canada 45–50, 246–50; US 246–50 *see also* phenomenological narrative study; scientific education (classroom discourse); Zeta (case study)
CCSS (Common Core State Standards), California 55, 63, 65, 66, 69
CELDT (California English Language Development Test) 59, 60
Chicago Public Schools (CPS) 240, 246–50 *see also* bilingual education study
child-parent relationships *see* parenting styles
child's temperament, bioecological model 198, 202–3
child-teacher relationships 201–2, 259 *see also* scientific education (classroom discourse)

Chinatown communities 5, 7; *Ibasho* 168 *see also* hybrid identities

Chinese Americans *see* United States

Chinese-heritage students 1, 2, 5; terminology 258–9 *see also* heritage language learners; struggling students

Chinese immersion programs, mainstream schools 18–20, 21

Chinese language, critical spatial theory 110, 112 *see also* heritage language learners

Chinese School Association in the United States (CSAUS) 12

Chinese vs. western comparisons: conceptions of creativity 213–15; models of learning 212–13; parenting styles 233–4; schooling systems 45, 56–7

Chinese Youth Leadership Program (CYLP) 5, 165–9, 171–6 *see also Ibasho*

Chineseness xiv, xvi, 5, 137, 259; distancing from 110, 144–5 *see also* identity; resistant attitudes

CHLSs *see* community-based heritage language schools

Chua, A. 88, 211, 219

classroom discourse *see* scientific education (classroom discourse)

classroom instruction methods *see* teaching methods

collaboration with parents 259 *see also* parental involvement in education

Common Core State Standards (CCSS), California 55, 63, 65, 66, 69

'The Communist and the Cowboy' phenomenological narrative study 187–8

communities of color 173

community, sense of 169–70 *see also Ibasho*

community-based heritage language schools (CHLSs) 12, 13, 14, 20–1; classroom instruction methods 18; ethnic identity 15–16, 18; language learning outcomes 16–17; resources and funding 17; teacher recruitment and training 17–18, 21 *see also* heritage language learners

community-based organizations (CBOs) 165, 166–7 *see also Ibasho*

Comprehensive English Language Test 91, **92**, 98

Confucian values 31, 212–13, 255

content-area classrooms 73, 74–6 *see also* academic essay writing study; scientific education (classroom discourse)

contexts, bioecological model 203–5

CPS (Chicago Public Schools) 240, 246–50 *see also* bilingual education study

creativity 6, 211–12, 219, 257; challenges and prospects for developing 217–19; Chinese vs. western models of learning 212–13; conceptions 213–15; novelty and practicality as markers 211, 212; parental involvement/styles 215–16, 218; stereotypes, educational 216–17, 218; test scores, looking beyond 263

critical spatial theory 4–5, 103–4, 107, 116–17; age on arrival 99, 106–14, **108**, 116–17; data collection/ analysis 108–9; inclusion 112, 114–15, 116; literature review 104–7; marginalization 105, 112–14, 116; participants 107–8, **108**; study results 109–15

critical thinking skills 144, 258, 260

CSAUS (Chinese School Association in the United States) 12

cultural brokers 173

274 Index

culture/cultural perspectives 9–12; creativity 219; distancing from Chinese 110, 144–5; maintenance of Chinese 6, 235 *see also* acculturation; Chinese vs. western comparisons; hybrid identities; identity
Cummins, J. 43
curriculum, learning across *see* learning across the curriculum
CYLP (Chinese Youth Leadership Program) 5, 165–9, 171–6 *see also Ibasho*

demand characteristics, child's temperament 202
demographic data 2; academic essay writing 61–3, **62**; Asian immigrants 239–40; bilingual education study 240, 242, 244, 246, 250; Canadian ELLs 153–4; heritage language learning 21; heterogeneity 100; parenting styles **228**, 228–9; US ELLs 55, 61–3, **62**, 201
dialects, Chinese language 11
dichotomies, foreign/U.S 145–8 *see also* hybrid identities
difference within difference 17, 25 *see also* heterogeneity/differences
disabilities, learning 60
disaggregating success *see* heterogeneity/differences
discourse, classroom *see* scientific education (classroom discourse)
disruptive behavior, teacher perceptions 78–9, 80–1, 84, 260; bioecological model 202; mathematics learning 125, **127**, **128**
domains, new literacy studies concept 42
drop everything and read (DEAR) time 34

dropping out of school/classes 17, 99–100, 125
Du, X. 42, 43–4

early education case study *see* Zeta (case study)
easygoing parenting styles 226
ecology, local language 244, 247 *see also* bioecological model
Education Longitudinal Study 123–4, 126
education outcomes *see* academic outcomes
educational models, Chinese vs. western 212–13
educational policies, mainstream schools 19
educational values, and parenting styles 224, 230–1, 236
effectiveness, educational 262
elementary school, phenomenological narrative study 183–4
ELS (Education Longitudinal Study) 123–4, 126
ELLs *see* English language learners
emotion-related language, bioecological model 204–5
emotional well-being 176, 235 *see also Ibasho*
English as a foreign language (EFL) 57
English as a second language (ESL): case study 25, 26, 28–34, **30**, 36–8; critical spatial theory 103–4; heterogeneity/differences 88–9, 97
English language learners (ELLs) 3, 240; Canadian Chinese immigrants 47; case study 33, 35, 37, 38 *see also* academic essay writing; bilingual education; scientific education
English speakers of other languages (ESOL) **30**, 88, 267

entrepreneurial families 91, 95–6, 97, 99 *see also* socioeconomic status

environmental contexts, bioecological model 198

ESL *see* English as a second language

ESOL (English speakers of other languages) **30**, 88, 267

essay writing study *see* academic essay writing study

ethics, research 29

ethnic identity *see* identity

ethnic language, terminology 21n *see also* heritage language learners

ethnoburbs (suburban residential and business areas) 59

ethnographic approaches 42, 168, 185, 190 *see also* bilingual education study; multimodal literacy theory

everyday life mismatches *see* scientific education, (classroom discourse)

exclusion, phenomenological narrative study 185 *see also* inclusion; marginalization

executive function, bioecological model 202–3

exosystems, bioecological model 203–4

expectations, parents and teachers 6; Canadian Chinese immigrants 158–9; case study 26, 27, 29, 36; creativity 213; heritage language learning 14, 15, 20; mathematics learning 124, **128**, 129; multimodal literacy theory 43; parenting styles 226

extracurricular activities 231, **232**

family as educator model 26 *see also* Zeta (case study)

family literacy practice: critical spatial theory 105; case study (Zeta) 32, 33 *see also* home language learning; homework

family rules, mathematics learning 124, **127**, **128**, 129

first language, terminology 21n

FOB (fresh off the boat). 160–1, 162, 258 *see also* racial discrimination

force characteristics, child's temperament 202

foreign/U.S. dichotomy, Chinatown communities 145–8 *see also* hybrid identities

funding, community-based heritage language schools 17

GAP test 91, **92**, 98

gender effects, mathematics learning 122, 124, **127**, 129

generational effects: mathematics learning 122–3, 125, **127**, 129; parenting styles 233

globalization 41, 254

Grandfather's Journey story (phenomenological narrative study) 183–4

guardians, academic essay writing 60 *see also* parental involvement in education

Guthrie, G. P., 241–2, 248

habitus 43, 160–1, 162, 258

Hanban language council 19

A Handbook of Teaching Cantonese-Speaking Students (California State Department of Education) 242–3

harsh parenting 226 *see also* authoritarian parenting

Heritage Language Journal 13

heritage language learners (HLL), United States 3, 11–13, 20–1, 256; community-based heritage language schools 15–18, 20–1; home language learning 14–15, 20; literature searching 13; mainstream schools 18–20, 21; resistance 110; terminology 21n

heritage students 1, 2, 5; terminology 258–9

heterogeneity/differences 1–3, 4, 5, 7, 259; achievement gaps 255–6; bioecological model 197–8; Canadian Chinese immigrants 88–9, 98–101, 153–4; creativity 211; heritage language schools 18; hybrid identities 137, 138–9, 143, 148, 149, 150; mathematics learning 120, 131–2; and model minority stereotype 155–8 *see also* individual needs and abilities; struggling students

hidden curriculum, Canadian Chinese immigrant study 158–9, 162

high school narrative, phenomenological narrative study 187–8

HLL *see* heritage language learners

home environment: educational values 230–1; mathematics learning 5, 121–6, **127–8**, 129–32, **130**

home language, terminology 21n *see also* heritage language learners

home language learning: case study 32, 33, 38, 39; entrepreneurial families 96, 98; heritage language learners 14–15, 20; parenting styles 230–1 *see also* homework

home literacy model 26 *see also* Zeta (case study)

homework: case study 28, 29, 31, 32, **33**, 35, 36; community-based heritage language schools 17; home language learning 14; mathematics learning 122, 124, 125, 126, **127–8**, **130**, 132; parenting styles 232

homogeneity, incorrect assumptions of *see* heterogeneity/differences

hooks/attention-grabbers, essay writing 66

Hough school, Chicago, case study 246–50

humor, conceptions of creativity 214, 218

hybrid identities, Chinatown communities 5, 137–9, 141–3, 148–50; distancing from Chinese identity 144–5; foreign/U.S. dichotomy 145–8; positioning theory 140–2, 144, 150; study setting/context 139–41 *see also* phenomenological narrative study

'I'm a Civilian' phenomenological narrative study 185–7

Ibasho (place to feel safe, secure, and accepted) 5, 164–5, 176–7, 260; building through CYLP 171–6; concept of 165–6; data collection/analysis 168–9; lack of in the United States 169–71; study setting/context 166–8

IDEA Language Proficiency Test (IPT) 29, **30**, 34

identity xiv–xv, 5, 260; academic essay writing 61–2; biracial 6, 257; Canadian Chinese immigrants 42–3, 44, 47, 51, 144–5 , 154; critical spatial theory 110; heritage language learners 12, 14, 15–16, 18–20, 21; multimodal literacy theory 42–3, 44, 47, 51; multiracial 6, 181, 186, 188–91; parenting styles 233–4; phenomenological narrative study 180–1, 183, 186, 188; pride in 174; situational 183, 186 *see also* hybrid identities

IFEP (initial fluent English proficient) label 60

immersion programs 19–20, 60

immigrant optimism 122, 123

inclusion, critical spatial theory 114–15, 116 *see also* exclusion
individual-environmental processes, bioecological model 198
individual needs and abilities 258–61
individual person characteristics, bioecological model 198, 202–3
initial fluent English proficient (IFEP) label 60
innovation, conceptions of creativity 213, 214, 217, 219
intergenerational effects *see* generational effects
International Baccalaureate (IB) program 155–6
international league tables 41
intragroup racial discrimination 160–1
IPT (IDEA Language Proficiency Test) 29, **30**, 34

Jane Schaffer writing instruction curriculum 66
Japanese concept of *Ibasho* 165–6
journal writing 34–5, 36, 42

K–12 schools *see* mainstream schools
Kids and Family Project (University of California-Berkeley) 6, 199, 204
kinetic diversity 100 *see also* heterogeneity/differences
Kress, Gunther 42

L2 literacy acquisition, Zeta 27–30, 33, 37–9
Lakeview Elementary School 78 *see also* scientific education (classroom discourse)
language ecology, bilingual education study 244, 247 *see also* bioecological model
language learning 3, 31–2; Chinese *see* heritage language learners; English *see* academic essay writing; home

language learning; literacy; multimodal literacy theory; scientific education (classroom discourse); Zeta (case study)
language policy and planning (LPP) 244
Latino community 7, 239–40, 246–50 *see also* bilingual education study
Lau v. Nichols law suit 239, 242, 250
league tables, educational 41 *see also* test scores
learning across the curriculum 2 *see also* critical spatial theory; heterogeneity/differences; mathematics learning at home; scientific education (classroom discourse)
learning disabilities 60
learning outcomes *see* academic outcomes
Lee, S. J. 89, 144, 181
Leung, A. K. 243
Li, G. 15
Li, M. 18
library books, home literacy use 32, 33
limited English proficiency (LEP) 27
literacy: Chinese 12, 20; English 27–8, 32, 33, 34–5, 57 *see also* academic essay writing
literacy events/practices, new literacy studies concept 42
literature reviews: bilingual education study 240–4; critical spatial theory 104–7; heterogeneity/differences 89–90; mathematics learning 121–3; multimodal literacy theory 43; scientific education (classroom discourse) 74–7
local language ecology, bilingual education study 244, 247 *see also* bioecological model
location *see* neighborhoods

278 Index

loneliness 169–70
longterm English learners (LTELs) 59
  see also academic essay writing

Maclean's magazine 1, 156–7, 161
macrosystems, bioecological model
  204
mainstream schools: English language
  learners 76–7; heritage language
  learning 14–15, 18–20, 21 *see also*
  academic essay-writing study;
  scientific education (classroom
  discourse); Zeta (case study)
Mandarin 11; academic essay writing
  59; Chinatown communities 140;
  heterogeneity/differences 90, 91–2,
  92, **93**, *94*, 95, 96–100; immersion
  programs 19 *see also* bilingual
  education study
marginalization 240, 242, 244; critical
  spatial theory 105, 112–14, 116 *see*
  also exclusion
mathematics learning 5, 120–1,
  131–2; data collection/analysis 126,
  130–1; databases 123; generational
  status 122–3, 125, **127**, 129; home
  variables 5, 121–6, **127–8**, 129–32,
  130; literature review 121–3;
  parental involvement 121–2, 124,
  128, 132; study methodology
  123–5; study results 126–31, **127–8**,
  130; theoretical frameworks 121
microsystems, bioecological model
  203–4
middle-class parenting styles 226, 227,
  236 *see also* socioeconomic status
middle school narrative, phenomenological narrative study 185–7
model minority stereotype xiii, xv, 3,
  5, 88; academic essay writing 55;
  bioecological model 197–8;
  Canadian Chinese immigrants 153,
  155–8, 161; case study 25;

Chinatown communities 137, 141;
  critical spatial theory 103, 106, 108,
  116; heterogeneity/differences 88,
  89, 155–6, 255–6, 259; *Ibasho* 165;
  parenting styles 224; scientific
  education (classroom discourse) 73
  see also struggling students
models of learning, Chinese vs.
  western 212–13
mother tongue: terminology 21n *see*
  also heritage language learners
motivation to learn, case study (Zeta)
  35–6
multicultural experience, and
  creativity 219
multilingualism, community-based
  heritage language schools 15 *see also*
  bilingualism
multiliteracies theory 42
multimodal literacy theory 3–4, 41,
  51; literature review 43; narratives
  of study participants 45–50, *46*;
  study methodology 43–4; study
  participants **44**; theoretical
  frameworks 42–3
multiple language social spaces 105 *see*
  also critical spatial theory
multiracial identity 6, 181, 186,
  188–91, 257 *see also* biracial
  identity; phenomenological
  narrative study
'My Other Dad Has a Motorcycle'
  phenomenological narrative study
  181–3

narratives, multimodal literacy theory
  45–50, *46 see also*
  phenomenological narrative study
National Assessment of Educational
  Progress Reading Report Card 156
National Council of Associations of
  Chinese Language Schools
  (NCACLS) 12

national curricula 263

National Education Longitudinal Study (NELS) 123, 124, 126, **127**, 130, **130**

National Longitudinal Survey of Youth (NLSY79) 121

NCACLS (National Council of Associations of Chinese Language Schools) 12

neighborhoods: *Ibasho* 171; mathematics learning 125, **127**, **128**, 129

nested contextual systems, bioecological model 203–5

new literacy studies (NLS) concept 42

New York Times, The 1

NLSY79 (National Longitudinal Survey of Youth) 121

Ngo, B. 89

North America *see* Canada; United States

Norwegian American Chinese identity 257 *see also* phenomenological narrative study

novel solutions 211 *see also* creativity

novelty, as marker of creativity 212

one-size-fits-all approach 258

one-way immersion programs 19

oral skills, parental involvement 31–2 *see also* language learning

originality, conceptions of creativity 213, 214

otherness 105, 138, 150

outcomes *see* academic outcomes

parachute kids 57, 60, 256

parental attitudes, heritage language learning 14, 15, 20 *see also* expectations

parental involvement in education 255; academic essay writing 60; bilingual education study 241–4;

Canadian Chinese immigrants 156–8; case study (Zeta) 37, 38; collaboration 259; Confucian values 31; creativity 215–16, 218; heterogeneity/differences 90; language learning 26–8; mathematics learning 121–2, 124, **128**, 132

parent-as-researcher participant observation 29

parenting styles 6, 224, 225, 232, 233, 235–6, 257; academic performance 234–6; bioecological model 200, 203–5; Chinese vs. western comparisons 233–4; and creativity 216, 218; data collection/analysis 229–30; educational practice 231–2; educational values 230–1, 236; effects on children 226; extracurricular activities 231, **232**; study methodology 227; study participants 227–9, **228**; study setting/context 227; theoretical frameworks 225–6; transgenerational similarities 233

peer exclusion, Canadian Chinese immigrants 159–60

permissive parenting styles 225

person characteristics, temperament 198, 202

phenomenological narrative study 5–6, 180–1, 189–91; biracial identity 257; elementary school narrative 183–4; high school narrative 187–8; middle school narrative 185–7; pre-school narrative 181–3

PISA (Program for International Student Assessment) 262

policies, educational 19

popularity, phenomenological narrative study 185

positioning theory, Chinatown communities 140–2, 144, 150

positive attitudes, heritage language learning 14, 15, 20, 21, 26

practicality, as marker of creativity 212

pre-school narrative, phenomenological narrative study 181–3

pride 50, 155, 174, 232, 248 *see also* *Ibasho*

professional development, English teaching staff 61

professional middle-class parenting styles 226, 227, 236 *see also* socioeconomic status

Program for International Student Assessment (PISA) 262

ProQuest database 13

racial discrimination, Canadian Chinese immigrants 158–62

racialized habitus 161, 162, 258

reading logs, Zeta 28, 32, **33**, 34

reading skills development, Zeta 32, 33 *see also* literacy

refugees 91

research ethics, case studies 29

resistant attitudes 110, 113, 116, 156, 231

resources, educational 17

Rosen, Jeffrey 64, 66–8

sacrificial parenting styles 232

sampling methodology, multimodal literacy theory 43–4

scientific education, classroom discourse 4, 73–4, 84–5, 259; data collection/analysis 79–80; disruptive and distracting behaviors 78–9, 80–1, 84; literature review 74–7; mismatches from everyday life experiences 74, 75–6, 81–4, *82, 83*, 85, 86; study setting/context 78–9

scientific learning, critical spatial theory 114–15

SDAIE (specially designed academic instruction in English) 59

Seal of Biliteracy (Illinois) 250

segmented assimilation 122–3

SEI (structured English immersion) 60 *see also* immersion programs

self-regulation skills, bioecological model 202–3

sense of humor, conceptions of creativity 214, 218

SES *see* socioeconomic status

shaming parenting style 226

sheltered English instruction (SEI) 59, 67 *see also* academic essay writing

sibling number, and home mathematics learning 125, **127, 128**

silently struggling students *see* struggling students

situational identity 183, 186

social relations: bioecological model 200–2; Canadian Chinese immigrants 156–8, 158–61; critical spatial theory 109–10

social spaces 103, 104–5 *see also* critical spatial theory

socialization 1, 2, 74, 76, 141, 205, 260 *see also* acculturation

societal level stereotypes *see* stereotypes, educational

sociocultural perspectives 6; critical spatial theory 104–5; multimodal literacy theory 43 *see also* bilingual education study; bioecological model; creativity; parenting styles

socioeconomic status (SES): bioecological model 197, 204; Canadian Chinese immigrants 154; Chinatown communities 137, 139; entrepreneurial families 91, 95–6, 97, 99; mathematics learning 124; parenting styles 226, 227, 236

socio-emotional adjustment, bioecological model 6, 199, 206 *see also* acculturation
spatial theory *see* critical spatial theory
specially designed academic instruction in English (SDAIE) 59
STARTALK 21
stereotypes, educational 41; creativity 216–17, 218; hybrid identities 137, 139, 141, 145, 149, 150 *see also* model minority stereotype
stigma, learning disabilities 60
stories, multimodal literacy theory 45–50, *46 see also* phenomenological narrative study
straight-line assimilation 122
structured English immersion (SEI) 60 *see also* immersion programs
struggling students xv, 4, 5, 7, 20, 60, 256; scientific education 74, 75, 77, 78
student demographics *see* demographic data
student retention, community-based heritage language schools 17 *see also* dropping out of school/classes
study skills approach to writing 58 *see also* academic essay writing
subject-specific instructional support 73, 259
supportive parenting styles 226 *see also* authoritative parenting
survey methodology, academic essay writing 61–3
suspension from school 125, **127**, **128**

teachers: community-based heritage language schools 17–18, 21; discourse with *see* scientific education; professional development 61; student relationships 201–2, 259 *see also* expectations, parents and teachers

teaching materials, community-based heritage language schools 17
teaching methods: community-based heritage language schools 18; research-based 66–8
temperament, bioecological model 198, 202–3
temporal contexts, bioecological model 198, 205–6
terminology 21n, 258–9
test scores, looking beyond 1, 4, 5, 7, 255, 256–7, 262–4; academic essay writing 56, 60; case study (Zeta) 26, 27, 31, 35–7, 39; multimodal literacy theory 41, 42, 45 *see also* whole person education
'The Communist and the Cowboy' phenomenological narrative study 187–8
'The Importance of Social Forgetting' (Rosen) 64, 66–8
The New York Times 1
tiger mothers xv, 88, 89, 98, 198, 226
time management, learning 231
time periods, bioecological model 198, 205–6
TIMSS (Trends in International Mathematics and Science Study) 262
'Too Asian' article (*Maclean's* magazine) 1, 156–7, 161
'Too Smart' article (*The New York Times*) 1
transgenerational *see* generational effects
translanguaging 241
Trends in International Mathematics and Science Study (TIMSS) 262
trilingual-tricultural high school, Hough school, Chicago 247–8
tutoring at home: entrepreneurial families 96, 98; parenting styles

230–1 *see also* home language learning

two-way immersion programs 19

Uchikoshi, Y. 243, 244

underachievers 3, 156, 161, 206

United States Census (2010) 59

United States studies *see* academic essay-writing; bilingual education study; bioecological model; creativity; critical spatial theory; heritage language learners; hybrid identities; *Ibasho*; mathematics learning; parenting styles; phenomenological narrative study; scientific education; Zeta (case study)

University of California-Berkeley's Kids and Family Project 6, 199, 204

usefulness, as marker of creativity 211, 212

Valley High School (VHS) 59, 61, 62 *see also* academic essay writing

vocabulary learning, case study (Zeta) 34–5, 38

Wang, P. S. 16, 17

Wang, Y. 15, 241, 242

Wang, Z. 57

Warner school *see* hybrid identities (Chinatown communities)

well-being 176, 235 *see also Ibasho*

western vs. Chinese comparisons *see* Chinese vs. western comparisons

'What Is the Point' phenomenological narrative study 183–4

whole person education 256–8, 260–1, 263 *see also* test scores (looking beyond)

Woodcock Reading Mastery Test 91, **92**, 98

writing ability, English language learners 57 *see also* academic essay writing; literacy

youth pop culture: and acculturation 111

Zach (case study) *see* phenomenological narrative study

Zeta (case study) 3, 25–6, 37–9, 256; parental involvement 26–8, 31–5, 37, 38; reading logs 28, 32, **33**, 34; research questions 31–7; study methodology/results 28–31, **30**; theoretical frameworks 26–7; Zeta's evaluation of learning 35–7

Zhang Jie (case study) *see* phenomenological narrative study